To Ginny and Gay,
in appreciation
for your friendship.
Diane Sasson

YEARNING FOR THE NEW AGE

RELIGION IN NORTH AMERICA

Catherine L. Albanese and Stephen J. Stein, editors

YEARNING

for the

NEW AGE

LAURA HOLLOWAY-LANGFORD

and

LATE VICTORIAN
SPIRITUALITY

DIANE SASSON

INDIANA UNIVERSITY PRESS

Bloomington & Indianapolis

This book is a publication of

Indiana University Press
601 North Morton Street
Bloomington, Indiana 47404-3797 USA

iupress.indiana.edu

Telephone orders   800-842-6796
Fax orders   812 855-7931

Manufactured in the United States of
America

Library of Congress Cataloging-in-
Publication Data

Sasson, Diane, [date]
    Yearning for the new age : Laura Holloway-
Langford and late Victorian spirituality /
Diane Sasson.
        p. cm. — (Religion in North America)
    Includes bibliographical references
(p.   ) and index.
    ISBN 978-0-253-00177-1 (cloth : alk.
paper) — ISBN 978-0-253-00187-0 (elec-
tronic book) 1. Holloway, Laura C. (Laura
Carter), b. 1848. 2. Religious biography—
United States. 3. Spiritual biography—
United States. 4. United States—Biography.
5. United States—History. I. Title.
    BL73.H65S27 2012
    204.092—dc23
    [B]
                                    2011042559

1 2 3 4 5   17 16 15 14 13 12

To Claudia J. Keenan,
For her help and friendship

Tell all the Truth but tell it slant—
Success in Circuit lies

Emily Dickinson

CONTENTS

FOREWORD

DIANE SASSON has crafted a riveting biography of Laura Holloway-Langford (1843–1930) that is also first-rate religious and intellectual history. Sasson's masterful account follows this gifted Southern woman who left the devastating circumstances of the defeated South following the Civil War and traveled across the nation and beyond, gradually gaining national and international attention and prominence. This is the tale of Laura Holloway-Langford's odyssey as a quintessential seeker, and of the excitement, the engagement, and at times the discontent she experienced as she moved through the new spiritual worlds of the late nineteenth century and of the opening decades of the twentieth century.

This account of Laura Holloway-Langford's journey documents her multiple diverse engagements with the religious and social movements of the late nineteenth and early twentieth centuries. Those decades were complex and transitional moments in American spiritual life and history; alternative religious movements as diverse as Theosophy and Spiritualism, Buddhism and Shakerism, appeared at times side by side on a national scene that was dominated by a diversity of Christian denominations. Holloway-Langford engaged these outsider groups in her own distinctive manner, providing in many instances critical input that influenced the subsequent paths of these movements in the United States.

Similarly, this biography tells of Holloway-Langford's engagement with the rapidly changing social world in America during the decades following

the Civil War—the Victorian era. This is the story of a Southern "lady"
and divorcée who successfully embraced a range of roles forbidden at
that time, including journalist, feminist, alternative religionist, and social
critic. She occupied a borderland position during much of her professional
life. Sasson's account of Holloway-Langford's accomplishments in these
diverse roles is highly instructive with respect to the challenges facing
creative women of the era. The sociological implications of her activities
and interests were radical in her time.

One of the unexpected developments in this story of the twice-married
Holloway-Langford was her extended and deep personal relationships
with the members of the celibate North Family of Shakers at Mount Lebanon, New York, a friendship extending for more than three decades, as
documented in various ways including personal correspondence that was
exchanged for many years. Holloway-Langford clearly shared the Shakers'
enthusiasm for spiritism. She was also a financial benefactor of sorts for
the community, purchasing a Shaker farm in Upper Canaan, New York,
in 1906 at a point when the members of the United Society of Believers
in Christ's Second Appearing—the formal name of the Shakers—were
experiencing very difficult times. Both sides of this unusual relationship
valued it highly.

But Holloway-Langford's engagement with the Shakers was merely one
aspect of her manifold religious interests, interests that were expressed
in her personal relationships with diverse religious figures; in her insa-
tiable appetite for the various expressions of the occult, the marginal, and
Eastern religious traditions; and in her confidence regarding a post-death
existence of some sort. This panoply of interests, for example, was responsible for her personal relationships with William Q. Judge and Helena
Petrovna Blavatsky of the Theosophical Society, as well as for her extensive international travel to Europe, where she met with diverse parties who
shared her concerns and curiosities regarding Buddhism and other Eastern religious traditions. Theosophy, or "divine wisdom," featured a body
of ancient teachings believed to have existed prior to any of the world's
religions, the source of all spiritual insight and knowledge. The goal or task
of Theosophists was to recover, revive, and represent this ancient wisdom.
In many respects, Holloway-Langford was far ahead of the majority of
her contemporaries in the United States in that her religious worldview

was not confined principally to the Judeo-Christian tradition. She sought and found spiritual insight from diverse metaphysical and Asian religious sources. In that respect she anticipated spiritual and religious viewpoints that would not be widespread in American culture until the 1960s, and that are increasingly common in the twenty-first century.

One other valuable dimension of this study deserves mention and attention, namely, the personal reflections provided by Diane Sasson regarding her years of engagement with this research project. Sasson's account of the ways that she was drawn into the work for this historical monograph is a revealing look into the ways that highly diverse personal factors influence the choice of topics and the investment of time and thought by professional historians. The result of this effort is a highly readable and insightful work that casts light both on its subject and on the process of historical reconstruction.

Catherine L. Albanese
Stephen J. Stein

ACKNOWLEDGMENTS

LIBRARIANS are truly the unsung heroes of book projects that are based on obscure or archival material. I cannot name all those who helped me, but my gratitude goes to librarians at the American Society for Psychical Research; Brooklyn Public Library; Columbia University Library; the Library of Congress; Nashville Metropolitan Archives; the New York Historical Society; the New York Public Library; and the Tennessee State Library and Archives. My special thanks go to the Interlibrary Loan staff at Vanderbilt University Library.

Other librarians have become friends and partners in my research. In particular, I thank Christopher Benda and Anne Richardson at the Vanderbilt Divinity Library; Christian Goodwillie, Curator of Special Collections and Archives at Hamilton College, and formerly at the Hancock Shaker Village; Jerry Grant at the Emma B. King Library at the Shaker Museum and Library in Old Chatham, New York; Carol Kaplan at the Nashville Public Library; Janet Kerschner at the Theosophical Society in America; Joan Sutcliffe at the HPB Library, Toronto; and E. Richard McKinstry and Jeanne Solensky at the Henry Francis du Pont Winterthur Museum and Library.

There must be special acknowledgment, as well, of all who labor to make available primary resources on the web. This book could scarcely have taken shape without the ability to search online nineteenth-century newspapers and magazines. In particular, documents posted on the web made it possible for me to study the early years of the Theosophical movement without travel to distant libraries.

Many individuals stimulated me to expand my thinking about Laura. Joseph Horowitz insisted that I see the Metropolitan Opera's production of *Parsifal*. By doing so, I came to better understand Laura's absorption with Wagner. Michael Gomes, at the Emily Sellon Memorial Library of the New York Theosophical Society, suggested sources and brought occult novels to my attention. Kathy Stumph, owner of Welcome Home, an antique shop in Chatham, New York, gave my research a special impetus when she handed me a treasure trove of Laura material.

I am pleased that this book is part of the Religion in North America series edited by Catherine L. Albanese and Stephen J. Stein. Catherine Albanese's comments on the manuscript kept me on Laura's track, steeling me against the temptation to pursue other interesting paths. Stephen Stein has encouraged my work in Shaker studies, inspiring me to persist through the lean as well as the fruitful years. At Indiana University Press, Dee Mortensen, Senior Sponsoring Editor, her assistant Sarah Jacobi, Angela Burton, Managing Editor, and Marvin Keenan, Manuscript Editor, initiated me into the mysteries of book production. Thanks to my copy editor Emma Young for her attentive reading of the manuscript. Finally, my appreciation goes to my husband Jack for his unfailing support, editorial comments, and computer ministrations.

I dedicate this book to Claudia J. Keenan. Curiosity about Laura brought us together, and over the last three years we have emailed each time a startling discovery turned up. Claudia unstintingly shared with me her knowledge, her ideas, and even her original research. She, no less than any of the others named here, bears no responsibility for any errors of fact or interpretation; but without her collaboration, writing this book would have been much less gratifying.

A NOTE ON NAMES

LAURA HOLLOWAY-LANGFORD was a woman of many names. She was born Laura O. Carter. When she married in 1862, she became Laura C. Holloway, the name under which she published until 1890, when she married Edward L. Langford and assumed his surname. To avoid confusion, I have chosen to call her "Laura Holloway-Langford," a form of her name that she occasionally used. In the notes, I abbreviate her name as "LHL," which I use in reference to correspondence irrespective of how the letter was addressed. The appendix contains a bibliography of her publications, arranged chronologically, with the author's name as it originally appeared (entries with no name listed were published anonymously). In notes referring to her writings, I put the name under which she published in brackets in the first reference. In quoted material, however, her name varies. For example, among Theosophists she was known as "Mrs. Holloway."

"Theosophy" or "Theosophist" with a capital "T" refers to the Society established by Helena Blavatsky and to its members. References to "theosophy" refer to the more general search for divine wisdom or enlightenment. Helena Petrovna Blavatsky signed correspondence "H. P. B.," and the Theosophical literature often refers to her by these initials. Likewise, in this literature the Master Morya is sometimes referred to as "M." or "Master M.," while Koot Hoomi becomes "K. H." or "Master K. H." In the text, I use full names, but the abbreviated forms appear in quoted material. Theosophical literature customarily refers to persons from India by their first name, a practice continued in subsequent historical writing. I prefer, however, to use surnames. For example, rather than referring to "Mohini," I use "Chatterji," a spelling I have chosen because it is the form under which he published, although Theosophists often spelled his name "Chatterjee." A list of abbreviations for manuscript collections appears at the end of the book with the notes.

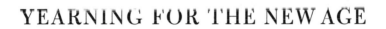

YEARNING FOR THE NEW AGE

Introduction

TO PRESIDENT Andrew Johnson she was a "little rebel." To Helena Blavatsky, founder of the Theosophical Society, she was a "bomb-shell from the Dugpa world." In occult fiction, she is portrayed as a busybody who fancied herself a mental healer. Some Theosophists labeled her a "Sex Maya." Brooklyn newspapers identified her as the "chief priestess" in the Wagner cult, but Henry Ward Beecher praised her as the most eloquent lecturer on the subject of woman in America.

Who was this person who evoked such strong and disparate reactions? Laura Carter Holloway-Langford (1843–1930) appeared to be a conventional Victorian woman. She was slender, with brown hair and blue eyes, polite and soft-spoken, but wielding a strong Southern accent. Today she is remembered as the author of a popular tome, *Ladies of the White House*, and as the founder of the Seidl Society, an organization that brought musical culture to women and children. She is also recognized as one of the first women to work in a newsroom, becoming an editor at the *Brooklyn Daily Eagle*. Beneath the veneer of professionalism and middle-class sobriety, however, Laura Holloway-Langford led a shadow life as a spiritual seeker. She was, by turns, a spiritualist, a Theosophist, a Buddhist, and so closely allied with the Shakers that some called her "Sister Laura."

Until recently most accounts of her accomplishments relied on embellished stories that she perpetuated, some of which are repeated in studies on the Theosophical Society, the Shakers, Buddhism, and Wagner.[1] It was only in 2007 that an accurate chronology of her life was established by

Claudia J. Keenan for the *Tennessee Encyclopedia of History and Culture*. About the same time, I published articles detailing her relationship with the Shakers and her attitude toward her Southern identity.[2] Yet the common thread in all these aspects of her life, her spiritual quest, has been unexplored.

Laura Holloway-Langford believed that a new era was emerging when universal truths would be acknowledged, moral purity would triumph, and harmonious social and economic relations would prevail. In this study, I trace her search for this "New Age" over more than half a century of American social and religious change.[3] Holloway-Langford's life can be a lens through which to view the emergence of a distinctively American spirituality in the late nineteenth and early twentieth centuries. Her attraction to alternative religions was inextricable from her desire for personal autonomy and her belief in women's social and economic rights. She was ambivalent about suffrage, but unequivocal about the necessity of transforming family and sexual relationships. At the same time, she embodied the internal contradictions that feminist women faced even as they aspired to take on new roles.[4] She rejected domesticity but married twice and was a devoted mother. In her writing and lectures, she voiced Victorian pieties about womanhood while she fought to free herself from them.

Laura Holloway-Langford claimed to be a delicate, "true" woman who worked outside the home only from necessity, but she was an ambitious journalist and a shrewd businesswoman. She portrayed herself as a humble worker in benevolent causes, but dreamed of creating powerful organizations that she could control. She allowed her desire for respectability to limit her potential, yet she welcomed new ways of understanding herself and her place in society. Rejecting creedal formulations and institutional religion, like other "restless souls," she set out on a path that led away from conventional Protestantism and toward a syncretic mix of Christianity, theosophy, and Eastern religious traditions.[5] She came to believe that hidden, esoteric truths were at the core of all sacred traditions and texts. For Holloway-Langford, the unity of East and West signaled the dawning of a New Age when the material world would yield to the spiritual.

This book focuses primarily on the years between 1870 and 1910, with the last chapter set in the 1920s. The story begins in Brooklyn of the 1870s, after Laura Holloway-Langford and her family left Tennessee in the aftermath of the Civil War. There, she found a home among ultraliberal Protestants—Congregationalists, Unitarians, and Free Thinkers—who rejected the Christian claim to an exclusive path to salvation. Struggling to reconstitute her life economically as well as socially, Holloway-Langford turned to phrenology, which asserted that the characteristics of each human body revealed truths about the moral, emotional, and intellectual makeup of the individual. Like many who were attracted to phrenology, Holloway-Langford was also a spiritualist, convinced that the "veil" separating the living from the dead could be lifted by those who possessed psychic powers. Among her close friends she was reputed to be a gifted clairvoyant. In the late 1870s she began a relationship with a community of Shakers, whose ideals of sexual purity and equality she admired. By the 1880s, Holloway-Langford's interest in spiritualism and the occult led her to join the Theosophical Society, where she discovered Eastern religious thought. A seminal event in her spiritual quest was a trip to Europe in the summer of 1884, when she became a disciple of Helena Petrovna Blavatsky and the Adept Brotherhood, the enlightened ones whom Theosophists called the Mahatmas. Among her most prized possessions were letters that she received from a Mahatma named Koot Hoomi. By the mid-1880s, she had adopted the mantra of the Theosophical Society, "There is no religion higher than Truth." After returning to the United States, she was among those who introduced a new vocabulary into American religious discourse, helping the public feel comfortable with ideas drawn from Eastern traditions.

Despite the influence of theosophy and Eastern religious ideas, Holloway-Langford's spirituality remained deeply rooted in the American experience. After the Civil War, during a time of great social fluidity, she questioned all hierarchies, whether religious, racial, or sexual. Even though she looked to the past for ancient wisdom, she cherished a hope, rooted in Protestant millennialism, that from the rubble of the old society a new world would be born. Like many feminists of her era, however, she did not look to political solutions to remedy social inequality, but instead believed that progress depended on individual self-reliance and self-development. Nevertheless, her view of marriage situated her among the "sex radicals" of the Victorian era.[6] She believed that neither religion nor law sanctioned marriage and that the only justification for sexual relations was spiritual affinity. Additionally, she was attracted to eugenic theories that claimed that only such marriages were capable of producing superior offspring. Some of her ideas were radical, but she, like many Victorian women, was deeply conflicted about sexual desire. She acknowledged its power, but argued that it must be directed toward spiritual rather than physical expression. She advocated women's control over their own bodies, but she shied away from any suggestion that women should be free to express their sexuality.[7] In her public persona and in her published writings, she endeavored to preserve the image of high-minded Victorian respectability. Consequently, only among spiritualists, Theosophists, and Shakers did Laura Holloway-Langford find a space where her "unorthodox gender politics" could be expressed.[8]

From the time that she moved north, Laura Holloway-Langford sought to reinvent herself. Through her constant refashioning of her identity, she created an elusive personality. She never gave wholehearted allegiance to any organization. In her later years she was disillusioned with both the Theosophical Society and the Shakers. Her loyalty was to the idea of a higher self. Thus, she is a transitional figure, one who reflects the breakdown of religious certainty during the Victorian era and the subsequent search for a synthesis that would usher in a New Age of spirituality.

Laura Holloway-Langford's spiritual quest is rooted in the social and cultural dislocation that she experienced in her early adulthood. Her story begins in Nashville, Tennessee, before the Civil War.

GROWING UP SOUTHERN

Laura O. Carter was born on August 22, 1843, the sixth of fourteen children and the eldest daughter of Samuel Jefferson Carter and Anne Catherine Vaulx. Although the family traced its ancestry to the tidewater Virginia Carters, her father had immigrated to Tennessee from the foothills of the Blue Ridge Mountains.[9] Originally the Vaulx family had been Episcopalian, but by the mid-nineteenth century it was affiliated with the Presbyterian Church, where Holloway-Langford received an orthodox Calvinist religious education.[10]

Laura Holloway-Langford was fortunate to complete her education before the Civil War, graduating from the Nashville Female Academy in June 1860. At that time, it was "the largest school for young ladies in the country," with a rigorous curriculum that included the study of the physical and biological sciences, physiology, mathematics, political science, and philosophy. Calisthenics was required, and students could choose to study French, German, or Spanish. Senior girls were also expected to demonstrate skill in art and music. In early 1860, the Academy employed two piano instructors who had studied in Paris at the Conservatoire Impérial.[11] Despite the modern course of study, the principal, Reverend Collins D. Elliott, held conventional ideas about a woman's place in the world. He believed that a girl should be educated "according to God's Word" and that "every fiber of her mind" should be directed toward marriage and motherhood. He assured parents that the "sweetly submissive and sublimely trusting lady heart" of the Academy's students would be protected from "strong-minded" women who might infect them with "mannishness of mind and soul." Accordingly, he fired a prominent teacher who suggested that by becoming educated young women might live independent of marriage.[12]

When Holloway-Langford was a student at the Female Academy, her father, Samuel Carter, was proprietor of the Nashville Inn, located at 55 Public Square, with the family residence nearby. He owned a farm three miles outside of town, but he was primarily a businessman who also traded land and raced horses at the Walnut Grove track which he managed. In the mid-nineteenth century, Nashville was no provincial backwater. With its wharf on the Cumberland River, the city was a bustling commercial, cultural, and political hub. It boasted four bookstores, where one could even find a translation of the Koran. Its theaters attracted major stage and musical performers, including Jenny Lind and Edwin Booth, who starred in *Richard the Third* and *Hamlet*. By the mid-1850s, Italian opera was performed regularly in Nashville.[13] Holloway-Langford not only had the opportunity to experience live music and theater, but she also met the actors and musicians who boarded at her father's hotels. In the 1850s, one of these was the young violinist Camilla Urso, who became her friend.

In the 1860s, Samuel Carter ran the St. Cloud Hotel. According to the *Nashville Daily American,* the hotel was a comfortable if not elegant establishment with a dining room and a bar. Centrally located near the Capitol, it was the "haunt of all the great men" and the place where members of the state legislature gathered to work out their strategies. The St. Cloud became even more prominent during the "troublous times." When, on February 25, 1862, Union troops arrived in Nashville, their commander, Brigadier General William Babcock Hazen, and his staff stopped at the hotel. A room was kept reserved for Andrew Johnson after he became military Governor of the state, and General George H. Thomas established his headquarters at the St. Cloud.

> Gov. Johnson sent forth his military edicts from its walls; Gen. Buell, when the city fell into his power, held court there. It had many gruesome aspects, too. The Government undertaker was stationed across the street and came there every day to receive the consignments of Federal corpses from neighboring battlefields. They came in, often three carloads at once, and were stacked up, one upon the other, like cord wood, with the greatest neatness and precision. The good people of the city would come to look at them and talk about them to each other; their dead foes.[14]

There were rumors, too, that Confederate spies infiltrated the public rooms of the hotel. Only a block away, the unfinished Maxwell House Hotel had been turned into a Union prison, and the First Presbyterian Church, catty-corner from the St. Cloud, was a federal military hospital.

The War divided the Carter family, with some members fighting for the Confederacy while others took up arms on behalf of the Union. Holloway-Langford's sentiments in the early years of the conflict were decidedly Confederate. Benjamin Truman, Secretary to Andrew Johnson, described her as "a vehement rebel, young, pretty, brilliant, vivacious, *petite,* and savage." Mr. Carter's "pretty daughter Laura" was even arrested for spitting on Union officers from the porch of the hotel. Told to behave herself because Andrew Johnson was a guest there, she replied that she would dance on his grave. When this was reported to Johnson, he responded: "Oh, you mustn't mind these little rebels. There is no harm in Laura. Dance on my grave, will she? She will plant flowers instead. I'll take care of her. Let her go."[15]

MARRIAGE TO A UNION OFFICER

Holloway-Langford's sentiments changed when she fell in love with a Union officer who frequented the St. Cloud. Captain Junius Brutus Holloway, from Richmond, Kentucky, was on the personal staff of General Don Carlos Buell. Laura had known Junius Holloway for just over three months when they were married on June 18, 1862. She had the distinction of being the first of many local girls to marry a "Yankee" during the occupation of Nashville.[16] Within weeks of the marriage, Holloway was captured by the Confederates. When released, he was arrested by the Union Army and accused of disloyalty. The Andrew Johnson papers recounted that "one of Samuel Carter's slaves later deposed that Holloway not only had said that he would 'rather go South and join the Southern Army' than take the loyalty oath but also that he had spoken of Union officers as 'Abolition Sons of Bitches.'"[17] Thus it appears that, despite their belief in the Union, both Laura and Junius had strong sympathy for the Confederacy. Junius Holloway was still in prison in June 1863, perhaps at the Maxwell House Hotel, when his wife wrote to Andrew Johnson on his behalf: "At the request of my Husband who is under arrest I write this note thanking you for the kind interest you have taken in him. . . . My Husband would write himself but he is not allowed the privilege. If you can spare a few moments, Gov., will you come down and see him? He is very unhappy about this unfounded arrest and wishes to see you. If you could leave your business for a few moments, you will confer a very great favor."[18] Later that month, due to her intervention, Junius Holloway was released without facing additional prosecution, but by late 1863 his military career was finished. The couple was reunited, however briefly. Their only child was born in Nashville in 1864. They named him George Thomas, after the general who led the Union army in the Battle of Nashville. The young family had no opportunity to establish a home of their own, probably living with the Carters at the St. Cloud Hotel.

Within four years, the marriage had dissolved. Laura closely guarded the details of their separation, but for the rest of her life she subtracted five years from her age in order to obscure this part of her history. There were reports of a divorce, although when and where it took place is unknown.[19] Junius Holloway remarried, and until his death in 1915 he worked in Washington, D.C., as a clerk for the U.S. House of Representatives, dealing with Civil War claims.[20] After she left Nashville, however, Holloway-Langford claimed to be a widow, a status that was all too common for women in the postwar years and which, apparently, was not questioned.

LEAVING THE SOUTH

In March 1865, when Andrew Johnson assumed the Presidency after the death of Lincoln, William Brownlow became governor of Tennessee. Samuel Carter, a Brownlow supporter, was elected to the state General Assembly representing Davidson County. On February 25, 1865, shortly after the Thirteenth Amendment to the Constitution was passed, the State of Tennessee, seeking readmission to the Union, voted to free the slaves. In a circular published in a local newspaper, Carter urged his constituency to accept Emancipation as "an accomplished fact" and to support the reorganized state government.[21] The Radical Party chose Carter as its candidate for a seat in Congress from the 5th Congressional District. However, in the election on August 3, 1865, Samuel Carter was soundly defeated by the Conservative Ticket candidate.[22] Nashville in the 1860s was not hospitable to homegrown Unionists, even those as deeply entrenched in the community as the Carters. The family was threatened by a "vigilante committee," and some of the younger children were prevented from attending school.[23] With Emancipation, Samuel Carter had lost much of his wealth. Violence escalated, and the city was flooded with refugees. Anson Nelson, a prominent citizen whom Holloway-Langford had known since her childhood, recalled Nashville in 1865: "During the latter months of this year, the city was full of thieves and robbers, and deeds of blood and robbery were frequent. It was unsafe to go out at night, without arms."[24] Holloway-Langford later said that her father was reluctant to leave Nashville, but that she and her mother persuaded him that they must do so in order to provide the younger children with an education.

In 1866, Laura Holloway-Langford and her son George, accompanied by Samuel and Anne Carter and their seven younger children, left Nash-

ville for New York. In the North, Samuel Carter struggled to find a job
and establish his sons in business. Holloway-Langford turned to President
Andrew Johnson for help, but she was not pleased with the job of store-
keeper that was offered. Believing that the hours were too long and the
pay too little, she again wrote the President, requesting that he find her
father a more "exalted, less laborious" position.[25] Despite these interven-
tions, Samuel Carter never regained his economic footing, and the family
was supported by the work of his children. The three youngest, Annie,
Ella, and Vaulx, were at school, but Samuel, Jr., who was sixteen when the
family arrived in New York, and, Frank, who was even younger, worked as
clerks. Irene was a stenographer, while Laura hoped to contribute to the
family income by her pen, first trying her hand at fiction and poetry before
finding her vocation as a biographer and journalist.

In 1870, the family moved to the "Heights" in Brooklyn, where Holloway-
Langford took her first position with a newspaper. After the death of
her parents, she was left to raise two younger siblings, as well as her son
George.[26] She left no account of how she managed her newspaper work
plus her domestic responsibilities, but the evidence suggests that she struggled both financially and emotionally. In 1878, Holloway-Langford was
boarding with a family at 179 Schermerhorn Street in Brooklyn, while
George, too old to share a room with his mother, lived with a Chinese
immigrant couple who ran a laundry. It was only in late 1883 or early 1884
that Holloway-Langford moved into her own home, at 181 Schermerhorn,
where she would live for more than two decades.[27]

These early experiences had a profound effect on Laura Holloway-
Langford, but her spiritual yearnings cannot be reduced to the exigen-
cies of personal trauma. Many Southern women suffered loss, dislocation, and poverty, yet they did not explore alternatives to conventional
Protestantism. The cultural milieu that Holloway-Langford encountered
in the North, however, exposed her to new ideas about both religion and
the place of women in society. During her first years in New York, she
lived near Union Square, within a few blocks of the Academy of Music.[28]
With a theater that seated more than 3,000, the Academy popularized
opera to American audiences. Close by, at East 14th and Irving Place,
Stephen Pearl Andrews resided at a boardinghouse where spiritualists
congregated. Andrews had founded the Free Love League, and was one

of the authors of *Love, Marriage and Divorce, and the Sovereignty of the Individual.* Holloway-Langford would have found especially interesting Andrews's defense of divorce and his belief that sexual relations should be based only on spiritual affinities.[29]

In New York, Holloway-Langford could walk to Cooper Union, which had been founded, in part, to provide vocational training for "respectable females of suitable capacity."[30] Open to the public were a reading room and library where she may well have done her early writing. Cooper Union was a magnet for proponents of new ideas. In 1867, "a mass demonstration of the colored people" of New York heard speeches by William Lloyd Garrison, Wendell Phillips, Horace Greeley, and Henry Ward Beecher, who addressed the audience about deprivation and suffering in the Southern states.[31] Labor organizations convened in its Great Hall, which was also the meeting place of the Working Women's Protective Association.[32] Women's rights were debated there, with the National Women's Suffrage Association sponsoring a lecture by Anna E. Dickinson in spring 1869.[33] Holloway-Langford also may have been among the hundreds who attended séances at Cooper Union, which in March 1869 hosted a celebration of the "Advent of Modern Spiritualism."[34]

By the time she moved from New York City to Brooklyn in 1870, Laura Holloway-Langford had left the social and cultural world of Nashville, Tennessee, far behind. She was ready to join ranks with women who were throwing off conventional sexual relationships as well as orthodox religious ideas. A new world had opened to her.

1

Sex, Suffrage, and Religious Seekers

In the decades after the Civil War, Brooklyn was a center for activist women who rejected Victorian notions of womanhood and who sought ways to express their spiritual yearnings beyond the bounds of mainstream religion. Overwhelmingly white, middle-class, and of Protestant heritage, this first generation of "New Women" broke down social and economic barriers and entered the work force as professionals and wage-earners. Many women lacked the opportunity for higher education, but a large number nevertheless followed careers as writers, journalists, and lecturers. Some obtained scientific and medical training allowing them to teach other women about their bodies and to lobby for sex education in the schools. Many women were active in movements for women's rights, while still others worked for an equitable economic system based on coop eration rather than competition. Despite their varying professional paths, they joined together to create organizations that supported women's quest for education, meaningful work, and self-development. These efforts to enlarge women's lives and to reform society were inspired and sustained by a changing religious climate. Rejecting traditional sources of authority and reformulating liberal Protestantism, such women were freed to envision a New Age of social, sexual, economic, and spiritual equality.[1]

Women's organizations created a social space where members could express and contest new ideas, and where they could experiment with new social, political, and religious roles. A number of scholars have detailed the role of such societies as sites for "intimate" practices of reading and writing and as forces in progressive politics.[2] Women's clubs, however, also nourished unconventional ideas and encouraged women to become religious and social leaders. Located between the private, domestic world of family life and the public world of work and politics, they established a milieu in which women could expand their religious knowledge and diversify their spiritual vocabularies.

Through the organizations they established and led, Laura Holloway-Langford and her friends transmitted radical ideas to the bourgeois women of Brooklyn. Unlike Helena Blavatsky, the founder of the Theosophical Society, or Mary Baker Eddy, who originated Christian Science, these women are largely forgotten; yet they were the cultural workers who disseminated new ideas to the American public. Because of their Anglo-Protestant heritage and their economic and social standing, they were able to "defy proprieties, pioneer new roles, and still insist upon a rightful place within the genteel world."[3] Through the reforms they championed, the speeches they gave, and the papers they published, Laura Holloway-Langford and her colleagues helped to make Brooklyn comparable to Boston as a center of feminist and religious ferment. Their patronage of alternative religious views lent respectability to ideas that were once deemed radical but that by the twentieth century had come to seem ordinary.

CHANGING RELIGIOUS IDEAS

By 1870, a generation of Protestants in Brooklyn had been raised on a heady diet of rationalism and Transcendentalism, seemingly contradictory philosophies that were nevertheless often intertwined in the minds of those seeking new forms of spirituality. For many seekers, Emerson was a touchstone for their inner lives. Religiously liberal women frequently quoted him, finding in his writings sanction for their belief in an indwelling God who could be known intuitively. Through Emerson and other Transcendentalists, many intellectual Brooklyn women were also introduced to Eastern philosophy. At the same time, however, they were influenced by intense forms of Protestant rationalism, exemplified by the

Free Religious Association that had been formed in 1867 and that opposed all forms of supernaturalism. Emerson was one of the Association's early members and a speaker at its first gathering. From its inception, the leadership of the Free Religious Association supported women's rights. Ednah Dow Cheney, a Boston social reformer and member of the New England Women's Club, was one of the founders. Speakers at the first convention included Robert Dale Owen, the utopian socialist and spiritualist; Lucretia Mott, women's rights activist; Thomas Wentworth Higginson, advocate of racial and sexual equality; and Isaac M. Wise, the liberal reform rabbi. At his temple, Wise had initiated accepting women as equals in the minyan required for synagogue prayers. Participants in the Free Religious Association were, for the most part, Unitarians, liberal Universalists, or Quakers, but the gathering included spiritualists, Jews, and the "unchurched." Professing an all-inclusive religion of humanity, the Association was also committed to the "scientific" study of religion.

Most Brooklyn women were not led to doubt the religious orthodoxies of their youth by studying the new biblical scholarship that challenged the supernatural claims of the Bible and the divinity of Jesus. Nor, with the exception of a few intellectuals such as Dr. Clemence Lozier, who advised alumnae of the New York Medical College to read "Darwin, Tindall, Herbert Spencer, Buckle, and Agassiz," did they read the original work of the seminal thinkers of their day.[4] Instead, they came into contact with these ideas through popular magazines, newspapers, and even in works of fiction. For example, The Phrenological Journal was widely read, and in one single issue in 1870 readers could have found articles discussing evolution, the marriage problem, communism and taxation, dreams, dress reform, and the relative influence of Confucius versus Muhammed.[5] The Phrenological Journal also kept close tabs on the Free Religious Association, and it reported how Octavius Brooks Frothingham, its first president, described the "religion of the future." According to him, it would be neither Catholic, nor Protestant, nor "technically Christian," but would be a democratic religion of humanity. The editor of the Phrenological Journal added his own version of the coming New Age: "We see [man] rising from his present sensualism into a higher mentality, and culminating in the perfect man God intended him to be. Buddhism, Mohammedanism, Judaism, Roman-ism, Protestantism will have their day, and man will outgrow his sectarian creed. Whether he can ever outgrow Christianity, is a question which no man of this generation can decide."[6]

Yet a number of Laura Holloway-Langford's friends believed that they had indeed outgrown Christianity, and they worked for social reforms that would create a society that eschewed claims of religious exclusivity. In 1863, when she was only twenty, Mary C. Putnam had severed her membership in the Baptist Church, declaring her disbelief in the "orthodox system of Divinity" and rejecting doctrines of the Trinity, the Atonement, and Eternal Punishment. Putnam, whose father was the publisher George P. Putnam, received a medical degree from the New England Hospital in Boston and a doctorate from the Sorbonne. Subsequently, she married Abraham Jacobi, a German-Jewish immigrant and distinguished pediatrician who was head of the New York Medical Society. The Jacobis professed no religious creed, and considered themselves citizens of the world of liberal ideas.[7]

Whether or not they affiliated themselves with a religious organization, progressive women in Brooklyn shared ideas that were widespread among the most liberal Protestants. They rejected Calvinism, especially the doctrines of original sin and the need for atonement. They decried sectarianism, and most believed that the "superstitions" of the past would be replaced by a universal religion. Rather than looking to the Church for answers, many women, like their male counterparts, turned to science as the source of knowledge. They had faith in evolution as the key to social and religious progress. Most of them discerned no contradiction between rational approaches to knowledge and a belief in a corresponding unseen world of the spirit. Many also argued that occult laws governed the spiritual world just as physical laws controlled the material world. During the last quarter of the nineteenth century, many progressive women in Brooklyn considered themselves mystics, spiritualists, psychics, students of the occult, Theosophists, Buddhists, or Vedantins, some identifying simultaneously with several of these categories. By the end of the century, a new metaphysical lexicon—which included terms such as materialization, karma, reincarnation, and astral bodies—was almost as familiar to this group of Brooklyn women as the vocabulary of sin and redemption had been to the previous generation.

Ann Braude has shown that American women who adhered to "hetero-dox" theologies also tended to support a reform agenda including women's rights.[8] Barbara Goldsmith has confirmed the connections between suffrage and spiritualism.[9] Likewise, Joy Dixon has demonstrated that theosophy and feminism in England often went hand-in-hand.[10] In the years immediately after the Civil War, many white, middle-class Brooklyn women held ideas about sexual relationships that would, in other parts of the country, have seemed even more radical than their religious ideas. They argued that sexual relations should be consensual and not under male control, that neither marriage nor motherhood should be the ultimate goal for every woman, and that divorce should be an option for a loveless marriage, which was considered death to the spirit. Yet far from advocating sexual permissiveness, many women were active in the social purity movement. They sought to apply the standards of sexual chastity to men equally as to women, redefining the ideal union between man and woman as spiritual. What they had in common was a rejection of Protestant orthodoxies that supported traditional gender arrangements, and they sought new spiritual understandings of what it meant to be a man or a woman.

BECOMING A WRITER

Laura C. Holloway-Langford's writing career debuted with an obscure novel, *Laure: the History of a Blighted Life,* by L. C. H., published in 1869 and reprinted in 1872.[11] Since the 1850s, the failure of marriage had been a major theme in popular domestic novels by women. Sometimes these were lightly disguised autobiographies, like the popular *Ruth Hall* by Sara Payson Willis Parton, in which the heroine is left destitute when her husband dies but after many tribulations gains fame and fortune as a journalist.[12] It would not be surprising, then, for Laura Holloway-Langford to hope that she might catapult herself from poverty by writing domestic fiction. Though originally advertised as an autobiography, *Laure* does not portray the external facts of Laura Holloway-Langford's life. Nevertheless, at an emotional level the book describes the suffering and shame that Holloway-Langford endured because of her marriage as well as her eventual realization that she was responsible for her own happiness.

The heroine of the novel is a French school girl who turns down the suitors chosen by her family in order to marry a mysterious American, Joseph B. Hilton (whose initials, of course, rehearse Junius B. Holloway). When he learns that his wife is pregnant, Hilton abandons Laure and returns to the United States. Infant daughter in arms, Laure pursues him, even though she admits that her "love and devotion had all been wasted upon one who was false and unworthy."[13] Hilton physically abuses Laure, threatens her life, and even kidnaps the child (whom the brave Laure steals back). Having heard that Hilton has died in the Civil War, Laure plans to remarry, but she is distressed to discover that he is still alive. None too soon for the reader, Laure realizes that she can depend only on herself. After a friend counsels her that it will be easier to find work in a city where she is not known and can portray herself as a widow, Laure moves to St. Louis, where she teaches French and music. At the novel's conclusion, the narrator states: "Hilton is still alive, a lonely and miserable man . . . poor and friendless. . . . As for me I am 'living my own life.'"[14]

What made it possible for Laura Holloway-Langford to live her own life was the success of her book, *Ladies of the White House*, first published in the same year as *Laure*. After leaving Nashville, she hit upon the idea of writing a collection of biographies of First Ladies. She was probably inspired by her friend, Martha Patterson, the daughter of Andrew Johnson who assumed the role of First Lady during her father's administration, due to the infirmity of her mother. With the help of President Johnson, Holloway-Langford obtained reminiscences from still-living relatives of the first families. When the book was complete, she mailed him a copy. From his home in east Tennessee, Johnson wrote: "I have no corrections to make & endorse as written. *God bless* you in all your efforts to make a good name."[15] The patronage of the President jump-started her career as a writer, and the success of *The Ladies of the White House* brought Laura Holloway-Langford to the attention of the New York literary world.

The first edition of the book, which was sold by subscription, became a bestseller, with sales reported to have reached 100,000 copies. The title page of the book quoted Schiller:

> "Honor to women! To them it is given
> To garden the earth with the roses of heaven."

In the introduction, Holloway-Langford wrote: "The Ladies of the White House have had no biographers. The customs of the Republic, which returns to private life those who have served it, effectually deterred the historian from venturing on such difficult and obscure ground. The space allotted to them has been confined to descriptions of their personal appearances on public occasions, or, perhaps, a mention of their names in sketches of their husbands." In subsequent editions, she argued that women's contributions to the nation should be included in the country's historical memory.[16] *Ladies of the White House*, then, was an early prototype for the later work of feminist historians. Yet, as Claudia J. Keenan has pointed out, Holloway-Langford's work also perpetuated the valorization of domesticity. She notes that while *Ladies of the White House* emphasized the "modesty, devotion, and faithfulness" of the Presidents' wives, it also portrayed them as having "been tested by life" and having overcome some "personal difficulty or sorrow." Keenan observes that Holloway-Langford's "own disappointments echo through her stories of the first ladies."[17] Identification with the lives of women who had overcome adversity would shape Holloway-Langford's lectures and writing for the next decade.

After the publication of *Ladies of the White House*, Holloway-Langford secured a contract for another book, *Homes of Famous Americans*. Once again she solicited President Johnson's help, writing a flirtatious letter asking him to send her a description of his home. Additionally, she appealed to his sympathy:

> My Friend, do not grieve my heart by a refusal to write, if need be, more than once about this matter. I try to be, and am, lively and full of hope, but my life is sadly checkered, and there has been much to suffer which should have been spared me. But I am inspired with a strong desire to achieve success, and . . . I will try to carve a name in history. And think of it: the very name I bear is not my own and I despise it.[18]

Yet it was under the name "Holloway" that she was establishing her literary reputation.

Although she continued to write some fiction and poetry, Laura Holloway-Langford soon assumed the professional identity of journalist, a career that did not require self-revelation. Many early female journalists used pseudonyms, which, even when the author's identity was known, nevertheless created a persona that provided distance between the personal and professional life. Sara Jane Lippincott, an editor of *Godey's Lady's Book* and the first woman on the payroll of the *New York Times,* wrote under the name "Grace Greenwood"; Jane Cunningham Croly, the first female journalist to syndicate her writing, used the byline "Jennie June"; Sara Payson Willis Parton, whose popular column ran from 1856 until her death in 1872, published under the name "Fannie Fern"; and Kate Hillard, early in her career, used the name "Lucy Fountain." Laura Holloway-Langford, too, occasionally published under "S. E. Archer," a pseudonym that disguised not only her identity, but also her sex. Later in her life Holloway-Langford asserted that journalism was an appropriate career choice for women because of "the anonymous character of newspaper writing," and she advised female writers to "learn to sink their personality."[19] She believed that as journalists women should not only conceal their personal lives but hide their opinions as well.

Before the war, women journalists had been primarily columnists or feature writers, but by the early 1870s they were also reporting hard news, including politics and international affairs. Mary Clemmer Ames covered Congress for the *New York Independent* and for the *Brooklyn Daily Union,* and Kate Field contributed to newspapers as a European correspondent.[20] Respectable women, however, worked from home or in a genteel editorial office. They did not risk their reputations by working daily in a newsroom, where the rough-and-tumble atmosphere might include crude language, alcohol, and hard opinions. Yet this is exactly what Laura Holloway-Langford did. Unable to earn sufficient income by freelance writing, by the early 1870s she had taken a position at the *Brooklyn Daily Union,* the newspaper owned by Henry E. Bowen. The press described her as a "true" daughter of the South who would like nothing more than to remain at home with her mother, but who, as head of a household, must earn a living.

> She is, perhaps, the only lady journalist who occupies a regular editorial position and is in her office every day. Her hours of toil are those of the other workers on the paper, although she is the only lady there, and the only consideration extended to her is to permit her to do a man's work, she exerts herself to excel in it, and long ago she made it pay pecuniarily. Her taste of journalism is almost unpardonable in a woman, unless she can sustain all her womanly attributes in the pursuit of her chosen work.

The article gave her credit for retaining her "honor," in part, it seems, because she portrayed herself as descended from "an old aristocratic Virginia family."[21]

THE LECTURE PLATFORM

In addition to newspaper work, Holloway-Langford attempted to establish a career as a lecturer. After the Civil War, women increasingly took to the lecture platform, not only as trance mediums or on behalf of social reform, but also as paid speakers.[22] The most successful women lecturers earned impressive sums: the flamboyant Anna Dickinson was said to make as much as $20,000 a year. Yet almost as soon as she began to speak publicly, Holloway-Langford found herself caught in the maelstrom of conflicting opinions over women's rights. Typically, she lectured on the trials and tribulations of women. Her first address on the life of Charlotte Brontë was given at Cooper Union on January 26, 1870, and was repeated at the Brooklyn Athenaeum on February 24 and in Clinton Hall on April 15.[23] The positive notices in the press focused more on Holloway-Langford's personal appearance than on the substance of her lecture: "Mrs. Holloway has made a loving study of the character and writing of her subject, and bears a strong resemblance to the wonderful little novelist. She is young and pretty, and is said to be a cultured elocutionist."[24]

The lecture, however, was not so well received by the progressive women of New York, because Holloway-Langford reportedly said that Charlotte Brontë "was a woman who had nobly achieved success without the ballot." Holloway-Langford may have been arguing that women need not wait for the vote in order to make more of their lives than marriage and motherhood, but the supporters of suffrage took offense.[25] According to the *Brooklyn Daily Eagle*, after the lecture at the Athenaeum, Holloway-Langford was confronted by "a savage set of sisters," but she successfully defended herself.[26] After praising the lecture, Parker Pillsbury, an editor of the suffragist weekly *The Revolution*, castigated Holloway-Langford for "her invidious, unjust and certainly unnecessary flights at the Woman Suffrage enterprise. . . . The better portion of the audience, heard her with silence mingled with surprise and sorrow. Can anybody doubt whether

Charlotte Bronte would be to-day . . . demanding the right of suffrage equally with men? For the Misses, as well as the Mr. Brontes?"[27]

Several newspapers, liking nothing better than to portray women as engaged in a cat fight, picked up the story. The *Boston Advertiser* reported that when Holloway-Langford had concluded her lecture at the Athenaeum, "a bevy of the strongest-minded waited upon her and asked that she would erase the obnoxious words. The lady, although astonished at their peculiar earnestness, quietly refused to unsay what she had said, or to keep unsaid what she desired to say from the platform. And thus the signal for war was given. The advocates, with the cry that they would 'make New York too hot' for the courageous little lady, began to persecute her in the most annoying way." According to the *Advertiser,* they obtained front row seats the next time she gave the lecture, and when Holloway-Langford "came to the passage which had so angered her now enemies before, [she] looked down into their eyes and repeated the terrible sentences slowly, defiantly and eloquently. They tried to hiss, but some of the lady's admirers knowing to the condition of affairs, drowned their stinging noise with the loudest of loud applause." *The Revolution* denied these reports, especially the rumors that Holloway-Langford "had been visited in person by some of the prominent leaders in the Woman's Suffrage movement and seriously threatened with hisses, if not severer violence, should she repeat some utterances in the lecture unfriendly to their enterprise, in her redelivery of it." In its own defense, *The Revolution* published a letter to Susan B. Anthony written by Laura Holloway-Langford, in which she denied "any complicity" in the newspaper accounts and wrote, "Towards you there can only exist in my heart, the warmest feelings of admiration, and I would deplore any event which would lessen your interest in myself."[28] Holloway-Langford stopped short of saying that she advocated suffrage, but she was careful to praise Anthony, whose backing could be important to her fledgling career. At this point, *The Revolution* called a truce, stating that its criticisms were "in the most friendly spirit; and, with an honest purpose to make the lecture and its author as useful and as widely known and as highly esteemed and admired as she could desire."[29] The following year, Holloway-Langford published a letter in *The Revolution* that phrased her hopes for working women in almost religious terms, but once again she avoided the issue of suffrage: "The poor, hard-working, long-suffering masses of working-women must toil on and toil unceasingly, and look to the future for relief. … But who knows but the last years of the century are to be its grandest; or that its closing decade will not mark the redemption of the working women from the thralldom of accursed customs?"[30]

The interchange between Laura Holloway-Langford and *The Revolution* was the beginning of a long, friendly relationship with Susan B. Anthony. Perhaps more important, it alerted Laura Holloway-Langford to the political milieu which she had entered. Behind the scenes of this dustup was the struggle between the National Woman Suffrage Association, led by Anthony and Elizabeth Cady Stanton, and the more moderate American Woman Suffrage Association. Formed in late 1869, just months before Holloway-Langford's lecture, the AWSA was headed by one of the best-known men in Brooklyn, Henry Ward Beecher, the pastor of Plymouth Church, whose patronage Holloway-Langford also sought. Years later, in a memorial to Beecher, she praised him for welcoming "Southerners who, as exiles from home, had come to dwell among his friends."[31] Ever aware of the importance of cultivating influential friends, Holloway-Langford did not want to be identified with any particular faction of the suffrage movement. She had also been shocked to discover that any woman who mounted the lecture platform, no matter what her politics, was prey for press ridicule. Laura Holloway-Langford, like many women of her generation, attempted to tread a middle path, not offending those in powerful positions while still claiming to fight for the rights of women.

PHRENOLOGY AND SOCIAL REFORM

After leaving behind the religious teachings of her youth, like many of her peers Laura Holloway-Langford turned to phrenology and spiritualism, the first for self-understanding, and the second for comfort in times of loss. Both phrenology and spiritualism were based on belief in a higher spiritual realm, but phrenology claimed that mental faculties, moral propensities, and personality were revealed by the physical characteristics of an individual's skull. Both had spread like wildfire throughout the United States beginning in the late 1840s and gradually declined by the end of the century. In the United States, the brothers Orson and Lorenzo Fowler had adapted the "science" of phrenology to American culture, turning it into a practical tool for self-development and the perfection of the American Republic.[32] In their lectures, books, and in the *Phrenological Journal,* the Fowlers applied the lessons of phrenology to health reform, education, women's rights, and temperance. They were also "among America's pioneer sex educators," campaigning "against the prudery, false modesty, and ignorance that made sex a forbidden subject."[33] Fowler and Wells, as the publishing company was known, brought out Robert Dale Owens's *Labor;* a new edition of Margaret Fuller's *Woman in the Nineteenth Century;* Andrew Jackson Davis's *Philosophy of Spiritual Intercourse;* and the first edition of Susan B. Anthony's *History of Woman Suffrage.* Most famously, it distributed the first and published the second edition of Walt Whitman's *Leaves of Grass.* The Fowlers were friends of many prominent members of the women's rights movement, including Susan B. Anthony, Paulina Wright Davis, Antoinette Blackwell, and Amelia Bloomer. Among the suffragists, Lucretia Mott and Elizabeth Cady Stanton were especially attracted to phrenology.[34]

In 1844, Charlotte Fowler, sister to Orson and Lorenzo, had married Samuel Wells, who ran three major areas of the business: the publishing company; an exhibition hall with a cabinet known as "Golgotha" containing skulls, busts, death masks, casts, drawings, and paintings of animal and human heads; and a personal consultation business where heads were "read" and the client was offered guidance that might range from educational and employment counseling to marital and sexual advice.[35] Charlotte Wells took an active part in the business. She wrote for the journal edited by her husband, gave tours of the phrenological "cabinet," and offered classes especially designed for women. She was convinced that phrenology could lead to social reforms and the increase of women's rights. Having "fully exercised her own inalienable right to work, Charlotte Wells went further than either of her brothers in her concept of woman as the medium through whose influence the millennium would eventually be achieved."[36]

Her husband was less interested in spreading the gospel of sexual liberation than in selling books. He suppressed Orson Fowler's book on sex, later published in revised form as *Sexual Science, Including Manhood, Womanhood, and Their Mutual Interrelations,* and forced Fowler out of the business.[37] In his own writing, Wells cocooned new ideas within a comfortable cushion of Christian orthodoxy and Victorian notions of gender. His *Wedlock; or The Right Relations between the Sexes* introduced the discussion of marriage with biblical quotations, including Paul's admonition that wives should "be subject to their own husbands in everything." Wells depicted marriage as a divine institution established for the purpose of procreation, and he argued that a successful marriage depended on male and female developing complementary attributes, rather than competing in the other's sphere. His ambivalence about women's rights is especially apparent in the chapter on separation and divorce, where Wells turned to scripture for evidence that "the only proper ground for a divorce is connubial infidelity." He nevertheless included detailed information on the grounds for divorce and women's rights to property in the various states, a tangle of information that in the mid-nineteenth century was difficult for the ordinary woman to obtain. He concluded with a plea for the legal rights of married women, and quoted Shakespeare on the need for "right and justice" for "poor woman."[38]

Christopher G. White has shown how Christians who were anxious over their inability to experience the "characteristic emotions of faith" found comfort in phrenology, which offered the possibility that neither the self nor the world was "fallen."[39] Nothing, however, suggests that Laura Holloway-Langford was apprehensive about the state of her soul. What troubled her was the direction her life should take, since her expectations for the future had been dashed. Was there something in her make-up that was to blame for her failures? What were her natural abilities, and how should she apply them? To her, phrenology was not only a mental philosophy; it was also a tool for self-examination. In January 1869, Holloway-Langford's head was "read" by no less than Samuel R. Wells.[40]

In his analysis, Wells gave Holloway-Langford the highest rating, a seven, for benevolence. But he also rated her brain as

LARGE.—With activity and quality 6 or 7, combine great power of mind with great activity; exercise a commanding influence over other minds to sway and persuade; and enjoy and suffer in the extreme; with perceptives [sic] 7, can conduct a large business or undertaking successfully; rise to eminence, if not pre-eminence; and evidence great originality and power of intellect, strong native sense, superior judgment, great force of character and feeling, and make a conspicuous and enduring mark on the intellectual or business world.

She was, stated Wells, characterized by a "predominance of mind over body." It is striking that Wells's evaluation must have boosted Holloway-Langford's confidence in her ability, not only to overcome adversity, but to pursue roles not usually open to women. Phrenology served to stoke her ambition and validate her desire to make a name for herself in the world.

Laura Holloway-Langford had already come to Wells's attention by publishing a poem in *The Phrenological Journal*. Wells was impressed with this young aspiring writer who claimed to be only twenty-one years old. Subsequently, he published many of her early writings, essays, and stories as well as poems. Charlotte Fowler Wells was also moved by the personal story Laura Holloway-Langford told—of an aristocratic Southern family brought to economic ruin by the war, of a young mother widowed and forced to support her family by her pen. However much Holloway-Langford disguised and embroidered her past, her story all the same brought to light the plight of many other displaced Southern women who were ill-equipped by education or upbringing to survive Northern urban life.

THE SOUTHERN WOMEN'S BUREAU

Sympathizing with women like herself who were formerly privileged but now found themselves displaced and facing poverty, Laura Holloway-Langford, assisted by Charlotte Fowler Wells, established the Southern Women's Bureau. The Bureau was composed "of some of the most energetic and estimable ladies in this city, many of them Southerners who have made their homes here."[41] Its purpose was "to assist Southern Women who desire to be educated in the various Professions and Arts and also for those who are already sufficiently cultured to accept positions of trust and responsibility, and a pecuniary return therefor, and to benefit the thousands of our women who . . . have been left in circumstances which require the utmost effort of brains and hands to secure the comforts of life." The Bureau offered job placement for those who are "competent WRITERS,

MUSICIANS, TEACHERS, PHYSICIANS, REPORTERS, ETC." It also aided those who needed housing and transportation, daunting problems when women could not live or travel alone without sullying their reputations. *The Phrenological Journal* added its endorsement, commending the Bureau as contributing to national reconciliation:

> If we are indeed to become a thoroughly united people, we must work to-gether, help each other, and bring the women as well as the men of North and South together in fraternal working relations. As yet, aristocratic and conservative customs prevent Southern women from engaging in such pursuits as have long been open to the women of the North. Through this bureau it is presumed progressive ideas will be disseminated in the South, and that much good may grow out of it.[42]

The first meeting of the Bureau was held on June 7, 1870, at the Cooper Union. Charlotte Wells was elected President and Laura Holloway-Langford Corresponding Secretary.[43] At the next meeting, on June 23, "about two dozen ladies met." Among these was Charlotte Beebe Wilbour, one of the founders of the first New York woman's club, Sorosis, and its president from 1870–1875.[44] Additionally, Wilbour was active in the National Woman Suffrage Association and a contributor to *The Revolution*. According to the *New York Times*, Holloway-Langford "read a paper on 'Woman's Labor in the South,' in which she dilated on the oft-told story of man's inhumanity to woman, and announced that the day was at hand when women would assert their rights and secure their proper position in the world." She excoriated opponents of women's rights as "tame, stay-at-home, slaving women who had no thought beyond their kitchens." After her talk, a list was compiled of women who needed work, and "the kind of work each was fit for, and those who could give work."[45] The *Brooklyn Daily Eagle* described Holloway-Langford's lecture as a "harangue . . . against the tyrant man. . . . Her hottest indignation was directed against the 'namby-pamby, good women,' who 'remain unspotted from the world.'" Holloway-Langford was portrayed as "urging the shrieking sisterhood" to "'write victory on their banners and add new lustre to the name of woman.'" The paper advised female readers to avoid the Southern Women's Bureau and to "quit the spouting platform . . . and try to become good women."[46]

In September 1870, Holloway-Langford published a version of this talk as "The Women of the South." She argued that women were in a state of transition to a New Age, but that Southern women lagged behind their Northern sisters because of the "baleful influence" of slavery. "The one has been reared in an atmosphere bracing and invigorating to both the physical and intellectual being, and taught early the dignity of well-directed labor; the other, under the enervating, exhausting influences of a Southern sun, accustomed always to be served by the hands of inferiors, and educated only in those trivial accomplishments that are said to adorn the drawing-room." Southern women, "homeless and destitute," had been propelled into a new era because of their fierce need to support their young. They had realized that the "cant" of "protection" was a "misnomer for insult." Women of the South, she argued, had been deserted by their men and left with the burden of sustaining themselves and their children. She urged Northern women to support their Southern sisters, until woman "stands the acknowledged equal of man."[47]

At its final meeting on December 8, 1870, the Southern Women's Bureau announced that Mrs. Laura C. Holloway would give a lecture "for the benefit of the Society's treasury, which is almost exhausted." The needs of Southern women in New York were "urgent," and those who had remained in the South desperately needed to "learn some trade or profession, whereby they can obtain profitable and useful employment."[48] On December 16, at Cooper's Union, Holloway-Langford spoke on "The Perils of the Hour." Tickets cost $3–10 each, a substantial sum. Surprisingly, given her earlier lectures and the purpose for which the Southern Women's Bureau was founded, this talk focused less on women's need for jobs than on the "perils" women faced when attempting to enter the masculine sphere of work. The "obstacles in the way of women" that Holloway-Langford enumerated were those women themselves had created. Women, she argued, should avoid places that were "peculiarly masculine," such as newspaper offices, which strong-minded women visited in order to torment the editors. They should not wear "demoralizing fashions," use slang, or adopt "the masculine sidewalk swell." They should give up the "idea that women are fitted to do men's work" and should not engage in arguments that widened the breech between men and women.[49]

After the harsh reaction in the press to her earlier lecture, with its emphasis on women's subjugation, Holloway-Langford chose a topic for the fund-raiser that she hoped would avoid controversy. In one sense this strategy seems to have worked. The *Brooklyn Daily Eagle* praised the talk, impressed in particular by Holloway-Langford's life story, which portrayed the pathos of fallen privilege and the tragedy of "the dependent" woman struggling against "the evils of society." Holloway-Langford was commended for presenting "examples of success under adverse circumstances." Without a full text of the lecture, the message Holloway-Langford intended to convey escapes scrutiny; however, the *Brooklyn Daily Eagle* reported that she had eschewed "the phantasies of the strong-minded" and instead advocated "the honor and usefulness of women in the domestic circle." It praised her condemnation of women who pursued "those artificial chimeras which find their sole aim and end in cosmetics and fantastic dress."[50] The lecture even drew comment from Brooklyn's most famous clergyman, Henry Ward Beecher, who reportedly called it "the most eloquent lecture given on the woman in America."[51] The positive press that Holloway-Langford's lecture received did not save the Southern Women's Bureau, which disappeared from the record.

In these enterprises, Laura Holloway-Langford was emblematic of white middle-class women in the post-bellum period who sought new opportunities for work and self-development but who were unsure how these desires meshed with the politics of suffrage. Suffrage was fraught territory: support it too strongly and risk being labeled "strong-minded"; attack it and be condemned by women who were among the brightest and most interesting in the country. Thus, in 1870 Holloway-Langford waffled, at first casting aspersions on suffrage in her Charlotte Brontë lecture; then, in response to criticism from progressive women, attacking male supremacy in her lecture on labor in the South; and finally, reacting to negative coverage in the newspapers, criticizing "strong-minded" women as their own worst enemies. When she moved to New York, suffrage was not an issue of particular importance to Laura Holloway-Langford. Her goal was to gain respectability and to get ahead economically and socially. But during her first years of public life in the city, she experienced the sting of criticism both from the supporters of suffrage and the "antis," and she had friends on either side of the issue.

THE BROOKLYN WOMAN'S CLUB

The Southern Women's Bureau was one example of the new kind of women's organizations that were created after the Civil War. For decades, middle-class American men had joined clubs to engage in conversation, to socialize, and to promote special interests—civic, literary, or religious— or to escape the domestic circle and relax in all-male company with a cigar and brandy in hand. Except when a spouse might accompany a club member to a dinner or other special event, women were excluded from these gatherings. To be sure, throughout the century women had formed organizations to perform works of charity or promote social change, but they did not call themselves "clubs." The very term seemed to suggest masculine vice and self-indulgence, while women usually justified their own organizations in terms of woman's piety and self-sacrifice.

The short-lived Southern Women's Bureau, however, was not a benevolent society, but rather a self-help organization in which women cooperated in order to overcome the limitations imposed by a male-dominated society. In this way it was similar to Sorosis, the club recognized as the first women's organization to shun benevolence as its purpose. Sorosis accepted only female members; its name, taken from the Greek for "aggregate," suggested the aim of sisterhood or unity among women. When it was formed in 1868 by one of the nation's best-known journalists, Jane Cunningham Croly, the purpose of Sorosis was avowedly secular.[52] Croly insisted that Sorosis promoted the intellectual and personal self-development of women so that they could move into the public sphere as paid professionals, not unpaid volunteers. Nevertheless, in describing the club's formation, she drew on a spiritual language that American women were presumed to share. She described an organization for those "whose deeper natures had been roused to activity, who had been seized by the divine spirit of inquiry and aspiration, who were interested in the thought and progress of the age and in what other women were thinking and doing."[53] The poet Alice Cary was elected president, with Croly serving as vice-president, and by March 1869 Sorosis had eighty-three members, who were identified not in terms of their husbands or their social positions, but by their professions: "six artists or workers in art, twenty-two authors, six editors, one historian, eleven poets, nine teachers and lecturers, eight well-known philanthropists, two physicians, four writers on science, besides others who are contributors to periodicals."[54]

Laura Holloway-Langford was not affiliated with Sorosis, but she was one of the early members of the Brooklyn Woman's Club, the second-oldest of the New York women's clubs and the third oldest in the country.[55] On June 18, 1869, ten friends met at the home of Anna C. Field and established the Club. In 1871, it had grown to about thirty women and included Holloway-Langford, who, by that time, was an editor for the *Brooklyn Daily Union* and becoming well known in local society.[56] The organization was initially called the Brooklyn Social Science Club.[57] Members met every other Friday afternoon "to discuss matters of interest to themselves, to read papers . . . or speak extemporaneously on any theme which they may consider as coming under the range of topics suitable for the occasion."[58]

In 1898 when Croly wrote her *History of the Woman's Club Movement in America,* she labeled the Brooklyn Woman's Club conservative, but during the 1870s, when Holloway-Langford and her friends were most active, it contained a strongly progressive, even radical, faction. Its members believed that women should use their energy outside the home to change society, and its projects offered practical help for women who entered the labor market.[59] In the fall of 1870, Anna C. Field proposed that the Club purchase a house as a residence for single working women who were "of moderate means but refined tastes."[60] Such a residence would bring together women from different social classes who for whatever reason needed to support themselves. The idea of "Boarding Houses Wholly for Women" was ridiculed by the *Brooklyn Daily Eagle,* which characterized the women who undertook this project as "dewomanized spinsters, matrons, and warring widows" whose aims had gone from "suffrage to salad, from destiny to hash, from women's duty to hall bedrooms on the third floor." What most upset the reporter, however, was the notion that women could live independent of men: Who, he asked, would put out the lights in the hall?

> No woman since the world began has been tall enough to reach up to an entry chandelier. Even if she could turn the gas out, she would be afraid to go up the stairs in the dark. . . . A woman could never keep a night key, or use it if she could keep it. . . . Some woman would have to be in control. The rest wouldn't submit to it. Women will never submit to women. They

always submit to a man, but not to their own sex. . . . Every woman would know whether the other's hair was real or artificial. False teeth will be mixed up. . . . The women that had real bustles would quarrel with those that made theirs out of paper. . . . No man being present to arbitrate between them, they would scratch out each other's eyes, turn up their noses at each other, go off and have a good cry, and declare they would tell their mothers.[61]

To such objections, one can imagine Holloway-Langford pointing out that many women, including members of the Brooklyn Woman's Club, already lived quite successfully without a man. Despite fears that such publicity might jeopardize their ability to raise money, the Club succeeded in purchasing and renovating a house at 80 Willoughby Street, which then provided fifty bedrooms for working women. This enterprise soon became a separate organization, the Business Woman's Union, with its own board of directors. By the mid-1870s, the tone of articles in the *Brooklyn Daily Eagle* had undergone a significant shift. In 1874, it reported that the purpose of the home was "the opening up of new avenues of employment, both remunerative and benevolent, and the furnishing of comfortable homes for self-supporting women at moderate cost." A private room with board ran between $4 and $6 per week. "The inmates of the home are teachers, clerks, telegraph operators, artists and dressmakers, all women of refinement and education." Additionally, Miss Laura F. Beecher, the superintendent of the house, offered the women free commercial education.

In spite of its positive tone, the article appealed to traditional gender distinctions: "For the want of good food, good beds and cheerful society, girls naturally good were constantly being driven to the bad, while others, more delicate, unable to bear the wear and tear of hard work, poor food, wet feet, and the thousand and one miseries belonging to the usual boardinghouses for the working classes, were prematurely dying of want and exposure." The "earnest hearted" women of the club sought donations from "fathers and husbands, who knew best what dangers and trials beset a woman homeless and alone, to stretch forth a helping hand for the sake of their mothers and wives."[62] The article downplayed the right of women to live independently, choosing rather to emphasize woman's delicacy and need for male protection.

Chances are good that Laura Holloway-Langford penned this item. In 1873 she had joined the staff of the *Brooklyn Daily Eagle,* after a Southern friend had put in a good word for her with the editor, Thomas Kinsella. She first worked as a reporter, but soon Kinsella gave her an editorial position dealing with "politics, local improvements, art, literary news, and, above all, the questions that relate to the progress and enfranchisement of women."[63] Thus, from the 1870s until early 1884, Laura Holloway-Langford not only wrote many of the articles about women's organizations but also exerted editorial control over coverage of women's issues.[64] Unlike the male reporters who were excluded from the Woman's Club, Holloway-Langford had access to inside information. Additionally, the Club could depend upon her to publicize its projects and to solicit community support. Undoubtedly, the presence of women in the newsroom and on the editorial staff of major newspapers such as the *Brooklyn Daily Eagle* changed how women's organizations were covered in the press and contributed to their rise in respectability in the eyes of the community. The positive coverage and public support came at the price, however, of portraying Club work in the rhetoric of Victorian womanhood.

The achievements of the Brooklyn Woman's Club, particularly during its early years, were impressive. It investigated laws relating to women in the state of New York. It promoted new ideas about early childhood education and in 1884 established the first free kindergarten in Brooklyn. By the early 1890s, an Association had been formed which included seven kindergartens that followed the principles of the German educator Friedrich Fröbel.[65] The Club advocated practical education for women and founded schools for the study of cooking and nursing. It supported orphan asylums and lobbied for penal reform: one of its first official acts was to send two representatives to London to attend a conference on prisons. Beginning in 1876, it mounted a campaign to have women seated on the Brooklyn Board of Education. Yearly petitions were presented to the Mayor, and often Laura Holloway-Langford represented the Club. In a June 1887 meeting in Historical Hall, she read letters from supporters, but said that the reasons given in letters by opponents were "so flimsy she would not read them." Holloway-Langford did say that one "writer made the objection that, if women were placed on the board, their husbands would have to go after them to take them home."[66] By the mid-1890s, five women were serving on the Brooklyn Board of Education.

Through honorary memberships, the Club recognized those whose achievements were a model for its members: George Sand, the French writer who defied conventional female behavior and dress; Emily Faithfull, a lecturer and publisher who advocated gainful employment for women; Maria Mitchell, an astronomer and first female member of the American Academy of Arts and Sciences; Frances Power Cobbe, the Irish suffragist who wrote about domestic violence and later founded the British Union for the Abolition of Vivisection; and Dr. Mary Putnam Jacobi, who in 1876 won the Boylston Prize at Harvard for an essay that contradicted the conventional opinion that women required rest during menstruation—the pseudo-medical justification used to exclude them from the workforce.[67] One of the few men especially honored at a Club reception was Moncure D. Conway, a second-generation Transcendentalist who helped introduce Eastern religious ideas to the United States.

SUFFRAGE DIVIDES THE CLUB

Despite its strong feminist impulse, the Brooklyn Woman's Club was divided over the issue of suffrage. Its Constitution, Article II, stated that the objectives of the Club were "the improvement of its members and the practical consideration of the important questions that grow out of relations of the individual to society and the effect of existing institutions upon individual development. It shall be independent of sect, party and social cliques, the basis of membership being earnestness of purpose, love of truth and a desire to promote the best interests of humanity."[68] Notwithstanding the emphasis on the "relations of the individual to society," the Club admonished members to avoid discussing religion and politics, including the issues of women's rights and suffrage. Yet many of the founding members were political activists closely connected to the struggle for the ballot. Still, Celia Burleigh, the Club's first president, felt compelled to state that although she was a member of the Equal Rights Association, the Brooklyn Woman's Club was a separate organization, and she "deprecated . . . the introduction of the suffrage question in their meetings."[69]

The issue of women's rights became increasingly divisive among Brook
lyn women. Victoria Woodhull, who in 1870 had been the first woman to
declare herself a candidate for President of the United States, was notorious for her defense of free love, a concept attacked by Henry Ward Beecher
from the pulpit of Plymouth Church. In November 1872, the association
between suffrage and scandal became even stronger, when Woodhull
accused Beecher of carrying on an affair with one of his parishioners,
Elizabeth Tilton, wife of Theodore Tilton and a founding member of the
Brooklyn Woman's Club. In 1873, Woodhull was indicted for publishing
this accusation, which was deemed "obscene."

Henry Ward Beecher wielded immense power in Brooklyn, and Club
members like Laura Holloway-Langford probably rallied to his defense.
However, many of them may also have known that Beecher was a phi-
landerer. Holloway-Langford's friend, the poet Edna Dean Proctor, was
rumored to have had an affair with him decades earlier.[70] Would members of the Club have disbelieved their fellow club member, Libby Tilton,
when she told her side of the story? Or, in this circle of women, were love
affairs tolerated, perhaps even accepted, as long as they did not result in
public disclosure? It is impossible to know for sure, but it is intriguing to
think that Laura Holloway-Langford, in covering women's issues first at
the *Brooklyn Daily Union* and then for the *Daily Eagle*, may have reported
on this scandal.

The more entrenched she became in Brooklyn society, however, the
more Holloway-Langford distanced herself from the radical causes of her
earlier years. In the late 1880s, she asked "Thirty of Our Most Famous
Women" whether they would vote if given the chance. Some women answered "yes" without hesitation, but others, including several of Holloway-
Langford's close friends, qualified their answers. Edna Dean Proctor claimed
to have no interest in the issue, but said she would vote out of duty. The
poet and spiritualist Ella Wheeler Wilcox said that voting would require
too much of her "vital mental force." Even "Jenny June" (Jane C. Croly),
the founder of Sorosis, which had become synonymous with "strong-
minded" women, gave an ambiguous assessment: she asserted that she
had never worked for suffrage and she did not support it for all women any
more than she did for all men, yet if given the right, she would vote. Most
surprising was Laura Holloway-Langford's response, which concluded

her article: "If the right of suffrage were extended to me, would I go to the polls and vote. *No!* I would shrink from it. I believe women's work and life should be in the peaceful, hallowed precincts of her own home. Men should face the storms and strife incident to anything pertaining to political life. Ideas sweetly and wholly feminine in woman is [sic] the rose bloom which jewels her existence."[71]

What are we to make of such a position? (The equivalent today might be Phyllis Schlafly, who, with law degree in hand, traveled around the country and urged women to stay home and oppose the Equal Rights Amendment.) Although it is possible that Laura Holloway-Langford became more politically conservative as she grew older, she never held strong convictions about suffrage. Like a chameleon, she adapted her stance to reflect the prevailing opinion of the time. Just a few years later, she was enlisted to procure a thousand signatures on a suffrage petition. Even as she rejected its premises, Holloway-Langford craved bourgeois respectability. Despite her role in breaking down barriers for women in journalism, she cultivated a public image as a "delicate and gentle" woman. In her scrapbook she preserved a clipping that captures some of the contradictions of her persona:

> Mrs. Holloway is not a "sorosister" by any means, but she has been of great source to her sex, in and out of journalism. While no lady in the land abhors the erotic insanity of Mrs. Woodhull's followers more than she, she is yet capable of drawing the line between what is simply meant to be sensational and what is likely to prove beneficial to womankind in general. The only inconsistency of which, in this direction, she pleads guilty, is that she is a member of the society for the suppression of corsets and still manfully boasts that she wears them.[72]

SPIRITUAL IDEAS IN THE BROOKLYN WOMAN'S CLUB

If Laura Holloway-Langford did not play a major role in the suffrage movement, she was active in bringing a spiritual dimension to Brooklyn Woman's Club meetings. On June 3, 1873, she led a program on "Universal Peace" attended by prominent members of Brooklyn society as well as by visiting Quakers from Philadelphia. The meeting opened with a poem written by Annie Matthieson to be sung to the tune of "America" ("My Country Tis of Thee"):

Life is a struggling note,
On Time's rough wings afloat,
One warring breath.
But in its music deep,
Harmonies biding sleep,
Ready to rise and leap,
And conquer death.

Let yon lives call them forth,
East, West, South and North!
Hand clasping hand,
Bridging the mighty sea,
Circling all—bond and free—
Till the wide world shall be
One Fatherland.

Laura Holloway-Langford, a native Southerner and former Confederate supporter, then presented an essay on "Peace," for which she received applause and a bouquet of flowers, perhaps signifying her acceptance among Yankee women.[73] This program was emblematic of the rituals of reconciliation that became commonplace after the Civil War.[74] Despite the fact that the Brooklyn Club had banned discussion of religion from its meetings, its members were comfortable with a non-sectarian religious language that obfuscated differences among the members. Yet the language of this song was drawn from spiritualism. It suggested a New Age when not only sectional divisions would be healed, with "bond and free" united, but also a time when the separation between the material and the spiritual worlds, between the living and the dead, would be overcome. By accepting the existence of universal harmonies, Holloway-Langford and her Club sisters were primed to be receptive to the religious movements of the coming decades.

Later on, Holloway-Langford also gave lectures to the Club that introduced members to the careers of Sir Edwin Arnold, author of *The Light of Asia,* the popular poem about the life of the Buddha, and Dr. "Henry" [Heinrich] Schliemann, "the oriental scholar" who excavated the ancient cities of Mycenae and Troy. According to an article in the *New York Star*, "Mrs. Holloway's lecture, 'The Light of Asia,' was a brilliant one, the result of many years of travel in Oriental lands."[75] During these same years, the New England Women's Club held a number of programs on Eastern religions. Lectures by non-members included Imogene C. Fales on "Asiatic and European Thought"; Mohini Mohun Chunder [Chatterji] on the "Wisdom of India"; Sanskrit scholar Charles R. Lanman on "Vedic Religion"; Charles Carroll Everett, Harvard professor of theology, on "Buddhism"; and several talks on psychical research.

In Brooklyn during the last quarter of the nineteenth century, clubs sprang up like weeds: some lasted for a season, others for a generation or more. Adherents of new ideas were particularly prone to form clubs. The Brooklyn Human Nature Club studied phrenology; the Brooklyn Philosophical Association, established in 1878, discussed new scientific, ethical, social, and religious subjects. The Brooklyn Ethical Association grew out of a Sunday school class on ethics taught by Lewis G. Janes at the Second Unitarian Church, where a liberal minister, John W. Chadwick, was pastor. The Club included members who differed in "theology, in politics, and in speculative views" but who were united in their commitment to the "scientific method, especially as inspired and illustrated by the evolution idea." They were especially interested in applying the idea of evolution to ethical, social, and religious questions, and they vigorously opposed those who claimed that evolution and theism were incompatible. In 1883–1885, the Club undertook a two-year course of study on the evolution and development of "Oriental religions" and included programs on most of the world's major faiths: fetishism, Confucianism, Brahmanism, ancient Egyptian beliefs, Buddhism, Zoroastrianism, and Hebrew religion, as well as a talk on "Our Aryan Home" and a presentation by Amrita Lal Roy, editor of the *Hindu Review*.[76] The Club's excursion into Eastern religion culminated in May 1897 when Anagarika H. Dharmapala, the founder of the Maha Bodhi Society, was present at a celebration of the Buddha's birthday. At the Pouch Mansion, an altar covered with yellow, Indian-figured silk had been constructed. The walls behind the altar were decorated with the flags of the United States, England, and Ceylon, as well as a "small piece of silk which the priest explained was the flag of Buddha. The air was heavy with incense. . . . Mr. Dharmapala secured silence by ringing a sweet toned silver bell, and then Miss Caroline B. LeRow . . . read a selection from the 'Light of Asia.'"[77] It may have been from this time that Laura Holloway-Langford acquired a studio portrait of Dharmapala, which she retained until the end of her life.[78]

Many of the new clubs included both sexes, but women-only organizations opened a space where women were judged not on their family background or sexual arrangements, but on their intellectual and professional achievements. In this setting, new ideas proliferated, not only through organized activities, but also through women's friendships and social networks. In the 1870s, there had been few religious or philosophical associations in which women could participate as equals. In later years, women who were part of what John Thomas has termed the "adversary tradition" had other options.[79] They could join organizations such as the Theosophical Society or the Bellamy Nationalist Clubs. If they were attracted to Eastern religions, they could participate in Buddhist or Vedanta Societies. They could attend congresses of liberal religion that became popular after the 1893 World's Parliament of Religions. They could lecture and teach mixed groups of religious seekers in seminars and conferences such as those held at Sarah Farmer's Green Acre Colony. But in the first decade after the War, it was the Brooklyn Woman's Club that mediated between Laura Holloway-Langford's past life in the South and her new identity as a progressive, professional woman. The Club located her socially, and at the same time provided a venue where she could express her unconventional social and religious ideas.

2

✐

"A Clairvoyant of the First Water"

Nineteenth-century Americans from all walks of life believed in signs, premonitions, dreams, waking visions, and messages received orally or "impressed on the mind," which were interpreted as evidence of a spiritual reality that existed alongside the physical world. They sought proof of immortality, not in scripture, nor theology, nor the reassurance of the clergy, but in communications from those who had "passed to the other side." In 1848, mysterious rappings were reported at the Hydesville, New York home of Margaret and Catherine (Kate) Fox. Soon, messages from the spirit world swept over the country, producing an industry of mediums, trance lecturers, and writers who supported themselves as professional spiritualists. Mainstream clergy denounced spiritualism, but many liberal congregations included members who followed unconventional religious paths. In Brooklyn, spiritualism was so widespread that the *Daily Eagle* regularly reported on it, albeit with bemused condescension.

Likewise, popular magazines were filled with discussions of supernatural occurrences. *Godey's Lady's Book* frequently printed short fiction with spiritualist themes. The *Atlantic Monthly* offered articles by authors who proclaimed the power of the spirits, as well as by skeptics such as Henry James. In 1869, it published the autobiography of Frederick W. Evans, who described his conversion to Shakerism. Angels, said Evans, had visited him nightly, revealing "the facts of the existence of a spiritual world, of the immortality of the human soul, and of the possibility and reality of intercommunication between souls in and spirits out of the mortal body."[1] Hardly an issue of *The Phrenological Journal* appeared without some reference to spiritualism, including a piece in 1870 by Harriet Beecher Stowe explaining how spiritualist ideas were being spread to millions of Americans through lectures, lyceums, and "spiritual picnics" for children. In Stowe's view, the popularity of spiritualism resulted from the failure of American Protestantism, which had not provided spiritual nourishment to satisfy the "yearning for the invisible."[2]

Laura Holloway-Langford's interest in spiritualism began early in life, setting her on a course that led to both the Shakers and the Theosophical Society. Prior to the mid-1880s, however, there was little exceptional about her religious quest. During the postwar years, many liberal Protestants turned to spiritualism as an alternative to the authority of church and clergy. In this cultural milieu, Holloway-Langford might hear a sermon by Henry Ward Beecher on Sunday morning; attend a Shaker meeting in the afternoon; and call up otherworldly spirits at home that evening. Yet as Ann Braude has detailed, spiritualism undermined the claims of Christianity. Believing that they could penetrate the "veil" separating the living from the dead, spiritualists dispensed with the theology of original sin, predestination, and final judgment. Even Christ's resurrection and the doctrine of atonement became "logically unnecessary." Instead, spiritualists proclaimed a benevolent deity and a "human moral order."[3] To their minds, both earthly society and the spiritual world were continually evolving, and they were instruments in the service of social and religious progress.

During the 1850s and 1860s, spiritualists had been deeply involved in social reform, especially abolition and women's rights. By the 1870s, however, they were less active in the public arena.[4] Nevertheless, when she moved to Brooklyn, Holloway-Langford became friends with progressive feminists whose efforts to change society were rooted in their spiritual beliefs. One of these was Imogene C. Fales, the founder of the American Sociologic Society, who promoted communalism over capitalism and spiritualism over materialism. In the *Religio-Philosophical Journal*, Fales wrote that the "New Age" would come into being when internal spiritual forces came into harmony with external social relations. In her view, this change would originate in the spirit world, the result of the "bride descending out of heaven." The "religion of the future," she asserted, would be a "spiritualized Christianity" that would transform both social institutions such as marriage and the capitalist economic system on the basis of equality.[5] Holloway-Langford also became friends with women writers who shared her metaphysical interests. Among these were the poets Louise Chandler Moulton, Ella Wheeler Wilcox, and Edna Dean Proctor; and the journalists Kate Field and Mrs. Frank Leslie (née Miriam Follin). This community, formed by reading and writing, constituted an informal spiritual network that encouraged Holloway-Langford's literary and religious aspirations.[6]

Despite such friendships, Holloway-Langford was leery of being identified with either radical political or spiritualist activity. As a divorced woman posing as a widow, her social status remained fragile. If she offered her services as a medium, she kept these activities private, avoiding open association with the vulgar world of trance speakers and the materialization of spirits. Additionally, as a journalist, she had an inside view of the scandals that rocked Brooklyn and that linked spiritualism with sexual misconduct. Her first position was at the *Brooklyn Daily Union,* the newspaper that had been edited by Theodore Tilton. When Holloway-Langford joined the *Brooklyn Daily Eagle,* its pages were dominated by stories about Tilton's lawsuit against Beecher.[7] Whether or not Holloway-Langford wrote about these events, she witnessed first-hand the damage to the reputations of her friends Lib Tilton and Henry Ward Beecher. By the time Victoria Woodhull resigned as President of the American Association of Spiritualists in 1875, Holloway-Langford no longer publicly identified as a spiritualist, confining her metaphysical pursuits to informal discussions with sympathetic colleagues.

SPIRIT GUIDES

During the late 1860s and early 1870s, however, Holloway-Langford had published spiritualist poetry and short fiction under her own name. In 1868 she wrote a poem, "The Angel Guide," in which, in a great city far from home, a troubled man sees in "waking vision" a "radiant" angel.[8] Two years later, she dedicated another poem to Belle, the granddaughter of President Andrew Johnson, expressing the hope that all her days would be sunny and that they would be reunited in "Summer-land."[9] As the spiritualist version of heaven, Summer-land had been described by Andrew Jackson Davis as a new Eden—an "inhabitable sphere" among "the suns and planets of space," a luminous region of eternal life glimpsed through clairvoyance.[10] Another poem welcomed paths "lost in brightness" and portals that open with "a sound like song" to reveal a "Morning Land."[11] In these poems, Holloway-Langford gave thanks "For the lifting up the curtain, For the drawing back its veil"—that is, for a glimpse of spiritual reality beyond the material world.

Like many spiritualists of Southern background, Holloway-Langford was more absorbed by communication with the dead than with radical social change. Yet the oppression of women was an issue that fully engaged her, and she disdained any organization that valorized traditional marriage. In the writings of spiritualists, she found discussions on how relationships between men and women might be reconstituted. Holloway-Langford agreed with Andrew Jackson Davis, who proclaimed that "the majority of marriages in this world" were a death to the spirit and that "you may clothe yourselves with the dark habiliments of wo [sic], when you consign at the altar, a heart to a living grave."[12] In common with many spiritualists, she claimed that traditional marriage was little better than prostitution and that marriage without love was legalized adultery. Nevertheless, she supported Mary Love Davis in "her troubles," when she was divorced by Andrew Jackson Davis, her husband of thirty years.[13]

In "Unequal Marriages," published in the Brooklyn Magazine, Holloway-Langford expressed sympathy for the theory of purified generation, the idea that when marital partners had been spiritually perfected they could engage in "pure" sexual relations that would produce superior offspring. In contrast, the offspring of impure unions would be physically, intellectually, and morally inferior.[14] Still, while she believed that sexual relationships should be the result of "elective affinities" rather than social or legal sanction, Laura Holloway-Langford was shrewd enough not to say so directly, choosing instead to publish her veiled critique of marriage under the pseudonym "S. E. Archer."[15]

For Holloway-Langford, the key to women's liberation was economic independence. Always self-protective, she employed fiction as a vehicle for attacking both marriage and the patriarchal family. In her early stories, young women not only fight for their independence, but they succeed through help from the spirit world. One heroine discovers a diary that her mother had written before her death, counseling that marriage need not be a woman's destiny. Emboldened by strength transmitted from beyond the grave, she defies her father and refuses to degrade her "womanhood by earning a home through marriage." Another deceased mother instructs her daughter how to escape a life of drudgery and dependence. In another story, a heroine fulfills her dream of keeping a lighthouse, which is "a stepping stone to a higher place." Alone and isolated from society, the woman nevertheless becomes "a beacon, shining out in precept and example as bright to others as her great lamp shines out in strong rays over the darkness of the deep, guiding wanderers home." The heroine understands that her freedom is inextricable from her pursuit of spiritual knowledge.[16] Indeed, these stories suggest that for a woman to achieve a higher self she must be liberated from traditional female roles. They encouraged female readers to reject male dominance—whether imposed by husband, father, or brother—and to turn to other women, both living and dead, for aid in achieving independence. The stories reiterate William Leach's observation that many women who were unable to completely throw off the claims of religion sought out the spirits, who "often divulged what people already thought, gave direction to their desires, or justified unconventional or even radical activity."[17] In effect, Holloway-Langford's stories suggested that women's progress was dependent upon their spirituality, rather than upon their efforts to gain political or social power.

In 1883, Laura Holloway-Langford published *Hearthstone, or Life at Home,* with advice on how to create the perfect home.[18] In the best-known book of this genre, *The American Woman's Home* (1869), Catherine E. Beecher and Harriet Beecher Stowe had argued that the family should embody the "end . . . which Jesus Christ came into this world to secure." By their definition, a good home was synonymous with a patriarchal Christian home: "It is the man who is the head and chief magistrate . . . ; not less is he so according to the Christian law, by which, when differences arise, the husband has the deciding control and the wife is to obey."[19] In *Hearthstone* Holloway-Langford did not denigrate marriage, but she nevertheless avoided framing home or heaven as Christian. Instead, she asserted that "the divine light within us, no matter whether we be of this church or of that, or of no church at all, burns up at this dark and desolate materialism." She counseled her readers to take comfort in knowing "that the dead are only separated from us for a brief interval, by a thin veil, through which we may, in happy moments, catch glimpses of them, and in hours of gloom and solitude feel their cheering presence."[20]

Holloway-Langford was convinced that even though all religions shared essential truths, spiritualism, by dispensing with creed and dogma, was in the forefront of progress.[21] Yet, despite the veneer of gentility that she maintained, spiritualism set her on a path toward deeper involvement with the occult.

THE SHAKER CONNECTION

Founded in the late eighteenth century by Ann Lee, a charismatic leader, the United Society of Believers in Christ's Second Appearing, commonly known as the Shakers, held that sexual transgression was the original sin. They gathered into celibate communities, where all goods were shared and where men and women assumed equal roles in governance. From its inception, the Society of Believers had cultivated Pentecostal gifts of the spirit, so it was not surprising that many Shakers interpreted the spread of spiritualism as part of God's plan to redeem the world.

In March 1872, Antoinette Doolittle, Eldress of the North Family at Mount Lebanon, addressed a joint meeting of Shakers and spiritualists in Troy, New York. She quoted the scriptural prophecy that there would be "a new thing in the earth. A woman should compass a man." According to Doolittle, woman was "gathering her forces for battle . . . against error." To Paul's injunction that women should be silent and subject to man, she retorted: "'Peace to the ashes of the dead.' We will not contend with Br. Paul for aught that he said or did, in his time, but will venture to say, that his day is over, as far as the woman question is concerned. His counsel in that respect does not meet the needs nor demands of the nineteenth century." She advised that those who wanted to turn back to an earlier time would have no more success than those who sought to restore the antediluvian world. Doolittle was convinced that in order for women to gain equal rights, theology must change. "As long as we have all male Gods in the heavens we shall have all male rulers on earth. But when the Heavenly Mother is revealed, and is sought unto as freely and confidingly as the Heavenly Father, then will woman find her proper sphere of action, and be able to fill that sphere."[22] Doolittle may have been aware that as early as 1859 a leading spiritualist, Emma Hardinge Britten, had posited the dual nature of God.[23] In any case, she believed that spiritualists who were committed to women's rights would also be receptive to Shaker theology of a Mother and Father in the deity.

On Saturday, November 22, 1873, ten Shakers arrived in New York City, where they lodged in the "New Hygienic Home," an institution that specialized in the water-cure treatment of "diseases peculiar to women."[24] The "Home" was run by the spiritualist Dr. Eli P. Miller, who believed that society's ills were due largely to "abuse of the sexual function."[25] The next morning they took the stage at Robinson Hall, the New York meeting place of the Society of Progressive Spiritualists. They were introduced by James M. Peebles, a former Universalist minister and a medical doctor, who had become a spiritualist leader.[26] Most likely Laura Holloway-Langford first met the Shakers at this event, drawn to it because of her interest in spiritualism, rather than in her role as an editor for the *Brooklyn Daily Eagle.*[27]

At the Sunday morning service, Antoinette Doolittle addressed the gathering. Although she presented a "clear, lucid advocacy of [women's] rights and interests," not all women were satisfied that their voices had been represented. The following day, the Elder of the North Family, Frederick Evans, received a letter from "the travailing Daughters of Zion, in New York City," who vehemently protested their treatment by male spiritualists. They wrote: "Not in the whole city of New York, or Brooklyn, do we know of a platform where Woman is invited to advocate the grand truths which for years have inspired her." They identified "man" as "the great red dragon who has usurped every place of honor and trust.... Does [woman] want a church? a man owns and controls it. A public hall? she must apply to a man. Even the deciding power of who shall supply the rostrum of the liberal Spiritualists is a man, or a woman whom man places in power." The Daughters of Zion accused their male counterparts of granting a public voice only to women like Victoria Woodhull who used their sexuality to gain power, in contrast to the Shakers, who judged a woman by the quality of her character and the purity of her life. Significantly, they quoted from *Revelation* 12 a description of the appearance of a woman clothed with the sun, "travailing in birth, and pained to be delivered," but opposed by a great red dragon, standing ready to devour the child. While Shakers pointed to this passage as a prophecy of the coming of Ann Lee, whose child, the Shaker community, was "caught up to God," the Daughters of Zion gave the passage a militantly feminist interpretation. The spiritualist women argued that in spite of their labor to bring forth a New Age for the nation, their birth pangs had been suppressed by male subjugation, which permitted them to bear only "monstrosities." Even women married to wealthy men, they asserted, were like prostitutes forced to exchange their bodies for the contents of their husband's "purse," and they lamented that "intellectual and inspired women have no foothold upon earth."[28]

Despite scholarly contentions that spiritualism provided women opportunities for leadership, these women from New York were furious that "the *Soul*-women of this movement" had not been notified that the Shakers were coming; that at the meeting, spiritualist women were not "given the liberty to express their glad welcome before the public"; and that they were not even allowed to greet their "Shaker brothers and sisters." The Daughters of Zion argued that this incident was emblematic of systemic mistreatment by men, who refused women equal power in spiritualist organizations and who aggressively dominated their Sunday morning meetings, preventing women from speaking. For such women, Shakerism represented a model of equality, visible in the meeting at Robinson Hall, where the Shaker brothers had been accompanied by an equal number of Shaker sisters, who shared the platform and were major speakers.[29] No wonder, then, that women like Laura Holloway-Langford believed that Shakers were in the vanguard of both spiritualism and the movement for sexual equality.

After this event, Laura Holloway-Langford initiated a correspondence with Antoinette Doolittle. In her first letter to Holloway-Langford, Doolittle sent pictures of herself and Elder Frederick Evans. She wrote:

> Dear Laura, I have done as you requested me to do—thought of you in
> my prayers and requested my loving companion and helper, Sister Anna
> White, to do the same. . . . I send my shadow to you as you request, but
> when you think of your Shaker friend Antoinette, remember her as one
> who is looking beyond all material forms—striving through faith in the
> dual God, a Heavenly Father and Mother, to peer through the misty
> clouds of earth caused by sin & disobedience to God's laws, into the
> spheres where the redeemed of all kindreds and nations dwell.[30]

To the Shakers, Holloway-Langford had represented herself not just as
a spiritualist, but as a clairvoyant who could traverse the boundary between the living and the dead. Throughout their relationship with her, the
Shakers were convinced that "dear Laura" was "in constant touch with
the unseen spiritual world, seeing and conversing with dear ones from
behind the veil."[31]

BEYOND THE SUNRISE

In fall 1883, John W. Lovell, one of the initial members of the Theosophical Society, published *Beyond the Sunrise, Observations by Two Travellers.*[32]
Reviews indicated that the book had been written by "two well-known
American writers who choose to remain anonymous." However, a letter
from Shaker Eldress Anna White in 1901 confirms that Holloway-Langford
was the author.[33] *Beyond the Sunrise* describes the uncanny experiences
connected with the death of Holloway-Langford's mother, and it presents
Shakerism as an option for women who are unhappy with family relations.
When her mother died on August 15, 1874, Holloway-Langford had written Eldress Antoinette Doolittle, who responded with a consoling letter.
She suggested that this "severe affliction may prove a blessing that will be
unveiled to your sight, when the bitterness has passed away," and advised
Holloway-Langford to look to Shakerism for comfort: "Under such spiritual auspices, when one loved Gospel parent passes on to their home in
the Spirit land, we find others who fill their places."[34] It was natural then,
that when Holloway-Langford wrote a book about spiritualism, she sent a
copy to Doolittle. Frederick Evans briefly reviewed the book in the *Shaker
Manifesto,* where he commented that "its presentation of Ann Lee's mission is bold and free."[35]

Beyond the Sunrise reiterates major concerns of Laura Holloway-Langford's life: a hunger for communication with the spirit world, indignation at the sufferings of women, and a desire to reorder sexual and family relationships. Written in the third person, the book presents the observations of Mona and Cleo, the "Two Travellers" of the title. The "Preface" reassures readers that although names and details have been changed to preserve anonymity, "almost all the occurrences herein narrated are strictly true." While it is impossible to verify this statement, many of the experiences related by the character Cleo are drawn from Laura Holloway-Langford's life.

The book begins by describing the large, comfortable drawing room of Mona and Cleo's home that reflects their culture and refinement. It is furnished with "massive carved furniture" and "long ebony book-cases, filled with the best classics of the language." On the polished floor is a Turkish carpet and on the wall hangs a Madonna by Carlo Dolce. "This bust, that statuette, that cup of jasper, those bronzes from Japan, that carved olive from Jerusalem, those curiosities from western Pueblos, fitted into their surroundings, betokening a sympathy for all things that represented the life of different peoples and expressed their love or labor."[36] The bond between Mona and Cleo demonstrates that women who forego marriage need not give up the dream of a happy home and a committed relationship. By sharing resources, they live independent of men. Their lives prove that women are capable of loyal friendship, "self-sacrifice, enthusiasm, heroism, if need be, each for the other."[37] The narrator remarks "that the love of woman for woman is pure as that of an angel" and that in order to fulfill "her own, true selfhood" woman must be liberated from the "ignorance and sensualism" of men.[38] Throughout the book Mona and Cleo address each other with terms of endearment. They are described as being "one in mind," even though Mona is "less hopeful and more self-contained than Cleo . . . who sat at her feet, her disciple in all things." Most importantly, Mona and Cleo share a spiritual affinity, believing in "the unseen powers of human beings."[39]

Each Sunday evening they invite a few carefully chosen friends to their home, where they escape the "unutterable weariness of our common-place daily lives" of work, "wear and waste." These gatherings are devoted to conversation about that "border-land, a mystic country, where matter ends and spirit begins, or rather where both meet and mingle."[40] However, the conversation of these friends frequently turns to the plight of women. Just as in her short stories, in *Beyond the Sunrise* Holloway-Langford links alternative spirituality to women's struggle for autonomy and personal self-development.

Mona establishes this theme in the book's first story. She tells of growing up on a farm on the Western Reserve, where her "slight and delicate" mother was so exhausted by frequent childbirth that she had no energy for a spiritual life. "I sometimes think," comments Mona, "it is better to never have motherhood than subject children to such deprivations." Mona's only brother, Jamie, was enraptured by music. One day as Jamie gazes "upward like one entranced," the family hears music hovering above his head. Soon afterwards, Jamie falls sick. While on his deathbed, that "strange music floated again on the air; it filled the room, it swelled louder and clearer, while the boy's eyes took a strange expression as of joyful recognition and perfect peace. Reaching up his hands, he whispered: 'I am going, mamma, going where the music comes from!'" From that time on, whenever the spirit of Jamie is near, Mona hears this music.[41]

Cleo describes her first intimations of a spirit world in a story about her mother.[42] At age five, Cleo's mother was placed in a boarding school, so her childhood was one of "loneliness and neglect." When she was fourteen, her father insisted that she marry, because he considered "his home, a great plantation occupied by his servants and himself, an unfit place for a young lady. So she married a lover much older than herself, but still only twenty-three years of age." Her mother's life, says Cleo, was "pathetic from beginning to end."[43]

In this account, Holloway-Langford disguised a more disturbing personal story. Her own mother, Anne Vaulx, was only fourteen when, on November 29, 1832, she married Samuel Carter, who was twenty-eight.[44] Already Samuel had fathered three children. Two survived; the youngest had been born May 3, 1831, to his wife Eliza Staggs, who died in the childbirth. Anne Vaulx, almost a child herself, assumed responsibility for the care of this young daughter and of Samuel's son, just four years old.[45] During the next thirty years, she bore fourteen children. Two children died in the first year of life, but most survived to adulthood. Anne Vaulx

Carter was only fifty-six when she died, leaving a son and a daughter in Holloway-Langford's care.

In *Beyond the Sunrise*, Cleo recounts how "the war came like a thunder bolt in a clear sky, and my mother's heart never had rest or peace again." When Cleo's father dies on a journey south, her mother insists on visiting her "old home" there. One night, the mother's specter appears in Brooklyn to bid her children adieu; the next day they receive a telegram confirming her death. Letters from Cleo's sister recount additional telepathic experiences surrounding their mother's departure that apparently are based on actual correspondence from Holloway-Langford's sister, Irene.[46] During the year after her mother's death, Cleo said: "I almost grew to hate the God who in mercy permitted me to live, and I would have been glad to have flung the empty gift of life at His feet with scorn and despair. But I plodded on, working hard through necessity, and holding on to those I loved with a tenacity that helped me if it did not them." Her sisters and brothers left home, marrying or going to college. "Mother grew nearer, singular as it may seem after they had all gone, and many and many an evening I would go to my room where I boarded, and sit in the dark the entire evening thinking of her.... Sometimes ... the demon of unrest would seize me, and I would ride for miles in the street cars, caring only to be out of the house." One night Cleo visited a woman who told her that the spirit of her mother had accompanied her: "She died away from you, but in some way you were aware of her death.... She has but one request to make now—that is, that you will not grieve and fret over her absence so much. It prevents her from getting as near you as she could otherwise." Looking at her host, Cleo was startled to see her mother's face. The woman took Cleo's hand and said: "She gave you this ring—her wedding ring—and she is glad you wear it. This is her proof to you that she is here."[47]

For three years, Cleo received no communication from her mother. Then one evening, while the "Two Travellers" sat alone in an empty house, "waiting Quaker like for the spirit" to advise them on purchasing it, Cleo perceived the shadow of a woman climbing a ladder to hang a picture on the wall. A pair of hands held up a portrait of her brother, whose face was surrounded by pale purple chrysanthemums, her mother's favorite flower. Over the picture she observed an arch "of gray and white and blue as a pomegranate blossom, and just in the centre of it I plainly saw the word 'Home' in brilliants. . . . I looked again, and there stood in perfect view the full form of my mother, smiling and brushing her two hands together as if she had soiled them with dust." Cleo understood the vision as a sign that she and Mona "were in sympathy and harmony with each other" and that they were meant to create a home together. Members of the Sunday-evening group who heard these stories proclaimed Cleo "a clairvoyant of the first water," a term which refers to a diamond that is translucent in clarity and therefore of the highest quality. In her friends' estimation, Cleo is "undefiled by false living." Her vision has not been clouded "by abuse of her gift. She is scarcely conscious of her great power, and never will be wholly so until her busy life is ended on earth, and her warm, loving heart is dead to those who need her in this world. Then, and not till then, will she know that she already is what she longs to be—a seer."[48]

CRITIQUE OF MARRIAGE

Beyond the Sunrise is not exceptional in the kinds of supernatural experiences it reports—premonitions of death, mental telepathy when people are "in rapport," messages from spirits of the dead, and miraculous healings. Such stories were ubiquitous in nineteenth-century spiritualist publications. The book is notable, however, for its pervasive unease about the relations between men and women and the deep distress that characters express over the failure of the family to sustain women. These issues are addressed most directly in a chapter that portrays Honor, a friend from Mona and Cleo's "outer circle," who is an austere woman with a "discordant nature."[49]

When Cleo remarks that Honor resembles the Shakers in her plain speaking, Honor acknowledges that she shares many of their beliefs, including celibacy. She finds idealization of the biological family and motherhood a travesty, completely at odds with her own experience as a forlorn child with no individual life of her own. "My rights, if I ever had any, were swallowed up in the interests of others. . . . My mother had so many babies that I marvel now that she ever gave me the slightest personal attention.

... We were herded as cattle, and as one of the herd I grew to girlhood, and finally to young lady-hood." She was forced to marry at age sixteen in order to have a home. "My father was glad to have me off his hands; and I, who had never been in general society, had never known a day's independence in my life, married a narrow-minded man, whose views of life were as contemptible as my father's in many ways. It came over me by degrees that I must bear the fate I had meted out to myself, and go on like the dumb driven cattle around me. It was hard to be an unhappy girl, but it was harder to be an unhappy wife." When she leaves her husband, she is ostracized by her family. Honor admits that she is hostile toward "the institution of family. There is no place in a household of growing children for thought or repose or solitude or genial company. What would Mona and Cleo's home be if they had a husband apiece and three or four children? They would be half starved intellectually, and wholly different from what they now are." Honor wants no part of a heaven imagined as a place where she is reunited with her family. "I prefer a desert, a wilderness, a veritable waste place for my heaven, where there will be neither parent nor child. Unless I can be with congenial natures I prefer solitude."

Honor believes that the Shaker Society offers a model of how the family can be restructured to reflect spiritual affinity rather than biological chance. She venerates Ann Lee because "she was large enough to see that there are two classes of people in this world—those who do and those who do not wish to live in family relation. The order she founded is the highest existing on the earth to-day. . . . Women find in the Shaker Society the recognition they get nowhere else." However, from Honor's perspective, Ann Lee was not so much a religious leader as a cultural rebel. "Her life was a protest against certain forms of tyranny. . . . She got out of thralldom, though you may say at a fearful cost; but she elevated her character and won self-respect."[50] Honor values celibacy as a means to personal freedom, but for her it has little to do with either religion or communal living.

In *Beyond the Sunrise,* other members of the group react to Honor's disquisition on the Shakers. Mona's sister, Una, defends marriage, claiming that Ann Lee's revelation supports it.

> Until her time, there had been only a masculine God. . . . She saw the two coequal principles running through nature, without which can be no life.

> Celibate as she was, Ann Lee discovered the law of marriage at its very
> fountain, in the Divine beginning. Her discovery of the feminine principle
> . . . means that womanhood, the highest development of the feminine
> principle, is the coequal and peer of manhood.[51]

Una believes that when the feminine principle is recognized, the existing
order of things will be revolutionized and an "era of justice" will com-
mence. Despite the fact that Una affirms that women can retain individuality in marriage, she reinforces conventional gender ideology: "Woman
is the interior, inspiring, spiritual part of married oneness . . . man is the
external, constructive, powerful portion of the dualism. . . . He goes out to
battle with the forces of the world; she makes the hearthstone the centre
of love and grace and beauty." Una is the only woman in the group who
claims to have found spiritual affinity within heterosexual marriage, a
relationship that she believes will continue even after death. Nonetheless,
she and her husband exercise "will-power to conquer animal propensities,
and so grow to be worthy [sic] the high destiny which is attainable by all
who faithfully strive to reach the life of the soul." From the beginning of
their marriage, they agreed "to have a separate room, to say nothing of a
separate bed." As portrayed by Una, the ideal marriage is one of the spirit,
not the flesh.[52]

Mona also questions whether celibacy is the only way for a woman to
become an equal partner with a man. She believes that if women find their
"true mates," marriage can be "beautiful, holy and enduring." Cleo, however, is skeptical. She remarks, "My real mate may be married or in heaven,
who knows?"[53] Even when one of the two male members of the group, the
"Professor," confides his story to Cleo and Mona, he confesses to feeling
torn between his spiritual development and his need for woman's companionship. He believes that the "conjugal union" should be "pure, holy, spiritualized affection . . . beyond and above physical attraction." He adheres to
the theory of pure generation: when men and women achieve the "highest
spiritual consecration" then "war, crime, ignorance, and misery" shall
become things of the past. "Then shall the children born on this planet be
beautiful as the gods and goddesses of the Greeks." At the same time, the
Professor asserts that "strong incisive, masterful manhood needs gentle
clinging attaching womanhood; neither can reach its highest development

alone." He asks, "Why should I desecrate my manhood any more than a woman should sully her womanhood? Would not the sin and shame of the inversion of purity be the same in the one as in the other?" Yet his God-created nature requires a "dearer self . . . the revelation of Deity through womanhood . . . my soul's own and only companion."[54]

After the Professor implores "the powers of love and wisdom" to reveal his "true mate," he sees her in a dream. A few weeks later, the Professor rescues a woman from a train accident. He realizes she is the woman who appeared in his dream. The doctors say she is dying, but the Professor exerts his will to bring her back to life. Their marriage is described as a "union of spirit with spirit," the joining of two pure lives which had been "neither dissipated nor degraded."[55] However ideal the Professor considers his marriage, his story nevertheless replicates the motif of the helpless female who succumbs to the force of a man's will. Even though the Professor is not a villain, his marriage is no model for women who seek to share power equally with their partner. For the female characters in *Beyond the Sunrise*, heterosexual relationships are fraught with danger. And for both men and women, a consummated heterosexual marriage is portrayed as incommensurate with a spiritual life.

In the book, Holloway-Langford presents few viable alternatives for feminist women. Mona evidences some knowledge of theosophy, having heard that "adepts" and "brotherhoods" in India and Persia use their will-power to "subjugate the body through the soul." She fears, however, that "many will use their knowledge of natural laws to bewilder and mystify the uninitiated and sometimes they may resort to jugglery to supplement the use of their curious lore." Additionally, she vows never to "bow down before a priesthood of these occult powers. Let all who will, learn that they, themselves, are the repositories of all force, and that wisdom may convert that force into power."[56] Thus, even before joining the Theosophical Society, Laura Holloway-Langford was wary of gendered hierarchies. Whether in the patriarchal family or in the relationship of a female student to a male spiritual master, she was primed to resist submission to male power.

In addition to disclosing the metaphysical ideas that preoccupied Laura Holloway-Langford, *Beyond the Sunrise* also opens a window into her personal experience. Like Mona and Cleo, she may have attempted to create an unconventional family with a female companion, finding that sharing a home with another woman solved the economic and social challenges of living without a male protector. For some years when she was in Brooklyn, the poet Edna Dean Proctor lived with her at 181 Schermerhorn Street. Dr. Lucy Hall may also have resided there for a time.[57] These arrangements came to be known as "Boston marriages," after the novel *The Bostonians* by Henry James, which described women sharing a home independent of male support.[58] *Beyond the Sunrise* portrays Mona and Cleo's home as ideal, preferable to either heterosexual marriage or celibacy. Their relationship is emotional and spiritual, not merely economic. In Laura Holloway-Langford's circle, erotic relationships between women were not uncommon. The historian Lillian Faderman goes so far as to assert that "from its inception, women's fight for the vote was largely led by women who loved other women."[59] Susan B. Anthony had romantic feelings for Anna Dickinson, as well as for Elizabeth Cady Stanton. Many loving friendships were affectionate, but not overtly sexual; others, however, were undoubtedly lesbian. For example, Elizabeth Rose Cleveland, the sister of the president and a literary collaborator with Holloway-Langford, was for twenty years the partner of a wealthy widow, Evangeline Simpson, to whom she wrote explicitly erotic letters.[60] Many married women, however, also sought the companionship of women. It is difficult to gauge the full nature of Holloway-Langford's relationships, but her life story suggests that female friendships were central to her emotional life.

A longing for home and reunion with family permeates Holloway-Langford's most personal writing. Many of the stories in *Beyond the Sunrise* are narratives of loss. The death of loved ones was a familiar experience to Holloway-Langford. Of five older brothers, one had died as an infant, another at age twenty, and Charlie, who was closest to her in age, died of tuberculosis in 1861. Her parents' last child, Mary Hays, born in 1863, had lived only two months. For Holloway-Langford, the death of her mother severed the last connection to family history and Southern culture. With her youngest brother and sister orphaned, her family's dissolution seemed complete. Socially dislocated, Holloway-Langford also had failed to establish a new family by marriage. By the time she wrote *Beyond the Sunrise*, she had fulfilled her promise to her mother, launching her younger siblings into the world. Ella Watson Carter had recently married the music critic

William J. Henderson. The youngest Carter child, Vaulx, who had been her mother's favorite, was a midshipman at the U.S. Naval Academy, where he played on its first football team. Even her own son, George, no longer depended on her, having entered West Point. Finally, almost a decade after the death of her mother, Holloway-Langford moved into a home of her own at 181 Schermerhorn Street, Brooklyn.

Laura Holloway-Langford had been sustained by women: first by her mother, then by friends. By the time that she wrote *Beyond the Sunrise,* she was free from caretaking responsibilities for the first time in her life, but she found that she was dissatisfied. She longed to live a life of greater significance beyond the newsroom of the *Brooklyn Daily Eagle.* As she entered middle age, her furtive explorations of the spiritual world did not quell her yearnings. The time seemed auspicious for new, even radical, choices about her life. It would be a member of the Sunday evening group, William Quan Judge, who, in consultation with the spirits, would give her the courage to venture onto a new path.[61] She was once again ready to refashion her identity—this time from a run-of-the-mill spiritualist to a pupil of the Masters—those wise men known variously as adepts, great souls, or Mahatmas—who were said to possess ancient metaphysical knowledge.

3

"Better Come"

Laura Holloway-Langford, like many women who joined the Theosophical Society, sought opportunities for leadership and creativity that were not easily available in Victorian society.[1] She wanted to
reveal her clairvoyant gifts openly, to test their powers, and to be re-
warded for them. Additionally, she longed to escape the persona that she
had so carefully constructed in Brooklyn, daring to hope that she might
refashion her personal life unhindered by bourgeois social expectations
and sexual mores.

Holloway-Langford did not meet Helena P. Blavatsky and Henry Steel
Olcott while they lived in New York, but she had heard about their claims
to occult knowledge from friends.[2] She also had read articles about spiritualism that Olcott, a former U.S. Army colonel and a lawyer, had written
for New York newspapers. Olcott later published these in *People from the
Other World,* where he recounted meeting Blavatsky at a séance in Chit-
tenden, Vermont, and described the extraordinary wonders she had performed.[3] In fall 1875, Olcott proposed the formation of an organization
to promote occult research. Of the sixteen people who agreed to found
such a society, only two were women: Helena Blavatsky and the well-
known clairvoyant Emma Hardinge Britten, author of a popular history
of American spiritualism.[4] On November 17, the Theosophical Society
was "fully constituted," with Olcott as President, Helena P. Blavatsky as
Corresponding Secretary, and William Quan Judge as Counselor.[5]

The original purpose of the Society was to discover and disseminate the laws governing the universe. In its first incarnation, "the Society reflected the organization and attitude of an exclusively male institution."[6] It resembled a Masonic order, with members pledging secrecy and its activities kept private. Fellows of the Society were expected to advance through three "degrees," demonstrating their progress in acquiring esoteric knowledge.[7] Although members were admitted without regard to race, nationality, or religious belief, there was no mention of universal brotherhood. Olcott recalled that "the little group of founders were all of European blood, with no strong natural antagonism as to religions, and caste distinctions were to them non-existent. The Brotherhood plank in the Society's future platform was, therefore, not thought of: later on, however, when our sphere of influence extended so as to bring us into relations with Asiatics and their religions and social systems, it became a necessity, and, in fact, the corner-stone of our edifice."[8]

In fall 1877, Blavatsky and Olcott were visited by James Peebles, whose frequent travels across the globe had earned him the title of "the spiritual pilgrim." Peebles described meeting spiritualists in Calcutta who were familiar with the writings of Americans such as Emma Hardinge Britten.[9] Olcott showed Peebles a photograph of two Hindu gentlemen he had met on a transatlantic voyage in 1870. Peebles recognized one of them as Moolji Thackersey, and he gave Olcott his address in Bombay. Olcott immediately wrote to Thackersey about the Theosophical Society and its love of Indian wisdom. As a result, Olcott established a connection with Hindu religious reformers, and in January 1878 the Theosophical Society embarked on an alliance with the Arya Samaj, an organization that sought to revitalize Indian society through study of the Vedas.[10] By the end of that year, the Society had established branches in London and Bombay. All told it had 175 members, more than forty of them in the New York area.[11]

Convinced that ancient wisdom was preserved in the traditions of "oriental" religions and disappointed with the progress of Theosophy in the United States, Helena Blavatsky and Henry S. Olcott decided that the future of the movement lay in the East. In December 1878, they set sail for India. After stopping over in London to visit the American medium Mary

Hollis-Billing, they arrived in Bombay in mid-February 1879.[12] According to Olcott, the Society in America had "dwindled to almost nothing," but Theosophy "began to revive from the moment its executive centre was shifted to India."[13] In 1882, the Society established its headquarters in Adyar, a suburb of Madras, and the movement spread rapidly across the Indian subcontinent.

Back in New York, Abner Doubleday and William Q. Judge were left in charge of the fledgling American branch of the Society.[14] Doubleday reported that although many people were curious about supernatural phenomena, few of them could be enticed to study occult literature or even to attend a meeting.[15] Thus, Judge must have been elated when, some four years after Blavatsky and Olcott left for India, he met Laura Holloway-Langford. Here was a woman who had rejected orthodox Christianity, yet who believed in spiritual reality. She was well-educated, but she craved a deeper understanding of esoteric traditions. Her explorations of spiritualism had made her receptive to the idea of clairvoyant communication. In other words, she was well prepared to embrace the teachings of theosophy. William Q. Judge persuaded Laura Holloway-Langford to join the Theosophical Society, a decision that would transform her life.

FROM SPIRITUALISM TO THEOSOPHY

During her early years in New York, Helena Blavatsky had considered herself a spiritualist. By 1877, however, when *Isis Unveiled* was published, Blavatsky had altered her beliefs.[16] She attributed the appearance of spirits either to the medium's double, or "astral body," or to a lingering remnant of a dead personality in the process of final disintegration. In her most daring departure from spiritualism, Blavatsky denied that spirits of the dead communicated with people on earth; instead, she proclaimed the existence of living adepts whose wisdom had been gained over many reincarnations.[17] In the early years, however, the distinction between spiritualism and theosophy remained hazy, and at first, rather than repudiating spiritualism, Blavatsky subordinated it within a larger occult worldview.[18]

Cathy Gutierrez rightly observes that theosophy was indebted to spiritualism for many of its adherents as well as for a "cultural ambience in which questions of hidden knowledge and occult practices could find a receptive audience." Additionally, she argues that theosophy's popularity indicated doubts about the concept of evolutionary progress, so that rather than looking forward to an age of perfection, theosophists searched for religious truths in the ancient past.[19] Such distinctions made little difference, however, to a seeker like Laura Holloway-Langford, who found it quite possible to simultaneously anticipate a millennial New Age and seek its truths in ancient wisdom. To her, theosophy appeared a natural step in the unfolding of spiritual progress. As R. Laurence Moore notes, "an interest in the mysteries supposedly unveiled by an occult society was a logical graduation for spiritualists who took seriously the caveat . . . that they ought to do something more than merely go through the dry exercise of watching mediums' performances."[20]

Stephen Prothero has argued that theosophy was "an attempt to reform spiritualism by 'uplifting' its masses out of their supposed philosophical and moral vulgarities—to transform the mass of prurient ghostseeking spiritualists into ethically exemplary theorists of the astral plane."[21] While Holloway-Langford never abandoned spiritualism, she was nevertheless mindful of the social ramifications of her affiliations. She was impressed by the intellectual caliber of those associated with the Theosophical Society: scholars who studied comparative religions, university professors who claimed the scientific method could test the reality of occult phenomena, linguists who translated the classics of Eastern spirituality, and poets and writers who found in theosophy a symbolic language for their art. Theosophy's emphasis on the active acquisition of knowledge appealed to her desire for self-improvement and social status. She had always felt herself above the common mold, and theosophy appeared to offer a means to prove it.

WILLIAM QUAN JUDGE

A lawyer, Judge resided at 116 Willoughby Street, Brooklyn, just about three blocks from where Holloway-Langford lived, but they did not meet until 1883. In 1875, after reading *People from the Other World,* Judge had contacted Olcott asking for the name of a medium.[22] Olcott suggested Helena Blavatsky. Under her influence, Judge began to study Hermetic traditions.[23]

He was convinced that through discipline and strength of will he could learn to exercise occult powers. His success, however, was limited.[24] Even Blavatsky found his efforts amusing. On June 14, 1877, she wrote to a relative in Russia: "There is Judge, who has simply become a holy Arhat. He sees visions and he flies; and he asserts that he passes out of the body every night and roams in infinite space. I ring a bell in Forty-seventh Street, in my room, and he hears it at Brooklyn, eight miles off; he starts off at once, and in two hours he appears at my call." She concluded, "See what fools they are, and how I lead them by the nose!"[25] In a letter dated August 1, 1881, Judge asserted that when Blavatsky lived in New York, he had heard from the Masters "*viva voca*," but that he and Olcott did not know their true identity.[26] He believed that sometimes these "Illuminated Ones" spoke to him in the deep of night, usually between midnight and 4 AM, and that at other times they occupied Blavatsky's body and spoke through her.[27] Blavatsky's letters prior to 1884, however, contain only a handful of references to Judge, and she appears to have valued him primarily as "a smart lawyer, and a faithful true friend to all of us," rather than as an occultist.[28]

Judge had not accompanied Blavatsky and Olcott when they moved to India. He had sworn never to be separated from his only child, and, even though his daughter died from diphtheria in September 1878, he remained in the United States. In deep mourning, Judge chose not to abandon his wife, a decision that he later termed "a fiasco." His state of mind was not helped by failing to hear from Blavatsky for almost a year after her departure. When he finally received a letter it was a "hellish epistle. . . . It would have driven off anyone else; though if it had . . . none of you would have cared a damn."[29] Months later he continued to smart from Blavatsky's "*awful* letter," writing to Olcott: "She accuses me in it of almost anything. Perfectly terrible."[30] However, when Judge informed Blavatsky that he was ready to give up theosophy, he received a reply from one of her Hindu followers, Damodar K. Mavalankar, who corresponded with Judge from October 1879 through June 1883, often at the request of Blavatsky.

Judge felt trapped by his marriage to Ella M. Smith, whose father, a Methodist minister, the Reverend Joseph Smith, lived with them, along with her elder sister, Joanna, and a nephew. Judge wrote Mavalankar:

> They are not only professing Christians, but are very bigoted and prejudiced knowing nothing of their own or anyone else's spirit powers and tolerating nothing on the subject. . . . And as for information about India,

China and Japan, it is positively shocking what false and foolish tales they have been told and really believe coming from those beastly missionaries in those lands. . . . They call all such people as you and M[orya] heathens and that in contempt. . . . Then my wife . . . is also a Christian of decided beliefs. She goes to church every Sunday while I stay away. . . . She hates T. S. and H. P. B. and does not want to converse on religious subjects. So of those subjects that lie near my heart and are constantly on my tongue we never speak except accidentally and then it always produced ill blood. You of course being a Hindu can hardly understand how a wife can believe contrary to her husband. But in America women are different and the fact is here the majority of men believe as they do just to please the wife. But I do not and therefore smothered doubt is always there. Now what a hell this is to live in.[31]

Yoked to a mate who had no sympathy for his spiritual yearnings and who refused to accompany him to India, Judge wrote Olcott that his head was "in the pillory." He wanted "to clear out of here and never be heard of again, burying myself in India and helping the cause, but if I did that, you see I could not come out openly, for being known, disgraceful things could be said of me."[32] He rejected his wife's desire for a new child, probably by refusing sexual relations, even though he was "pestered to death to procure another."[33] Yet he continued to be tortured by fantasies of "adultery or fornication."[34] He longed to leave "without notice or on a pretended trip to some other place and never come back till I had the truth and light—or death."[35] All told, his correspondence during these years presents an overwhelming sense of desolation, fueled by a commingling of spiritual and physical desire and frustration. At times, self-annihilation seemed to Judge the only solution. He wrote to Olcott that he was constantly "assailed by doubts and that black despondency which produces the absurdity of suicide."[36]

Damodar Mavalankar's letters fueled Judge's determination to find a way out of his predicament. From the fall of 1881 through 1882 he undertook several risky and ultimately failed business ventures in Venezuela and Mexico.[37] But despite his best efforts, Judge wrote Olcott that he remained "stuck here, stuck, stuck, stuck fast."[38] By the time Judge returned to Brooklyn in early 1883, his law practice had lapsed, he was deeply in debt, and his health had been undermined by Chagres fever. During the spring of 1883, Judge was consumed by self-loathing. He wrote to Olcott: "They told me once I put myself in hell, and no one else could get me out. Well, here in hell I lift up my eyes to those that are above and do not deny them. . . . I cannot leave here till all my debts are paid, and that looks very far away." Nevertheless, he clung to his dream, writing Olcott that thoughts of the occult Masters were "here in my head all the time, and cannot if I would, and I would not, drive them out." He concluded, "You cannot measure the disgust I feel for this country and society. It is rotten to putridity, and seems to grow worse daily. I feel its deposits on myself too, and am restive with a constant longing to escape."[39] Judge feared that Blavatsky's "Hindoo" disciples would scorn his inability to command his wife to accompany him to India: they would, Judge wrote, laugh at him as "a man . . . who cannot get his own wife to agree with him on matters of philosophy and religion."[40]

Judge did not meet the culturally sanctioned ideal of masculinity as it was understood either in the East or the West. In India, a man was expected to wield the power of patriarchy over his family. In America, a husband was expected to shoulder responsibility for women and children, to provide for their material needs, and to remain stoic in the face of setbacks. Especially among those of Judge's social class, a husband was nevertheless expected to honor his wife's desires. In an age of hard-driven capitalism, Judge displayed traits that were often gendered as feminine: artistic talent, a craving for the approval of others, strong emotional enthusiasms, and, most significantly, a deep spirituality. It was these qualities in Judge that Theosophy called out to, and these which seemed to him his real self.

DISCOVERING THEOSOPHY

William Q. Judge met Laura Holloway-Langford in January 1883 when they were both dissatisfied with their lives and anxious about their futures.[41] Throughout the early 1880s, Judge had been a member of a spiritualist circle that included Mary Hollis-Billing, who had communicated messages to him from the spirit world.[42] When Holloway-Langford invited him to participate in her Sunday-evening salon, he may have been seeking another medium to guide his future course. The most immediate effect of Judge's participation, however, was that he introduced theosophy and the idea of the adepts to the group. Under Judge's influence Holloway-Langford began to read the works of A. P. Sinnett. On September 23, 1883, the *Brooklyn Daily Eagle* published a long article, "Buddhism in India," that presented Sinnett's *The Occult World* and his *Esoteric Buddhism* as major turning points in the history of world literature. Probably authored by Holloway-Langford, the piece ascertained the existence of adepts and argued that "occult science" had revealed knowledge far beyond that of physicists or followers of Darwin. Theosophy claimed both to revive ancient wisdom and to teach the "laws of practical occultism" that she believed were superior even to the most advanced thinking in all fields, including science.[43]

The discovery of theosophy helped Laura Holloway-Langford make sense of extrasensory occurrences, both as she had personally experienced them and as they had been reported by family and friends. As a result of this new perspective, her clairvoyant experiences changed. No longer did the spirits of her mother and other dead relatives appear to her. In their stead emerged the "astral forms" of living beings that brought knowledge and guidance. She reported that one of these was a Hindu, another was European, and a third was an "elemental" who accompanied Judge, teaching him and guiding his development. Holloway-Langford later claimed that although Judge had no "special knowledge of this being," Blavatsky herself had attested to its reality. Additionally, Holloway-Langford maintained that it was through her mediation that Judge had "spiritual experiences richer and deeper than any he had ever known."[44] Because Judge, as Holloway-Langford depicted him, was not endowed with gifts of clairvoyance or clairaudience, he depended on her for communications from the Masters. Holloway-Langford's portrayal of her own powers of clairvoyance as far superior to those of Judge was, of course, self-serving. Judge's letters to Olcott during this period, however, confirm his lack of self-confidence, indeed, his desperate need for spiritual encouragement.

Given Judge's emotional fragility, it is easy to understand how profoundly he was affected by a June 1883 letter from Mavalankar, on which was scribbled: "Better come M."[45] Judge interpreted this note as a summons to India from the Master Morya, a "Mahatma" who had appeared to Olcott in New York. It confirmed in Judge's mind that his fate was linked with the Theosophical Society. Still, Judge hesitated, writing to Mavalankar that he was willing to work his passage to India, but that it seemed to him "mean" to run away from his wife, leaving her without support when, at his solicitation, she had given up a "good paying position as a teacher" to marry him. He admitted, however, that he wished to disappear and be presumed dead, "but I do not want to leave behind a memory for men to point the finger of scorn at."[46]

In November Judge's confidence was bolstered when Olcott issued a charter for a New York branch of the Society called the "Aryan Theosophical Society." Judge was elected president.[47] According to Holloway-Langford's later reconstruction, "one night in the winter of 1883" Judge announced to the Sunday evening group his plan "to make a change in his life, which might bring shipwreck to his domestic and business relationships." He was convinced that fate was "moving him to prepare for an enlarged field of labor in the cause he loved." Holloway-Langford claimed that Judge revealed "more of his mind" to her "than to other members of the group." He surely told her about the cryptic message from "M.," and he probably confided his anguish over his marriage. Holloway-Langford, especially given her own troubled marital history, would have lent a sympathetic ear when Judge turned to her for "advice and comfort." She encouraged Judge to "sever his relationships . . . in America, and . . . bid farewell to his past,"[48] and she claimed to have seen an "astral light" confirming that she was destined to follow him to Europe.[49] The occult experiences Laura Holloway-Langford reported during 1883 and early 1884, whatever their exact nature, were certainly momentous, for William Q. Judge seized upon them to justify a theosophical mission abroad.

Marlene Trompe has detailed the ways in which men and women engaged in indecorous conduct during séances or while under the influence of the spirits. She argues that even though such behavior did not jeopardize their social standing, it nevertheless "shaped new conceptions of feminine sexuality and marriage."[50] In the case of Laura Holloway-Langford and William Q. Judge, the crossing of boundaries in the world of the spirit led directly to the violation of Victorian moral and social codes. With the encouragement of Holloway-Langford and the spirits speaking through her, Judge decided that his marriage would no longer impede his spiritual path; likewise, Holloway-Langford was determined to escape the confines of the life she had fashioned as a respectable widow. Together they hoped to invent new identities far beyond the censure of family and friends in Brooklyn.

SEEKING NEW LIVES

While Judge was making plans to leave New York, "Laura Carter Holloway" was admitted as a Fellow of the Eastern Division of the Theosophical Society, Third Degree, Third Section. Her certificate was signed by H. S. Olcott, President; H. P. Blavatsky, Corresponding Secretary; and William Q. Judge, Recording Secretary, New York.[51] In addition to progressing through "degrees" of occult expertise, members were classified by "Sections." The identity of those in the "First Section" was secret and composed "exclusively of initiates in Esoteric Science and Philosophy, who take a deep interest in the Society's affairs and instruct the President-Founder how best to regulate them." Members in the Second Section had "proved by their fidelity, zeal, and courage, their devotion to the Society" and had "become able to regard all men as equally their brothers irrespective of caste, colour, race, or creed." The Third Section was composed of those "on probation, until their purpose to remain in the Society has become fixed, their usefulness shown, and their ability to conquer evil habits and unwarrantable prejudices demonstrated."[52] Holloway-Langford's ambition was to join the inner group of initiates who had access to secret knowledge. She hoped that the Mahatmas would accept her as a "chela," a disciple, so that she could carry out their work.[53] Both the precise nature of "chelaship" and how it might be confirmed were unclear, an issue which set the stage for much of the internal Theosophical drama in which Holloway-Langford was to play a pivotal role.[54]

Laura Holloway-Langford did not radically change her beliefs, as might occur in a religious conversion; instead she broadened her perspective to include a focus on Eastern religions and a more active pursuit of occult knowledge. By affiliating with the Theosophical Society, she promised to "struggle against the evil around us" and to labor for universal brotherhood, believing "that every one of us and every member of the race to which we belong, should stand in his true and sacred relation to every other human being."[55] Given her longstanding commitment to religious universalism and sexual equality, she assumed that, despite the gendered language of "brotherhood," Theosophists were pledged to the equality of all people, including women. Yet, as James Santucci has pointed out, in the early years the Theosophical Society's attitude toward sexual equality was ambiguous.[56] During its first decade, leadership in the Society was overwhelmingly male. Of more than forty-five Executive Officers in 1880, there were only two women: Helena Blavatsky and Emma Coulomb.[57] Likewise, the movement's membership was predominantly male until the end of the nineteenth century.[58] It was not until the revisions of the Rules in 1888 that members pledged to seek universal brotherhood irrespective of sex. Consequently, Laura Holloway-Langford joined the Theosophical Society at a time when a role for women was not clearly established.

By early 1884, both William Q. Judge and Laura Holloway-Langford were at crucial points in their lives. Judge undoubtedly thought they were of similar age, but Holloway-Langford was actually eight years his senior, having turned forty in August 1883. She was at the peak of her reputation as a writer, and, although not wealthy, she had a steady income from her books. On February 11, 1884, Thomas Kinsella, the editor of the *Brooklyn Daily Eagle* and Holloway-Langford's mentor, died suddenly. Shortly thereafter, Holloway-Langford left the newspaper, possibly fired by a new editor who opposed women working in newsrooms. Whatever the reason, she found herself free of professional and personal responsibilities for the first time in her adult life. She was in a position to reinvent herself as an occultist.

William Q. Judge remained in debt and his wife still refused to accompany him, but he sailed for London in late February, with plans to travel from there to India. The funds for his travel must have been supplied by friends sympathetic to his theosophical aspirations, perhaps even by Holloway-Langford. In London for about a month, Judge visited English Theosophists, went sightseeing, and awaited word from Henry S. Olcott and Helena Blavatsky. During this time, he frequently wrote Holloway-Langford, describing his daily activities. Despite having resolved his personal dilemma, Judge's self-doubts continued, as did the urge toward suicide. He wrote that his thoughts "have dwelt upon the Masters, upon you, upon the situation. . . . Dear friend, help me. . . . You are now either up or awake as it is 11:30 here a.m. . . . Goodbye, Love to the whole Δ and may we soon be able to see clearly what the whole affair is to be."[59] The Δ apparently referred to Holloway-Langford and two other members of the Sunday-evening salon, because Judge declared: "Surely I will never meet again three souls so kind to me as you three and never again one like yours until I meet myself. . . . Give my love to the other two sides of the triangle."[60] After visiting the Assyrian and Egyptian artifacts at the British Museum, he wrote Holloway-Langford: "Oh, how I longed to have you there with me that you might relate what dim shapes you would see flitting about, harmless, sad, wondering where the past had gone; questioning why the rites of the ancient days proceeded no more, and looking with still greater wonder upon us, the modern barbarians.... I want very much to learn what is the connection between me and you and Egypt's past."[61] Holloway-Langford and Judge were convinced that they had spiritual affinities based on a previous existence and that it was "karma" that they should now be reunited. They conjured up imaginative past lives where they might safely transgress boundaries of propriety. Such role-playing excused their developing relationship, while at the same time it enacted a commitment to a common future.[62]

Judge sought confirmation of Holloway-Langford's revelations from the English Theosophists. When A. P. Sinnett described his vision of an adept who had light hair and great beauty, Judge felt certain it was the same figure that had appeared to Holloway-Langford. Judge also reported that Holloway-Langford's perceptions of Blavatsky were accurate: "What you saw of her prostration was right. [Sinnett] says she is very sick, and oh, how tired." In Judge's estimation, the English Theosophists he had met, "notwithstanding their large opportunities," were not "as advanced" as Laura Holloway-Langford, and he wrote her, "they have not got your powers."[63]

Emboldened by Judge's confidence in her gifts, Holloway-Langford on March 29 wrote to Mavalankar in Adyar, India, requesting that she be "enrolled as a pupil" of the Masters. She also revealed to him that Judge had mailed her copies of Sinnett's letters from the Masters, whom he called the "Mahatmas."[64] Mavalankar's reply, which did not reach Holloway-Langford until mid-May, warned that "many people seem to confound physical seeing with knowledge.... True perception is true knowledge." He continued: "One may see a thing and not know it, while he may know a thing and yet not see it." Mavalankar cautioned Holloway-Langford that she might not be prepared to understand either her own visions or the Mahatma letters received by Sinnett.[65]

Holloway-Langford later quoted extensively from this letter in her sketch "Teachings of the Master," which she published in 1886 in Judge's journal, The Path. In it, an unnamed female "Soul" was transported telepathically to the presence of a "Master," who spoke to her in Mavalankar's words. The Soul, as Holloway-Langford refers to herself, was a "Babe" or a "little child clinging to [the] garments" of her Master. On this journey, she learned that "fiery is the furnace of probation" where the neophyte will be opposed by "enemies of the spirit" and "the demons of worldliness, inconstancy, suspicion and faint-heartedness." The student must learn the language of the "arcane knowledge of occultism," but proof "of the existence on this earth of the Wisdom Teachers" would come only through intuition.[66] In this sketch, Holloway-Langford portrays the "Soul" in terms that are culturally feminine. The Soul must place itself in a state of complete dependence on the Mahatmas. Knowledge, the Master taught her, comes neither through intellect nor through occult phenomena, but by faith guaranteed by intuition.

While she waited in Brooklyn for acceptance as a pupil by the Masters, Judge was summoned by Olcott and Blavatsky to Paris. On March 28 he accompanied them to apartments at No. 46, Rue Notre Dame des Champs.[67] Judge had planned to leave immediately for India, but Blavatsky and Olcott demanded that he remain in Paris to help with writing *The Secret Doctrine*. Judge went to work, selecting and collating material from *Isis Unveiled*. He wished Holloway-Langford were there to assist him. He wrote her: "For this work you are peculiarly fitted; and even if you worked at it with the intention of returning to New York that would be good Karma for you. I am fitted also for certain portions of the work, and together we would revel in knowledge and advance hand in hand along the path." Judge found other confirmations that the adepts endorsed his decision to leave New York. Blavatsky informed him "that the Master had told her in India, that he was doing or 'about to do something with and for me.'" Additionally, the young Brahmin chela Mohini Mohun Chatterji, who had accompanied Blavatsky to Europe, substantiated the existence of the Hindu adept and "an English Adept or European with rather light hair" that Holloway-Langford had seen. Despite these encouragements, Judge remained depressed: "For several days I have had … the most awful blues that ever were. So bad indeed that H. P. B. was very much worried. It seemed impossible to stave them off, and as they were accompanied with an uncontrollable desire to weep, I was in a bad way. … I trust you are not the cause of my depression, although if so that is better than any other cause."[68]

Judge was anxious to get Blavatsky's blessing for Laura Holloway-Langford to join him, promising to write her "just what she says. I have no doubt of all this and that Karma has brought us together and will keep us the same."[69] On April 24, 1884, Judge wrote Olcott, who was in England, describing Blavatsky's enigmatic reply to his request: "'The Master will marshal a procession before us containing good and bad, leaving to our Karma to make the proper selection.'" But Blavatsky had also reported that when Holloway-Langford's name was mentioned, the Master replied, "'She may come.'" Judge continued, "If we get her we will have acquired the very first and best of seers and the purest of persons. She has money and will be no expense. She dislikes parade and knows more what she ought to do than we can tell her. But . . . meanwhile keep confidential what I have told you. I am writing to tell her to come as soon as she can."[70] On the same day, Blavatsky dictated a letter to Holloway-Langford. In it, she responded both to letters that Holloway-Langford had written describing her psychic experiences and to Judge's entreaties. Blavatsky wrote:

> I told [Judge] to tell you that you were *not* mistaken, and that what I
> learned from him and from your letters was not only real, but also interest-
> ing to even me who have seen so many mysterious things . . . . In looking
> up to the Mahatmas and aspiring to be their disciple you will have the
> surest guides and the greater safety—'for those who know the truth
> of all things will teach you.' I am not permitted to reveal all that I now
> know or could discover. Time and your own powers will reveal all to you.
> Meanwhile you will be receiving from Judge what proofs he can give you.
> And I trust the time is not far distant when you will be engaged also in
> the grand work of benefitting Humanity by forwarding the Theosophical
> movement.

Although Judge had been the scribe, Blavatsky added a note in her own hand: "I will remain in Paris until July or later; I will be happy to see you—which may easily happen if you *come to England in May*—for then you can come over here and go to India with W. Q. J."[71] This was the sign for which Laura Holloway-Langford had been waiting. Within a few weeks she was on her way to Europe.

Judge's spirits were buoyed, and he wrote to Olcott: "I expect Mrs. Holloway here in a short time, and if she comes we can get a lot of the *Secret Doctrine* ready for H. P. B. . . . . I will bet my head to a lemon that I have got now a magnificent coadjutor, *if not a successor to* H. P. B. and one who has trained scientific methods of literary work, as well as psychical abilities of the kind that make H. P. B. so remarkable." Judge continued: "I thought in the street yesterday I heard the Master say Mrs. H. would be a successor and then they would let H. P. B. vanish. Two hours after in the parlor in talking to Wagnalls, who extolled the character of Holloway . . . H. P. B. leaned back and said, 'O my God, if I shall only find in her A SUCCESSOR, how gladly I will PEG OUT!'"[72] Judge interpreted Blavatsky's remark as "a curious 'scientific coincidence.'" More likely, however, Blavatsky spoke ironically, fed up with hearing men sing the praises of the American psychic.

EUROPEAN JOURNEY

Laura Holloway-Langford asked a friend, the poet Louise Chandler Moulton, if they might travel together to Europe. Moulton declined, but promised "I shall *never* speak of anything you say to me about your plans or your reasons for them to Miss Proctor, or anyone else."[73] As noted earlier, Holloway-Langford may have been sharing her Brooklyn home with Edna Dean Proctor, but since most of Holloway-Langford's close friends were also spiritual seekers, it seems unlikely that they would disapprove of her desire to meet Helena Blavatsky. Holloway-Langford's relationship with William Q. Judge, however, was an entirely different matter, especially if she was contemplating following him to India. Although her friends were critical of marriage, they were much more likely to advocate celibacy as a solution than to support women's sexual freedom. Cleo, the character in *Beyond the Sunrise* who most closely resembled Holloway-Langford, responded to the declaration that each woman has a "spiritual mate" by laughing and asking what would happen if her "real mate" were married. It was no coincidence, then, that Holloway-Langford wrote these lines in 1883, at the very time she was developing a relationship with a married man.

Laura Holloway-Langford arrived in Paris in late May or early June 1884. Shortly thereafter, she crossed paths with a friend, Oliver Otis Howard, a Union General who had become Commissioner of the Freedmen's Bureau and who, because of his piety, was known as the "praying general." Holloway-Langford explained to him that American newspapers had sent her to investigate the Theosophical Society and to "examine the pros and cons concerning them and make a report to the friends who sent her."[74]

On one occasion, she implied that she had accompanied General Howard and his family to Europe, and another time she said that she had traveled with a friend and her young son.[75] Later she claimed that she had left the United States to recover from an illness that she feared might prove fatal. Despite these conflicting stories, it is clear that Laura Holloway-Langford left Brooklyn in pursuit of a career as an occultist. Whatever its other dimensions, her friendship with William Q. Judge was a passport to Helena Blavatsky, A. P. Sinnett, and leading Theosophists. It is also clear that she concealed this information from family and friends in New York.

Unbeknownst to her, Laura Holloway-Langford had arrived in Europe at a time when the Theosophical Society was coming under intense scrutiny. Doubts had been raised both in India and in Europe about Helena Blavatsky and about claims of communications from adepts. Additionally, A. P. Sinnett was engaged in a struggle for leadership within British Theosophy. Into this volatile milieu stepped Laura Holloway-Langford, a woman who, in her own mind, was a sophisticated professional and a gifted clairvoyant. She did not see herself as a novice, but rather as one who was offering her talents to the Theosophical cause at considerable self-sacrifice. After spending a couple of weeks in Paris, Holloway-Langford headed to England, probably accompanied by Olcott and Judge, arriving on June 13.[76] It was not long before Judge sailed for India, leaving Laura Holloway-Langford on her own in London, where she was already making a striking impression among the British Theosophists.[77]

4

⚬ஃ⚬

"The First Bomb-shell from the Dugpa World"

In the spring of 1886, Helena P. Blavatsky felt that "fierce waves" of evil spirits were "heaving and spreading and beating ferociously around the [Theosophical] Society."[1] She had left India at the end of March 1885, some months before the Society for Psychical Research labeled her a fraud. The Society for Psychical Research had been founded in London in 1882 with the goal of examining paranormal phenomena through scientific methods. In December 1884, its representative, Richard Hodgson, had arrived at the Theosophical Headquarters in Adyar, India, where he conducted a three-month investigation. A report presented to a General Meeting of the Society for Psychical Research in June 1885 concluded that Blavatsky was neither "the mouthpiece of hidden seers" nor "a mere vulgar adventuress; we think she has achieved a title to permanent remembrance as one of the most accomplished, ingenious, and interesting imposters in history."[2]

Blavatsky later alleged that the defamation of the Theosophical Society began when Laura Holloway-Langford arrived in Europe in the summer of 1884. She called Holloway-Langford the "first bomb-shell from the Dugpa world," sent "by the opposing powers for the destruction of the Society."[3] Blavatsky also accused the prominent British Theosophist A. P. Sinnett of betrayal because he had "welcomed and warmed" the American in his "own breast."[4] A middle-class, middle-aged journalist, Holloway-Langford was an unlikely candidate for a she-devil; nevertheless, Blavatsky came to view her as a snake that had insinuated itself into the Society, corrupting the hearts of its followers and undermining their loyalty. Some later Theosophists labeled Holloway-Langford a "Sex Maya," using the Sanskrit term for "illusion." They contended that she had disguised her true nature and had tempted male members of the Society to abandon the truths of Theosophy. Even when the story of Laura Holloway-Langford was rendered in less dramatic terms, she was portrayed as a failed disciple of the Masters, an aspirant with a flawed character who had flirted briefly, if intensely, with Theosophy, but who quickly abandoned it for the comforts of bourgeois life in Brooklyn.

For many years, Holloway-Langford would puzzle over the meaning of her experiences in Europe. During the first two weeks of June 1884, she mingled with Theosophists in Paris, but rather than remaining there with Helena Blavatsky, she proceeded to London, where A. P. Sinnett and his wife, Patience, had invited her to be a guest in their home.[5] Sinnett introduced her to the posh world of British occultists, and he persuaded her to assist in psychic experiments by becoming a medium for his communications with the Masters. When Blavatsky arrived in London, she demanded that Holloway-Langford cut off her relationship with Sinnett and instead live with her at the home of Francesca Arundale, a spiritualist who had become a Theosophist. Having little knowledge about politics within the Theosophical Society, Holloway-Langford found herself in the middle of a bewildering internecine struggle for power between A. P. Sinnett and Helena Blavatsky. In the ensuing "flapdoodle," to use one of Blavatsky's favorite words, tensions over class and race that had been simmering within the Society erupted.

Additionally, Holloway-Langford's presence highlighted unresolved questions about gender.[6] Despite the movement's commitment to universal brotherhood, it was unclear whether a woman, other than Blavatsky herself, might attain the designation of "chela," or disciple of the Masters. Even Blavatsky did not claim to be "head" of the Theosophical Society, stating that "a society, the central feature of which is the Masters, could never be under the leadership of a woman."[7] Laura Holloway-Langford had given up a thriving career in Brooklyn in the belief that as a Theosophist she could recreate her life free of the cultural constraints of Victorian womanhood. She looked to Helena Blavatsky as a model for female autonomy. During the summer of 1884, however, she discovered that the

Theosophical Society did not provide a clear path for female leadership. Rather than escaping the limitations imposed by her sex, Laura Holloway-Langford became entangled in controversies where gender was employed as a tool to control the behavior of both male and female members of the Theosophical Society.

THE MAHATMA LETTERS

The uproar that Holloway-Langford's Theosophical apprenticeship created is preserved in about thirty letters from the Mahatmas written between early July and mid-October 1884. Except for two letters from Master Morya, all the letters came from an adept named "Koot Hoomi." Laura Holloway-Langford received at least ten letters from him, while nine were sent to Helena Blavatsky and about a dozen more were directed to other Theosophists. Many of these letters were presumed to have been written in Koot Hoomi's hand, often in blue pencil. Helena Blavatsky claimed that sometimes others were communicated to her telepathically, explaining that she often saw the "orders, and the thoughts and words" of the Master and then was able to "precipitate" them into the form of the letter. At other times, however, the Master sent her "the paper and the message already done."[8] Exactly how the letters were transmitted remains a mystery, but Theosophists accepted that only those at the highest level of psychic development could send or receive messages.[9]

Although the originals of Mahatma letters survive, there is no consensus about their origin or author. Many scholars argue that Blavatsky and her assistants produced them,[10] while those sympathetic to the claims of Theosophy believe that, whatever their channel of communication, the letters expressed the thoughts of living Masters. Even if Blavatsky wrote the letters, however, the problem of what kind of evidence they constitute remains unresolved. Theosophists, including Blavatsky, did not deny that occult communications often came through the hand of a disciple. The accuracy of such messages, she conceded, varied according to the expertise of the person who received them. Sometimes admonishing, sometimes encouraging, the letters restricted the recipients' behavior while shaping their attitudes toward other members of the Theosophical Society. The letters, written and preserved in English, set specific boundaries on the vagaries of occult communication. Most importantly, they controlled the narrative, both the story as understood by the actors in it and as it was later reconstructed by historians of the Theosophical Society.

The letters confront us—as they confronted Laura Holloway-Langford and other Theosophists—with the question of how to assess assertions of supernatural revelation. Catherine Wessinger has noted that authority derived from occult sources must be accepted on faith, thus opening the door to conflicting claims to authority.[11] Yet the Mahatma letters posed some special problems. Were communications genuine *only* when they came through Blavatsky's mediation, or might other disciples, like Laura Holloway-Langford or A. P. Sinnett, receive knowledge directly from the Masters? When letters purporting to be from the Masters appeared, how could one be sure they were genuine? Might some of these be "false" messages, either because of faulty transcription or because they were sent by evil spirits? Written documents have the power to contain meaning and to fix signification, but many of the revelations from the Masters were ambiguous or self-contradictory. Who had the authority to interpret them?

By the time Laura Holloway-Langford appeared on the scene, a set of conventions had developed around letters from the Masters. Among Theosophists it was understood that they communicated with only a few of the most advanced disciples; that written messages from them carried greater authority than other forms of communication, such as dreams or visions; and that contact between a Master and a disciple required facilitation by Helena Blavatsky, who was the chosen instrument for esoteric knowledge. During the summer of 1884, however, A. P. Sinnett defied these conventions. Claiming to have received messages directly from the Masters, he began to make his own demands, even presuming to judge for himself whether a communication was authentic.

These challenges to the authority of the Masters and of Blavatsky were mounted amidst uncertainty about the future of Theosophy. Blavatsky had come to Europe in spring 1884 in order to shore up support for the Theosophical Society, but as the year progressed, her attention turned increasingly to protecting it from attack. In England a committee of the Society for Psychical Research began to interrogate members of the Society, while in Adyar, India, Emma and Alexis Coulomb, former employees at Theosophical headquarters, accused Blavatsky of deceiving her followers. At the same time as she struggled to defend Theosophy from outside attacks, Blavatsky was confronted by internal dissent among her followers.

The Mahatma letters written during these months reveal the tensions in the relationships among Laura Holloway-Langford, A. P. Sinnett, and the Hindu lawyer and philosopher Mohini Mohun Chatterji. Blavatsky acted as puppet-master, manipulating the strings from behind the stage. First Sinnett, then Holloway-Langford refused to cooperate fully with her aims. Initially, Mohini Chatterji was a willing participant, but by 1885 he too was tired of the game. The stage for this drama was set by colonialism, with its attendant assumptions about the mystic East and the rational West. Against this backdrop of sexual, racial, class, and cultural conflicts, Laura Holloway-Langford confronted the Masters.

ALFRED PERCY SINNETT

A. P. Sinnett (1840–1921) was an English journalist who moved to India in 1872 in order to edit *The Pioneer*, the most prominent English-language newspaper in that country. In February 1879, shortly after Blavatsky and Olcott arrived in Bombay, they received a letter from Sinnett, who proclaimed his interest in occult phenomena and offered to publicize the mission of the Theosophical Society. Later that year, Blavatsky and Olcott visited Sinnett and his wife Patience at their home in Allahabad, "the winter capital of the viceroy and his government," where they were introduced to important members of Anglo-Indian society.[12] On December 26, Blavatsky and Olcott initiated the Sinnetts into the Theosophical Society. Some months later, Sinnett submitted inquiries about the nature of the cosmos to Helena Blavatsky, who transmitted them to the Adept Brotherhood. In October 1880, through Blavatsky's mediation, he began to receive a stream of communications from the Master Koot Hoomi.[13] Sinnett published two books based on the teachings in these letters, *The Occult World* (1881) and *Esoteric Buddhism* (1883), which, along with Blavatsky's writings, were largely responsible for publicizing Theosophy to the English-speaking world.

In November 1882, A. P. Sinnett lost his job as editor of *The Pioneer*, apparently "because of his Indian sympathies and his public espousal of

Theosophy."[14] He and Patience returned to England in early 1883. There Sinnett discovered that some Theosophists questioned his reliability as a conduit for esoteric knowledge. In particular, he was criticized for publishing a letter purportedly written by the Master that quoted verbatim from a lecture given in 1880 by the American spiritualist Henry Kiddle. Furthermore, Anna Kingsford, who in 1883 had become President of the London Lodge of the Theosophical Society, disparaged *Esoteric Buddhism* for its reliance on the Mahatmas, whom she judged to be coarse and materialistic. She argued that the truths of all religions found their most perfect form in Christian rather than in Buddhist esotericism.[15]

By early 1884, the Sinnetts had moved into a new home at 7 Ladbroke Gardens, where each Tuesday afternoon they invited those interested in occultism to gather. In *The Early Days of Theosophy in Europe*, Sinnett wrote that the movement had begun at "the upper levels of society." He believed that its influence should be "left to filter downwards with social authority behind it, instead of beginning on lower levels and trusted to filter upwards." Sinnett was not pleased to learn that Blavatsky and Olcott planned to visit England. He continued:

> I knew that the Theosophical movement had now taken root in London on a social level that would be quite out of tune with the personalities of the two "founders," especially with that of Colonel Olcott. Madame Blavatsky's manners were very rough. . . . Our experience in introducing her to Anglo-Indian friends had not been encouraging. One had to know her very thoroughly to be able to ignore characteristics that were repellent rather than attractive. . . . But Madame Blavatsky in London amidst the flood of people mostly belonging to the upper strata of society; I knew that trouble must ensue.

Sinnett was convinced that, even more than Blavatsky, Henry Steel Olcott would set back the "cordial relations" with the people he had been cultivating: "The superficial aspects of his personality were of a kind quite certain to set the teeth on edge with Englishmen of the type of those who were leading the Psychic Research movement."[16]

If, to Sinnett's mind, Helena Blavatsky and Colonel Olcott were not the best representatives of Theosophy, Indian disciples raised a different problem. Their presence suggested that all "occult wisdom was eastern in its origin," a premise rejected by Sinnett. Why, he reasoned, should esoteric knowledge not be equally available to Westerners, especially since European civilization, in his opinion, was more advanced in every way than that of Asia? Sinnett was convinced that the Indian disciples were jealous because he had been chosen by the Adept Brotherhood as its intermediary to Europe. He asserted that Indians "resented the idea that the arcane knowledge of the East should overflow into the western world." He quoted Frederic W. H. Myers, one of the founders of the Society for Psychical Research, who expressed gratitude to the adepts for selecting Sinnett as their intermediary, because he was "congenial" to "Western minds."[17]

Early in 1884, Blavatsky informed Sinnett that the Master Koot Hoomi was sending "his chela," Mohini Mohun Chatterji, who would answer all questions that the London Theosophists had raised about Sinnett's books. She continued:

> You better show to Mohini all the Master's letters of a non-private character . . . so that by knowing all the subjects upon which he wrote to you he might defend your position the more effectually—which you yourself cannot do, not being a regular chela. Do not make the mistake . . . of taking *the Mohini you knew* for the Mohini who will come. . . . The ambassador will be invested with an *inner* as well as with an *outer* clothing.[18]

Blavatsky thus directly challenged Sinnett's assumption that he was the principal spokesperson for Theosophy in Europe. Sinnett was not a "regular" disciple; moreover, the authority to interpret and correct his own writing was being given to an Indian rather than a European. It was no wonder, then, that Sinnett reacted with ambivalence to the arrival of Chatterji, whom he considered his racial and social, if not intellectual, inferior.

MOHINI MOHUN CHATTERJI

Mohini Mohun Chatterji (1858–1936) belonged to a prominent Bengali family that for several generations had mediated between Hindu religious traditions and Christianity. In 1882, he joined the Theosophical Society and became Assistant Secretary of its Bengal branch. On September 17, 1882, Koot Hoomi accepted him as a disciple in a letter addressed directly to him, establishing a year's probation during which time Chatterji was ordered to undermine the "pernicious superstition" of Christianity and to convince unbelievers that Blavatsky and Olcott acted under the direct orders of the Mahatmas. He was warned not to doubt these Masters, even though their actions might appear strange.[19] There is little evidence to support J. Barton Scott's contention that Koot Hoomi was Chatterji's "true guru" and that "his astral discipleship" predated Blavatsky's influence.[20] Instead, Chatterji initially had little interest in either the Mahatmas or occult phenomena. He even questioned what good the Mahatmas could do for India or humanity, receiving a severe reprimand from Koot Hoomi: "Take care Mohini Mohun Chatterjee—doubt is a dangerous cancer. One begins by doubting a *peacock,* and ends by doubting—."[21]

Despite Chatterji's misgivings, he was put to work defending the Adept Brotherhood. He was ordered by Koot Hoomi to write an account for *The Theosophist* of his conversation with a peddler who seemed to confirm the Adept Brotherhood's presence in Tibet. Paul Johnson suggests that Blavatsky used Chatterji to concoct a story about adepts in Tibet in order to hide their true residence in Kashmir.[22] Whatever the purpose, Chatterji was enlisted in the creation of an increasingly complex Mahatma narrative. In "The Himalayan Brothers—Do They Exist?" he admitted that two years previously, like other "Europeanized graduates of Universities," he had looked upon the existence of the Mahatmas "with incredulity and distrust." He declared, however, that now he believed Koot Hoomi was a living person.[23] Despite the ongoing efforts of Blavatsky to convince him of the reality of the Mahatmas, Chatterji continued to be more interested in early Indian metaphysics than in communications from Tibetan Masters.[24] Initially attracted to Theosophy because of the value it placed on ancient Hindu traditions, he quickly realized that his status within the Theosophical Society was contingent on his public corroboration of the existence of the Adept Brotherhood.

Chatterji accompanied Olcott and Blavatsky when they arrived in France in mid-March 1884. While in Paris, he received a letter from the Master Koot Hoomi, instructing him how to behave in front of Europeans. He was told that "appearances go a long way." He was instructed to greet Blavatsky *"as though you were in India, and she your own mother.* You must not mind the crowd of Frenchmen and others. You have *to stun them....* You will thus salute her on seeing and taking leave of her the whole time you are at Paris—regardless of comments and *her own surprise.* This is a test."[25]

On April 5, Chatterji and Olcott left Paris and traveled to England, where, on the evening of April 7, they attended an important meeting of the London Lodge. Blavatsky had remained in Paris, but at the last minute she decided to make a surprise appearance. Charles W. Leadbeater recalled that Blavatsky slipped into the back of the room, but that she soon grew impatient and "jumped up from her seat, shouted in a tone of military command the one word 'Mohini!' and then walked straight out of the door into the passage. The stately and dignified Mohini came rushing down that long room at his highest speed, and as soon as he reached the passage threw himself incontinently flat on his face on the floor at the feet of the lady in black."[26] The Master Koot Hoomi had ordered Chatterji to prostrate himself before Blavatsky as an indication of the veneration Indians gave her; however, Chatterji's action also replicated the relationship between the white colonialists and their Indian subordinates. It would have been unimaginable for A. P. Sinnett or any other European Theosophist to behave in such a manner, precisely because they considered themselves Blavatsky's equal, if not her superior. But because they saw Chatterji as a subaltern, his behavior struck British observers as both thrilling and appropriate. Although exotic, it conformed to racial, social, and political hierarchy.[27]

After Blavatsky had assumed the platform, Frederic Myers, who was a member of both the Theosophical Society and the Society for Psychical Research, asked for documentary evidence from India as to the existence of the Mahatmas. Blavatsky turned to Chatterji, who "described a recent appearance of the astral figure of one of the Mahatmas at the Headquarters at Adyar."[28] Blavatsky was a skillful manipulator of cultural representations; she well knew that in London metaphysical matters would be given greater credence when mouthed by an "oriental." In a letter from about this same time, Koot Hoomi excoriated Chatterji for frivolous behavior, reminding him that he was living among people who under other circumstances would have shown him contempt and that all Hindus would be judged by his behavior. The Master and Blavatsky agreed that Europeans would view Mohini Chatterji as "*the* representative of India to be *regenerated*."[29]

After coming to London in April, Chatterji had resided at Sinnett's home, where he was employed in copying letters. In William Q. Judge's opinion, Chatterji would have been better off elsewhere: "Sinnett wants to extract from a 'native,' as he once called him, all he can, now that he sees that native under the shadow of a great name."[30] For his part, Sinnett may well have resented the attention Chatterji received from the well-heeled

Londoners who congregated at his home. Isabelle de Steiger, in her *Reminiscences*, paints a vivid picture of Mohini Chatterji, whom she said "had the features of a dark 'Christ.'" He had "long, smooth, shining black hair, which was parted in the Christ fashion in the middle, and hung in waves on to his shoulders, where it rested in thick curls." He was dressed in a "long tunic of rich black velvet; with a full skirt, girded at the waist" and trimmed with "thick glossy black fur." Steiger continued:

> We understood that he had a wife in Madras or Bombay; but nobody asked any private questions, and we all knew little of Indian domestic life. He was "Mohini," a Messenger from the Mahatmas, conveyed by Madame Blavatsky as a sort of personal secretary and general assistant to the British Theosophists; and as he was eminently Oriental and looked as beautiful as such a position in life should entitle him, he pleased us all. He pleased me extremely.[31]

Charles W. Leadbeater described how at one of Sinnett's receptions, Oscar Wilde, "habited in black velvet, with knee breeches and white stockings . . . came up to Mohini, was introduced, bowed gracefully, and in retiring said in a very audible stage whisper to Mrs. Sinnett, 'I never realized before what a mistake we make in being white!'"[32] Even the Russian writer Vsevolod Solovyov, who later denounced Blavatsky, had been fascinated when he met Chatterji in Paris, noting especially his "most magnificent velvety eyes with a deep and gentle expression." When Solovyov tried to shake hands, however, Chatterji refused. Blavatsky explained that as a chela, he was "just the same as a monk, an ascetic, you understand; he has to keep off all earthly influences; do you know, he never so much as looks at a woman?"[33]

Before joining the Theosophical Society, Mohini Chatterji had been a modern young man who emulated European dress, interests, and attitudes. He was a graduate of Calcutta University, a school established by the British in 1857 as the first modern university on the Indian subcontinent. He had studied modern European languages, Western philosophy, and law, preparing him for a career under the British Raj. In Europe, however, Chatterji was expected to fulfill Western expectations about the mysterious East. On the one hand, he was to display India's spiritual superiority, while on the other hand, he was to pose as a backward "native" in need of Western regeneration. It is difficult to know how much Chatterji consciously performed the "Indian guru," but descriptions of him by

European observers as well as the Mahatma letters suggest that he played a role designed for him by Blavatsky. In July, at Prince's Hall, Piccadilly, Chatterji read a paper on the wisdom of the ancient Aryans, and "intense interest [was] excited in the audience at the strange sight of an Indian, preaching the superiority of the Eastern wisdom over that of the whole world in the world's great metropolis."[34] In London, it was Chatterji more than either of the founders of the Theosophical Society who became the most effective spokesperson for Eastern religious traditions.

HAUGHTY ENGLISHMEN

In their letters to A. P. Sinnett, the Mahatmas explicitly addressed the racial prejudices of Anglo-Indians toward those they termed "Asiatics." Koot Hoomi once commented that Sinnett was among only a few "haughty" Englishmen who might accept a "nigger" as a spiritual guide.[35] And once, when Sinnett rejected his advice, Master Morya wrote: "You are at liberty to regard me as a 'nigger' and savage, Sahib," an ironic inversion of the term "Master." He implied that even though Sinnett might acknowledge Indians as spiritual Masters, in the outer world Sinnett considered himself to be the overlord.[36] Sinnett had welcomed occult teachings from Eastern sages, but "Hindus" appearing in London in their material bodies were considerably less welcome to him than "astral" gurus. Later he would argue that the downfall of Theosophy had been caused by the arrival of "deputations from India" and the mixing of the "Hindu element" with the European.[37]

William Q. Judge wrote Laura Holloway-Langford about Sinnett's reaction to one of the young Indians whom Blavatsky had sent to London. Judge reported that Sinnett had said "he couldn't imagine why they sent him, nor what they expected him to do." Judge went on to say that Sinnett was more interested in discussing "what name the grandsons of the Duke of Edinburgh would be able to bear" than in offering hospitality to a "native."[38] As a Brahmin and a chela of Koot Hoomi, Mohini Chatterji received a relatively more cordial welcome by Sinnett, but the latter nevertheless failed to treat him with the same consideration he would have extended to a European guest. In mid-April Sinnett received the last letter he would get from a Master until Laura Holloway-Langford arrived. Morya again addressed Sinnett as "Sahib," reprimanding him for giving Chatterji an unheated room: "He suffered greatly from cold in that high room where there is no fireplace in your house, and K. H. had to surround him with a double shell against a death cold that threatened him. Remember Hindus are exotic plants in your inclement pays [country] and cold, and those who need them have to take care of them."[39]

Not only did Sinnett reject Indians as his equals, but he also continued to be embarrassed by the eccentricities of the founders. Whereas members of the London Lodge were expected to wear formal dress to their meetings, Olcott would appear in company wearing "his extravagant Asiatic undresses."[40] Blavatsky, her large bulk contained in a flowing caftan, was uncouth and unpredictable. In contrast to Blavatsky and Olcott, Laura Holloway-Langford was well-dressed and eminently presentable. With her trim figure, Southern accent, and good manners, she lent a much-appreciated air of refinement to the gatherings at Sinnett's home. As an American, Holloway-Langford was not burdened by British social class distinctions. All the same, she had a strong sense of proper behavior and a long-standing desire to be accepted among the well-to-do. It was impossible for her or any white American to be entirely free of racial prejudice, but compared to others of her time and place, she had progressive notions about racial equality.

Yet Holloway-Langford was an Anglophile, as were many educated Americans, and she was delighted to have been admitted to Sinnett's upper-crust social circle. She later recalled that during the summer of 1884, London "society was on the qui vive [alert] and the receptions given by Mr. Sinnett at his pleasant residence in Ladbroke Gardens . . . were attended by many representatives of the literary and scientific circles of that city."[41] After returning to the United States, Holloway-Langford frequently alluded to famous men and women whom she had supposedly visited while in Europe, but whom she had in fact met only among large gatherings of Theosophists. Later, Blavatsky concluded that during 1884 the three disciples, Laura Holloway-Langford, Mohini Chatterji, and A. P. Sinnett, were all tested by the Masters and all found wanting. The evidence suggests that each of them faced cultural and personal conflicts that challenged both their character and their commitment to Theosophy. It was much easier, they found, to adhere to abstract tenets of universal brotherhood than to overcome ingrained notions of race, class, and gender.

THE PERILS OF MEDIUMSHIP

Laura Holloway-Langford arrived in London from Paris in mid-June 1884. Intent on getting her writing project under way, Blavatsky had decided to try her as a probationary disciple. Although Holloway-Langford knew little about Theosophy beyond what she had read in Sinnett's books, Blavatsky thought that her experience as a writer and an editor could be useful. A letter from Koot Hoomi to Blavatsky confirmed that the adepts had sent Holloway-Langford to Europe so that she could write a book for them, which they wanted "published before the end of the year." The letter also contained a warning: "Unless she does Mohini's bidding—who will have direct orders from me—and follows out strictly the path prepared for her under M's orders she will make of it a wretched failure."[42] Blavatsky seemed to have envisioned a collaboration, in which Mohini Chatterji would supply the metaphysics that Holloway-Langford would shape into a form appealing to English-speaking readers. It was clear, however, that Chatterji was the "regular chela," who would train Laura Holloway-Langford, a probationary "Western chela" who Blavatsky hoped would prove more malleable than A. P. Sinnett.

Blavatsky wanted Laura Holloway-Langford to begin writing immediately for the Theosophical Society, but Sinnett desired her help in reestablishing contact with the Adept Brotherhood, which had threatened to cut off communication with him over a controversy in the London Lodge. Sinnett wrote in *The Early Days of Theosophy in Europe* that Holloway-Langford "was a remarkable clairvoyant and pupil of the Master K. H. Her coming from America had been heralded by impressive stories concerning her psychic gifts and relationship with the Higher world and we found her an extremely attractive personality."[43] Within a short time of her arrival at his home, Laura Holloway-Langford agreed to sit as a medium for Sinnett, who put her into mesmeric trances.[44] Almost as if in response to his wishes, she began to use her consciousness as a channel for messages purported to come from the Master. At first she simply repeated words that were given by one claiming to be a chela of the Mahatma. Then, on July 6, she lost consciousness, and in a deep trance took on the persona of Koot Hoomi himself, speaking in his voice in the first person. Sinnett was delighted, convinced that he had found a medium through whom he could communicate with the Masters directly.

Assuming the familiar role of a spiritualist medium, Holloway-Langford apparently was unaware that she had crossed inviolate boundaries. While Blavatsky only transcribed his words, Koot Hoomi had possessed Holloway-Langford's body and had spoken through her voice. The gender-bending itself was shocking, especially since the Theosophists believed that the adepts were real men, not spirits.[45] Additionally, Holloway-Langford had collapsed the distinction between spiritualism and theosophy. And most significantly, she had directly challenged Blavatsky's power to control communication with the Adept Brotherhood.

In the meantime, Blavatsky had arrived in London in order to attend a June 30th meeting of the Society for Psychical Research. The meeting had not gone well. Olcott had given a rambling speech that he illustrated by "a little Indian convoy consisting of a figure of Buddha ... on little wheels. By moving it about it was supposed to represent some idea connected with the Buddhic faith."[46] The assembly erupted in laughter. Sinnett reported that when the party arrived back at his home, "Madame Blavatsky was bleached white for the intensity of her feelings. In tones rising even higher as she went on she denounced her unhappy colleague in language so violent that I was really afraid it would penetrate the next house."[47]

A few days later Blavatsky learned that Holloway-Langford had been possessed by Koot Hoomi while in a trance. In no mood to tolerate more nonsense from her followers, she contacted the Master for advice. He responded by saying that Holloway-Langford had given "bogus and fancy messages to Mr. Sinnett. . . . Let Mrs. H[olloway] sit no more for anyone—for her clairvoyance is entirely untrustworthy owing to various bad influences: it will soon come back to her." He scolded Patience Sinnett for saying that Holloway-Langford's writing project was unimportant, and he upbraided Mr. Sinnett for resenting "words uttered by Mohini under my direct influence."[48] Within the Sinnett household, Laura Holloway-Langford found herself caught between the authority claimed by Chatterji, as the Indian chela of the Masters, and by Sinnett, whose claim to preeminence in England was based, in large part, on his presumption of racial and class superiority.

At this point, Koot Hoomi wrote Blavatsky a letter that he later claimed should have been kept private. She, however, gave it to Sinnett, who passed it along to Holloway-Langford. The Master wrote that Holloway-Langford *sees* better than she *hears*. She has either to allow herself to be developed gradually and listen to the advice of our chelas or—to give up the thing— which would be a pity. She does not discriminate well between the things shown to her *by chelas sent*—& the transference of ideas from the mind of the one she sits for & which, of course, reflect that one's personal preju- dices, preconceptions, & inherent likes and dislikes.

Koot Hoomi described Holloway-Langford as "a very impressionable sen- sitive as well as a born clairvoyant," but he admonished her for "playing with fire recently by acting the *medium* for a bhuta," an earthbound spirit, at Sinnett's home. He also warned Sinnett that his "unsatisfied desire" was "begotten of selfishness & bigotry; & to encourage a hope that it might be gratified would be to add to, not curtail, the being's time in Kama-loka," the astral region of desire similar to purgatory. Additionally, Koot Hoomi instructed Mohini to stop Holloway-Langford from "meddling in this business" and to resume "writing séances" with her at the home of Fran- cesca Arundale, away from Sinnett's influence.[49]

Holloway-Langford was deeply offended by what she took to be ac- cusations of social, perhaps even sexual, impropriety, and she threatened to have nothing more to do with Theosophy. Koot Hoomi, in an attempt to restore her confidence in the Masters, wrote Blavatsky a second letter, which he instructed her to give to Holloway-Langford. This letter reas- sured Holloway-Langford that she had done nothing that anyone disap- proved of, except for injuring herself. Koot Hoomi blamed Sinnett and Blavatsky for inflicting "useless & most cruel suffering . . . upon one so gentle & tender hearted, & so well disposed to all of you." Furthermore, he reprimanded Sinnett for allowing Holloway-Langford to read what the Master had written about her without considering the "danger of an unexpected shock to such a highly nervous & sensitive being."

At the same time, Koot Hoomi warned Holloway-Langford that con- tinuing to act as a spiritualist medium was dangerous: "Fatal error! She has, she does wrong, a most serious one to herself: for she has thereby been for years *systematically destroying her health*." He asserted that by con- versing with "astral vampires" she had yielded to "unclean Shells" which had absorbed her vitality and caused her to become "highly nervous & sickly sensitive. The more they are encouraged the more serious it becomes for her, & *they may even kill her* if she heeds us not." While Koot Hoomi attempted to console "the poor suffering heart," he explained that the Masters could not have "*direct dealings* with her, for she is a woman as yet uninitiated & unprepared by a special & severe training & physiological re-formation." They could communicate with her only by intermediate agencies, and if she would trust them like a child heeding a parent, then she would find happiness, knowledge, and safety. Koot Hoomi concluded: "The golden chalice is held to her lips—let her not dash it to the ground. She talks of going back to America! For humanity's sake, if not for her own, she should live & work, and if needs be—*suffer.*"[50]

A crucial document in delineating the clashes of personalities and ideas that occurred during the summer of 1884, this letter has not been published. Whether or not Holloway-Langford accepted Koot Hoomi's view of spiritualism, she was hurt and troubled by his suggestion that she might never be accepted as a chela. Consequently, she neither made copies of the letter nor did she refer to it in her writings. Nevertheless, aware of its importance, she safeguarded it until the end of her life.

MAHATMA MANIPULATIONS

The two letters described above reveal the complex rhetorical tactics employed in the Mahatma letters. Koot Hoomi had refused to contact Sinnett or Holloway-Langford directly, but he attempted to control their behavior by correspondence addressed to Blavatsky. However, when Holloway-Langford reacted with vehemence, refusing to believe messages delivered orally by Blavatsky, Koot Hoomi instructed that his second letter be shown to her. Thus, the Mahatma letters were neither private correspondence, nor were they entirely public. Every communication from a Master was presumed to be important, but the letters served more of a social function than an esoteric one. They were instruments for criticizing members of the Society, for establishing who was in and who was out of favor, for rewarding and punishing, and for manipulating the relationships among Theosophists.

Written in mid-July 1884, these letters sought to undermine Sinnett's influence on Laura Holloway-Langford. To accomplish this goal, Koot Hoomi attacked her in gendered language that suggested her relationship with Sinnett was sexually impure. Indeed, later Theosophists believed that these letters proved that Holloway-Langford was a loose woman who had aroused destructive sexual energies. In particular, they cited the reference to Sinnett's "unsatisfied desires." This interpretation was strengthened by a letter from Koot Hoomi to Holloway-Langford in late August confirming that she had been possessed by a "bhuta attached to Sinnett who was under the influence of elementaries." He continued: "Your ex-friend *is a shell*, & one more dangerous for you than ten other shells—for his feeling for you was intense & earthly."[51] Holloway-Langford must have been shocked by Koot Hoomi's declaration that serving as a medium put her life at risk. Almost as alarming to Holloway-Langford, however, was the Master's attempt to intimidate her by damaging her social and sexual status; she was humiliated by the insinuation that by acting as a medium for A. P. Sinnett she had transgressed both spiritually and sexually. Already, as a single woman, she had jeopardized her reputation by traveling alone in Europe. In these letters the Master deliberately exploited her anxiety by employing language which, even if metaphorical, nevertheless cast doubt on her character.

In the second letter, Koot Hoomi asserted male dominance and female inferiority by appealing to patriarchal power: he was the father, Holloway-Langford the child. He portrayed the female body as particularly vulnerable to the deleterious effects of shells, the "earth bound remnants of humanity." Indeed, the vampire image conjured sexual associations, especially the nineteenth-century notion of the debilitating, even life-threatening, effect of frequent sexual activity. Koot Hoomi claimed that by engaging in "intercourse" with "elementaries," Holloway-Langford had harmed herself both physically and mentally.[52] She had demanded "direct dealings" with the Masters, but Koot Hoomi declared this impossible without "physiological re-formation."[53] What such "re-formation" would entail was unstated, but the letter implied that a woman could become a disciple of the Adept Brotherhood only by evolution into a sexless being. In this view, female sexuality was so powerful that, particularly in a premenopausal woman, it must be neutralized before an adept could communicate safely through a female chela. Koot Hoomi thus argued that it was impossible for Laura Holloway-Langford to have received messages from the Masters while at A. P. Sinnett's home, because her female body had, even if unintentionally, aroused desire and attracted unclean spirits. Little wonder, then, that Holloway-Langford was confused and distressed by the Master's messages.

THEOSOPHY VS. SPIRITUALISM

Laura Holloway-Langford had become mired in a situation fraught with sexual tension. She also had entered the contested terrain of the relationship between spiritualism and theosophy at a time when Blavatsky was at pains to distinguish them. Holloway-Langford, however, saw no inconsistency in being an aspiring chela and acting as a medium. In London, she had been in touch with spiritualist friends, particularly a "Mrs. B.," probably Mary Hollis-Billing, who was also a friend of Francesca Arundale,[54] as well as with the famous British spiritualist Stainton Moses, who was convinced that Holloway-Langford was a real medium.[55] Thus, it was not only Sinnett who was encouraging Holloway-Langford to use her psychic gifts. The Masters disapproved, and insisted that she must "separate herself for a few months from any contact with her old associations and their influence."[56]

Still, Holloway-Langford continued to deny that Blavatsky had accurately relayed orders from Koot Hoomi. She reasoned that if her mediumship in New York had led her to Europe, how could it now be dangerous? She insisted that if the Masters had something to tell her, they should write her directly, without intermediaries. She would believe them only if she received letters addressed to her personally. At one point, in exasperation, Koot Hoomi wrote to Blavatsky: "She is worse than a child—she would have *profs* [sic] in us as a Christian would have his in Jesus."[57]

Master Morya refused to write Holloway-Langford, but he responded indirectly to her through a letter to Blavatsky. He declared that she must stop troubling the Masters about unimportant matters. She should accept Blavatsky as their spokesperson without requiring "autographs from Masters." He asserted that Holloway-Langford had lost confidence in her own ability because of Sinnett's magnetic influence, which had "dragged her down from the lofty plane of seership to the low level of mediumship." Morya continued:

All you women are "Zin Zin" [crazy] fools to yourselves and to please a kind and affectionate friend, ready to sacrifice your own salvation.... Did not she, herself, feel that after she had sat near [Sinnett] for half an hour or so her *visions* began changing character? Ought this not be a warning for her? Of course she is serving a purpose and knew it in Brooklin [sic] but was made to forget by the other two magnetisms.... Yes, she is good and pure and chela-like; only terribly flabby in kindness of heart.[58]

In this letter, Master Morya made a brilliant rhetorical move. Like Koot Hoomi he attributed Holloway-Langford's difficulties to her gender, but he went a step further: "All you women are 'Zin Zin' fools." In this passage, he conflated Blavatsky and Holloway-Langford as two of a kind. By implication they were both seers, a comparison that would flatter Holloway-Langford. At the same time, he depicted them as sharing the shortcomings of their sex: they both sacrificed themselves in order to please others because they had too much "kindness of heart." Just as Holloway-Langford had tried to please Sinnett, Blavatsky also had been too lenient in her relationship with Holloway-Langford, who deserved a more severe reproof than Blavatsky had been willing to give. Through this message, Morya deflected Holloway-Langford's anger away from Blavatsky. The Master's scorn toward women's foolishness included them both.

The need to separate Sinnett from Holloway-Langford had become urgent. Blavatsky issued a direct order to Sinnett, said to come from the Master, which brooked no misunderstanding of what was required. "Mrs. Holloway" was ordered to "*sleep* at Mrs. Arundale [*sic*] *every night . . .* in short *to live* at their house. . . . Now if she contravenes the Master's orders which are those of Mahatma K. H. I wash my hands of all. But I must tell you plainly that Mrs. H. having been sent from America here by the Master's wish who had a purpose in view—*if you make her go astray* and force her unwittingly into a path that does not run in the direction of the Master's desire—then all communication *between you and K. H. will stop.*"[59] In this message, Blavatsky's strategy of attributing responsibility for hard decisions to the Master seemed to unravel. She spoke in the first-person, "I," in casting the blame on Sinnett. By implication, she portrayed Holloway-Langford as a passive instrument whom Sinnett could make "go astray." It was Blavatsky's own voice threatening that if he persisted, Sinnett would lose what he most desired: communication with the Master Koot Hoomi.

Holloway-Langford yielded to these demands and moved to the Arundale home, where, not coincidentally, Blavatsky was residing. Sinnett, however, continued to rebel; he was convinced that Blavatsky was jealous of Holloway-Langford's gifts and wanted to prevent her from becoming an independent link between himself and the Adept Brotherhood. According to his memoir, on July 17 "Mrs. Holloway" visited him and proclaimed that she "meant to give up the whole business in disgust."[60] It was this threat that triggered the first letter that Laura Holloway-Langford received directly from the Master Koot Hoomi. He wrote, in a tone much more conciliatory than in the letters written to Blavatsky:

> The book [*Man: Fragments of Forgotten History*] is a project undertaken; why not complete it? Its existence will depend upon you for you alone can create it, and the materials are in no other hands. But should you refuse to go on—do not deceive yourself with the false idea that you are unable to do what you have done.
>
> The real reason is loss of confidence and you are responsible for the influence that you permit others to exert over you. Shall you be tried in the balance and be found wanting? Will you go back to the old conditions of things in America? It is our wish to take you out of them.[61]

The Master thus encouraged Holloway-Langford to give up the passive role of spiritualist medium, to resist domination by others, and to take responsibility for her own choices. In order to write the book, he implied, she must relinquish Victorian notions of female spirituality, exerting her own will independent of the expectations of others.

KOOT HOOMI ADMONISHES SINNETT

Sinnett had not heard from Koot Hoomi for more than three months, but on July 18, the day after Holloway-Langford's threat, he too received a letter. The Master addressed him as "My poor, blind friend," and in strong language warned Sinnett that his arrogance and prejudice could separate him permanently from the Adept Brotherhood. He charged that Sinnett had "felt the profoundest contempt for us all, of the dark races; and had regarded Hindus as an *inferior* race." His Western mind had subjected him to "furies called Doubt, Skepticism, Scorn, Ridicule, Envy and finally Temptation." According to Koot Hoomi, rather than opening himself to intuition, Sinnett had clung to his intellectual nature, believing in "cold, *spiritually blind* reason." Instead of being haughty and proud, he should strive to be meek, gentle, and humble. Koot Hoomi once again rebuked Sinnett for his treatment of Chatterji, and complained that he had also "ungenerously snubbed" Olcott. Even though the Master admitted that the "Buddha with wheels" incident was unfortunate, he asserted that Olcott had acted from his heart, while Sinnett had set himself apart as socially and intellectually superior.

But it was Sinnett's relationship with Holloway-Langford that most challenged Koot Hoomi's authority. The Master denied that he had ever transmitted messages to Sinnett or anyone else through Holloway-Langford. He judged her to be "an excellent but quite undeveloped clairvoyante" whose progress had been compromised by Sinnett's imprudent meddling. He chastised Sinnett:

> You have proudly claimed the privilege of exercising your own, uncon-
> trolled judgment in occult matters you could know nothing about. . . . If,
> throwing aside every preconceived idea, you could TRY and impress your-
> self with this profound truth that intellect is not all powerful by itself; that
> to become a "mover of mountains" it has first to receive light and life from
> higher principle—Spirit, . . . then you would soon read the mystery right.
> You need not tell Mrs. H. that she has never seen correctly, for it is not so.
> Many a time she saw correctly—when left alone to herself, never has she
> left one single statement undisfigured.[62]

Koot Hoomi apparently distinguished between Laura Holloway-Langford's authentic visions of the Adept Brotherhood while she was in New York, and her illusion, encouraged by Sinnett, that she, by herself, possessed the psychic power to initiate communications with the Masters.

Despite such withering attacks from the Master, Sinnett had too much at stake to leave the movement. Holloway-Langford, in contrast, had less invested in Theosophy and could well have shifted her allegiance back to spiritualism. Both Holloway-Langford and Sinnett were learning, how-ever, that the Mahatmas could be pressured into communicating with them directly. The Masters' power resided in giving or refusing messages and in the recipients' confidence in their authenticity. By withholding his belief in the legitimacy of the Koot Hoomi letters communicated by Bla-vatsky, Sinnett provoked the Master into corresponding with him. Despite its unpleasantness, the controversy over his use of Holloway-Langford as a medium had led to the desired result, a resumption of communication with the Master.

At the same time, the presence of Laura Holloway-Langford had brought to the surface Sinnett's assumptions of both sexual and racial superiority. Previously, he had been compelled to submit to a woman, Blavatsky, for access to the great souls. In contrast, he controlled Laura Holloway-Langford, whom he hoped to use as a passive instrument subject to his mesmeric will. In addition to getting out from under the thumb of the "Old

Lady," as he called Blavatsky, Sinnett had also, in some sense, gained ascendancy over the Masters. In Sinnett's mind, despite their occult knowledge, the Masters remained "Asiatics," a class of people whom, in Koot Hoomi's opinion, Sinnett had "not yet learnt even to tolerate, let alone to love or respect."[63] Through Holloway-Langford, Sinnett had been able to summon the Masters, interrogate them, and goad them into writing letters to him directly. Unwilling to give up these advantages without a fight, Sinnett refused to deem the messages he had received through her as bogus. Moreover, he declared that Blavatsky was fabricating letters from Koot Hoomi in order to frighten Holloway-Langford into obedience. Thus, at one fell stroke Sinnett challenged Blavatsky's integrity and questioned the power of the Masters themselves. Laura Holloway-Langford's trance possession had inadvertently raised issues more important to Theosophy than the sexual peccadilloes of its members. At stake was the locus and nature of spiritual authority.

When Sinnett persisted in doubting the authenticity of any communication transmitted by Blavatsky, she accused him of "bamboozling" himself and engaging in self-deception. She asserted that Sinnett believed that a letter came from the Master only if it dovetailed with his own ideas. If a letter contradicted his "notions of the fitness of things," Sinnett rejected it as counterfeit. She continued: "If you—the most devoted, the best of all Theosophists—are ready to fall a victim to your own preconceptions and believe in new gods of your own fancy dethroning the old ones—then . . . Theosophy has come too early in this country."[64]

THE USES OF GENDER

In "The Ordinary Business of Occultism," Gauri Viswanathan argues that within the colonial context, spiritualism and occultism loosened "boundaries between closed social networks," but that it was possible to reimagine colonial relationships precisely because the next step—of sexual contact, resulting in racial "degeneration"—was avoided. While in India, Sinnett may have been willing accept an inversion "of the relations of domination and subordination" wherein "masters were those who guided initiates into unseen phenomena, which remained the uncolonized space."[65]

However, when he returned to his native shore, Sinnett reasserted his racial, sexual, and class privileges, refusing to submit either to "Asiatic masters" or to a woman, particularly one of such questionable status as Helena Blavatsky. Perhaps Sinnett is best understood as a spiritual colonizer. His desire was not, as some later interpreters would have it, sexual possession of spiritual mediums; rather he craved command of psychic space. As the European, he felt entitled to control Laura Holloway-Langford, a woman with whom he shared racial and cultural identity. He believed that neither Chatterji nor the Masters, as members of inferior races, had a right to dominate her. Koot Hoomi, however, directed Sinnett to rely on intuition instead of reason. Additionally, he advised him to cultivate a gentle spirit that would eliminate social and cultural prejudices. From Sinnett's perspective, however, the Master was demanding that he relinquish manhood as it was constructed in the West.

By submitting to Sinnett's will, Laura Holloway-Langford had acquiesced in a pattern of gendered behavior that the Master found contrary to the qualities needed by a chela. On the one hand, the Masters prohibited her full access to occult knowledge because of her female body, and they expected her relationship to them to be submissive and docile. On the other hand, they demanded that she throw off patterns of conduct that were expected of a well-bred woman in the West. The Masters and Blavatsky challenged the boundaries of gender, while at the same time they reinforced them in order to regulate behavior. Their gender ideology was inconsistent, not one fixed by either Western or Eastern culture. Gender for them was an instrument that could be used to manipulate their followers by raising their anxieties, whether by challenging Sinnett's understanding of Western manhood or by casting doubt on the chastity of Laura Holloway-Langford. By focusing on Holloway-Langford as a force of destruction, Blavatsky was able to deflect criticism, and, for a short time, obscure problems within the movement, while leaving unresolved issues of race, class, and gender that would continue to trouble the Theosophical Society. It was Laura Holloway-Langford's misfortune to become a pawn in a struggle for power not only between Helena Blavatsky and A. P. Sinnett, but also between conflicting gender and cultural ideologies. In the coming months, these conflicts would be played out not only in the lives of Theosophists but also in the pages of popular fiction.

5

Fantasizing the Occult

During the London season of 1884, theosophy was in vogue. Interest in Eastern metaphysics had been mounting since 1881, when A. P. Sinnett had published letters from Koot Hoomi in *The Occult World*. The appetite for the supernatural was further whetted when, in 1883, Sinnett's *Esoteric Buddhism* appeared. The following year, persons from "upper levels of society" gathered weekly at his home, which, according to Sinnett, "became the vortex of the whole movement."[1] That spring London society was abuzz when word spread that the founders of the Theosophical Society had arrived in England. Genuine inquirers, as well as the merely curious, sought glimpses of Blavatsky, dressed in black and rolling a tiny cigarette; of Olcott in oriental costume; and of Mohini Mohun Chatterji, with his large, soulful eyes. Often accompanying Blavatsky was a less exotic figure, a slender, attractive woman, bearing the soft accent of the American South. She was, it was rumored, a psychic who possessed unusual powers. This person was, of course, none other than Laura Holloway-Langford. This panoply of personalities, with their claims about mysterious sources of knowledge, attracted the imagination of writers who portrayed them in popular novels.

Literary representations reveal how the public perceived this cast of characters, but they also express contested ideas about gender and sexuality. Victorians lacked an adequate language outside the vocabulary of religion and morality to discuss relations between men and women, not to mention same-sex relationships. In fiction, however, these topics could be explored through plot and characterization in ways that were forbidden in polite conversation and that rarely appeared in other types of theosophical writing. Fiction could expose sexual exploitation; it could complicate the portrayal of masculinity and femininity; and it could contest heterosexual norms.

Even before the formation of the Theosophical Society, esoteric ideas had been transmitted through fiction. Hundreds of people attended lectures on theosophy, and many more read Blavatsky's *Isis Unveiled* and *The Secret Doctrine*; but far greater numbers, both in Europe and the United States, absorbed ideas about the occult through reading popular literature, where they encountered new spiritual ideas and vocabulary. Yet it was not always easy to distinguish between occult fiction and other types of esoteric writing. Before they became fictional characters, Helena Blavatsky, Mohini Chatterji, and Laura Holloway-Langford had fashioned public personae. Blavatsky transgressed gender expectations, her persona fluctuating between a woman of great spiritual power and an authoritative public presence that was perceived as masculine.[2] Chatterji, with Blavatsky's encouragement, played a part designed to exploit European Orientalism. Laura Holloway-Langford cultivated the role of a professional psychic and lent occult pursuits an air of middle-class respectability. In some sense, then, Blavatsky, Chatterji, and Holloway-Langford were imaginative creations well before they appeared in the pages of fashionable novels. This was doubly true of Koot Hoomi, who first came to life in the writing of A. P. Sinnett.

THE CHARACTER OF KOOT HOOMI

The prototype for theosophical fiction was an enormously popular book, Sir Edward Bulwer-Lytton's *Zanoni* (1842). Along with other writings by Bulwer-Lytton, this novel spread ideas about the existence of living adepts who preserved ancient wisdom, and it was influential in crystallizing Helena Blavatsky's conception of the Mahatmas. In *Isis Unveiled* (1877), Blavatsky wrote: "No author in the world of literature ever gave a more truthful or more poetical description of these beings than Sir

E. Bulwer-Lytton, the author of *Zanoni*." She quoted approvingly long passages from the novel in which the character Mejnour, a member of an ancient brotherhood, gave instructions on how to penetrate the barrier that separates us from other worlds:

> The soul with which you listen must be sharpened by intense enthusiasm, purified from all earthly desires. . . . When thus prepared, science can be brought to aid it; the sight itself may be rendered more subtile, the nerves more acute, the spirit more alive and outward, and the element itself—the air, the space—may be made, by certain secrets of the higher chemistry, more palpable and clear. And this, too, is not *magic* as the credulous call it. . . . It is *but the science by which nature can be controlled.*[3]

In the novel, Blavatsky found confirmation that there existed "Oriental Fraternities," whose members were small in number since "the slightest touch of mortal passion unfits the hierophant to hold communion with his spotless soul." She wrote that Bulwer-Lytton in *Zanoni* revealed that these Masters rarely share "knowledge of the most solemn importance" except for "the instruction of some neophytes."[4]

A. P. Sinnett in *The Occult World* pondered whether fiction could reveal occult knowledge. He concluded that Bulwer-Lytton had been initiated into a secret brotherhood, but that in *Zanoni* the author "preferred to throw out his information in veiled and mystic shape." By disguising his meaning, he avoided the wrath of "bigots in science, religion and the great philosophy of the common-place," while those in sympathy with him would understand the occult significance.[5] To Sinnett, the character of Mejnour represented a "great adept of Eastern occultism, exactly like those of whom I have to speak." Mejnour, then, was an ancestor of Koot Hoomi. And Sinnett readily acknowledged that early information about the adepts had come from "a mass of literary evidence." In *The Occult World*, however, he proposed, for the first time, to reveal directly to the public factual information about their existence and their teachings.[6] Thus, Sinnett admitted that both *Zanoni* and *The Occult World* presented the same knowledge, albeit in different forms.

Whereas *Isis Unveiled* made only passing reference to unnamed adepts, Sinnett introduced a specific character, the adept Koot Hoomi, who was to play such a crucial role in theosophical history. Critics recognized that although *The Occult World* was not fiction, it "reads like a romance."[7] Much like a novelist, Sinnett created a biography for the Master, supplementing information contained in the Koot Hoomi letters. According to Sinnett, Koot Hoomi was a native of Punjab who had been attracted to occult teachings at an early age. After studying in Europe, he had returned to the East and had been initiated into esoteric knowledge. At that time, he was given a mystical Tibetan name, Koot Hoomi Lal Sing. This information was crucial in gaining credibility for the story that followed, since readers must accept Koot Hoomi's ability to write in English and his familiarity with European literature.

In his first letter to Sinnett, Koot Hoomi mentioned Bulwer-Lytton's novel *Vril: The Power of the Coming Race,* which, he said, contained truth about the *vril,* known to him as the *akas,* a kind of energy-filled ether that permeates the universe. Like Blavatsky and Sinnett, Koot Hoomi made little distinction between the truths of fiction and other forms of discourse. He recapitulated some of the teachings of Mejnour, arguing, for example, that although misguided experimenters persisted in using the methods of physical science to test phenomena, occult study was a separate science that adhered to its own laws and methods. Koot Hoomi sought to distinguish himself from Mejnour:

> I hope that at least *you* will understand that we (or most of us) are far from being the heartless morally dried up mummies some would fancy us to be. Mejnour is very well where he is—as an ideal character of a thrilling, in many respects truthful story. Yet, believe me, few of us would care to play the part in life of a desiccated pansy between the leaves of a volume of solemn poetry. We may not be quite "the boys" to quote --'s irreverent expression when speaking of us, yet none of *our degree* are like the stern hero of Bulwer's romance.[8]

Koot Hoomi portrayed himself as chaste and abstemious—not quite one of the boys—but nonetheless a living man with feelings and a sense of humor, not a static, idealized fictional figure. Indeed, as the theosophical narrative developed, Koot Hoomi assumed human complexity. He indulged in gossip; he made mistakes in fact and in judgment; he got angry; and he often contradicted himself. The Mahatma letters thus created an intriguing character in the theosophical narrative, but the fallibility of Koot Hoomi also troubled many readers who sought wisdom in his writings.

MR. ISAACS AND THE ADEPTS

Only three years after the founders arrived in India, Francis Marion Crawford published *Mr. Isaacs: A Tale of Modern India,* a novel which introduced a character based on the Master Koot Hoomi. Crawford had gone to India in 1879 to study Sanskrit and edit the *Indian Herald* in Allahabad, where he must have been acquainted with A. P. Sinnett, who was editor of a competing English newspaper. The narrator of the novel, Mr. Griggs, was, like Crawford, born in Italy of American parents. He was also a journalist who reported for a fictional newspaper, the Allahabad *Daily Howler.* The early scenes of *Mr. Isaacs* were set in Simla, where "among the rhododendron trees Madame Blavatzky [*sic*], Colonel Olcott and Mr. Sinnett move mysteriously in the performance of their wonders."[9] Twice while Crawford was in India, in December 1879 at Allahabad and again in September 1880 at Simla, Blavatsky and Olcott visited A. P. and Patience Sinnett. Although Crawford did not meet them, he had heard about the founders of the Theosophical Society from his American uncle Samuel Ward, a spiritualist who had been interested in theosophy since the 1870s when he lived in New York. When his nephew moved to India, Ward suggested that he write a novel about the Adept Brotherhood. The sympathetic portrayal of the adepts in *Mr. Isaacs* astonished Blavatsky, who said that in India Crawford had been a "sworn enemy of Theosophy." Ward, however, was not surprised, because he believed that "Koot Hoomi helped project [the novel] upon paper."[10]

Crawford's knowledge of theosophy came primarily from reading. As Koot Hoomi himself noted, Crawford's novel was inspired by *The Occult World.* Not surprisingly, Koot Hoomi judged Sinnett's work superior, with *Mr. Isaacs* being only "the western echo of the Anglo-Indian Occult world."[11] In an 1884 interview in Paris, Blavatsky claimed that in the novel some passages about the astral body had been taken from articles in *The Theosophist,* and she found that Crawford's book had been "written on an imperfect knowledge of our society and of the great mysteries."[12] When she reviewed the novel in *The Theosophist,* Blavatsky expressed gratification that her own ideas, even when inaccurately conveyed, were being spread through popular fiction. "This is another proof of the fact that the Theosophical movement, like one of those subterranean streams which the traveler finds in districts of magnesian and calcareous formation, is running beneath the surface of contemporary thought, and bursting out at the most unexpected points with visible signs of its pent-up force."[13]

At the same time, she offered a shrewd appraisal of the novel. The plot revolved around Mr. Isaacs's infatuation with Miss Westonhaugh, a young English woman. Mr. Isaacs failed to follow the advice of the adept Ram Lal, which would have prevented Westonhaugh's death while on a tiger hunt. Cutting through the Victorian cant that identified spirituality with (white) woman's purity, Blavatsky pointed out that although the Muslim protagonist, Mr. Isaacs, has three wives, their "conjugal claims are ignored, and their personalities shoved away out of sight, because the author makes Mr. Isaacs to love and be loved by a paragon of English maidens."[14] She was particularly distressed that these racist and ethnocentric views were expressed by the Mahatma figure, Ram Lal. Despite the fact that Crawford depicted him as "an adept of the higher grades, a seer and a knower of men's hearts,"[15] Ram Lal advocated a path shaped less by theosophy than by Western literary paradigms of the eternal feminine, especially the beatified Beatrice who guides Dante toward heaven. Blavatsky wrote: "It was less a sin for our author to make his hero [Mr. Isaacs] relinquish fortune and the world's caresses to become a Chela, in the hope of passing aeons of bliss with the enfranchised soul of his beloved one, than to put into the mouth of *Ram Lal,* the adept 'Brother' . . . language about woman's love and its effects that no adept would by any chance ever use."[16]

Blavatsky did not, however, mind that Crawford based his adept brother on Koot Hoomi. Instead, she was delighted that he had made "our Brothers conceivable human beings, instead of impossible creatures of the imagination. *Ram Lal* walks, talks, eats, and—gracious heavens!—rolls and smokes cigarettes."[17] Like Koot Hoomi, Ram Lal had been Western-educated, holding a medical degree from the University of Edinburgh.[18] He was also a Buddhist, who spoke "with an accent peculiar to the Hindoo tongue. His voice was musical and high in pitch, though soft and sweet in tone."[19] Crawford described Ram Lal as a shadowy figure who could vanish like a whiff of smoke or could project his astral body to places far away from his physical location. When in Tibet, he appeared to be a shining silver statue, but when away from home his turban and long caftan, even "the skin of his face, the pointed beard and long moustache, the heavy eyebrows" were studies in greys.[20]

Blavatsky lamented Crawford's depiction of the adept as a ghost-like, joyless being. "The animated mummies whom novelists love to make the types of occult learning, doubtless had never any other feeling than that of the stone or the salted herring; but the real adepts as we are reliably informed—are the most happy of mankind, since their pleasures are connected with the higher existence, which is cloudless and pangless."[21] The Master Koot Hoomi, too, was distressed that people identified him with Ram Lal, whom he called "the 'all-grey' adept, of Mr. Marion Crawford."[22]

Such fictional portrayals of the adepts stimulated debate in theosophical publications about their nature. Were the Masters real men with the full range of human emotions? Or were they phantoms far removed from the material world? Perhaps more importantly, did they possess a universal wisdom that transcended the limitations of a particular race or culture? Blavatsky implicitly acknowledged that in whatever form of literature they appeared—whether in their letters or as characters in fiction—the Mahatmas were the product of imaginative elaboration. Joy Dixon has observed how in their letters the Mahatmas "played with notions of their own fictitiousness in sophisticated ways," calling attention to their personae as inventive guises. For example, Koot Hoomi declared: "Having been 'invented' ourselves, we repay the inventors by inventing." Dixon also quotes A. O. Hume, who wrote to Koot Hoomi: "Even when I was fully persuaded you were a myth . . . even then my heart yearned to you as it often does to an avowedly fictitious character."[23] Both the adepts and those who received their correspondence acknowledged that they were participating in the construction of an ingenious narrative. Yet the power of the Mahatmas was not necessarily diminished by the realization of their invention. It should not be surprising, then, that those who study the Theosophical movement struggle to distinguish between fantasy and facts in the primary sources. Even Blavatsky recognized that the adepts were more at home as characters in fiction than as figures in history.

MADAME TAMVACO AND MRS. EDYE

An Australian writer who had moved to England in the 1870s, Rosa Campbell Praed was fascinated by spiritualism and telepathic communication. In spring 1884, like many literary types in London, she joined in the mania for theosophy. Her observations of the founders and their entourage became the subject of two novels: *Affinities: A Romance of To-day,* published in 1885, and *The Brother of the Shadow: A Mystery of To-day,* which appeared the following year.[24] Both novels exploit the trope of the struggle between an innocent young woman and an unscrupulous man who exercises occult power over her. Theosophical entreaties to seek the higher life intersect with warnings about the preservation of female purity. The novels suggest that sexual desire, whether on the part of man or woman, is the chief enemy of spiritual progress, an idea widely accepted by women like Laura Holloway-Langford. In these novels, the language of theosophy becomes code for exploration of female sexuality, which when repressed leads to illness, but when expressed heterosexually subjects women to male domination. Some occult novels, however, hinted that relationships between women could offer a solution to the conundrum of female sexuality.

Praed freely admitted that she had taken notes on her exchanges with Oscar Wilde, the Irish poet and playwright, whom she met at Theosophical gatherings.[25] Likewise, she recorded conversations with Helena Blavatsky, Laura Holloway-Langford, Mohini Chatterji, and others, which she reproduced in her novels. Henry S. Olcott recalled that in July 1884 Praed had attended an afternoon reception at the house of Francesca Arundale and that the novel *Affinities* brought the scene back vividly to his mind: "I can see the lion-faced H. P. B. sitting there, smoking her cigarettes...; the while, an insinuatingly kittenish and supple-framed American lady sitting on the arm of her chair, and now and then snuggling her face under the old lady's double-chin, to her evident disapproval."[26] The depiction of Laura Holloway-Langford as "kittenish" echoes Blavatsky's denigrating descriptions, but the scene that Olcott paints of her "snuggling" up to Blavatsky suggests an unexpected closeness in their relationship.

In *Affinities,* Praed recreated the social world of theosophy and the eccentric characters who hovered around Blavatsky: an American dowager hopes for a glimpse of Hindus in turbans; members of the Society for Psychical Research crave phenomena but are on the lookout for trickery; a tiresome American professor spouts esoteric theories; and a foreign princess is involved in political intrigue. The novel also depicts theosophical "conversaziones" in London, where there were no astral bells or "flowers raining down from the ceiling," but where "the Prophet of Nazareth" was presented as the ultimate adept, an initiate of the ancient mysteries who exemplified self-sacrifice, purity, and truth. Disappointed, an "advanced young woman" had cried out, "'Why, it's nothing but Christianity, after all: and this is the nineteenth century! We did not come here in evening dress for this!'"[27]

In *Affinities,* the character of Madame Tamvaco, who is described as being indeterminate in age and nationality, was based on Blavatsky:

> The thickness of jaw, the massive conformation of the face, and something fixed, cold and tragic in her full gaze, suggested the Egyptian Sphinx; other peculiarities pointed to a Kalmuck origin. . . . These eyes, light in colour, were extraordinarily deep and luminous. They seemed to draw the light into themselves like a jewel of which the depths appear unfathomable, and exercised on the beholder a fascination akin to that of the serpent. . . . The whole countenance, if wanting in feminine sweetness, was noble and mysteriously attractive. She wore a loose garment of some clinging black stuff. It was fashioned like the robe of some ancient priestess, and had loose sleeves which left bare a white and shapely arm. She was short and stout, and in ordinary dress her figure would have been quite devoid of dignity, but her straight draperies seemed to impart to it something of classic ease and uprightness.[28]

Accompanying Mme. Tamvaco is Mrs. Edye, a character based on Laura Holloway-Langford:

> This lady—an American, to judge by her accent, which, to use a vulgar phrase, might have been cut with a knife—wore a high-necked cashmere gown that draped her slim, angular, but not ungraceful, form in straight folds from the waist, and suggested the divided skirt, and theories concerning the dress of rational woman. She did not, however, despise ornaments, for diamonds twinkled in her ears and round her throat, and the frizz of fair hair above her forehead was decidedly after the prevailing mode. It was certain that she had a very distinct personality, and the sort of gaze which seemed to indicate that she knew what she wanted, and that her aims were somewhat higher than those of the herd. She was undoubtedly interesting; and, notwithstanding her lankness, her unpleasing voice, and the peculiarity of her attire, was feminine and even spiritual in appearance.[29]

Praed also portrayed Mrs. Edye as an "unpliable-looking lady," a do-gooder who does not wait for an invitation before meddling in other people's lives.[30] She considers herself "a doctor on the occult plane," whose cures are superior to those of physicians who can make a diagnosis but cannot heal conditions "which the ancients believed were afflictions from the gods."[31] She has strong ideas about marriage, believing that laws of "spiritual chemistry" dictate that in matrimony the "affinities must be regulated" so that an "impure magnetism" does not injure the other partner, preventing spiritual progress. She exclaims: "There's a great deal written about the sacredness of marriage and the union after death; but it's all a question of affinities. If you have been in contact with a person only upon the physical plane, you cannot be together upon the spiritual one."[32]

The plot of the novel revolves around a young woman, Judith Fountain, who is clairvoyant and attuned to the occult. After inheriting a small fortune, she marries a poet, Esmé Colquhoun, whose finances are in ruin. Like Oscar Wilde, upon whom the character was based, Colquhoun disregards conventional mores. He is the lover of a married woman, Mrs. Christine Borlase, a painter who claims that "human passion is but the stream in which pure, divine passion is reflected."[33] Although Borlase breaks off her physical relationship with Colquhoun, their spiritual kinship is unaffected by his marriage. Because Judith shares only a physical affinity with Colquhoun, she is slowly wasting away. When Judith says that she married for love, Mme. Tamvaco exclaims: "This fever which wastes the flesh and burns the soul is Love! You would not listen to me. . . . Never yield your will to another. Fly any influence which threatens to overpower it."[34] She tells Judith that because Colquhoun has captured her imagination, her aura has been infected by his malevolent magnetism. Judith, then, is to blame for her weakened state: she has married for mere physical attraction and the impurity of her desires has attracted an evil that is consuming her.[35]

Another character, Major Graysett, has fallen in love with Judith. He ponders whether it is moral for him to encourage Judith to abandon Colquhoun, but decides to intervene because his love is uncontaminated by lust. Resolved to rescue her from Colquhoun, he seeks help from Mrs. Edye, who declares that her mission is to heal the soul through the body. "When I saw that poor young thing for the first time the other evening . . . I said to myself, 'There's a case for you.' And I'm going to take charge of her, just right away—Madame Tamvaco and I have settled it all." She tells Graysett to prepare to go on a journey with Judith, and she promises to accompany them to a "high mountain place" where Judith will be healed.[36] Only a few minutes later, however, Graysett feels the hand of Mme. Tamvaco on his arm. Her "whole demeanour had changed. Her face was grave, even sad; and her glorious eyes seemed to have borrowed the far-off lustre of the stars."

> "Go," she said very gently. "Go to her whom you love. It is near the hour of your appointment."
>
> "Madame," he exclaimed questioningly; "you will help her? You will save her?"
>
> "She is saved," replied Madame Tamvaco solemnly.[37]

But when Graysett reaches Judith, he finds her dead. Although Judith has, indeed, escaped her enslavement to Colquhoun, no one can accompany her on this journey. Praed uses Mrs. Edye's naiveté as a foil to Mme. Tamvaco's wisdom. In contrast to Mrs. Edye, Mme. Tamvaco does not claim that she can control or determine events that are part of a larger cosmic drama. Neither Mrs. Edye nor Mme. Tamvaco can save Judith, who is at once responsible for her own fate and a victim of the vampire-like husband who drains her life force. According to Praed, female sexuality is dangerous, and not only to men, but to women themselves. Additionally, women are responsible for the spiritual condition of men. Mme. Tamvaco declares that Colquhoun's character was determined by woman's influence. Because Judith's love was contaminated by sexual desire, she could not save either herself or Colquhoun. Thus, the novel shows that heterosexual desire, even in marriage, places women in mortal danger and destroys their only power—a spirituality born of sexual purity.

The *Dublin Review* warned readers that *Affinities* "was so profoundly uninteresting that none but the patient critic is likely to pursue it to the end."[38] True as this assessment may be, the novel reveals the personalities of major Theosophical figures and the sexual metaphysics that they promoted. Because few letters or other documents preserve Laura Holloway-Langford's own voice, the novel's portrayal is an important source of information. Praed's observations from the summer of 1884 are consistent with what is known from other sources: Holloway-Langford claimed to be a psychic healer; she espoused the necessity of spiritual affinity in marriage; and she pronounced opinions with the supreme confidence of a

missionary offering a promise of salvation. Although exceedingly percep-
tive about other people, she was a narcissistic personality who often did
more harm than good. Thus, Praed portrayed Laura Holloway-Langford
as expressing the strengths and weaknesses of the American character, its
boundless self-confidence as well as its naiveté.

MRS. LAKESBY

In July 1885, not long after the publication of *Affinities,* A. P. Sinnett
released his own theosophical novel, *Karma.*[39] Having encountered financial difficulty, Sinnett hoped that fiction would attract larger sales than his
other metaphysical writings. He loosely based the novel on the events of
August and September 1884, when Theosophists gathered at the home of
Mary and Gustav Gebhard in Elberfeld, Germany. Set in a German castle
reminiscent of the Gebhard's home, the novel portrays Helena Blavatsky
as a male occultist, the Baron Friedrich von Mondstern. Although he disguised Blavatsky's identity, Sinnett had no compunction about depicting
Laura Holloway-Langford, who in the novel appears as the character Mrs.
Lakesby. He describes her as "a little woman, bright and attractive though
no longer in her first youth, a widow of many years' standing, with brown
wavy hair and large blue eyes, very quiet and demure in manner as a rule,
with features not regular enough to be admired in detail, but producing a
pleasant ensemble; a thoroughly wholesome, nice little woman, ready to
like and be liked by the people she might be living with."[40] She was also
a clairvoyant who was in touch with "great spirits who teach her all sorts
of things," not one of those professional mediums who perform tricks
like "looking about into other people's rooms." But like "all sensitives . . .
whether they are ladies and gentlemen, or paid mediums," Mrs. Lakesby
could be difficult to handle.[41] She prefers to communicate with friends
who have passed on to "another sort of life," but nevertheless she agrees
to demonstrate thought-reading for those gathered at the castle.[42] She can
see into their minds, can visualize their homes, learning of illicit loves and
betrayals. She even transmits a message from a long-dead mother. She
describes her ability to leave her physical body: "I can ooze out somehow,

by making an effort I can hardly describe, and then, once in astral form, one can go anywhere by *merely* willing to."[43] Her psychic powers have been honed through her earlier reincarnations, and when in trance she travels back in time picturing the previous lives of her friends, whose spirits sometimes speak through her.

The Baron, who is a member of a mystical brotherhood and more advanced in his understanding of the laws of the occult than others in the group, warns Mrs. Lakesby about the dangers of speaking to specters. He cautions her that by communicating with the lower qualities of the spirit, she retards the spiritual progress of those who have passed on while at the same time she opens herself to dangerous astral influences. Mrs. Lakesby should, the Baron admonishes, devote herself to the great cause. This path, however, is difficult and its rewards often do not come in this life.[44] Many of the ideas that Mrs. Lakesby expresses more closely resemble spiritualism than theosophy. Despite Blavatsky's attempts to distinguish the movements, the line between them remained blurry even for many members of the Theosophical Society. A letter in the October 1887 issue of *Lucifer* questioned how Mrs. Lakesby was able to carry on conversations with souls of the dead and learn about their previous lives. Didn't Theosophy hold that when the body dies, souls lose their individual identity, existing in a semi-conscious state until their next materialization? Blavatsky replied that although Mrs. Lakesby might imagine that she had contacted spirits, she would have communicated only with their elemental natures, which were inferior even to their lowest selves while on earth. She noted that in the story the Baron discredited Mrs. Lakesby's views of the astral plane and its inhabitants, and Blavatsky urged readers to remember that *Karma* was a romance, not a statement of Theosophical principles.[45] This response resembles her warning that Sinnett had been duped by Laura Holloway-Langford when she claimed to have channeled voices of the Masters, insisting that Holloway-Langford had only been in touch with "shells," the earthly remnants of departed spirits.

Like most other theosophical novels, *Karma* reinforces the contention that spirituality and sexuality are incompatible. Nonetheless, its characters do not comply with conventional moral standards. Although the young man Annerly, who possesses psychic powers, relinquishes his love for a woman in order to pursue esoteric knowledge as the Baron's pupil, another character divorces his wife so as to resume a relationship with the young woman whom Annerly had loved.

The *Dublin Review* offered another scathing appraisal of this example of occult fiction. After quoting some of Mrs. Lakesby's conversation, it observed: "Spiritual society does not seem to improve the diction any more than the morals of those who frequent it."[46] In the United States, critics found the novel dull, saying it demonstrated spiritualism to be a worthless waste of time.[47]

Helena Blavatsky, however, was more favorably impressed than other reviewers. She was pleased that the characters were not caricatured, as she felt they had been in Praed's *Affinities*. In particular, she commented on Sinnett's portrayal of Laura Holloway-Langford, writing him: "In *Karma* the original of Mrs. Lakesby is neither flattered nor her defects exaggerated. You have taken but the real existing features as though from life, passing all the very prominent defects in *charitable* silence. But, is it only 'charitable silence,' my dear Mr. Sinnett? I am afraid you are still somewhat under the spell."[48] In this rather ambiguous and contradictory assessment, Blavatsky suggests that Sinnett's depiction had been colored by his persistent admiration for Holloway-Langford.

Blavatsky declared that the genre of a written work did not determine its truth. "You will do more good by fancy novels in which truth and *such truths* are found in apparent fiction, than by works as the *Occult World* in which every word is now regarded by all except theosophists—as hallucination and the cock and bull stories of confederates."[49] She suggested that because the reading public made little distinction between novels and works that preserved the words of the Masters, fiction might be a preferred means of spreading theosophical ideas. At least novels would not attract the kind of scrutiny exerted by the Society for Psychical Research in examining the Mahatma letters.

ANANDA

Of all the Theosophists, none made a more vivid impression than Mohini Chatterji.[50] Blavatsky had deliberately exploited European perceptions of the East as a land of mystery and wisdom, and she had presented Chatterji as its representative to Europe. Chatterji appears in *The Brother of the Shadow*, a popular novel by Rosa Campbell Praed, where he is represented as an exotic, ethereal figure. The novel reproduces Western Orientalism, with no acknowledgment of the contradictions between the man and the role he had assumed. Nevertheless, it is valuable in probing the intersection of race and gender in occult literature.

The Brother of the Shadow, published in 1886, may have been inspired by gossip about A. P. Sinnett's efforts to hypnotize Laura Holloway-Langford. The character of Ananda, based on Mohini Chatterji, however, holds most interest for the modern reader. In the novel, Julian Vascher sends his wife, Antonia, from Allahabad, India, to France, where she is to be treated for a painful neuralgia by a friend, Dr. Lemuel Lloyd. The doctor has been experimenting with the treatment of disease by electricity, clairvoyance, and mesmerism.[51] Lloyd's greatest desire, however, is to communicate with the Tibetan Masters, but he has been barred from contacting them because of his "grosser contact with the world."[52] In the novel, Lloyd's devotion to science and his sensuality represent Western materialism that thwarts spiritual development.

Lloyd is contrasted with his assistant, a young "Hindoo" named Ananda who has recently arrived in Europe from India. Ananda is "slight and with a physique almost feminine in its delicacy. A striking, indeed a god-like, head crowned his spare form. The face was oval, the skin a pale olive, the features of the purest type—instinct with sensibility, the eyes full and dark, the irises of wonderful clearness, . . . the whole countenance so tender, so spiritualised, and withal so intellectual, that to watch its play was a delight."[53] Like Chatterji, Ananda was a Brahmin who had received a superior education at the University of Calcutta. He was also a Buddhist and a disciple of the adepts of Inner Asia, with whom he communicated telepathically.[54] Ananda had developed these higher powers, including the ability to project "the Astral Double," because he had conquered sexual desire, "the most dangerous temptation that can assail the occultist."[55]

Much like A. P. Sinnett, Lloyd concludes that only through a medium with a "sensitive, etherealized temperament with psychic faculties ready to burst into play" will he be able to contact the Masters.[56] Ananda describes Antonia to Dr. Lloyd: she is not only beautiful, but "as sweet and sensitive as a musical instrument to the touch of the performer. I know no more. She is passive. No hand has swept the strings."[57] Such passages in the novel suggest that not only will Antonia be a responsive psychic instrument, but that, although married, her sexuality has not been awakened. Antonia has led a married life, but Lloyd believes that when separated from her husband she will be "untainted by any grossness of living." Once she regains "her magnetic atmosphere," her soul will penetrate "unknown regions" and "unfold to him the pages of the Astral Book."[58] Ananda, however, fears "the supremacy of Lloyd's earthy propensities. . . . He knew the dangers of mesmeric rapport to one not wholly purified from desire, the subtle intoxication of the senses which it produces, the paralysis of the will on one part, and on the other, its liability to intensify itself in the physical direction."[59]

Antonia and Ananda had known each other in India, where they had shared spiritual affinities. When Antonia arrives at Lloyd's chateau, Ananda greets her with yellow roses. Antonia recites to him verses from Kālidāssa's famous poem, "Kumārasambhava," which celebrates the beauty of sexual love: "The God of Love passed by. The flowers thrilled into beauty and fragrance; the bee drank honey out of the same flower-cup with his mate; the embrace of the creeper in the blossom became closer to its beloved tree." Ananda had taught her the poem, which he chants with her in Sanskrit. He cautions Antonia, however, that the lover in the poem prefers the absence of his mistress to her presence.[60] Praed thus suggests that the ties between Antonia and Ananda surpassed all earthly bonds, including those of marriage.

Dr. Lloyd prescribes treatment with an "electric bath," which he requires Antonia to take each day before he mesmerizes her.[61] The novel links Antonia's depression to sexual repression; thus, it may not be far-fetched to suggest that Dr. Lloyd's "electric bath" may employ sexual stimulation. The first electric vibrator had been patented in 1880, and although physicians had often employed "pelvic massage" in treating female complaints, electricity dramatically increased the ease with which women reached orgasm.[62] Whether or not Praed had the electric vibrator in mind, she portrays Dr. Lloyd as using his scientific knowledge to dominate Antonia sexually. The electric bath creates receptivity, making her drowsy, passive, and open to Lloyd's suggestion. As a result of these treatments, the depression and irritability that Antonia had felt in India depart. The improvement in her "nervous malady" is, however, also the result of separation from her husband. "I am happy without him," Antonia declares.[63] Thus, the novel hints that Antonia's illness had been induced by unfulfilled sexual needs, which have been remedied by Dr. Lloyd's treatments. Predictably, Dr. Lloyd falls in love with Antonia. Although he claims to use his mesmeric power only for metaphysical inquiry, "the *woman* clung to his imagination."[64]

In the novel, Praed has presented three types of male–female relationships: the conventional marriage, in which the woman is sexually repressed; an abusive relationship, where a woman is overpowered and victimized by a man; and a relationship of equality, based on sexual purity and spiritual affinity. The relationship between Antonia and Ananda transcends race and culture, but it is based on underlying orientalist suppositions. Ananda's spirituality is passive and enveloping, never coercive. It is portrayed as incommensurate with Western constructions of masculinity. Unlike the European husband or would-be lover, he responds to the beauty of nature and poetry. Having been purified of all base desires, Ananda is an asexual being. Thus, Praed feminizes the non-Western man of color, as Bulwer-Lytton and Francis Marion Crawford had done in their depictions of the Mahatmas.

Like the Mahatmas, Ananda possesses metaphysical knowledge. When Lloyd puts Antonia into a deep trance, she reports a vision of an Egyptian priest who wears a red cap and carries a snake-staff. Lloyd is elated, but Ananda warns him that the "mesmeric rapport" has awakened an "evil germ" and that the figure "was a black magician, a follower of the left hand path, a Brother of the Shadow."[65] Ananda tells Lloyd that "'there is a law of correspondences in the occult world which cannot be violated. . . . These black magicians in the East aim only at internal enjoyment, sensuality, the things of the flesh, which red, the blood-colour, typifies.'"[66] Praed offers a psychological interpretation, implying that Antonia has intuited Lloyd's true nature, which she has projected onto the form of an Egyptian Brother of the Shadow. Indeed, this figure mirrors Lloyd's desires, assuring him that sexual fulfillment, not asceticism, is the path to occult knowledge. Sensing the danger, Ananda prays to his Master to protect Antonia: "Guard her against the evil will of him who has strayed into the Left Hand Path and would turn his powers to baseness."[67] When Antonia's husband, Julian Vascher, arrives from India, Lloyd calls on the power of Black Magic to destroy him. However, Antonia, in her purity, has gained the strength to repel the evil from her husband and to turn it back on Dr. Lloyd, killing him.

The popularity of *The Brother of the Shadow* was due less to its esoteric content than to its eroticism inflected by sadism. For Praed, writing about the occult was a means to explore indirectly the dilemmas posed by sexual domination and submission. Contradictory views of female sexuality drive the novel's melodramatic plot. On the surface, the novel reiterates the cliché that sexual purity is the only path to spiritual development. A subversive subtext, however, suggests the mental and emotional harm done to women by an ideology that enshrines sexual repression. To complete the dilemma, Praed portrays heterosexuality as inherently dangerous for women. Whether under the influence of a husband or a necromancer, women are at the mercy of male power.

Other late Victorian women writers also used esoteric fiction as a vehicle for transgressive sexual ideas only hinted at in *The Brother of the Shadow*. Marie Corelli's novel *A Romance of Two Worlds* suggests that relationships between women could avoid the destructive paradigm of submission and dominance that characterized heterosexuality.[68] It hints that women can find fulfillment—sexual, emotional, and spiritual—in relationships with other women, which also foster rather than hinder women's acquisition of occult power. Whether or not they were members of the Theosophical Society or held to its precepts, women novelists like Rosa Campbell Praed and Marie Corelli found in occultism a symbolic language through which to explore the construction of sexuality and desire.

GENDERING THE OCCULT

The pursuit of the occult, even among Theosophists, was gendered masculine. In fiction, European male characters sought the secrets of the adepts in order to increase their worldly power. Through their occult training, they strengthened their will, which they imposed on others, especially women. In contrast, psychic abilities in female characters did not increase their power over others; instead, they increased women's vulnerability and made them susceptible to male domination. To be sure, neither Mrs. Edye nor Mrs. Lakesby—the characters based on Laura Holloway-Langford—were portrayed as passive mediums. Both characters displayed an ability to see into the human heart. Yet this trait was gendered female, stripping it of any authority to command people or determine events.

Despite the fact that occult novels reproduced late Victorian gender relations, they also hinted at a loosening of attitudes toward female sexuality and marital relationships. Mrs. Edye's notions of spiritual affinities warned about the dangers of traditional marriage, just as Laura Holloway-Langford was known to have done. The gothic trappings disguised more serious questions raised by these novels about compatibility in marriage and a woman's right to escape an abusive spouse. Of the female characters, only those based on Helena Blavatsky did not display weakness that was deemed feminine. Yet in *Affinities* Blavatsky was represented as androgynous, and in *Karma* she was transformed into a man, as Baron Friedrich von Mondstern. A. P. Sinnett could not imagine that Blavatsky, as a woman, could be portrayed in the novel as a member of the occult "Brotherhood." Moreover, although clearly male, adepts were never depicted as "one of the boys," both because spirituality was gendered feminine and because as non-Europeans they did not partake of Western masculinity. To the European writer, whiteness was the color of dominance and masculinity, and it was identified with worldly rather than spiritual power.

At the same time, however, the fictional representations of the adepts and Blavatsky reflected the metaphysics of theosophy, which viewed androgyny as characteristic of the higher self. The indeterminate gender of the adepts and Blavatsky, their incorporation of both masculine and feminine characteristics, confirmed that they were spiritually advanced beings. Yet, in occult fiction as well as in the early Theosophical Society, there was uncertainty about the relationship between gender and spirituality.[69] Often the dichotomies of Victorian culture—West/East, European/Asian, male/female—prevailed, despite the ideal of a universality that transcended race and culture, gender and sexuality.

6

"Our Golden Word: Try*"*

Theosophists esteemed the written word with an almost Protestant faith in its power, and they produced an array of metaphysical treatises, memoirs, and novels. Additionally, they penned a plethora of letters, which were passed from one person to another, keeping the founders in touch with followers on several continents. Even communications from the Adept Brotherhood occurred in writing rather than orally or through music, meditation, or images.[1] A disciple of the Brotherhood was expected to adopt vegetarianism and celibacy, but a prime qualification for the chela was literary skill. Helena Blavatsky might eat meat with relish, chain-smoke, and curse like a sailor, but these shortcomings were outweighed by her prodigious religious imagination and her talent as a writer. Since the appearance of *Isis Unveiled* in 1877, she had been the driving force behind the Theosophical Society's publications, authoring many of the articles that appeared in the movement's journals. While occult phenomena generated excitement, Blavatsky recognized that it was through the written word that Theosophy could enter the discourse of the modern world. The future of Theosophical movement, she knew, hinged less on messages from the Masters, which followers tended to treat as inviolate, than on the creation of texts that could be edited, debated, criticized, and rewritten.[2] It was her need for an experienced assistant who could aid in the production of metaphysical documents that led her to accept Laura Holloway-Langford as a probationary disciple.

NEGOTIATING WITH THE MASTERS

The Masters had assigned Holloway-Langford the task of writing a book in collaboration with Mohini Chatterji that would correct errors in the works of A. P. Sinnett. Because of the controversy over her role as a medium, however, she had threatened to give up this project. In letters, Blavatsky and Koot Hoomi sought to soothe her wounded pride, complimenting her abilities and affirming her good intentions, while reassuring Holloway-Langford that the summer's troubles were part of a larger cosmic plan. One letter suggested that she had been sent to test Sinnett and other members of the Society in England. Another said that, having been specially chosen by the Masters, she should not be discouraged. Additionally, Blavatsky sent her a note addressed to "Dearest Daughter of God," asking "whether Barkis is still willing."[1] Blavatsky's nickname for Holloway-Langford, "Barkis," referred to the faithful servant in Charles Dickens's novel *David Copperfield*.

Holloway-Langford, however, had not come to Europe to "serve" either Blavatsky or the Masters. More in the habit of giving orders than taking them, she seized the initiative, composing a letter to Koot Hoomi that asked:

1. Will you lead me by correspondence?
2. Will you make a book for me?
3. Have I been compelled to advance theosophically or have I done it myself?
4. Can a person earn a living & still be a novice?
5. Can I write a novel with your help?
6. Can my case be made an exception & my time of probation shortened?
7. Will you help me pay off a debt under a "solemn promise" (or contract) that I shall then go to India?
8. What are my chances of chelaship, and can you accept me before returning to America?
9. Will you help me write a poem?

In recounting this letter to Blavatsky, the Master added: "Etc. Etc. Etc. ... I repeat [these questions] so that the questioner may realise how much 4 pages of note-paper may be made to contain—when the woman-child, nervous & restless . . . was left to herself. . . . If we wished to paralyze her Personality & use her as an unconscious medium we might make her write books she would not be the author of, & poems that were not her inspiration." But, he asserted, such actions would violate the laws of karma. The Master concluded that Holloway-Langford could be transformed in her next rebirth from the "feeble worm of today" into a "strong adept" only if she took responsibility for her own actions and avoided "self-inflicted punishment."[4]

In their correspondence, Koot Hoomi and Holloway-Langford spoke different languages: he drew on the idiom of karma and reincarnation, while she employed the lingo of business and law. Experienced in negotiating book contracts, Holloway-Langford wanted to fix in writing the terms of her relationship to the Masters. To her it seemed logical to ask them for an agreement about the work she was expected to produce, what help they would give her, who would hold the copyright, and how much she would be compensated. Yet it seems far-fetched to think that she really believed that adepts living in Tibet negotiated financial arrangements with their chelas. More likely, Holloway-Langford was modeling her behavior on Blavatsky, whom she had observed manipulating messages in order to produce material results. She knew that neither her letters to the Master, nor his to her, were private correspondence. Blavatsky and others would be privy to their contents. If, in some mysterious way, her letter resulted in repayment of her loan (perhaps a mortgage on her Brooklyn house) or other financial compensation for her writing, she would not question how the desired result was achieved. In her letters, Holloway-Langford tested the limits of what might be attained, not only spiritually but also materially, through correspondence with the Masters.

In another letter to Blavatsky, Koot Hoomi responded to Holloway-Langford's list of questions and demands. He accused her of trusting only truths that were revealed directly to her and that she had not yet "assimilated all that can be extracted from Mohini's teachings." Although she had made progress, he was uncertain whether "she is, or is not our chela." Koot Hoomi predicted that if she continued to "give herself up as even a conscious medium," she would remain "a partly grown psychic vine," bearing "mildewed grapes" for a revolting wine served up to the public. To his mind, Holloway-Langford was a "nature-child" who required "fatherly restraint upon her latent natural impulses," and he refused to offer assurances about her future. He noted that "books may be written anonymously & yield great profits"; nevertheless, he mocked Holloway-Langford's notion that she could "make money, sell her books and live from January to December—by magic." He asserted that she must "tread the stony way" alone and that her spiritual progress depended on her own effort. No exceptions could be made to the "immutable Law of Cause & Effect." She would be accepted as a regular chela only when she had proved herself. He continued:

> No one of us was ever permitted to know the time, least of all to dictate time, place or circumstances, as to the beginning or conclusion of our chelaship. There is but one law for all. Let her forget if she can that she is L. C. H. to think of herself only as a slave to duty, as we are—the path of which is revealed by the Atma. Let her ask nothing but the *privilege of showing what she can do unaided.* . . . Our golden word of course: *Try.*"[5]

Repeatedly, Koot Hoomi asserted that chelaship was not a profession, but a spiritual practice that required the eradication of self, control of the mind and the senses, and devotion to duty irrespective of any expectation of personal reward. Holloway-Langford, in contrast, had an essentially secular conception of her undertaking. She perceived herself as an employee, not a disciple, who was discussing contractual rights with an employer. She was a practical American who had no intention of becoming a "slave" working without pay in obedience to a master, spiritual or otherwise. Her position echoed Cleo's comment in *Beyond the Sunrise* that she would never bow down to an occult priesthood. Koot Hoomi may have had these attitudes in mind when, sometime later, he told Henry Steel Olcott that Holloway-Langford's "faults are those of her, and your, country."[6]

TWO CHELAS: EASTERN AND WESTERN

Blavatsky claimed that *Man: Fragments of Forgotten History* was written by a secret method. The "writing séances" had taken place in the upper room of the home of Francesca Arundale, who observed the two chelas, Mohini Chatterji and Laura Holloway-Langford, at work. She recalled that they "were told to look back into the far past and sketch out the history of the long distant ages." Completed work was sent to the Masters, apparently through Helena Blavatsky, and corrected copy was returned to the chelas. Arundale remembered an incident when Holloway-Langford could not discern what she was supposed to write. She said: "'I cannot see it,' and pushed the papers away from her. The table was covered with sheets of foolscap on which they had been writing, and at last she or Mohini . . . took up the page again, and on the margin was written in the clear handwriting of the master in blue pencil the one word 'Try.'" Arundale remarked that shortly after the book was finished, a "psychic misunderstanding arose and Mrs. Holloway returned to America. I liked her very much and I saw her once astrally at night, but I have neither seen nor heard from her since."[7]

Laura Holloway-Langford had expected more help from the Masters than simply the injunction to "Try." Joscelyn Godwin has pointed out that the word "Try" was a code for "the essential difference between occultism and spiritualism." It embodied the "doctrine of the occultist," who must develop the will and overcome obstacles by "repeated and patient effort."[8] Holloway-Langford, however, still thought of her role as that of a spiritualist medium. She may have envisioned receiving a book via the slate-writing technique that had been popularized by Mary Hollis-Billing, or perhaps she thought that her task would be to transcribe dictation from the Masters in a kind of automatic writing. She had not anticipated that the Masters would expect hard work, self-development, and study. She was instructed to set aside fixed hours each day,

> all alone, in self-contemplation, writing, reading, the purification of your motives, the study & correction of your faults, the planning of your work in the external life. These hours should be sacredly reserved for this purpose, & no one, not even your most intimate friends or friend, should be with you there. Little by little your sight will clear, you will find the mists pass away, your interior faculties strengthen, your attraction towards us gain force, and certainty replace doubts.[9]

In the production of *Man: Fragments of Forgotten History*, Koot Hoomi acted as an editor. He suggested topics for the writing, and he made the final decisions about the book's title and who would be credited with its authorship. The Master instructed Holloway-Langford to "Make Preface explaining the origin of the Book—Enough to interest the reader without divulging the whole process—a page of 'Zanoni.'"[10] By invoking the popular occult novel by Sir Edward Bulwer-Lytton that had introduced the idea of wandering ancient seers, Koot Hoomi suggested that the Preface introduce the Adept Brotherhood as the source for the teachings in the book. Additionally, he was instructing Holloway-Langford to find a "hook" that would have wide appeal to English readers.

As a result of Koot Hoomi's advice, Holloway-Langford wrote two prefaces that told how a chela from the East and one from the West had received a call from the adepts. The language was overwrought, sentimental, and laced with antiquated usage in order to give an air of sanctity. The Eastern Chela was portrayed as a male "pupil," while the Western Chela was a female "soul." In the "Preface by the Eastern Chela," Holloway-Langford imagined a little shepherd boy in the Himalayas who, "sustained by the traditions of his race," became a mystic. He was summoned to travel westward and instructed: "Take this mutilated scroll, an unknown, though kindred spirit will bring the missing fragments, and then will be revealed to thee things which thou hast till now sought in vain. Take no thought for the morrow nor tarry here a single day; thy path of duty leads to the West." Obedient to the Master, the "faithful pupil found himself among the ill-fated splendour of Paris. . . . Ghost-like the ascetic haunted the homes of wealth and pleasure, everywhere regarded more as the mysterious hand that recorded the doom of the Assyrian monarch than a human being willing to work and bear." Then one evening, he heard the call of his missing soul mate. "The two strangers met and were strangers no more, the fragments united together, the torn scroll became whole. The mystic scroll was all in quaint characters and in an unknown tongue. Many an anxious day and many a watchful night has it cost the fellow-students, united in a strange land, to decipher its meaning. The following pages represent the result."[11]

The Western Chela, in the meantime, was in her room, on a snowy winter day in New York, feeling helpless in the face of human suffering. Suddenly she sensed the presence of an Eastern sage. He had long, flowing hair and carried a "book-like parchment" and a small wooden staff that emitted fragrant incense. He wore sandals and a "yellow Tibetan bodice" under a long white robe that was trimmed with Himalayan fur. In his soft voice, he taught her an unknown doctrine, which was the "essence of all doctrines, the inner truth of all religions—creedless, nameless, untaught by priests, because it is of the spirit and not to be found in temple or synagogue. It is the still small voice heard in the whirlwind and felt in the storm." She had involuntarily appealed to him when her thoughts had turned to the helpless and the homeless. He told her: "Your heart breathed its prayer; your soul registered it in the atmosphere about you; and the spirit was refreshed by so pure a breath wafted from the lower kingdom to the higher; from the body to the soul and thence to the region of spirits." Evening after evening, he came and instructed her from the writings of the ancient volume. One day the sage no longer appeared. She realized that the Master had departed, but that he waited for her in a foreign land. She was afraid and hesitated. When spring came, she heard his voice summon her. She answered in an echo of biblical language: "Master! I come! Thy will be done!" And she obeyed.[12]

As Holloway-Langford framed the book, Chatterji, the Eastern Chela, was the bearer of ancient knowledge. He required her help, that of the Western Soul, to decipher the mutilated scroll. The frame was constructed almost as a romance: neither the Eastern nor the Western Chela can be made whole until they are reunited. The Preface also implied, however, that there were two kinds of knowledge. The one possessed in the East was spiritual and mystical; that in the West was rational and practical. The two must be joined before the inner essence of truth can be revealed.

The Preface was an odd introduction to a work that, for the most part, contained abstract and abstruse teachings. Chunks of material were lifted from previous Theosophical works, including Mahatma letters and writings by Blavatsky, much of which appeared in quotation marks but without attribution. After the controversy over Sinnett's apparent plagiarizing of Henry Kiddle (see chapter 3), Mohini Chatterji was uneasy about using such materials. He questioned the Master about the propriety of reproducing teachings that were contained in letters written to others. Koot Hoomi replied that Chatterji was free to use any "secret doctrines" that appeared in his letters, since those were "theosophical property." The Master concluded: "You are at liberty to even copy them verbatim and without quotation marks—I will not call it 'plagiarism,' my boy."[13]

Some sections of the book display Holloway-Langford's journalistic style, while other sections, more abstract and metaphysical, apparently were written by Chatterji. The text was interlaced with quotations from English literature, ranging from Shakespeare's *The Merchant of Venice* to Milton's *Comus*, all with citations of author and title. Furthermore, there were numerous quotations from the Bible, probably contributed by Holloway-Langford. Mohini Chatterji supported the book's arguments with references to Eastern texts such as the *Rig-Veda* and *Atharva-Veda*, as well as with philosophic arguments, including algebraic equations. The authors attempted to weave these disparate sources into a narrative of the history of man as a seven-fold being corresponding to a seven-fold universe. Such a project depended on a conviction that—when understood esoterically—all sacred texts, all great literature, and all science contained the same universal truths.

THE EVOLUTION OF SEX

In a chapter called "The Evolution of Sex," Holloway-Langford attempted to synthesize theosophical ideas with her conviction that the relations between men and women must be transformed. Much of the chapter's content echoes the writings of Blavatsky, who almost certainly discussed with Holloway-Langford the topics the book should cover. Still, Holloway-Langford's own analyses are discernible, especially in passages that address issues of women's equality. Following Blavatsky's elucidation of Kabbalistic traditions, Holloway-Langford posited an original fall, not from the Garden of Eden, but from a state of bisexuality, when male and female were one. In *Isis Unveiled* Blavatsky had claimed that Adam was originally an androgyne and that before sexual differentiation creation was spiritual and a product of the will. Only after the rending of Divine Unity did male and female become separate beings who engaged in physical procreation.

Holloway-Langford expanded this metaphysics to coincide with Victorian gender ideology. According to her, male and female first became distinct in their mental attributes. The male mind favored the "general and the abstract," while the female evolved "a tendency towards the particular and the concrete."[14] Bodily differentiation followed, with the development of the sex instinct resulting in male dominance. She blamed Christianity for codifying discrimination against women in "systems of ecclesiasticism." Injustice to the female sex, according to Holloway-Langford,

> reached its culmination in the enthronement of a personal God, with a Son to share His glory, but wifeless, motherless and daughterless. The materiality of man is nowhere so emphatically expressed as in his conceptions of a Supreme Father. He has eliminated from his ideal god all the attributes of woman; in his miraculously begotten Son alone are to be found some of the finer elements of womanhood.[15]

Blavatsky, too, had written that the God of the Unitarians was a bachelor, while that of other Protestant sects was a "spouseless Father."[16] But unlike Blavatsky, who identified female power with nature, Holloway-Langford accepted the widespread nineteenth-century identification of the male sex with the physical world and the female with the spiritual. To her, the descent into materialism was a result of Christianity's elimination of the female, and thus the spiritual, from the godhead. In Christ, however, she saw the restoration of feminine attributes in the divine.

After presenting some historically dubious material exonerating the place of women in other religions, Holloway-Langford blamed the evils of the world on the "subjection of woman and interference with her liberty of person and of conscience." The result had been to make "the world a prison-house for humanity . . . given to disease, want, and death." She asserted that women would not be liberated by "laws and enactments." Thus, in *Man* she reiterated her conviction that suffrage, in and of itself, would not remedy female oppression. Both her feminism and her disdain for politics found ready acceptance among Theosophists. As Diana Burfield observes, "Many Theosophists who had little interest in women's suffrage and the political aims of the women's movement" nevertheless were sympathetic to the views on the status of women and relations between the sexes put forward by the feminists.[17] Holloway-Langford, however, not only advocated women's equality, but she identified male sexual desire as the cause of women's oppression. In *Man: Fragments of Forgotten History*, she declared: "So long as a man is hampered by the indulgence of any weakness, and, above all, when he is guilty of subjugating another human being to sexual selfishness—so long will it be wholly impossible for him to advance his work and spread true wisdom."[18]

Holloway-Langford's own point of view had been influenced by personal experience as well as by contact with perfectionist religious groups such as the Shakers. She believed that the institution of marriage, as presently constituted, made sexual equality impossible, preventing social progress. Thus, in contrast to the Kabbalists who sought to repair the world through reuniting male and female, Holloway-Langford rejected sexual union, even as a metaphor, as a path to spiritual development. She wrote that "the married relation which accentuates the differences between man and woman is utterly incompatible with the higher life. Adeptship is the peculiar heritage of the celibate." She asserted that when humans became fully enlightened "immaculate conception" would become possible, writing: "This knowledge of spiritual reproduction is one of the highest secrets of Adeptship, but until its day arrives the duty of every spiritual-minded man and woman is to accelerate the advancement of the race by individual purity, which is the first step in the path which leads to Adeptship."

In the meantime, the adepts "keep alive the race ideal and possibilities" by propagating spiritually rather than physically, and by infusing "truths into the inner mind of the neophyte."[19] Holloway-Langford envisioned these spiritual progeny neither as clones of the adepts (whom she regarded as exalted male figures), nor androgynous beings, but rather completely sexless creatures. She believed that the fall from Eden had resulted in a devolution into sexual, racial, and national differentiation. In the New Age, Eden would be restored. Every boundary would dissolve, and sex itself would be eliminated as humans evolved into a purely spiritual state. When all had reached the level of the Adept Brotherhood, not only would exploitation and discrimination disappear, but the physical body itself would vanish.

These ideas were far from original to Laura Holloway-Langford. According to Siv Ellen Kraft, Blavatsky and many of her followers accepted Victorian notions that sexual indulgence would lead to debilitation, sickness, and even death.[20] At the very time that Holloway-Langford was working on *Man*, Blavatsky published an article in which she claimed

that the "future occultist" would have a virgin birth. Even though Blavatsky asserted that this day was "very, very far off," she termed its arrival
a "Kingdom of Heaven" on earth.[21] Four years later, Blavatsky expanded
her ideas in *The Secret Doctrine,* where she made a strong distinction between the soul, which was infinite and eternal, and the body, which was
the site of animal instinct. In order for the body to be a vehicle for the
evolution of the soul, asserted Blavatsky, it must be disciplined and sexual
energies transformed into mental powers.[22] In Laura Holloway-Langford,
Blavatsky found an eager pupil who was already predisposed to accept sexual purity as a solution for female subjugation. Decades later, Holloway-
Langford would produce another book, *As It is Written of Jesus the Christ,*
where she applied these ideas to the Christian gospel.

NEVER TOUCH MOHINI

An incident that occurred during Laura Holloway-Langford's collaboration with Mohini Chatterji on *Man* highlighted the contradiction between the Theosophical Society's universal ideals and its notions about
human sexuality. In the later part of August 1884, about the time she was
completing work on *Man,* Holloway-Langford received a letter from the
Master Koot Hoomi containing a reprimand: "You were told ere now
never to touch Mohini; you have done so out of sheer malice and brought
upon yourself the displeasure of one of our chiefs."[23] Holloway-Langford's
version of the incident was that "I had offered my hand forgetting that he
was forbidden to touch a woman's hand even in friendly greeting." When
the letter containing this incident appeared in print in 1923, Theosophists
were certain that this was another example of her sexual licentiousness.[24]

It seems more likely, however, that in 1884 the Theosophical movement
had not resolved the question of whether a woman could be an instrument
for esoteric knowledge, or, indeed, whether a woman could be in communication with the Masters. To be sure, the Society had been inspired by
a woman who was the channel for supernatural communication, but, as
many who knew her remarked, Blavatsky seemed neither male nor female.
More recently, James Santucci has characterized Blavatsky as a Magus or
Shaman, whose "androgynous personality and psyche" contributed to her

power.[25] In the early days of the Society in India, however, even Blavatsky was sometimes excluded from participation in meetings because of her sex, and separate branches of the Society for Hindu "Ladies" were established.[26] The restrictions on women were made explicit by Koot Hoomi, who wrote in 1882 to A. P. Sinnett that his wife could have no contact with the Master's chela: "I have not the slightest objection to Mrs. S. your lady seeing either of them; but I pray her not to address them, since they are forbidden by our religious laws to speak with any lady—their mothers and sisters excepted."[27]

In England, however, Laura Holloway-Langford did not expect to be bound by Indian customs, even though she was described by the Master as a "feminine personality." In one letter, Koot Hoomi instructed Blavatsky to tell her that "Djual Khool [one of Koot Hoomi's disciples] is not allowed to correspond with female chelas—you will explain to her *why*."[28] The Masters refused to be explicit about their "policy"; it was left to a woman, Blavatsky, to offer the details. In a letter to Francesca Arundale, Koot Hoomi reported that Holloway-Langford said that her ways were not those of the Indian Masters and that she could not comprehend them. She described Blavatsky's conversation with her about these matters as "rude and indelicate." He asked Arundale to explain to Holloway-Langford that the conflict was rooted in the differences between East and West. If she truly desired to become a chela, he said, she must be more like Blavatsky, who never considered "the propriety of things" when carrying out a Master's order. "In the eyes of you, the civilized and cultured portion of mankind, it is the one unpardonable sin; in our sight—i.e., uncultured Asiatics—it is the greatest virtue." Holloway-Langford, however, had let her "womanly pride and personality . . . get mixed up . . . in a question of pure rules and discipline. . . . To say nothing of the relative decency or indecency of any social custom of any country, there are rules of conduct controlling chelas which cannot be departed from in the slightest degree."[29] Whether or not Holloway-Langford had touched Chatterji's hand inadvertently, there is little evidence to support allegations of any overt sexual misconduct on her part. There were, however, conflicting expectations for behavior all around. If Holloway-Langford had offended Eastern sensibilities, so Blavatsky had offended Western ones, perhaps by making explicit taboos regarding the female body.

As a probationary candidate Holloway-Langford would not yet have taken a vow of celibacy; however, the Masters never doubted her sexual "purity." Nevertheless, it would not be surprising that physical contact between a male and female chela who worked together in close proximity would be carefully regulated. Also lurking in these texts is the blood taboo present in many religious traditions, including Hinduism. A menstruating woman was by definition "impure" and was forbidden to handle sacred objects, participate in holy rites, or touch the body of a holy man.[30] If communication with a Master was understood as a kind of "touching," this would explain why, in theory, great care must be taken before he established a direct link through a woman.

In *Man: Fragments of Forgotten History*, Holloway-Langford addressed the prohibitions surrounding menstruation: "The infringement of the wise rule which separated women from all men, during this period, has not only blunted the moral sensibilities of men and women, but is a constant torture to all finer natures; and persons at all gifted with clairvoyant perceptions find the influences surrounding women during the period under notice particularly distressing."[31] Menstrual blood, steeped in earthly materiality, was so incompatible with the spiritual plane that its presence interfered with, or perhaps even distorted, clairvoyant sensibilities. As is always the case, such blood taboos functioned to restrict the range of female action. The threshold that she crossed when she touched Chatterji, then, was less about sexual temptation and more about her refusal to stay within the boundaries prescribed by the Masters for female behavior. Additionally, the Mahatma letters revealed how language was used as a tool to make invisible, and thus to control, female sexuality. They addressed Holloway-Langford as "child" and as "babe." If the spiritually undeveloped chela corresponded to the physically immature girl-child, the problem of mature sexuality could be skirted—at least on a metaphorical level. It is not clear whether Holloway-Langford realized that the religious prohibitions regulating contact with a menstruating woman implied that the only way a woman could overcome her inherent disability was to shuck off the body itself. In *Man* she had faulted all the "modern religions" for requiring that a woman "must unsex herself before she can enter the kingdom of heaven."[32] But the solution she proffered was little different: men and women in their more evolved state would be equally "unsexed." The case of Laura Holloway-Langford as a disciple in collaboration with Mohini Chatterji raised the question of whether, at this stage in the Theosophical movement, any woman, except Blavatsky herself, could hope to be granted equal status as a "regular chela."[33]

Laura Holloway-Langford had offered her talents to the Theosophical Society with the understanding that the ideal of universal brotherhood, despite the gendered language, fully included women. She had looked to Helena Blavatsky as a model for overcoming the limitations imposed by Victorian notions of the woman's sphere. If, as Helen Sword has argued, spiritualism offered women like Holloway-Langford an opportunity for "gender bending ventriloquism," then Holloway-Langford certainly believed that Theosophy would provide even greater freedom for women to pursue an occult career.[34] In New York, Holloway-Langford had been active in efforts to eradicate harmful ideas about the female body and to provide sex education for young women.[35] Yet within a short time after arrival in England, she had been confronted by ancient sexual taboos that to her mind were evidence of an inferior religious understanding.

A BOOK THAT CAN "LOWER THE MASTERS"

The sheer audaciousness of the undertaking in *Man* is remarkable. The usual pattern in such works was for an Eastern seer to transmit knowledge mediated through the pen of the Western writer—the model Sinnett had followed in his books. In this experiment, however, two flesh-and-blood writers, of different sexes, different religions, and different cultures—not to mention different temperaments—were expected to narrate the evolutionary history of the race—biological, cultural, linguistic, and religious—and to synthesize the essence of knowledge into a single perspective and voice. If it had succeeded, the book would have made an argument for the unity of all knowledge; it would have demonstrated that it was truly possible for humans to transcend their locations in time, history, and culture. In other words, it would have validated the claims of theosophy. Unfortunately, the two chelas, Laura Holloway-Langford and Mohini Mohun Chatterji, did not succeed in this grand plan.

At first, Blavatsky had high hopes for the book. Despite her later claims to the contrary, she and Olcott, through the Masters, corrected and approved the version that went to the publisher in late 1884. While in Elberfeld, Germany, in August 1884, Holloway-Langford received instructions from Koot Hoomi about how to make final revisions on the book. She, Chatterji, and Henry S. Olcott were to take turns reading it aloud to Blavatsky, who was sick. The Master Morya and Djual Khool would be present, and if corrections were needed, they would communicate them to Blavatsky. Koot Hoomi praised Holloway-Langford, apparently encouraging her to remain in Europe or travel to India in the service of the Theosophical Society: "You have done good work, child. I am satisfied. Be strong; do not think of home; all is well that ends well. Trust to the future and be hopeful."[36] About the same time, he informed Olcott that the Masters were "satisfied with [Holloway-Langford's] book, her first attempt at expounding occult doctrine. Be kind and brotherly to her always. She is honest, candid, noble-minded and full of zeal."[37]

It was not long, however, before Blavatsky sent A. P. Sinnett a message from Koot Hoomi that attempted to repair her relationship with him by disparaging the book:

> I had to leave [Holloway-Langford] under her self-delusion that this new book was written with the view of 'correcting the mistakes' of *Esoteric Buddhism* (—*of killing it*—was the true thought); and it was only on the eve of her departure that Upasika [Blavatsky] was ordered to see that Mohini should carefully expunge from it all the objectionable passages. During her stay in England Mrs. H. would have never permitted you to see her book before the final publication. But I would save five months labour of Mohini and will not permit it to remain unpublished.[38]

In the hope that Sinnett would be willing to revise the book for its second edition, Blavatsky sent him a long list of corrections, which, however, Sinnett did not make.

In November 1885, Blavatsky wrote a letter addressed "To the Theosophists," where she claimed there was "*a mystery* connected with the writing and publication of MAN which I am not at liberty to make public in all its details." She went on to explain that the book was written by two chelas; the Eastern Chela was a "pucka disciple," that is a genuine chela, and the other was a "Western Chela—a candidate who failed." She had left the manuscript "in a chaotic half-finished condition and went away from London, leaving the 'Eastern Chela' in a very perplexed state. Those who had ordered the book to be written *to try the psychical developments of Chela* and *Candidate*—would have nothing more to say about it. . . . In the *Secret Doctrine,* all the errors and misconceptions shall be explained away and corrected, I hope."[39]

By December Blavatsky had received a letter from Gerald B. Finch, President of the London Lodge, in which he said that *Man: Fragments of Forgotten History* was a work which "can only lower the Masters." Blavatsky wrote Sinnett, claiming that even Chatterji confessed that the book was *"good for nothing."* She judged that four chapters written entirely by Chatterji were good, but that the parts written by Holloway-Langford, where "the spring of inspiration has let loose its waters," were "rough, unsystematic," and "like a meaningless jibbering of a schoolboy." Though mandating that Mohini must revise those sections where "his *collaborator* gave original ideas," the Masters had told Blavatsky that the book must be published before Christmas. Blavatsky encouraged Sinnett to talk to Chatterji: *"He* will tell you HOW it was written for he is now free to speak." In this letter, Blavatsky attempted to placate Sinnett, who had been angered by the idea that *Man* corrected errors in his own books. At the same time, she sought to undercut his admiration for Laura Holloway-Langford, whose "probation," Blavatsky declared, was now finished.[40]

In later years, Blavatsky tried to distance herself even further from *Man,* disclaiming any direct involvement in its composition. In 1887, in *The Theosophist,* she asked: "What had I to do with the 'states of consciousness' of the . . . authors?"[41] Yet she could hardly disavow the book completely, since it had been written under her supervision. In fact, the failure was more Blavatsky's than it was Holloway-Langford's. Blavatsky had tried an experiment in using the expertise of a student of Eastern religion and a professional journalist to produce Theosophical texts. Perhaps if Chatterji had been allowed to write alone, the book would have had metaphysical coherence. If the task had been left up to Holloway-Langford, the book would have resembled a novel, a narrative about spirit guides leading the "soul" or the "pupil" to occult knowledge. The result, however, was a confusing hodgepodge of genre and perspective. Blavatsky's anger at Holloway-Langford was spurred by the realization that it was up to her to produce the definitive statement of the Theosophical movement. Others might help, they might verify references, organize the material, and edit the work: but she must be the one to produce the text. It was a burden that she did not welcome, but composing *The Secret Doctrine* became the major task for her remaining years.

FIGURE 1

Laura C. Holloway-Langford. Portrait by G. Frank E. Pearsall,
Brooklyn, was probably taken when she was in her thirties.
Courtesy, Women of Protest: Photographs from the Records
of the National Woman's Party, Manuscript Division,
Library of Congress, Washington, D.C.

FIGURE 2. ABOVE

Helena Petrovna Blavatsky
with Fan, London, 1884. Courtesy, The Winterthur Library:
The Edward Deming Andrews
Memorial Shaker Collection.

FIGURE 3. RIGHT

Eldress Anna White, North
Family Shakers, Mount Leba-
non, New York . Courtesy,
The Winterthur Library: The
Edward Deming Andrews
Memorial Shaker Collection.

FIGURE 4

William Quan Judge and Henry Steel Olcott, pictured in a
photograph owned by Laura Holloway-Langford. Courtesy,
The Winterthur Library: The Edward Deming Andrews
Memorial Shaker Collection.

FIGURE 5

Mohini Mohun Chatterji. Photograph taken in London, 1884.
Courtesy, The Theosophical Society in America Archives.

FIGURE 6

Portrait of Koot Hoomi painted by Hermann Schmiechen,
London, July 1884, from the clairvoyant description
given by Laura Holloway-Langford. Courtesy,
The Blavatsky Archives Online.

7

The Lady Mrs. X

During 1884, Helena Blavatsky came under increasing scrutiny from both those who wished to prove the reality of psychic power and skeptics who doubted her claims. By late that summer, she decided that it would be prudent to avoid transmitting letters from the Masters. Yet the Adept Brotherhood was not ready to forego all communication with disciples. In a letter, probably written to Francesca Arundale, Master Morya puzzled over how "Esoteric Teachings" might be conveyed to A. P. Sinnett, who had been the "chosen correspondent." The obvious channel was Mohini Chatterji, but Morya judged that he had "not reached that stage of physiological development that enables a chela to send and receive letters. His evolution has been more upon the intellectual plane." Additionally, he predicted that Chatterji would succumb to the "seductive influences" of the Western world, destroying his inspiration and resulting in his failure as a chela. But, said Morya, there was someone else who might take Blavatsky's place, and "if given such powers," this person would "conceal it to the last."[1]

Master Morya apparently referred to Laura Holloway-Langford, whom Blavatsky had decided to try as a mediator for occult communications. Holloway-Langford was acknowledged to be clairvoyant, and she proclaimed her willingness to sacrifice for the movement. Even though she was not so advanced in her chelaship as Chatterji, she possessed important advantages. She was socially adroit, moving easily among the better classes in British society. She could be counted upon not to make a fool of herself in the way that Henry Steel Olcott had done. Long skilled in keeping secrets, she knew how to be discreet. Additionally, while Europeans tended to view Indian "natives" as irrational and untrustworthy, they assumed that she was a person of honor and integrity. It is impossible to know how deeply Laura Holloway-Langford was involved in the production of occult phenomena, but the evidence strongly suggests that for a short time she was privy to some of its mysteries.

MRS. X TESTIFIES

Laura Holloway-Langford proved her usefulness to the Theosophical Society when she testified before a committee of the Society for Psychical Research. The presence of Blavatsky, Olcott, and their Indian followers in England presented an opportunity for the Society for Psychical Research to interrogate Theosophists who claimed to have seen the Mahatmas. In December 1884, a "Private and Confidential" document was sent to Society members and associates. It contained forty-two appendices with the texts of the interviews that had taken place the previous summer and fall. Among those interviewed was Laura Holloway-Langford, who was designated "the lady hereafter styled Mrs. X."[2] Not only did Holloway-Langford request that the committee disguise her identity, but she also asked that her testimony not be made public. The committee honored this request, and her statements were omitted from the report that Richard Hodgson made to the S. P. R. in 1885.[3] As a respectable "lady," Holloway-Langford was granted the privilege of privacy accorded few Theosophists.

Even though unpublished, her testimony supporting the existence of the Adept Brotherhood was important, because members of the Society for Psychical Research deemed it more credible than that of either A. P. Sinnett or Mohini Chatterji. Sinnett's experiences with the Masters were attributed to "an accidental hallucination" caused by an "abnormal state of mind."[4] Chatterji's testimony was also judged worthless, even though in England he had become the spokesperson for all things Hindu. As an Indian, he was considered gullible and easy to deceive. Humiliated and angered by the report, Chatterji later crafted a rebuttal, stating that neither the Mahatmas, nor occult phenomena, nor even Blavatsky herself was central to theosophy.[5] In contrast to the other witnesses, Holloway-Langford was considered "an exceptionally conscientious, accurate, and trustworthy informant," who had not been contaminated by "oriental superstition."

The report details Laura Holloway-Langford's description of a Tibetan Master who had appeared in Brooklyn and instructed her in occult teachings. She stated that he had directed her to travel to Europe and offer herself to Blavatsky as a student. The confidential report continued:

> She reports herself to have distinctly and repeatedly seen Koot Hoomi in "astral body," in a country distant from India, before she had even seen his picture (which she subsequently recognised), and without discovering who he was; that she acted on communications made to her in these interviews; and that these communications were afterwards confirmed by letters in the Koot Hoomi handwriting, addressed not only to Madame Blavatsky and others, but to Mrs. X. herself, under such conditions that no other person, as she maintains, could possibly have had a hand in them.

The committee concluded that Holloway-Langford had seen Koot Hoomi in dreams. Nevertheless, it judged her testimony to his existence reliable in the "First Degree," because she had "no previous inclination to mysticism, nor acquaintance with Eastern modes of thought." Additionally, she had been directed to Theosophy by phenomena before she had met Blavatsky. The report recounted Holloway-Langford's description of how Koot Hoomi had transmitted a letter to her at the Arundale home in London: "Mrs. X. saw a red mark growing between her pillow-case and the pillow, shortly after she had risen, and before anyone had entered the room. This turned out to be a letter in the K. H. handwriting."[6]

Holloway-Langford later described the incident in detail. She wrote that at the Arundale home, her bedroom adjoined Blavatsky's, but without a connecting door:

> While dressing in my room, I had a sudden sense of an electric signal; something unexpectedly shocked me, and I put down the hair brush I held in my hand and turned toward the door. No one had knocked, yet I was in a state of expectancy and felt that either I should see someone, or hear something. . . . Suddenly an impulse moved me to go to the side of the bed. . . . I lifted the small pillow which I had used, and under it lay a sealed envelope, addressed to me. . . . Had it been there all night? I do not know, but

I think not. . . . I knew, however, that it was the work of a Great and Living Soul, who . . . had given me and others through me, this signal proof of his desire to help us in our effort to learn the spiritual side of nature, and to understand the laws governing it.[7]

The "Private and Confidential" report of the S. P. R. contained an additional reference to Laura Holloway-Langford's experience, noting that in August 1884 she had accompanied Helena Blavatsky, Mohini Chatterji, and Francesca Arundale to Cambridge. Blavatsky had been invited there to testify about the existence of the Mahatmas. According to Marion Meade: "At her meetings with the Society for Psychical Research [Blavatsky] went out of her way to be helpful, declining to perform phenomena, she disarmed her interrogators by stating that the Society's purpose was to promulgate religious doctrines, not to prove she possessed supernormal powers."[8]

Holloway-Langford later offered her own account of the visit to Cambridge. She claimed that despite the fact that Blavatsky had made a good impression on the committee, she had a premonition about what was to unfold. When Holloway-Langford remarked that Blavatsky had received a "'most kind welcome from delightful people,'" Blavatsky replied, "'You Americans are always ready with pretty speeches.' She then added sadly, 'but the Karma of the Theosophical Society cannot be changed by any display of psychic powers on my part. I am here to select the instrument through which the society is to suffer. . . . Hodgson will be the man the S. P. R. will select to go to India.'"[9] Of course, when Holloway-Langford wrote this account in 1888, Richard Hodgson had already published his report labeling Blavatsky a fraud. In her retrospective depiction, however, Holloway-Langford turned Blavatsky into a Christ-like figure who, in full knowledge of the future, accepted martyrdom for the sake of occult truth.

In his testimony before the Society for Psychical Research, the prominent British Theosophist Bertram Keightley recounted another incident that occurred on the visit to Cambridge, which Holloway-Langford did not relate to the committee. He stated that on Sunday evening, August 10, "we were sitting around the table having just finished tea, when a note fell bearing the initials of Mahatma K. H. The note was found under Mrs. X.'s chair, near whom it fell and whom it especially concerned." Holloway-Langford and Chatterji said that they had seen something fall, and Keightley testified that he then saw a note on the floor, which Chatterji picked up. It read: "You came together—why should you separate before you are all ready. You are all wanted here for a purpose." It was signed by the Master Koot Hoomi and was written in his hand. Keightley declared that although Holloway-Langford had planned to leave the next day, in response to the note, she decided to remain in Cambridge.[10] Mundane messages, such as these, were not uncommon. In this case, however, Chatterji and Holloway-Langford apparently cooperated in the transmission of a letter in order to support her desire not to return to London ahead of Blavatsky.

THE MASTERS' POST OFFICE

In the weeks previous to the visit to Cambridge, Holloway-Langford had begun to communicate directly with the Masters. During July 1884, the home of Francesca Arundale, where Laura Holloway-Langford, Mohini Chatterji, and Helena Blavatsky were living, became the central post office for this correspondence. In her memoir, Arundale stated that outgoing mail to the Masters was placed in a particular drawer in Blavatsky's room, but incoming letters were received in many ways. Once, Arundale discovered a Koot Hoomi letter addressed to Sinnett on the top of a box. Another time she recalled leaving a letter in her pocket, having neglected to put it in the "usual drawer." Nevertheless, Blavatsky handed her an answer to it from Koot Hoomi.[11]

Holloway-Langford published two accounts of how she, in defiance of Blavatsky, initiated contact with Koot Hoomi. Neither narrative is reliable as history: dates are confused, separate incidents are conflated, and dialogue has been imaginatively recreated. Even so, these recollections reveal Holloway-Langford's self-perception of her relationship with the Masters. The first version, written in 1888, recounts how Holloway-Langford boldly approached Blavatsky demanding that she convey a letter to Koot Hoomi. Blavatsky was infuriated at her audacity, but impressed by her progress as a disciple. Holloway-Langford recalled:

> She railed at me, flew into a rage, demanded to know by what right I intruded upon her and ordered her to send letters to the Mahatmas. When she had concluded I quietly asked her to send it, adding that it was

important."Nothing that concerns the emotions of people is important," she retorted. "You all think that if you make a prayer it must have an immediate personal response from Jehovah. I am tired of nonsense." I coolly laid the letter on the table, sat down near to and facing her, and looked at my letter. She opened a drawer of the desk, which I saw was empty, and told me to put it there. I pushed the letter from the table into it and closed it myself. She leaned back in her chair, looked with some interest at me, and remarked that my will was developing. . . . Days after I met Mme. Blavatsky in the hall as she was going out to drive with one of the guests, and she put out her hand for me to assist her down the step. As I took her hand, I smilingly said, "Where's my letter?" She looked at me steadily for a moment, and it suddenly occurred to me, but why I do not know, that it was answered. I ran my hand into the pocket of my dress and there was a letter folded and sealed in a Chinese envelope.[12]

In 1912, Holloway-Langford wrote another article, "The Mahatmas and Their Instruments," in which she stated that the "one wish of [her] life was to be recognized" by receiving a letter from an adept: "Then as now I loved the Masters. . . . And, loving them, it seemed but natural that I should ask for aid, and offer to serve with their permission in the order and on the plane to which I belonged." In this account, Holloway-Langford claimed the Masters chose her as their instrument because of her love for them. At the same time, she portrayed herself as initiating the relationship, asserting that the Masters "could be reached through love. What mattered it that the laws governing the transmission of messages was [sic] not understood? What fear could be felt when affection alone inspired the writer and influenced the agent?"[13]

In the earlier anecdote Blavatsky had disparaged Holloway-Langford's emotional petition as a "prayer," not to the Master but to a Christian God, from whom she expected an "immediate personal response." Indeed, the extant examples of her letters to the Masters suggest that Holloway-Langford did not seek metaphysical knowledge so much as personal advice, consolation, and encouragement. In the quarter century between the two versions of this incident, Holloway-Langford increased her emphasis on her "love" for "the Great Souls." Certainly, any notion of a personal, emotional relationship between a Mahatma and a chela was completely at odds with the Theosophical understanding of the Adept Brotherhood, whose function was to reveal esoteric knowledge, not to give or receive love. Over the years, Holloway-Langford increasingly viewed her occult experiences through the lens of Christian rhetoric and belief, merging her love of the Master Koot Hoomi with love for Christ, thus reinterpreting the Masters of Wisdom in a way that would be acceptable to many Americans. These accounts also reveal the egotism that characterized Holloway-Langford's personality. She possessed an unwavering faith in her spiritual superiority, which she believed entitled her to become the Master's disciple.

KOOT HOOMI'S PORTRAIT

Laura Holloway-Langford's role as a channel for a portrait of Koot Hoomi offers additional evidence that Blavatsky had decided to test her as a mediator for the Masters. Hermann Schmiechen was a German painter living in London who had joined the Theosophical Society. He agreed to take part in a "psychical experiment" to see if images could be transferred to his mind from those who had seen the Masters. Working with a profile of Master Morya provided by Olcott, Schmiechen began to paint his portrait. Olcott visited Schmiechen's studio several times, where he observed "the gradual development of the mental image which had been vividly impressed upon his brain, and which resulted in as perfect a portrait of my Guru as he could have painted from life."[14] Subsequently, Schmiechen was asked to paint the Master Koot Hoomi's portrait. Blavatsky, in a letter from Master Morya, had been told: "Take [Holloway-Langford] with you to Schmiechen & tell her *to see*. . . . Say to S[chmiechen] that he will be helped. I myself will guide his hands with brush for K.'s portrait."[15] This letter confirmed what Holloway-Langford later claimed—that she was the psychic who saw and communicated to Schmiechen the image of Koot Hoomi.

Decades later, she recounted sitting with Patience Sinnett on the platform where Schmiechen worked. Blavatsky, who sat facing them, ordered Holloway-Langford to smoke a cigarette. Although never having smoked and fearing it would make her ill, she took the cigarette and discovered that it produced "a curious quieting of nerves." She lost all sense of other people in the room as she focused on the easel. Quite likely Blavatsky had given Holloway-Langford something more than tobacco, possibly hashish, which enhanced her ability to "see" the Master.[16] When Holloway-Langford uttered in German "beginnen," Schmiechen quickly sketched a head.[17] Holloway-Langford then saw Koot Hoomi standing motionless beside the artist. Blavatsky called out to her, "Describe his looks and dress." Holloway-Langford compiled:

> He is about Mohini's height; slight of build; wonderful face full of light and animation; flowing curly black hair, over which is worn a soft cap. He is a symphony in greys and blues. His dress is that of a Hindu—though it is far finer and richer than any I have ever seen before—and there is fur trimming about his costume. It is his picture that is being made, and he himself is guiding the work.

While Schmiechen painted, Mohini Chatterji had been quietly pacing the floor at the rear of the apartment. Observing him, Holloway-Langford noted "a similarity of form between the psychic figure of the Master" and Chatterji, as well as "a striking resemblance in their manner." When she noted this likeness to Patience Sinnett, Chatterji looked at her with alarm. At that point, the Master caught her eye and "conveyed to her mind the conviction that her discovery was a genuine fact." From this time on, Holloway-Langford believed that the chela Mohini Chatterji was even more "closely related" to the Mahatma Koot Hoomi than was Blavatsky herself. "No sooner was this conviction born in her mind than she encountered a swift glance of recognition from the shadow form beside the easel, the first and only one he gave to anyone during the long sitting."[18] Not only did Holloway-Langford declare that she saw the astral form of Koot Hoomi, but she also implied that it had been projected into the physical body of Mohini Chatterji, who, in effect, had become the Master's double.[19]

Through Laura Holloway-Langford's mediation, Hermann Schmiechen produced a portrait of Koot Hoomi that bore a remarkable likeness not so much to Mohini Chatterji as to nineteenth-century images of Jesus. Perhaps influenced by the German artist Heinrich Hofmann, Schmiechen painted Koot Hoomi as a bearded European with long wavy hair and a serene expression. In 1932, the Theosophist Brian Ross produced a similar sketch of the Master Koot Hoomi. Ross's drawing, however, bears an uncanny resemblance to a later, 1941 painting by Warner E. Sallman, whose "Head of Christ" is "one of the most familiar pictures of Jesus of all times."[20] Most Christians today would be shocked to learn of the link between Koot Hoomi and this familiar image of Jesus, but followers of the Ascended Masters would not be surprised. They continue to conflate both the wisdom of Koot Hoomi and of Jesus—identifying them as the two "World Teachers"—and their visual representations. Thus, contemporary New Age artists depict Koot Hoomi as a blond, blue-eyed Jesus.[21]

PHENOMENA AT ELBERFELD, GERMANY

Laura Holloway-Langford's final test as a probationary chela occurred in Elberfeld, Germany, while visiting Gustav and Mary Gebhard. Mary Gebhard had been a student of the renowned Kabbalist Eliphas Lévi. She had established an "Occult Room" in her home where friends could pursue esoteric interests.[22] In August 1884, Helena Blavatsky, Mohini Chatterji, Bertram Keightley, and the Arundales planned a holiday in Elberfeld and invited Laura Holloway-Langford to join them. She, however, had made arrangements to travel on the continent with the Sinnetts. Koot Hoomi was adamantly opposed to this idea. He instructed Blavatsky to tell Holloway-Langford: "If she goes with the Sinnetts . . . or follows them out of England or stops with them she is lost."[23] Still, Holloway-Langford was obdurate, insisting that it would be impolite to refuse the Sinnetts' invitation. At this point, Koot Hoomi contacted her directly, without Blavatsky as intermediary. On a note delivered by the postman, he wrote in blue pencil: "Why must you be so faint hearted in the performance of your duty. Friendship, personal feelings and gratitude are no doubt fine noble feelings but duty alone leads to the *development* you so crave for. *Try to show them* the truth for the last time. I *desire* you to go to Elberfeld. I desire you to change Magnetisms as little as you can. Private K. H."[24] Nevertheless, Holloway-Langford refused to accept responsibility for this change in plans. She demanded that Koot Hoomi provide an explanation to the Sinnetts. On that point Koot Hoomi relented, but he warned her to forego "feeble controversies: either you desire further development under our guidance, or you do not. If the former you cannot meet Mr. Sinnett for some time—not till next year probably. . . . Your actions will determine whether this will be *the last letter* of instruction you will receive from me or not."[25]

In effect, Laura Holloway-Langford had gained the upper hand with Koot Hoomi. In exchange for agreeing to go to Elberfeld, she forced him to acknowledge that she acted only in response to his command. Needing her cooperation, Koot Hoomi declared that Holloway-Langford was to be left "strictly alone." He wrote Blavatsky: "Whether she goes, or remains, her subsequent fate is in her own hands.... I said to her, 'Try' & shall say no more." But he also praised "her richly gifted nature," and attempted to shame Holloway-Langford into compliance: "You may tell her this—that for one so emphatically determined in some of her moods; one who asserted so often that she was ready at a moment's notice to go to Tibet in search of me, saying 'Here I am—will you teach me Master?' ... she acts with remarkable inconsistency." He then implored Blavatsky to "be kind and gentle with her.... She suffers, and patience was never a word for her. ... Poor weak nature. Loving, good, truthful & honest to all but to herself." Holloway-Langford and Koot Hoomi were playing a cat-and-mouse game, each trying to outmaneuver the other. When Holloway-Langford protested that he had no authority over her because she was not a chela, Koot Hoomi retorted that she had pledged her loyalty to him "unconsciously & when out of the body."[26] Koot Hoomi had regained the advantage, since Holloway-Langford could not counter this assertion without doubting the Master's claim to supernatural knowledge.

While the Sinnetts set off for Switzerland, Holloway-Langford accompanied Blavatsky's band to Elberfeld.[27] During her seven weeks in Germany, Holloway-Langford became more deeply implicated in the transmission of letters from the Masters. On the evening of August 25, Gustav Gebhard's birthday was celebrated in grand style. When the Gebhard family and its guests had assembled in the drawing room, Blavatsky announced that she "felt the presence of the Masters," who wanted "to do something." The group requested that they deliver a letter to Gustav Gebhard "on a subject on which he should mentally decide himself." Blavatsky then exclaimed that she had seen a ray of light shooting in the direction of a large oil painting. "This statement was immediately corroborated by Mrs. H—.... Mme. B. then required Mrs. H— to see and say what was going on, when Mrs. H—said that she saw something forming over the picture." After searching unsuccessfully for the letter, Rudolf Gebhard finally saw it drop from behind the picture onto the piano. The letter, addressed to Consul G. Gebhard, complimented his growing sympathy for Theosophy in flowery and obsequious language, and it reassured him about a son who was in America, which was the information Gebhard had mentally requested.[28]

Despite her part in these phenomena, Holloway-Langford was disgruntled that her own birthday, on August 22, had been ignored. She received a long letter from Koot Hoomi chiding her for wishing to be noticed. He wrote:

> To the profane a birthday is but a twelvemonth-stride toward the grave. When each new year marks for you a step of evolution all will be ready with their congratulations; there will be something real to felicitate you upon. But, so far, you are not even one year old—& you would be treated as an adult! Try to learn to stand *firm* on your legs, child, before you venture walking. It is because you are so young & ignorant in the ways of occult life—that you are so easily forgiven. But you have to amend your ways and put L. C. H. and her caprices and whims far in the back-ground before the expiration of the *first year* of your life as a chela if you would see the dawn of the second year.[29]

The letter infantilized Holloway-Langford, linking her concerns with childish "caprices and whims," words that suggested feminine weakness. At the same time, it confirmed that the Master considered Holloway-Langford a "chela." He warned her, however, that she must continue to resist the influence of A. P. Sinnett, and she must "wage battle" against old friends like Oliver Otis Howard, who was also visiting at Elberfeld and who might tempt her to once again act as a medium.

CONDUIT FOR THE MASTER'S LETTERS

On September 10, 1884, Blavatsky learned about an article published in the *Madras Christian College Magazine,* alleging that the Koot Hoomi letters were fraudulent. In response, she resigned as Corresponding Secretary of the Theosophical Society.[30] She knew that in the looming crisis of credibility, A. P. Sinnett, whose books had publicized the Mahatmas in the West, would be assailed by her critics. For his part, Sinnett was disgruntled, both with Koot Hoomi, who had interfered with his holiday with Holloway-Langford, and with "The Old Lady," as he called Blavatsky, who had persuaded Mary Gebhard not to invite him to Elberfeld.[31] Sinnett had grown tired of conforming in exchange for the promise of future communications from the Masters. Fearing that he might not remain loyal, Koot Hoomi wrote Holloway-Langford: "Better send for Mr. and Mrs. Sinnett as soon as you can. A general consultation is necessary. His [Sinnett's] own reputation is at stake. I will make his visit harmless. He is a changed man."[32] Holloway-Langford immediately sent a telegram to the Sinnetts, inviting them to join the Theosophists gathered at Elberfeld. It was Blavatsky's reputation, however, that was at risk, and Sinnett was being summoned to rally in her defense.

In the previous months, Sinnett had received only three letters from Koot Hoomi. The first had excoriated him for his racial and cultural prejudices. A second letter had been more conciliatory, suggesting that he and Holloway-Langford had been separated not because they were suspected of inappropriate behavior, but because their psychic development required it. In a third message, the Master had rejected Sinnett's request to publish more Mahatma material, and he contradicted Sinnett's description of Holloway-Langford as a "pleasant companion," asserting that she was "showing her white teeth."[33] Not long after he arrived at Elberfeld, Sinnett received a long letter from Koot Hoomi that was written "on four small folded sheets of L. C. Holloway note paper." The envelope was addressed to "A. P. Sinnett, Esq., c/ of L. C. H." and was conveyed to him by Holloway-Langford.[34] Sinnett recalled:

> A curious situation had developed, though I never could understand it fully. Madame Blavatsky . . . must have somehow got into disgrace with the higher powers, for the Masters sent communications over her head, without her knowledge, through Mrs. Holloway, whose psychic condition enabled them to deal with her in this way. A letter for me quite without Madame Blavatsky's knowledge had come this way, and it showed that I was definitely wanted, though it failed to clear up the situation fully.[35]

Blavatsky knew that Sinnett doubted the authenticity of any communication that she transmitted. Consequently, she had entrusted Holloway-Langford with the task of conveying the letter to Sinnett, tricking him into believing that she had no part in the transaction and that the Master had chosen a new instrument, Laura Holloway-Langford, to transmit his messages.

In this letter, Koot Hoomi warned Sinnett that "the air is full of the pestilence of treachery; unmerited opprobrium is showering upon the Society," and that the conspirators' arrows were aimed at him. They would, said the Master, try to shake his confidence "with pretended letters alleged to have come from H. P. B.'s laboratory." Koot Hoomi blamed Sinnett for publishing letters that should have "been limited to an inner and very SECRET circle." In order to prepare Sinnett to respond to investigators, the Master rehashed old controversies, explaining how he inadvertently had transmitted words to Sinnett that had resulted in a plagiarism charge. The conflict over Holloway-Langford, Koot Hoomi now claimed, was not due to Sinnett himself, but to a "colony of Elementaries" who quartered in his house. The letter instructed him to purify the house by burning wood fires and incense sticks, and forbidding "mediumistic sensitives" on the premises. Sinnett was also given "talismans" to ward off evil spirits. Then, most curiously, the letter asserted that there were "two distinct personages" answering to the name Koot Hoomi. Mistakes and inconsistencies in the communications, the letter implied, were the fault of another, false, Koot Hoomi, whom Sinnett had failed to distinguish from the true Mahatma. The letter alternated between flattery—Sinnett was addressed as one of "the great and prominent heads of the movement"—and threat: if he did not stay in London as Koot Hoomi's "mouthpiece and secretary in the *Circle*" the Master would "have positively *no time* to correspond" with him. Underlying the letter was a fear that Sinnett, too, might renege on his support for the Mahatmas, particularly since the events of the summer had aroused his suspicions about spurious messages from the Masters.[36]

In response to this letter, Sinnett demanded that Laura Holloway-Langford send his reply to Koot Hoomi. She declined, telling him to give it to Blavatsky himself. Koot Hoomi then intervened, writing the following letter to Holloway-Langford, which she was to "show to no one":

> You are very wrong in making such answer to A. P. Sinnett. Mix no more her [Blavatsky's] name with phenomena if you would not injure her.

> If S. gives you a letter addressed to me take it in silence and place it under the cloth on the spot . . . without attracting to this H. P. B.'s attention.

> I want from you *silence* and no more. I will try during the day to have his letter taken and send an answer. I will write to you in London. But Sinnett

must *never know* that I do not correspond direct with you. Silence will do it. I want to protect H. P. B. and would not have you say an untruth.[37]

Koot Hoomi wanted to guarantee that if A. P. Sinnett were approached by the Society for Psychical Research, he would testify that Holloway-Langford, not Blavatsky, had been involved in the transmission of Mahatma letters at Elberfeld. Holloway-Langford, however, refused to be the go-between. Instead of placing Sinnett's letter "on the spot under the cloth" as she had been ordered to do by the Master, she gave it directly to Blavatsky, saying that she "preferred not to be mixed up with Mr. S's correspondence."[38] If Blavatsky was testing Holloway-Langford to see if she might serve as the mediator for communications, she had failed the trial.

LEAVE-TAKINGS

Shortly after the Sinnetts reached Elberfeld, Blavatsky left, with Laura Holloway-Langford in tow. They arrived in London on the 6th of October. A. P. and Patience Sinnett soon followed. If the Koot Hoomi letters in early October 1884 were intended to force Sinnett to defend Blavatsky from accusations of fraud, the strategy had backfired. Sinnett wrote Koot Hoomi in Elberfeld, demanding that Holloway-Langford be permitted to spend one final week at his home before she left for New York. Since he believed that her psychic development had increased to the level needed to receive letters directly from the Masters, he wanted a last chance to use her as a medium. Now that Blavatsky was vulnerable, Sinnett thought he could outflank the Masters. He issued an "ultimatum" to Koot Hoomi, that if his request for a visit from Holloway-Langford was not granted, he would not support Blavatsky and the Masters before the London Lodge. The ploy, however, did not work. Shortly after his return to London, Sinnett received a letter by regular mail from Koot Hoomi.[39] The Master explained that "for reasons perfectly valid though not necessary for me to enter into in detail, I could neither answer your letter at Elberfeld, nor transmit it to you through L.C.H. Since it has become impossible to utilize the main channel—H.P.B. thro' which I have hitherto reached you . . . I employed the common post."

Koot Hoomi then upbraided Sinnett, whom he accused of possessing "an uncharitable spirit." He was told to broaden rather than narrow his sympathies: "Try to identify yourself with your fellows, rather than to contract your circle of affinity. However caused—whether by faults at Adyar, or Allahabad, or by my negligence, or H. P. B.'s viciousness—a crisis is here, and it is a time for the utmost practicable expansion of your moral power." Sinnett was told that because he had written books that revealed "treasures" of occult knowledge, he had been noticed by the guardians of the occult, who would test him. "Remember that my Brother and I, are the only among the Brotherhood who have at heart the dissemination (to a certain limit) of our doctrines, and H. P. B. was hitherto our sole machinery, our most docile agent." Koot Hoomi reminded Sinnett that he had told him that "were H. P. B to die before we found a substitute," the power would vanish with her. If Blavatsky now died, the Master asserted, Sinnett would be "the one who killed the rude but faithful agent," because his books and the Holloway-Langford affair had led outsiders to suspect her. Koot Hoomi claimed that he had control neither over Blavatsky nor over Holloway-Langford, who "is far, far from being ready; moreover she understands neither herself nor us. Verily *our* ways are not *your* ways, hence there remains but little hope for us in the West." He continued: "My friend, this is treading upon dangerous ground. . . . Friend, beware of Pride and Egoism, two of the worst snares for the feet of him who aspires to climb the high paths of Knowledge and Spirituality. You have opened a joint of your armour for the Dugpas—do not complain if they have found it out and wounded you there."[40]

Meanwhile, Laura Holloway-Langford chose loyalty to the Master over her friendship with A. P. Sinnett, whom she did not see again. With Blavatsky's encouragement, she made plans to return home. She wrote her "Beloved & Revered Master" that she had completed the task assigned to her, having submitted *Man: Fragments of Forgotten History* for publication in London. She sought his permission to sail for New York. Additionally, she asked his blessing for her to continue work on a book about Helena Blavatsky. In blue pencil, this request was marked "approved." Holloway-Langford also solicited the Master's consent for her to write a Theosophical novel and to maintain literary collaboration with Mohini Chatterji. Koot Hoomi noted: "Perhaps." She went so far as to suggest

how Blavatsky's reputation could be defended against the Coulomb accusations and the investigations of the Society for Psychical Research,
writing that members of the Theosophical Society should be asked to sign
a card expressing their faith in Blavatsky, for publication in the *London
Times* and in *Light,* the journal of the London Spiritualist Alliance. She
further recommended the formation of "a *secret occult society*" consisting "exclusively of those who possess either psychic or literary powers &
who put implicit faith in the Masters." If possible, its members would be
celibate. She advised that initially this society would consist of herself,
Mohini Chatterji, and Mary Gebhard, with Helena Blavatsky serving as
an ex-officio member.[41]

Despite the upheavals of the past months, Holloway-Langford did not
doubt her clairvoyant gifts, believing that she, along with Chatterji and
Mary Gebhard, was a chela who had been initiated into esoteric knowledge not available to ordinary Theosophists. Whether Holloway-Langford
consciously proposed a society composed only of women and a man of
non-European descent is unknown. At some level, however, she may have
realized that as long as the Theosophical Society was dominated by men,
the roles permitted women would be limited. She also recognized that
Chatterji was likewise an outsider, and one who was not considered fully
a man by European Theosophists. Koot Hoomi, however, did not consent
to the formation of a separate group, commenting in blue pencil "Society
useless."[42]

Holloway-Langford's final request in her last letter to Koot Hoomi
was that she be allowed to carry on correspondence with him through
Blavatsky, "who has kindly consented to help me in so doing." Just a few
days previously, Blavatsky had declared she would have nothing more to
do with sending letters to the Masters. Nevertheless, the Master replied,
"Yes, occasionally," adding the following condition:

> Courage & fidelity, truthfulness & sincerity always win our regard. Keep
> on child, as you have been doing. Fight for the persecuted and the wronged,
> those who thro' self sacrifice have made themselves *helpless.* Whether in
> Europe or China I will correspond with you thro' her—but not unless you
> keep to yourself faithfully the secret. You may show the letters but *never re-
> veal* the way they come to you. You will have to pledge yourself solemnly to
> that effect before I begin. Blessings on you child & keep off shells. K. H.[43]

Holloway-Langford knew how the Master's letters were transmitted. She had also gained the respect of members of the Society for Psychical Research. Blavatsky and Koot Hoomi feared that once outside their orbit of influence she might reveal embarrassing information. The Master's power over Laura Holloway-Langford depended on her willingness to acknowledge his authority as a source of esoteric knowledge. Still desiring to learn the laws governing the universe, she accepted a truce with Koot Hoomi. In exchange for future communications from him, she agreed to be silent about her knowledge of occult phenomena.

For a short time, Blavatsky had contemplated letting Holloway-Langford replace her as the conduit for communications from the Masters. She had allowed her to participate in the production of some minor phenomena. Holloway-Langford, however, had balked when instructed to act as the Master's post-mistress for letters to and from A. P. Sinnett. If she had accepted this task without questioning its methods or purposes, Laura Holloway-Langford might have found, at least in the short run, the occultist career she had sought when she came to Europe.

On some level, Blavatsky feared Holloway-Langford. She was not, as some observers suggested, jealous of her psychic powers. Rather, Blavatsky knew that while Holloway-Langford might appear malleable, she was crafty, always working to skew opinion and events in her own favor. Additionally, she was obstinate and self-righteous. In some respects, she resembled Helena Blavatsky: both were experts in manipulating others to their own advantage. Notorious for her scathing remarks about other women, most of whom she considered silly fools, Blavatsky never doubted that Laura Holloway-Langford was a woman of ability and determination. Yet Holloway-Langford lacked Blavatsky's daring, her disregard of bourgeois manners, and her willingness to cross cultural and social boundaries. Most significantly, however, Holloway-Langford did not possess Blavatsky's intellectual depth or imagination.

Nevertheless, Laura Holloway-Langford had demonstrated remarkable mettle in dealing with Blavatsky and the Masters. She had refused to channel the ideas of others without offering her own contributions. She had not hesitated to suggest how the Theosophical Society might be better organized or what face it should present to the public. Shaped by the confidence of Protestant America, she was an independent woman who, despite the assaults on her character during 1884, retained a belief in her cultural superiority. Concluding that she would always put her own interests ahead of those of the Theosophical Society, Blavatsky decided that Holloway-Langford would be much less likely to cause trouble in the United States than in Europe or India. It was a relief to her when Holloway-Langford left England on October 18, 1884. Her departure, however, was one more signal that the heyday of occult communication was coming to an end. A cloud hung not only over the head of Laura Holloway-Langford for her failure as a chela, but also over Blavatsky and the future of the Theosophical Society.

8

Disseminating New Ideas

Laura Holloway-Langford, William Quan Judge, and Mohini Mohun Chatterji each left their homelands expecting new lives as Theosophists. In their efforts to negotiate the volatile terrain of a movement marked by internal dissent and outside opposition, they faced disappointments—in themselves, in Helena Blavatsky, and in the Theosophical Society. Nevertheless, each of them contributed to the spread of theosophical ideas: Holloway-Langford through her writing, Judge as the leader of the American Section of the Society, and Chatterji through a lecture tour in the United States. By the late 1880s, Holloway-Langford and Chatterji had resigned from the Theosophical Society; yet they both remained theosophists in the larger sense of the term, persisting in the search for divine wisdom. Only Judge maintained his commitment to Theosophy as an organized movement, although near the end of his life he too broke away from the parent organization to form an independent group.

Laura Holloway-Langford's foray into the Theosophical movement was a brief but formative experience. In 1884, she had toyed with the idea of joining William Q. Judge in India, where they would become partners, at least spiritually if not also physically, and where they would devote their lives to the pursuit of esoteric knowledge. Blavatsky, however, had concluded that the American psychic caused more trouble than she was worth and had dispatched her back to Brooklyn. Arriving home in late October 1884, Holloway-Langford was demoralized and uncertain about how to continue her spiritual quest without the imprimatur of the Theosophical Society.

Judge's plans had also been thwarted. Within weeks of his arrival in Adyar, India, Emma Coulomb published excerpts from letters that accused Blavatsky of deceit. A few days later Judge removed and burned the "Shrine" from the occult room at the Theosophical Headquarters.[1] Shortly after these events, he decided to depart for home, not waiting until Blavatsky and Olcott returned to India.[2] He left Adyar in late October and, after spending some time in England, arrived in New York on November 26, 1884.

Judge's reasons for leaving India after only three months remain obscure. There were rumors that a German Theosophist, Franz Hartmann, had dropped upon Judge's nose a bogus Mahatma letter ordering him back to America.[3] Judge, however, denied this, writing Blavatsky: "I did not leave India because I got a message from a Mahatma. *I never got any messages from any Mahatma either pretended or real while I was in India....* I tell you neither you, nor Olcott, nor Holloway, nor deceit, nor trick, nor message, nor devil, nor Hartmann, had anything to do with my departure from India."[4] What seems clear, however, is that Judge had abandoned his family and career following a dream that had then been shattered by what he had learned—either about the Theosophical Society or about himself. He had risked his own reputation in a bungled attempt at defending Blavatsky, and he wanted nothing to do with the impending investigation by the Society for Psychical Research.[5]

Laura Holloway-Langford had been chastened by being branded a failed chela; only a few intimates in the United States knew about this debacle, however. In contrast, Judge's flight to India and his humiliating homecoming were known both within the Theosophical Society and to family and friends in Brooklyn. After returning to New York, Judge suspected that either the leaders of the Society had told "great *lies*" or the Mahatmas were "absolutely useless as guides."[6] Whatever his doubts, Judge soon turned his energy to building the American Section of the Society, established in October 1886, "on the proper lines, eschewing phenomena and preaching Universal Brotherhood and trying to spread Theosophy."[7] In contrast, Holloway-Langford kept her European adventure shrouded in mystery while she concentrated on reestablishing her career as a writer. She made no secret of having met Madame Blavatsky and other famous Theosophists; nevertheless, she shielded her private life from scrutiny by presenting herself as an objective reporter who had little personal involvement in the events she portrayed.

A NARROW, PRESBYTERIAN CHARACTER

On October 18, the same day that Laura Holloway-Langford set sail for America, Helena Blavatsky began a campaign to undermine her reputation and to shape how the summer of 1884 would be remembered. To A. P. Sinnett, she quoted Holloway-Langford's "parting words": "'Do me the justice . . . to tell Mr. Sinnett, that to the last I was living here on two planes—the physical and the spiritual. Judging me from the physical he could not, of course, understand me, for I was living on the spiritual. To the last *I have been acting under the direct orders of Master,* and could not therefore, do as he . . . would have liked me to.'" Blavatsky asserted that she, herself, was *"perfectly indifferent"* to Sinnett's relationship with Holloway-Langford, but she nevertheless tried to plant doubts in his mind about her credibility, writing that the American had been "greatly disturbed (mentally) all the time. . . . But I hope she will be calmer now and rest."[8]

Shortly thereafter, Blavatsky began to express her hostility more openly. On November 9, while on board ship en route to India, she wrote Sinnett that, even though Laura Holloway-Langford had been on probation as a chela, the test had been "performed over my long suffering back." She accused Holloway-Langford of conspiring with Frederic Myers and the Gebhards to disgrace her. "You will see what splatters *I* will receive as an effect of the causes produced by that probation business. I wish I had never seen the woman. Such treachery, such a deceit I would never have dreamt of. I was also a chela and guilty of more than one flapdoodle; but I would have thought as soon of murdering physically a man as to murder morally my friends as she has." Additionally, Blavatsky enclosed a communication from the Master, which, she related, had been impressed "in *relief* between the wall and [her] legs" in the ship cabin. Having previously depended on Holloway-Langford to furnish her with writing paper, Blavatsky recounted that she had had to borrow it from a fellow passenger in order to transcribe the message.[9]

In this letter, Koot Hoomi painted a damning portrait of Laura Holloway-Langford, whom he described as a "creature of Attavada," a follower of the doctrine of self who had bewitched Sinnett. He quoted *The Light of Asia,* where Edwin Arnold portrayed the narcissistic self as female: "The sin of Self, who in the Universe, / As in a mirror sees her fond face shown." He belittled Holloway-Langford's intellectual interest in theosophy, averring that reading Sinnett's books had "aroused" her to "spasmodic, hysterical curiosity." Despite the hyperbolic language, Koot Hoomi did not accuse Holloway-Langford of sexual misconduct. He declared that she was "naturally good and moral" and that her higher, not her lower, nature had been infected by the "venomous seed" of the "deadly upas-tree of Evil."[10] According to the Master, Holloway-Langford's purity was "of so narrow a kind, of so *Presbyterian* a character . . . as to be unable to see itself reflected in any other but her own *Self.* She alone is good and pure. All others must be suspected. A great boon was offered her—her wayward spirit would allow her to accept of none that was not shaped in accordance with her own model." Hence, Holloway-Langford was willing "to upset the whole structure in which *she* had no part . . . if she did not find the system and Society at the level of *her* expectations."[11]

According to the Master, Holloway-Langford was a puritanical bluestocking who sought to apply the conventional standards of Christian morality to the Theosophical Society. Koot Hoomi believed that adherence to a notion of absolute moral law was a defect, not a virtue—whether in a man or a woman. He claimed that Holloway-Langford had mistaken her own behavioral standards as universal, when, in fact, they were the internalized verities of middle-class Brooklyn society with deep roots in American Protestant culture. His description of her suggests that although she sought a New Age, her rigidity limited her openness to fresh ways of thinking. In contrast to later depictions, this portrait of Laura Holloway-Langford indicated that her failure as a chela was not due to moral transgressions, but instead to her inability to fully reinvent herself.

Blavatsky continued to fear that male Theosophists would fall victim to her wiles, even if her only contact with them was epistolary. She claimed that Holloway-Langford was "dancing the war-dance around Olcott," who remained "fast friends with her. . . . It is a *weekly correspondence* incessant and endearing, charming to behold she is his *dear* agent in Brooklyn, for things occult etc."[12] She was also incensed that Holloway-Langford had told William Q. Judge about "what happened in London & involved the reception of numerous letters from both Mahatmas." Blavatsky wrote to Judge: "Oh gods what a dirty world what false people! Look at Mrs. H. Do you still admire her?" Once again, she blamed Holloway-Langford for the strife among Theosophists in the summer of 1884, claiming that she had "tried to bamboozle the Mahatmas but came out second best." According to Blavatsky, Holloway-Langford had set "Sinnett against Olcott & me & the Mahatmas and O[lcott], me & the Arundales against Sinnett." She warned Judge that just as Christian missionaries had conspired with former Theosophists against her in India, so religious leaders in the United States were collaborating with traitors like Holloway-Langford. In particular, she feared that Holloway-Langford's "pious friend" General Oliver Otis Howard might lead a priestly conspiracy against the Theosophical Society.[13] When the Gebhards concluded that she had "played tricks upon them," Blavatsky blamed the insinuations of the "kitten-like Mrs. Holloway."[14]

LOYALTY TO JUDGE

Despite her denigration of Laura Holloway-Langford, Blavatsky had entrusted her with the important task of negotiating with J. W. Bouton, the U.S. publisher of *Isis Unveiled,* who Blavatsky hoped might publish *The Secret Doctrine.* When Blavatsky complained to William Q. Judge, he reminded her that in 1884 she had appointed Holloway-Langford as her representative to deal with Bouton. Holloway-Langford had employed a lawyer in New York, and thus, said Judge, "you are bound by your own acts." He added, "I thoroughly agree with what you say about her," but he continued in a nonjudgmental tone: "I understand that *she is writing a book on the theosophical movement, to be embellished with pictures. She is great on catching the passing emotions of the people, for a sale.*"

Judge was contending with more pressing issues. Someone had been sending telegrams that issued "ridiculous orders. . . . The last was the other day from Baltimore reading 'Your enemy is a woman; now as then she has betrayed you. Now you know why the Master did not cure you in India. H. P. B.'" Judge asked Blavatsky to write an authoritative letter denying that she was the author of these messages. Realizing that Blavatsky would jump to the conclusion that Laura Holloway-Langford was the culprit, Judge added "I do not connect *L. C. Holloway with it.*"[15]

In a letter to Olcott, however, Judge did not rule out the possibility that Holloway-Langford was capable of such guile: "I *think* [the telegram] was from C [Elliott Coues]; if not then Mrs. Holloway. It is all damned rot. Mrs. Judge opened that message."[16] The telegram apparently was sent to Judge's home, where his wife may well have identified Holloway-Langford as the woman who betrayed her husband. It is possible that Holloway-Langford was stirring up trouble out of pique for Judge having returned to his family, but it seems more likely that rumors about Judge's relationship with her were widespread in Theosophical circles and could be used by enemies who wanted to undermine his leadership in the Society.

On returning to Brooklyn, William Q. Judge visited Laura Holloway-Langford "to deliver a pair of (drawers?) which Miss Arundale bought her in London," an errand that seems surprisingly intimate.[17] Holloway-Langford described to him her conflicts with A. P. Sinnett. She also may have permitted Judge to read letters from Blavatsky and Koot Hoomi. Initially at least, Judge seemed to have accepted Holloway-Langford's version of these events rather than Blavatsky's description of the "Sinnett–Holloway imbroglio."[18] In April 1886, Judge founded a journal, *The Path,* which he edited until his death ten years later. Much of its content was written by Judge himself, both under his own name and under several aliases, but Holloway-Langford also contributed to *The Path,* where she published the article "Teachings of the Master."[19] In August, Judge gave Holloway-Langford a birthday present: a copy of *Light on the Path* by Mabel Collins that he had signed.[20] Although they gradually grew apart, Laura Holloway-Langford and William Q. Judge had forged a friendship that survived the vicissitudes of the Theosophical Society.

In 1887, *The Path* announced a forthcoming book, *The Yoga Way.* The author was said to have had an exceptional opportunity to study psychic phenomena and to have experienced "the wondrous and touching sympathy of the Esoteric Teachers." The book was to be issued by The Eastern

Publishing Company, which had been established recently in New York in order to circulate "occult and Theosophical literature in this country." A full-page advertisement in *Programmes for Brighton Beach Music Hall 1890–1891* identified the writer as one of the authors of *Man: Fragments of Forgotten History*. Other than announcements that the book was forthcoming, however, no record of *The Yoga Way* exists.[21] Perhaps becoming preoccupied with the Seidl Society (see chapter 9), Laura Holloway-Langford abandoned the project, or perhaps no copies of *The Yoga Way* have been preserved.

Whatever the case, Holloway-Langford never lost interest in theosophy, even though she was disillusioned with the Theosophical Society. Throughout her life, despite increasing poverty, she subscribed to occult periodicals. She kept abreast of the internecine battles within the Society in the 1890s through "Strictly Private and Confidential" pamphlets issued by the Eastern School of Theosophy (previously known as the Esoteric Section).[22] She maintained her support for William Q. Judge when Annie Besant accused him of misusing the Mahatmas' names and handwriting, and she approved of Judge's decision to create the Theosophical Society in America independent of Adyar and the leadership of Henry Steel Olcott. William Q. Judge died in March 1896, just shy of his 45th birthday. Emil August Neresheimer, a close friend and colleague in the Theosophical Society in America, was appointed a co-executor of Judge's will. Neresheimer recalled examining the private papers that Judge had left in the office of *The Path*. "Many of these consisted of letters from members and friends, having no bearing on the affairs of the Society." Neresheimer continued: "I packed these letters into sacks which I sealed and afterwards burned in the furnace of my home on Long Island."[23] If Judge had retained correspondence from Holloway-Langford, it was probably destroyed. On some level, however, Laura Holloway-Langford continued to consider herself a Theosophist. In 1899, she was among a small group of Judge's friends who rejected the leadership of Katherine Tingley and formed a separate organization called the Theosophical Society of New York. This branch continued for many years, centered on *The Word,* a journal edited by Harold W. Percival that was devoted to "Philosophy, Science, Religion, Eastern Thought, Occultism, Theosophy, and the Brotherhood of Humanity."[24]

REMINISCENCES

In public, Laura Holloway-Langford never disparaged William Q. Judge, Helena Blavatsky, or the Adept Brotherhood. Despite the fact that before leaving England she had gained the Master Koot Hoomi's approval to write about Theosophy, in the 1880s Holloway-Langford produced only a few minor articles on the topic, including three sketches of Blavatsky. These pieces were originally intended to be part of a book, but her project was preempted by A. P. Sinnett's *Incidents in the Life of Madame Blavatsky*, published in 1886. Written in order to defend Blavatsky from "the attack . . . instituted by the S. P. R.," *Incidents* focused heavily on occult phenomena and paid scant attention to the struggles within the Theosophical Society, skipping entirely the controversies of 1884.[25]

A quarter of a century later, Laura Holloway-Langford resumed writing about Theosophy, penning important reminiscences of the movement's founders: Henry Steel Olcott, William Q. Judge, and Helena Blavatsky. Most of this work was published anonymously, because, according to the editor of *The Word*, Holloway-Langford did not wish "to be known to the public as a psychic." In "Colonel Olcott: A Reminiscence," she recounted an afternoon in fall 1906 that she spent with him on his last visit to the United States. Recollecting old times and friendships, Holloway-Langford asked:

"Have you no word now for that devoted co-worker . . . toward whom . . . you were hostile . . . ? Do you not mourn him at all, that dear old friend of the long-ago?"

"You speak of Judge," he slowly replied. . . .

Then, as he seemed lost in reverie, I laid my hand upon his arm, and said in a low tone: "Henry, at such a time as this, and for the sake of the memory we shall both retain of this meeting . . . will you not tell me that your old feeling for him survives?"

"Yes, yes," he interrupted, "I know how you feel about him and always have felt." Then, taking my hand in his, he gave my face a searching glance, before he answered, in a manner subdued and most impressive:

"We learn much and outgrow much, and I have outlived much and learned more, particularly as regards Judge. . . .

"I know now, and it will comfort you to hear it; that I wronged Judge, not wilfully or in malice; nevertheless, I have done this and I regret it."

Thanking Olcott for his "brave recantation," Holloway-Langford declared that the "old days will seem nearer to me now that I know in your heart you feel right again toward him."[26]

The following month, Holloway-Langford published "William Quan Judge, A Reminiscence," in which she affirmed that Judge had been "a natural mystic." She praised him most highly, however, for his loyalty to Helena Blavatsky which was "untarnished by quarrels or contradictions, and unbroken by doubt or misgivings of any kind whatsoever," even when others were casting "mud and . . . slime" upon her. It was Judge, Holloway-Langford believed, whom Blavatsky intended to be her successor to lead the Theosophical Society. She recalled visiting Judge a few days before his death, although whether in person or only in spirit is unclear. She described him as "full of spiritual stature, erect, and strong, of bearing serene and abounding vitality." In "psychic vision" she saw an "astral form" wearing "vestments" of the "order of the Hierophants" hovering around him. Judge, she asserted, had joined the Fraternity of "sages and martyrs who, impelled by their love of men to come and dwell among them, have suffered and died for their redemption and salvation."[27] Unlike some later Theosophists who maintained that in India Judge had been initiated as an adept, Holloway-Langford did not claim that Judge had acquired occult power. In her eyes, Judge was less an adept than a manifestation of the Christ spirit.[28]

In several articles written between 1912 and 1917, Laura Holloway-Langford explored the complexities of Helena Blavatsky's personality. She described Blavatsky as "a volcano in petticoats; a woman, but masculine in her mental attributes."[29] She defended Blavatsky's "irascible" temperament as "natural" for one so deeply involved in occult work. She expressed a judgment, shared by many later biographers, that in her lack of feminine characteristics Blavatsky "was not like women generally." Holloway-Langford pronounced her "a cosmic woman—combining in her individuality characteristics common to all nationalities and all strata of society; not a personality merely, but a composite Being, the resultant of many reincarnations: the finished product of no one material existence."[30]

What is most striking in these articles is Holloway-Langford's determination to ignore thirty years of dispute about the character of Helena Blavatsky and the claims of occultism. She neither raised questions about Blavatsky's integrity nor did she reveal that Blavatsky had deeply wounded her. Her tone was that of an amused if admiring observer. Surely, in retrospect, Holloway-Langford felt betrayed by Blavatsky, who had derailed her ambitions, undermined her self-confidence, and humiliated her in front of friends. If so, she kept these feelings private. Her self-protective stance is unfortunate, because it prevented her from offering an analysis of the early days of the movement. Likewise, Holloway-Langford kept mum about whatever she knew about the Masters and their messages, about the production of occult phenomena, and about the jealousies and rivalries that animated members of the Society during the 1880s. Nevertheless, scholars have drawn on her memoirs for evidence about the early years of the Theosophical Society. It is important to realize, however, that Holloway-Langford's reminiscences, although autobiographical, are literary creations, not history.

BUDDHISM IN BROOKLYN

Laura Holloway-Langford wrote little about Theosophy in the years immediately after returning to the United States. However, she produced a large quantity of work, publishing six books in 1885 alone, mostly biographical compilations of letters and collections of materials written by others.[31] She picked subjects that reflected her own spiritual interests but framed them to enhance their appeal to the general public. For example, she edited *Songs of the Master,* a collection of poems inspired by her failure as an occultist. Within the context of Theosophy, the term "Master" had a specific meaning; but in her preface, she wrote that the songs represented "the love and tenderness of man for the Christ in his aspects as Child, Teacher, Friend and Master. Its conception came one cheerless afternoon as the shores of England were receding from sight and while the solitude of the ocean oppressed the spirit with a sense of great loneliness: a loneliness which brought thoughts of Him who was all his life a wanderer and a stranger on land and sea."[32] The meaning of the "Master," then, remained ambiguous. Holloway-Langford included some poems that presented Christ as a personal savior as well as others that interpreted the "Master" to be a non-sectarian "Christ Spirit" dwelling within each individual. Nevertheless, this book suggested that in a moment of personal despair, Holloway-Langford returned to her Christian roots for consolation.

By this time, however, Holloway-Langford had broadened her understanding of Christianity to preclude claims of exclusivity. If all religions
contained the same core truths, she found no need to choose among them.
Interest in Eastern traditions had been growing among religious liberals
since 1844, when a translation of Buddhist scripture had been published
in the Transcendentalist journal *The Dial*. Some years later, Thomas Wentworth Higginson, in a sermon on "The Sympathy of Religions" and in
articles on "The Character of Buddha" and "The Buddhist Path of Virtue,"
had advocated openness to other religious teachings.[33] Edwin Arnold's
The Light of Asia had been immensely popular, selling up to a million copies in the United States after its publication in 1879.[34] During these years,
Laura Holloway-Langford maintained her social and cultural identification with Christianity, but she was more likely to categorize herself as a
Buddhist than either a Christian or a Theosophist. In Brooklyn, however,
this label denoted little more than someone who had taken up vegetarianism and believed in reincarnation.

Buddhism and Theosophy were commonly conflated in the popular
mind. The conversions of Olcott and Blavatsky to Buddhism had been
widely publicized, and the vocabulary of "karma" and "reincarnation" had
become ubiquitous among spiritual seekers influenced by the Theosophical movement. To be sure, a number of Americans had called themselves
Buddhist since the 1870s, but the first formal conversion within the United
States did not occur until 1893.[35] Anagarika Dharmapala, who had joined
the Theosophical Society in Ceylon, founded an international Buddhist
organization, the Maha Bodhi Society, in 1891; a U.S. branch was formed
in 1894. In 1893, when Dharmapala arrived in New York on the way to
the World's Parliament of Religions in Chicago, he was the guest of the
Brooklyn Theosophical Society, which had its headquarters at the home
of Duncan C. Ralston.[36] A noted Theosophist, Ralston was the father of
Maude Ralston, who in later years became Holloway-Langford's close
friend and literary collaborator.[37] A photo of a group of Theosophists gathered at the Long Island home of Emil A. Neresheimer included Dharmapala, William Q. Judge and his wife, and Maude Ralston.[38] Despite these
connections, there is no evidence that before the mid-1890s any Theosophist had officially converted to Buddhism inside the United States.

The fullest information about Brooklyn Buddhists in the late 1880s
comes from an October 1886 article in the *Daily Eagle* that portrayed Bud-

dhism as a "negative" religion that created a "languid Oriental state" of "Asiatic indolence" similar to the effect of taking "haschish [sic]." The writer maintained that the elimination of a personal God attracted "skeptics who merely comply with the religious etiquette and worship in which they were born and bred, but who have never had implicit faith in the dogmas taught them." He claimed that "a notable strain of Buddhism" had sounded from Brooklyn pulpits: "The Radical Unitarians, some of the Universalists and not a few of the Broad Church Episcopalians and Rationalistic Congregationalists have strongly marked Buddhist features." The article identified William Q. Judge as the only Brooklyn Buddhist to have taken "pansila," which, the author explained, was "the highest esoteric initiation," and he described Judge as both the President of the Aryan Theosophical Society in New York and "the leading spirit and instructor of the Buddhists in Brooklyn." According to this article, a "new impetus was given to the Buddhist movement in Brooklyn" by literary ladies who had traveled to Europe, particularly "Mrs. Holloway," who had been converted while there "to total abstinence from meat and wine." These "Brooklyn Buddhists" reportedly met "regularly on Sunday evenings at each other's houses. . . . Before they learned from the Buddha 'a more excellent way' [they] used to hold similar weekly meetings for the esoteric communications and lunar experiments of Spiritualism. Some of them do not love Spiritualism less though they love Buddhism more."[39]

Sometime later the newspaper published a correction, apologizing for having left the impression that the purpose of the Theosophical Society was to promote Buddhism and noting that a separate Buddhist organization would be established in the fall of 1887, which would include Chinese and Japanese Buddhists as well as Americans.[40] Despite these caveats, there does seem to have been continuity between the spiritualist circle of 1883, where William Q. Judge had first met Laura Holloway-Langford, and the semi-private meetings of Theosophists in Brooklyn in the late 1880s. By fall 1890, the Brooklyn Theosophists were better organized, and they established public meetings on Monday evenings, welcoming all those who were interested in pursuing Theosophical texts.[41] The first book studied was Sinnett's *Esoteric Buddhism,* followed by *The Key to Theosophy* and *The Secret Doctrine.* The Society denied that it had "either doctrines or dogmas" and emphasized that these "books are not studied as authoritative," but that each seeker should "accept only what appeals to him."[42]

THE BUDDHIST DIET-BOOK

In late 1886, Laura Holloway-Langford published *The Buddhist Diet-Book,* which displayed on its cover an inverted seal of the Theosophical Society. In the book's "Preface," Holloway-Langford claimed to have discovered vegetarianism at Ladbroke Gardens, Elgin Crescent, and Platz Hof Strasse, but she designated these as Buddhist houses, rather than the homes of the Theosophists A. P. Sinnett, Francesca Arundale, and Mary Gebhard. To confuse matters even more, she remarked that her "Hindoo friends" would attribute the blessings she had received from vegetarianism to her "good Karma."[43] Either Holloway-Langford assumed that few readers had any knowledge of Eastern religions, or, perhaps more likely, she herself did not distinguish among Buddhism, Hinduism, and Theosophy. Her justification for vegetarianism was theosophical rather than Buddhist: she claimed that humankind had originally been all spirit, not needing food, but that it had evolved downward into a state of material being that was characterized by the eating of flesh, which was impeding humanity's astral progress. She added a list of pragmatic arguments that might convince her American readers of the need for a vegetarian diet: animal food was expensive, it filled the blood with impure substances leading to disease and a shortened life, and it brutalized those who slaughtered animals. Still, it is striking that while purporting to offer a Buddhist book, Holloway-Langford neither referred to the first precept of Buddhism—to refrain from taking any life either human or non-human—nor did she mention the suffering to animals caused by eating meat.

The timing for the book was auspicious: the American Vegetarian Society had just been organized, with Holloway-Langford's Shaker friend, Elder Frederick Evans, as one of the founding members.[44] To be sure, there had been earlier interest in vegetarianism, which was often associated with radical social reform. In the 1830s, some Shakers had adopted the theories of Sylvester Graham, who argued that vegetarianism diminished sexual desire. In 1854, Dr. Russell Thacher Trall had published *The New Hydropathic Cookbook,* where he argued that water-cure establishments should offer a table of fruit and bread.[45] Vegetarianism was even associated with spiritualism. Victoria Woodhull had included it in her 1872 presidential platform, and *Woodhull & Claflin's Weekly* had published articles on diet reform. But it was not until 1889 that the first vegetarian magazine, *Food, Home, and Garden*, was launched.[46]

Unlike earlier works, *The Buddhist Diet-Book* was directed at women who faced the practical challenges of putting food on the table for their families. Holloway-Langford explained that the Buddhist cook used "preserves, herbs, curries, and sweet condiments, many of which would be pleasant surprises to the Westerners who know as yet little of the possibilities of scientific vegetarian cookery."[47] Readers who expected to discover new methods of cookery or interesting combinations of ingredients were surely disappointed by Holloway-Langford's book, which featured recipes for creamed soups, potatoes, and boiled vegetables—dishes already familiar to the American housewife. Only two recipes had a mildly Eastern flavor: one a sauce seasoned with curry powder and the other an Indian pickle that included more spices than would be common in Western preparations of pickled vegetables. It seems that a hint of curry was as far as Asia had penetrated the kitchens of Anglo-Indians like the Sinnetts.

Just as Laura Holloway-Langford had little personal experience with Indian cuisine, she also had no direct engagement with Buddhist history or sacred texts. She wrote one article, heavily influenced by *The Light of Asia*, comparing Buddhism to Christianity, arguing that the Buddha's "mission was exactly the same as Christ's, which was to call men back to a spiritual state from the condition of materiality." She admitted that the doctrine of reincarnation was a serious stumbling block to many Christians, but she found the moral systems of the two traditions indistinguishable: "There is not a shade of difference between the teachings of Jesus and Buddha in these respects. Buddha taught that the kingdom of Heaven is within; that if a man possess all the virtues and yet lack charity, he is wanting in the essential thing." She maintained that the Buddha and Christ were parallel manifestations of the same Spirit and that the religions they founded were identical esoterically: a good Buddhist was also a good Christian, and vice versa. She claimed that the religions differed primarily in their understandings of how one obtained the afterlife, whether it was once and permanently, or as a "slow ascent up the evolutionary spiral." Finally she suggested that those who obtained the key to Christ's "veiled esoteric truths" would find that "the normal, spiritual evolution taught by Buddha was part of Christ's teachings." In other words,

Holloway-Langford implied that Christ's teachings had been misunderstood by the religious institutions that took his name, but that when the esoteric knowledge of true Christianity was revealed, it would be identical to Buddhism.[48]

WOMEN'S MAGAZINES AS A VEHICLE FOR NEW IDEAS

In January 1887, the first issue of a new journal, *The Lady's World: A Monthly Magazine of Home Literature,* was published by the Home Library Association, an organization established in 1884 by the Chicago publisher R. S. Peale. A cooperative venture, the Association bought books in quantity, including entire editions of popular works, and made them available at wholesale prices. In 1886, it published *The Home Library of Useful Knowledge. A Condensation of Fifty-Two Books in One Volume: . . . Embracing the Most Approved and Simple Methods of Self-Instruction in All Branches of Popular Education.* Agents of the Association canvassed neighborhoods, selling memberships, books, and magazines. The Association's purpose was to enable middle-class families, not just the wealthy, to acquire a home library, but it appealed to the desire for upward mobility by those who lacked opportunities for higher education. In particular, women were targeted as being responsible for the education of their families.[49]

Laura Holloway-Langford was engaged to edit *The Lady's World.*[50] She spent two weeks of each month in Chicago, a sixteen-hour journey from New York by train.[51] Beginning in June 1887, the name of the periodical was changed to *The Home Library Magazine.* Published in an attractive large format, each issue contained several full-page engravings plus dozens of smaller ones.[52] By October 1887, Holloway-Langford had ambitious plans for the magazine's future. Claiming that the Association had 200,000 members, she proposed sending each one a free copy of the magazine, to induce them to subscribe at a cost of $3 per year, with premiums offered for multiple subscriptions. She believed that *The Home Library Magazine* could become the "best home periodical in either hemisphere."[53] It must have come as a great disappointment when, at the year's end, *The Home Library Magazine* was merged with *The Woman's World,* published by Cassell & Co. in London.[54]

At first glance, *The Home Library Magazine* appears to be a typical Victorian monthly devoted to female fashion and homemaking, replete with pictures of women in elaborate costumes and in sentimental poses. On closer examination, however, it becomes clear that Laura Holloway-Langford had created a periodical aimed not at the Victorian "true" woman, but one designed to support the emerging identity of the New Woman. Within its pages there is scarcely any mention of marriage or motherhood, and only an occasional nod to piety. Domesticity, to be sure, is a central focus, but it too has been transformed, with women encouraged to take up skills and occupations usually considered masculine. Wood carving and fly fishing were suggested as "Pastimes for Ladies," while an article on "A Parisian Ladies' Atelier" described women studying painting with live models. A series of articles written by Holloway-Langford's brother, Vaulx Carter, who was an engineer, presented the basics of drafting and the use of tools for building with wood—information evidently deemed as useful to women as to men.

The achievements of women, many of whom led unconventional lives, were given prominence. The magazine contained a full-page illustration of Sappho, an article on the women of Greece, and pieces devoted to contemporary vocalists and actresses. Many of these articles had been previously published; in these cases it was Holloway-Langford who selected them for inclusion in *The Home Library Magazine*. Other articles were solicited from her friends, such as one by Rose Elizabeth Cleveland on Joan of Arc, about whom she wrote: "Her power was but the power which many another woman may have—the power of a buoyant, masterful faith in God, in herself, in humanity, and a will to come to the rescue."[55] Holloway-Langford was beginning to stamp her own imprint on the magazine. For example, she initiated a series of articles on women's contributions during the Civil War, asserting that their work and sacrifice had been overlooked. Unfortunately, only one of these articles reached print before the magazine ceased publication.

Each issue of *The Home Library Magazine* contained at least one explicitly feminist article or editorial. In "How Women May Earn a Living," Holloway-Langford recommended that women acquire training as stenographers, bookkeepers, bookbinders, and librarians, but she warned that many jobs—such as telegraphy and typesetting—paid women much less than men for the same work. She advocated establishing a "Ladies' Association" to give women "scientific training in horticulture and arbori-culture, poultry-raising, dairy work, bee-keeping."[56] In an editorial, she returned to a theme of her early essays—the duties of mothers to their daughters, exclaiming: "What if some mother should be bold enough to begin the reformation of the world in her own home. What if some daugh-ter should lift the standard of life for herself to a point where she could not speak of marriage as a speculation in which girls must engage as soon as they are out of school!" She disputed the widespread notion that women have no other choice than to marry and asserted that even a life of poverty was "not so hard as the fate of those who marry for convenience." She warned that marriages of expediency damaged both women and society, because they produced inferior offspring, resulting in "the unmistakable deterioration perceptible in the race to-day." She declared that if women gained self-respect and independence, they would change their views of marriage. She concluded: "Home is the place to begin the reformation, and mothers are the natural leaders. Until they begin it there will be noth-ing done."[57] Holloway-Langford had redefined the meaning of home and family. Rather than a place that conserved the sanctity of marriage, it be-came the site of revolution against its constraints. She envisioned mothers as the educators and liberators of the next generation of women. Through *The Home Library Magazine,* she encouraged women to believe that even without access to public life they had the power to change the world.

The fiction that Holloway-Langford selected for *The Home Library Magazine* also suggested new paths for women's lives. A chapter from the popular novel *All Sorts and Conditions of Men* by Walter Besant was published in each issue under the name of the novel's main character, "Angela Messenger." A highly educated woman and a university gradu-ate, the heroine had inherited a great fortune, which she used to found a "Palace of Delights," a school of art, dance, and music that exposed young women to culture and rescued them from lives of poverty.[58] Angela Mes-senger was a model for the New Woman; she relied on her own judgment and creativity to realize her ideals, even though by the novel's conclusion she had also gained a husband. Holloway-Langford must have believed that *The Home Library Magazine* would have a long run, since it would have required more than four years for the entire novel to be published.

In January 1888, Oscar Wilde became editor of *The Lady's World* (London), renaming the magazine *The Woman's World*.[59] The relationship between these magazines and those edited by Holloway-Langford is not clear, but their content overlapped. For example, "The Position of Women," an article that appeared in the first issue of Wilde's journal, had previously appeared in *The Home Library Magazine*. Scholars cite this article as evidence that Wilde promoted the New Woman and that he turned *The Woman's World* into a site for the negotiation of gender and sexual identity. However, it had been Laura Holloway-Langford who had provided the material that Wilde adopted.[60] In contrast to Wilde, who appealed to the upper classes, Holloway-Langford in *The Home Library Magazine* reached out to American women who lacked both social status and inherited wealth. In many cases, they were the first generation of women to receive more than rudimentary education. In her editorship of the magazine, Holloway-Langford advocated a pragmatic feminism that encouraged all women to seek economic independence in order to control their sexuality and thus advance themselves and civilization.

The Home Library Magazine was more revolutionary in its treatment of gender than of religion. Holloway-Langford published several articles about India and the Himalayas, including a report on a convention of "Pundits, public instructors and princes, for the purpose of discussing plans for the revival of Sanskrit literature," which, she claimed, would open up to the West "the history of the human mind."[61]

More interesting is a sketch that Holloway-Langford wrote under the pseudonym S. E. Archer. She described an incident that recounts the trip that she and Helena Blavatsky made from Elberfeld, Germany, to London, October 5–6, 1884.[62] In "A Day in an Old Holland Town," she portrays two unnamed travelers who missed their train connection and found themselves stranded on the border between Holland and Prussia. The character based on Blavatsky was ill, and no one in the frontier town could understand any of the seven languages that she spoke. The women obtained a room in an antiquated inn, where the food was unrecognizable and where Blavatsky "was much too large for her bed." The following day, Blavatsky, "smoking and fuming," frantically tried to pantomime their situation to the dense Dutch. Just in time, one of them understood that they needed transportation to the depot. Shortly thereafter a man appeared at the inn driving a hearse. Blavatsky mounted the seat with the driver, while Holloway-Langford perched on a stool in the back, both of them laughing until they cried but arriving at the station in time to catch the train for Rotterdam. This vignette captures Blavatsky's personality, and it suggests an intimacy with Holloway-Langford that is lacking in other accounts of their relationship. Despite the fact that Holloway-Langford was accused of gravely offending Blavatsky and the Masters while in Elberfeld, the two women are portrayed as warm companions, sharing a room at the inn as well as frustration and laughter. It makes us realize how much Holloway-Langford might have contributed to history's understanding of Blavatsky, if she had not been at such pains to keep her experiences in Europe private.

Holloway-Langford also persuaded Mohini Chatterji to contribute a poem for the March 1887 issue of her magazine. In "Duty and Sacrifice," a lover longs for death, but then imagines his beloved's "grief-laden face" and her "beauty steeped in pain." He concludes:

> I cannot die, tho' death be near
> For sweet is death but thou more dear.[63]

Readers would undoubtedly have read Chatterji's contribution as a sentimental love poem. It was probably inspired, however, by Sultan Bahu, a seventeenth-century Sufi mystic from the Punjab, whose verses, often sung to music, proclaimed that the absolute love of God can result in union with the Divine.[64] Chatterji's poem also suggested the Bodhisattvas, the enlightened ones, who in Buddhist traditions sacrificed themselves by remaining embodied rather than escaping through death. Still in this world, they devoted themselves to alleviating the suffering of others through compassion.

MOHINI CHATTERJI AND THE SPREAD
OF EASTERN RELIGIOUS IDEAS

Laura Holloway-Langford and William Q. Judge, like most American Theosophists, had only a superficial acquaintance with Eastern metaphysics, and they played a minor role in the diffusion of Buddhism and Hinduism in the West. Indian Theosophists, such as Mohini Chatterji, however, provided an important link between Asia and the United States.

Theosophists agreed that Chatterji was "one of the most brilliant Hindu members of the early Theosophical Society."[65] Unlike Blavatsky or Olcott, he possessed a deep knowledge of ancient philosophy and literature. Some scholars have even suggested that it was only after Chatterji joined the Theosophical Society that the Mahatma letters to A. P. Sinnett began to address Hindu religious ideas.[66] Be this as it may, there is no doubt that Chatterji was one of the primary conduits for the Hindu concepts and vocabulary that entered Theosophical thinking and writing. Although largely unrecognized, Chatterji played a major role in spreading Eastern religious ideas to the American public. Through his lectures and translations of ancient texts, he opened the way for the popularity in the 1890s of Vivekananda, Abhedananda, and other followers of Ramakrishna.[67]

In 1883 and 1884, Clara Erskine Clement Waters and her husband, Edwin Forbes Waters, the publisher of the *Boston Daily Advertiser*, had attended gatherings at the London home of A. P. Sinnett where they had met many Theosophists, Mohini Chatterji probably among them. After returning to the United States, the Waters had been reinitiated into the Theosophical Society by William Q. Judge, who believed that their influence on intellectual people would produce great results for the Society in Boston. Hungry for more knowledge, they plied Judge with questions about "the laws of Occultism, the residences of the Mahatmas, how they appear, all the fine 'ramifications' of Karma etc. etc."[68] Mrs. Waters arranged for Arthur Gebhard, who was then the business manager of Judge's *The Path*, to instruct a group of spiritually minded Boston women in Eastern lore.[69] Under his guidance, these Bostonians investigated Sinnett's *Esoteric Buddhism* and attempted to develop their own sixth sense. They were thrilled by Gebhard's accounts of abandoning the life of an Epicurean, being initiated into "the mysteries of the Theosophical Cult," taking up vegetarianism, donning a Brahminical robe, and devoting himself to the life of a chela in pursuit of occult powers. Waters, "eager for further enlightenment," wrote to Theosophists in London, "begging that they would spare to us the young Brahmin, Mohini Chatterji, their best exponent, to instruct us further in the Hindu philosophy."[70]

At first Chatterji declined, not wanting to get embroiled in controversies over control of the Theosophical Society in the United States, but in the fall of 1886 he accepted the invitation.[71] His coming was heralded in American newspapers. The *St. Louis Globe-Democrat,* drawing on information published in the *New York Sun,* reported that Chatterji had been teaching in Europe under the approbation of the "Brotherhood in Thibet [*sic*]," which apparently had approved him to continue his work as a "Guru" in the United States. As he had been in England, likewise in America, Chatterji became a voice for all things Eastern: the article suggested that the "Hindoo" might teach "Aryan literature," mysticism, and esoteric Buddhism, as well as the doctrines of karma, reincarnation, and the principles of Lord Buddha.[72] The major New York newspapers noted his arrival in the city on November 22, but they portrayed him as a philosopher rather than as a Theosophist.[73] In Boston, Chatterji offered twice-weekly classes on the *Bhagavad Gita,* and his students "became fairly steeped in Indian lore." They saw him as a Christ figure, a "pure and selfless creature," while Arthur Gebhard now appeared to have been a mere John the Baptist who had prepared the way for the spiritually more advanced Chatterji.[74] The *Chicago Tribune* reported that Mohini Chatterji had "astonished Boston with his wisdom."[75] The *Brooklyn Daily Eagle* described young women who proclaimed themselves "to be Buddhists in religion, adopting their new opinions somewhat on the same principle as the latest fashion in dress." According to this account, "the beauty of Buddhism—the 'Light of Asia'—the wisdom of Vedas and the sublime morality of Indian theosophy" had become the "New Craze" in Boston.[76] Louise Chandler Moulton, a poet and friend of Laura Holloway-Langford, remarked that "perhaps nothing else has ever taken hold of [the city] as did Theosophy. If you went out to drink five-o'clock tea and shake hands with your neighbors, you found the company broken up into groups, and in the centre of each one some eloquent woman discoursing of reincarnation, Karma, and Devachan."[77]

Chatterji also lectured on Eastern religions to groups outside of Boston. At New York's prestigious Nineteenth-Century Club, an organization established in 1883 by Courtland Palmer and devoted to Free Thought, Chatterji spoke to a large audience. Members of the club had anticipated hearing "the tenets of the old new faith expounded by a genuine Hindu, a master of the cult," but Chatterji spoke "most eloquently on every other subject but Theosophy." Nevertheless, the *New York Times* reported that

the evening was one of the club's most successful of the season and that
Mohini Chatterji would soon open a school in the city, "where he will
probably stick more closely to his subject."[78]

Since returning to the United States, Laura Holloway-Langford had kept
in touch with Chatterji, whom she considered a close friend and brother.[79]
The day after his talk at the Nineteenth-Century Club, she hosted a reception at her home in Brooklyn where he was the guest of honor. Chatterji
"talked informally to the thirty people present about Theosophy and its
relations to Western civilization. The Brahnim [sic] is an old friend of Mrs.
Holloway. She studied theosophy under his tutelage."[80] In another notice
of the event, the *Brooklyn Daily Eagle* reported that after lunch, Chatterji
talked about spiritual mysteries, asserting that "whatever was impossible
was necessarily true, and that whatever could be explained by reasoning was necessarily false. . . . All religions were absolutely true, because
they were not rational." He spoke about reincarnation, and frequently he
quoted from the Bible. "At 5 o'clock PM Mr. Chatterji, looking decidedly
weary, left Mrs. Holloway's to attend a dinner party in New York."[81]

In March 1887, Chatterji was among prominent clergymen invited
to celebrate the 150th anniversary of the founding of Boston's Old West
Church, an Independent Congregational Church established by the father
of James Russell Lowell. The strong impact of his message can be gauged
by the fact that it was the only presentation that newspapers quoted in
full. Chatterji first described the effect of reading *The Precepts of Jesus:
The Guide to Peace and Happiness*, a book written by his great grandfather, Ram Mohun Roy. Much like Thomas Jefferson's *Bible*, this work,
published in 1820, attempted to find the essence of Christianity by ex-
punging all supernatural elements and focusing on the words of Jesus.
Chatterji told those gathered in the Old West Church that he was, for the
first time, publicly expressing his "personal gratitude" to the Christian
scriptures for providing a "philosophy of great excellence" that was "free
from the ambiguities and complexities of the older systems." He reminded
the congregation of his great-grandfather's Unitarian sympathies: "Fifty-
four years ago . . . one of my ancestors died in Bristol, surrounded by Christian people, in the unity of God. Therefore, it is to me a special matter of
delight to have this opportunity of addressing you as a man, a brother, and

a Christian."[82] Surely most members of the audience understood Chatterji to say that he accepted the superiority of the Christian Bible over Hindu religious texts and that he had become a Christian.

Yet Chatterji was Christian only in the manner that his ancestor had been.[83] Like Ram Mohun Roy, Chatterji refused to posit the superiority of one faith over another. Instead, he asserted that each religious tradition contained within it the same profound universal truths, irrespective of the texts, symbols, and forms through which those truths were communicated. Therefore, he argued that it was senseless to search among strange lands and scriptures for spiritual nourishment: religious seekers should delve into the riches of their own traditions. Chatterji avowed that Christ taught the essential verities—the brotherhood of man and the fatherhood of God. Anyone who believed these truths was, in the broadest sense, a Christian. He did not, mean, however, that he had relinquished his own religious heritage in favor of Christianity.

Ednah Dow Cheney, Boston reformer, Transcendentalist, and Free Religionist, explained Chatterji's religious evolution, while at the same time she extolled the religious tolerance of Americans:

> Having passed through a period of doubt and agnosticism, as he says most young Brahmins do, he is now a devoted Brahmin, accepting revelation as authoritative, but not confining it to the sacred books of his own nation, but believing that the divine light shines through all sacred books and all religions. While we may not accept his beliefs, we cannot but admire the breadth and the catholicity of this thought. . . . It indicates a wonderful advance in freedom of thought and in real liberality in religion; that those whom in our childhood we were taught to renounce as heathen are now welcomed among us to teach us of their wisdom as well as to learn of ours.[84]

In April 1887, Chatterji spoke at the South Congregational Church of Boston, where Edward Everett Hale, a leading Unitarian minister, presided. At a time of economic anxiety, when the newspapers were full of stories about labor strikes and threats from anarchists, Chatterji's lecture reassured his audience that religion was interior and spiritual, rather than external and political. He warned that change in the world would come only through a spiritual transformation, when people recognized that they were children of one God: "Universal brotherhood is not to be attained by any steam-roller of monotony imposed on all the race. . . .

You cannot inaugurate the brotherhood of humanity by making all men rich or all men poor. No socialism, no communism will do. . . . The true brotherhood is in mutual helpfulness, and not in the equal distribution of wealth."[85] His message was intrinsically conservative, and it reassured Americans that they had little to fear from Hindu religious influences. His stance was at once familiar to evangelical Christians and one which would come to dominate New Age religions in the next century: the world would be transformed through changing the heart and the imposition of mind over matter, not through politics or revolution.

Chatterji continued to lecture occasionally, but within a few months he turned his attention to literary endeavors. In January 1887, he published a substantial piece on solar myths in *The Theosophist*, responding to articles by Max Müller and Andrew Lang.[86] Much of his effort was devoted to producing *The Bhagavad Gîtâ: or The Lord's Lay: With Commentary and Notes, as well as References to The Christian Scriptures; Translated from the Sanskrit For the Benefit of Those in Search of Spiritual Light*. Published in October 1887, it was an outgrowth of the classes that he had taught in Boston, at which he had offered his own translation of the *Gita*.[87] In the preface, Chatterji asserted that "the word of God does not change with the change of time. As it was in the beginning, so it is now, and will be to the end." By superimposing the Christian Bible onto the *Bhagavad Gita*, he attempted to demonstrate that they were not contradictory, but that they embodied "the same Truth." Chatterji concluded the volume with this statement: "Human nature is one, God is but one, and the path of salvation, though many in appearance, is really one."[88]

In the American press, notices of *The Lord's Lay* were less than glowing. A reviewer in the *New York Times* criticized Chatterji's inclusiveness: "Like many Orientals he seems to find room for pretty much every system in his own. . . . He does not try to deduce the morality of the Bhagavad Gîtâ from our Scriptures; neither does he claim the Indian dialogue a forerunner of or influence upon the New Testament. He takes a neutral ground which will not be very satisfactory to Western minds, anxious as they generally are to have things historically correct, tabulated, and in sequence."[89] Another article suggested that Chatterji had sacrificed intellectual rigor in his desire to appeal to liberal Christian readers, asserting that "it would be hard to find any two religions that have less in common than the ancient Hindu and the Christian."[90] The *Christian Union* warned readers to beware of the "seductive charm" lurking in Chatterji's translation. The reviewer did not deny parallels to Christian scripture, but he insisted that whatever insights might be found in the *Gita* were only "dim and flickering shadows of truth." He rejected Chatterji's contention that separate spiritual paths could lead to salvation, and he asserted that only Christians basked "in the complete light of God's revelation."[91]

Mohini Chatterji had resigned from the Theosophical Society in 1887, and in September he sailed for Europe after spending less than a year in the United States.[92] European Theosophists who saw him after his return were disturbed by his appearance. The Christ-like Chatterji no longer looked the part. The Theosophist Isabelle de Steiger recalled that his long, waving black hair had been cut short, and instead of wearing the black velvet and fur robe, he was dressed in a cheap suit of yellow, black, and white plaid. "Poor Mohini!" she exclaimed: "East and West had met, but what an embrace!"[93]

Chatterji might well have parlayed the adoration of female spiritual seekers into a full-time occupation. The Orientalism of the West, however, made it almost impossible for him to remain affiliated with the Theosophical Society unless he was willing to play the role of a sage from the mystic East. Some Theosophists found it difficult to accept Chatterji's defection from the Society, spreading a rumor that he had been lured away by the Catholic Church. William Q. Judge's *The Path*, however, printed a rejoinder, reporting that Chatterji had visited Jesuits in Italy in order to examine a manuscript that he thought similar to the Vedas, but that he had not converted to Catholicism.[94] After more than five years in the West, Mohini Mohun Chatterji rejoined his family in Calcutta and resumed his profession as an attorney.[95] He maintained a life-long interest in religious mysticism and in poetry, both ancient and modern.[96] He continued to be a serious student of Hindu traditions, publishing a number of philosophical and metaphysical works. In the 1890s, he translated into English one of the classic works of Vedanta, the *Crest-Jewel of Wisdom of Shree Shankaracharya*.[97] These accomplishments, however, were ignored in accounts of the Theosophical movement, even though some of his books were published by the Society's presses. In 1935, C. Jinarajadasa reported that Chatterji, although blind, was still teaching a small group of disciples.[98]

During the 1880s, liberal religionists in Boston and New York had flocked to hear words of wisdom from Mohini Chatterji, but his message did not reach mainstream America. In fall 1893, however, Americans responded enthusiastically to Swami Vivekananda's opening address at the Chicago World's Parliament of Religions. His words echoed the message that Chatterji had earlier proclaimed: "As the different streams having their sources in different places all mingle their water in the sea, so, O Lord, the different paths which men take through different tendencies, various though they appear, crooked or straight, all lead to Thee."[99] Although many participants still clung to their belief in the superiority of Christianity, Catherine Albanese asserts that the World's Parliament of Religions "stretched the liberal fabric of the Protestant umbrella in directions that, at least potentially, wore thin the Christian certitude of possessing the unique—and most highly evolved—religious truth."[100] The road to the World's Parliament had been smoothed by earlier representatives of Eastern religions who, like Mohini Chatterji, had close ties both to Theosophy and to Indian reform movements. Sara Bull, who became Vivekananda's "most important American disciple," had "discovered the attractions of Asian religion as early as 1887, attending readings of the *Bhagavad Gita* offered by an Indian Theosophist named Mohini Chatterjee."[101] When she died, Bull left much of her $500,000 estate to "Hindu friends in India," including Chatterji.[102] In 1894, Sarah Farmer, another woman who had gathered around Chatterji in Boston, established the Green Acre Conference in Eliot, Maine, which became one of the major venues for spreading knowledge of Eastern religions. During the first summer of its operation, the Monslavat School of Comparative Religions, headed by Lewis G. Janes, President of the Brooklyn Ethical Association, hosted Vivekananda, Dharmapala, Annie Besant, and other prominent Theosophists, spiritualists, and pioneers of the New Thought movement.[103]

Beginning in the mid-1880s, metaphysical publications popularized Chatterji's words, which both comforted spiritual seekers and were congenial to former Protestants who still were attuned to the notion of grace abounding. Chatterji was reported to have said: "The yoke of God is very light indeed. None need do any special thing for him; but in the performance of the ordinary acts of life he is fully worshipped if they are performed for his sake alone. The interior spirit is superior to all works."[104] After the dawn of the new century, his words were picked up by writers who advanced the view that not only were psychology and religion compatible, but that they pointed to the same path for self-development. The 1905 *Psychological Yearbook* quoted Chatterji, in what would become a mantra for the New Age: "The spirit in the individual is really identical with the spirit of God. The Deity stands in relation as a giver to man,—granting what is asked. God is, and the ego is, and they are one being,—consciousness."[105]

FEMINIST ASPIRATIONS

Laura Holloway-Langford sympathized with the new metaphysics, but after resigning from the Theosophical Society she increasingly pursued her spiritual interests in private. She never discussed openly her disappointment with Blavatsky or the Society, turning her attention instead to literary work. While Mohini Chatterji played an important role in disseminating new religious ideas, Holloway-Langford was more effective in promoting feminist aspirations. She had hoped to bring new ways of thinking about gender to thousands of American women through *The Home Library Magazine,* but its publication lasted only a year. In 1888, she brought out *The Woman's Story, as Told by Twenty American Women.* The book consisted of a short biographical sketch of each writer, a photograph, and a sample of her work. Still, Holloway-Langford found herself at loose ends. She needed a focus for her energy and ambition. She also wanted to carve out a sphere of influence where she could exercise her talents. It was then that she hit upon the idea of establishing an organization under her direct leadership and control that would open opportunities for women to participate fully in the cultural life of Brooklyn. A few months later she would found the Seidl Society, her most significant achievement.

9

Music of the Spheres

In May 1889, Laura Holloway-Langford created the Seidl Society. Taking its name from the conductor Anton Seidl, the Society was established to promote musical culture among "all classes of women and children" and to produce "harmony over individual life and character."[1] Convinced that music was a spiritual force with the power to dispel the divisions created by sex, race, or social class, Laura Holloway-Langford envisioned the Seidl Society as a public space where she could implement her ideals. The Society opened the world of classical music, particularly the "new music" composed by Richard Wagner, to people who ordinarily had little opportunity to hear it. Through educational programs sponsored for its members, the Seidl Society was also a vehicle for the spread of esoteric religious ideas. From its inception, the Society was avowedly feminist in its aims, and it showcased the ability of women to manage a complex nonprofit organization whose activities were far more demanding than those undertaken by ordinary women's clubs.

HOLLOWAY-LANGFORD'S MUSICAL LIFE

Of all the arts, it was music that most inspired Laura Holloway-Langford. In her youth she had studied piano at the Nashville Female Academy, where one of her classmates was Camilla Urso, a musical prodigy who was born in France in 1842. As a child, Urso had played the violin on tour in

Europe and the United States, but in 1856 she settled in Nashville, where her mother taught French and where she occasionally performed, accompanied by George Taylor, a piano instructor at the Academy who became her husband and father of her two children. By 1863, however, Urso had left Nashville (and apparently her husband as well) to resume her musical career as one of the first women to become a professional violinist. Laura Holloway-Langford would have heard Urso play in the 1880s and 1890s at the Metropolitan Opera House, Steinway Hall, or the Brooklyn Academy of Music. At home in Brooklyn, Holloway-Langford hosted musical evenings where she and her friends performed. Later she recalled that her son George had been inordinately fond of orchestral music, but that the most musical member of her family was her sister Anne Catherine. In 1880, another sister, Ella Watson Carter, married William James Henderson, who gained prominence as a music critic, first for the *New York Times*, 1887–1902, and then for the *New York Sun*.[2]

Laura Holloway-Langford had long believed that music was the link between the material and the spiritual worlds, an idea familiar to spiritualists, who typically opened their circles with the sound of the flute, harp, or guitar. Holding hands, members of the circle often joined in song. Through music, they sought to come into harmony with each other and with the vibrations emanating from other realms. Thus, when she wrote *Beyond the Sunrise*, Holloway-Langford had music mark the presence of spirits. The character Cleo proclaimed in the book that the "music of the spheres" was not a myth, although she feared that most people had forgotten how to hear it. Cleo was certain that if people could be "keyed in harmony" they would feel "the rhythm throbbing through the universe."[3] As a Theosophist, Holloway-Langford understood the universe to be layered across space and time, with levels of reality coordinated and held together by an ethereal substance.[4] She believed that this substance was manifest in music which was "the most perfect symbol" for "expressing Theosophy or Divine Wisdom."[5]

After she returned to Brooklyn from Europe in fall 1884, Laura Holloway-Langford was a regular patron of the Metropolitan Opera House. Of twenty-one librettos in her personal library, twelve were for Wagnerian operas, most of which were performed at the Metropolitan between 1886 and 1891.[6] There she heard the Hungarian conductor Anton Seidl, who had joined the Metropolitan Opera in 1885 and who was "looked upon as a repository of Wagnerian tradition—a prophet, priest, and paladin."[7] A newspaper article in 1888 remarked that at her home Holloway-Langford maintained a fine conservatory whose "walls have echoed the divine notes of... [Adelina] Patti, [Etelka] Gerster, [Clara Louise] Kellogg, and [Amalie] Materna, while the sweet violin strains of Ole Bull and [Rafael] Joseffy have charmed its mistress and her guests."[8] Undoubtedly Laura Holloway-Langford had heard these great stars perform at the Metropolitan Opera House or at the Academy of Music, not in her own conservatory. Inaccurate as the article may be, it nevertheless demonstrates that in the public mind Holloway-Langford was known to be a patron of music culture even before she founded the Seidl Society.

If in the winter Holloway-Langford attended opera, the summers found her at Brighton Beach, a mecca of popular culture, with a racetrack, a seaside theater, and a music hall. She had resumed her friendship with Edna Dean Proctor, whose brother had married the daughter of Charles Storrs. Storrs was president of the Brighton Railway Company, which had been organized in 1880 to build a line along the shore of Coney Island to Brighton Beach. Additionally, Storrs had helped develop this property into a summer resort.[9] Laura Holloway-Langford often accompanied the Storrs family to the beach, where, in the summer of 1888, a new musical pavilion had been opened, with Anton Seidl conducting members of the Metropolitan Opera Orchestra. As thrilled as Holloway-Langford was to attend these performances, she also recoiled at the need for a male companion. Wealthy women might spend their summers in hotels near the beach, with husbands joining them for weekends, but single, working women like Holloway-Langford or Edna Dean Proctor could not take the train by themselves, spend a day in the Brighton Beach Hotel, enjoy an evening of music, and return home without undermining their reputations.

THE SEIDL SOCIETY

The impetus for establishing the Seidl Society arose out of Holloway-Langford's determination that single women participate fully in the cultural life of Brooklyn. With her characteristic approach to solving a problem without directly challenging the social structure, Holloway-Langford contacted the Brighton Beach Railroad Company, a co-sponsor of the concerts. The *Brooklyn Daily Eagle* recounted that "the luxury of listening" to Anton Seidl's concerts at Brighton Beach

> was at that time accessible only to women with escorts. Mrs. Holloway conceived the idea of so arranging matters that women and children could, without violating social proprieties, and without escorts, listen to the music. The Brighton Beach railway company entered into the project in the spirit in which it was submitted to them. They furnished a special car and made such other provisions as were necessary to insure all possible comfort and convenience. Out of this germ sprang the Seidl society.[10]

Colonel Edward Langford was Secretary and Treasurer of the Brooklyn & Brighton Beach Railroad running from Prospect Park to the Brighton Beach Hotel, which was owned by the Railroad.[11] He had been instrumental in getting Seidl to play at Brighton Beach in 1887 and in building the music hall for his orchestra.[12] He was therefore the person to whom Laura Holloway-Langford submitted her request that the railway set aside special cars for unescorted women. She also asked that mothers with children be given free use of its transportation facilities three days each week.[13] Edward Langford approved the scheme, which would publicize Brighton Beach and its music program. In the summer of 1888, to his delight, women filled the railway cars and substantially increased concert attendance, a profitable arrangement for both the Brighton Beach Railway and the hotel.

The following spring Laura Holloway-Langford founded the Seidl Society as a woman's cultural organization. Its constitution echoed the charter of the Brooklyn Woman's Club, declaring that the Society was "independent of sect, party, or social clique," with participation limited to women.[14] A candidate for membership was required to submit her name in writing and "be vouched for by two members who must know her personally."[15] For an annual fee of $5, Seidl Society members received admission to all summer and winter concerts. Holloway-Langford persuaded the Brighton Beach Hotel to designate Friday afternoon as club day, when the hotel's corridors, parlors, and meeting rooms would be reserved for use by the Society. Members first assembled to "listen to a short address by some woman prominent in the literary, social, or philanthropic world," followed by an informal social hour. Later they occupied "their seats in the music hall, with every feeling of safety for those who wish to remain or come only for the evening concert."[16] The members of the Society sold tickets, publicized events, arranged decorations, and ushered at two concerts each day during the summer months.

Laura Holloway-Langford was determined that the Seidl Society would not be just another woman's club. She dreamed that it could change the cultural and social landscape of Brooklyn. The Society's inaugural dinner was held on June 15, 1889, with 380 women in attendance. The guest of honor was Auguste Kraus Seidl, the composer's wife.[17] Shortly thereafter, Holloway-Langford hosted a reception at her home where she solicited support for establishing a summer Wagner Festival modeled on Bayreuth. She hoped that Mrs. Seidl might prevail on Cosima Wagner to give her approval for such an undertaking, even perhaps attending as a guest of the Seidl Society.[18]

The work of the Seidl Society soon grew beyond its original mission. Holloway-Langford established a Seidl Society Library, and she initiated a series of publications sponsored by the Society.[19] In addition to the summer performances at Brighton Beach, the Society sponsored winter concerts at the Brooklyn Academy of Music, a venue that was used mainly for theatrical, social, political, and religious functions and was not expressly adapted for music. Holloway-Langford proposed raising funds to build a Wagner Opera House, which could offer a full season of performances, with the capacity to stage Wagner's operas as well as attract major orchestras to Brooklyn. As the *Daily Eagle* noted, "other cities half as large have such halls and patronize them, too."[20] Glowing from her initial successes, she imagined this building as the cultural center of the city and as the home of the Seidl Society. The next spring, the Society undertook its most ambitious project, the *"Parsifal* Entertainment." At a time when other women's clubs were becoming increasingly conservative, the Seidl Society was in the forefront of opening opportunities to women.

MARRIAGE: A COMPLETE SURPRISE

Soon, Edward Langford began accompanying Laura Holloway to social occasions sponsored by the Society. On May 2, 1890, about two years after they met, they were married. Edward Langford was a member of Holy Trinity Protestant Episcopal Church in Brooklyn Heights—its building a masterpiece of gothic revival architecture and its congregation composed of the Brooklyn elite. Perhaps harking back to the church of her youth, Laura Holloway asked a Presbyterian minister, the Reverend James M. Sherwood, to perform the wedding ceremony.[21] The *New York Times* noted that "the marriage was a complete surprise to some of the most intimate friends of each. The Colonel is on the shady side of fifty, and is known as a confirmed old bachelor. Mrs. Holloway, too, was thought to have abandoned all idea of venturing again into the uncertainty of matrimony." The article recounted an anecdote taking place during the run-up to a much-anticipated "Entertainment" sponsored by the Seidl Society.

> Mrs. Holloway had charge of the decorations. . . . She had present several well-known gentlemen to help her out in the more laborious part of the work. Two of them were bachelors and one of the bachelors was Col. Langford. He was on the go constantly and did great work. Mrs. Holloway was delighted and turning to a reporter who was present she said: "If I had a few more old bachelors like these I would get through my daily work very quickly." In a month she had as much of her wish as the law in this part of the country permits.[22]

In 1889, Edward Langford had supervised the Brighton Beach concerts, but after her marriage, Laura Holloway-Langford increasingly assumed this responsibility. She negotiated the artistic program with Anton Seidl and the musicians, she made financial arrangements with the Brighton Beach Hotel and Railroad, and she managed a substantial budget. During one nine-week season, for example, the Society took in $34,000 while charging only 25 cents for concert tickets. At the end of that summer, the Society's books were balanced, which the *Brooklyn Daily Eagle* deemed "a remarkable feat of managerial skill."[23]

Despite the immense amount of labor that she put into the Seidl Society, Laura Holloway-Langford was typical of female benevolent workers who donated their talents without pecuniary reward. In the past, she had argued that women should be employed as paid professionals, not as unpaid volunteers. However, her economic and social status had changed with her marriage to Edward Langford, and she no longer needed to work for compensation. Ironically, her unpaid work for the Seidl Society brought greater social prestige than had her contributions as a journalist. Nevertheless, during 1892 and 1893, Holloway-Langford was able to parlay her position as president of the Seidl Society into paying editorial work. In the early 1890s, Isaac K. Funk had undertaken the publication of his first *Standard Dictionary of the English Language.* He hired over "Two Hundred Specialists and Other Scholars" of "the Most Recent Advances in Knowledge," including F. Max Müller for "Buddhistic Terms"; William Q. Judge for "Theosophic Terms"; Benson J. Lossing for American History; and Anton Seidl, William J. Henderson, and Laura C. Holloway-Langford for Music. Of the seventy-seven specialists listed for major departments, Holloway-Langford was the only woman, surely a result of her insistence on equal billing with Seidl and Henderson, whose names lent prestige to the project. Much of the drudgery of the editorial work, however, fell on her shoulders.[24] The *Washington Post* wrote that Laura Holloway-Langford had "proven her ability to be a force in music culture as well as editor and author."[25]

Additionally, she was employed in another musical project. In an opening ceremony of the Chicago Columbian Exposition, or World's Fair, on June 3, 1893, a choir of 1,200 children from the public schools performed under the direction of William Tomlins. The songs came from the *Children's Souvenir Songbook,* which contained a selection of poems written by the country's premier poets and put to music by its best composers. Her name does not appear in connection with this publication, but it was Laura Holloway-Langford who chose the poems for the book. Despite her professional expertise, Holloway-Langford's work was invisible, with William Tomlins credited as editor of the *Children's Souvenir Songbook.*[26] Neither this project nor the position with the *Standard Dictionary* would have come her way, however, were it not for the public prominence that Laura Holloway-Langford had achieved as an unpaid cultural worker as president of the Seidl Society.

THE SEIDL SOCIETY AND FEMINISM

The Seidl Society was apolitical, but its activities reflected Laura Holloway-Langford's interests: the rights of working women, the plight of homeless children, and the spread of new religious ideas. From its inception, the Seidl Society was identified as a feminist organization. In summer 1889, Holloway-Langford invited two of the country's best-known proponents of suffrage to speak to its members. Elizabeth Cady Stanton was the guest of honor at a luncheon on July 12, and on August 30 Susan B. Anthony spoke to three hundred women on the topic "Woman's Mission." In her invitation to Anthony, Holloway-Langford had written: "Not nearly all our members are suffragists, but all of them honor you as a great and noble representative of the sex. You can do more good by meeting this body of musical and literary women than by addressing a dozen out-and-out suffrage meetings."[27] In her lecture, however, Anthony challenged Holloway-Langford's premise. The *Brooklyn Daily Eagle* reported that Anthony was not "diverted from her great mission" by trifles such as Wagner's musical dramas. She attributed women's subordination and financial dependency to their lack of the ballot, and with a backhanded reference to Anton Seidl she "rebuked her fellow lunchers for supposing that 'the object of a woman's life is to help a man.'"[28]

One of the speakers the following summer was Anna Dickinson, the suffragist and celebrated lyceum speaker turned actress. When, sometime later, Dickinson was hospitalized in a mental asylum, it was Laura Holloway-Langford who issued an appeal to those "who appreciate the public services and private character of this noble and gifted woman— now suffering the combined misfortunes of ill-health and poverty"—to donate to a fund.[29] She hoped to raise $20,000 so that Dickinson could travel to Europe, where she could recover at the famed thermal springs in Carlsbad, Germany.

Initially, the press mocked the Society by portraying women worshiping at the feet of their god, Herr Seidl. One writer admitted that men were jealous of Seidl and that they were "inclined to tell scandalous stories of the handsome, long haired musician."[30] The *Daily Eagle* took note of the new Society in a mocking tone that recalled its earlier attitude toward the Brooklyn Woman's Club:

> Who would not like to be an orchestral conductor and rule over the
> stormy democracy of fiddles and drums? Who would not like to be a hand-
> some man? Who then would not like to be Anton Seidl? He has taken the
> City of Churches captive. The Seidl Society is organized for his worship,
> and irrepressible Laura C. Holloway is the chief priestess in the cult whose
> temple is Coney Island. I believe in woman's rights. I believe women are
> as good as men, and "a deal better"; I believe in their going where they like
> and how they like, without chaperons or escorts. The American woman
> can take care of herself and the police will take care of the masher. But
> they must allow us poor males something. According to what I hear

smoking is to be confined to a sequestered spot in the gallery. . . . Coney
Island is a place of amusement, and the concerts are part of the fun. Now,
if a man, bad as men are, cannot enjoy his after dinner cigar while listening
to the orchestra, he will be perilously apt to keep away. . . . Women can do
anything, but, I doubt whether they will make the Beach a focus of culture
on such hard and fast lines.[31]

The author professed to be a feminist, but he resented a cultural elitism
that he associated with female do-gooders who, to his mind, were intrud-
ing on male space.

In another article, the *Brooklyn Daily Eagle* made fun of the women
who, the author said, worshiped Seidl but excluded him from their opening celebration because he was a man. The women "gave him a big letter
S made of daisies, as a hint that it regarded him as a good deal of a daisy
himself." In other words, the article implied that Seidl lacked masculinity
and that he was complicit in the feminization of Brighton Beach. Real
men were the "coarse half of humanity that goes to Coney Island to drink
beer and swim." Despite his ambivalence about Seidl and classical music,
the writer conceded the need for the Society: "By joining an association
like this a woman, if she be unmarried or unengaged, need not sit pining
at home for healthful recreation or refined pleasures because no 'young
feller' offers to act as escort. In union there is strength, and the several
hundred devotees of Brighton Beach music are, in their corporate capacity
at all events, quite well able to take care of themselves."[32]

Other newspapers, however, praised the salubrious female influence,
describing how members of the Seidl Society required strict decorum
in the Brighton Beach Pavilion. The women were on hand for a matinee
and evening performance every day of the week. They enforced regula-
tions against smoking and ensured that latecomers were seated only in the
interval between numbers. Most notably, a sign proclaimed that talking
during the performance was a breach of politeness that would not be tolerated. "The gentlewomen, who man the aisles, maintain a vigilant outlook
and are always ready to pounce upon any bold spirit found infringing in
the slightest degree."[33]

The Seidl Society had been formed out of a feminist and egalitarian
impulse, to give women an equal opportunity to enjoy excursions to the
beach and to participate in musical culture irrespective of their marital or
economic status. According to the *Daily Eagle,* the Seidl Society attracted

"some of the richest women in Brooklyn and many women who earn their own living."

> It is thus enabled to throw chances for education and culture as well as business opportunities in the way of women and girls who become acquaintances of members of the society, and who will take help from women whom they feel to be their friends which self respect would not allow them to take from organized charity. During the excursions last Summer members were required to go to the beach with the poorer women whom they invited and to look out for them during the day.[34]

For the fall and winter 1890 season, the Seidl Society reserved the Family Circle at the Brooklyn Academy for women who were self-supporting, with each Society member having the privilege of inviting suitable candidates.

Holloway-Langford believed that "rich women and poor met on equality on the ground of their common womanhood and their common love of music."[35] Women, she thought, were by nature more spiritually inclined than men, so that no matter their social class, they would be elevated by exposure to classical music. Less-privileged women would also be uplifted, socially and culturally, by their association with members of the Seidl Society. She invited Grace Dodge, the first woman to serve on the New York School Board, to give pointers on how to relate to women from the working class. Dodge had founded the New York Working Girls' Society in 1885 "to provide a place where working women could 'have a good, useful time in the evening,'" while preserving their "social purity."[36] When she spoke to the Seidl Society, Dodge urged members to "treat the working girls as friends, talk with them of books, clothes, and other things about which they talk with each other, and do with them rather than for them."[37]

Sisterly solidarity in the Seidl Society, however, was short-lived. Despite the fact that the Society never "tolerated anything that savored of class or social distinctions," few elite women volunteered to accompany working-class women on the train or in the hotel. Consequently, there were too few chaperones to keep track of the women invited to the beach. *The Brooklyn Daily Eagle* reported complaints from hotel patrons that the "poor women did not conduct themselves with the same circumspection which would be required of the paying patrons of the [hotel]. Some of them were reported to wander off, indulge in beer and then thrust themselves into the presence of guests of the house."[38] Not all women came to the beach to be uplifted culturally or morally, and apparently a few failed to meet the standard of social purity. In response to this article, Laura Holloway-Langford denied that the Seidl Society was abandoning philanthropic projects, pointing to continuing excursions for children, but she wrote: "Individual members differ in their preferences; some devote themselves to the musical interests of the Society and take no part in the philanthropic work." She avoided, however, answering the charge that poor women had not conducted themselves with propriety.[39] Holloway-Langford remained convinced that music was a universal language that could transcend disparities in wealth or social standing. The women of the Seidl Society learned, nevertheless, that it would take more than a few summer concerts to overcome the gap that separated their lives from those of the working-class women of Brooklyn.

Yet Laura Holloway-Langford never wavered in her support of women who earned their own living. In one telling incident, she went toe-to-toe with the manager of the Brighton Beach Orchestra, who had hired a woman harpist, Inez Carusi, but paid her only $40 a week, whereas her predecessor, a man, had received $54 per week. Carusi protested, and Holloway-Langford exerted the power of the Seidl Society to demand that the injustice be rectified. When asked what would be done if Carusi were fired for complaining, Holloway-Langford replied: "'That will not happen. . . . The Seidl Society is composed entirely of women; women have worked for it and sustained it, and this woman will be sustained in her position . . . not because she is a woman, but because she is a musician. . . . This woman will remain at her post until the season closes.'"[40] Laura Holloway-Langford prevailed, even though in the music world women were routinely prevented from joining orchestras because they were not members of the union, which only admitted men. The conflict over the female harpist and the Brighton Beach Orchestra demonstrated Holloway-Langford's prescience in creating an all-woman organization that could wield power on issues important to its membership.

CHILDREN, RACE, AND CULTURE

Even though in later years the Society cut back on its outreach to working-class women, it continued to sponsor summer outings for children. In the 1870s, when working for the *Brooklyn Daily Union,* Holloway-Langford had convinced businessmen to support "Fresh Air" picnics for working children of all races.[41] As president of the Seidl Society, she continued to imagine ways that poor children could be given holidays. In its first summer, the Society conveyed 3,500 people to Brighton Beach, many of them children from public institutions. Because of Holloway-Langford's leadership, the Seidl Society provided outings for children from Howard Orphan Asylum for "colored" children, an institution named for Oliver Otis Howard. Since the time that he headed the Freedmen's Bureau, Howard had been committed to the education of former slaves. He was one of the founders of Howard University, which was named for him, and he had served as its first president. He was also Holloway-Langford's good friend. It was not a matter of chance, then, that the Seidl Society supported the Howard Orphan Asylum.

The *Brooklyn Daily Eagle* gave the August 15, 1889, outing for children from this orphanage front-page billing, describing a "jubilant and happy" gathering at the beach, where the president and ladies of the Seidl Society provided refreshments. The children then consumed a "sumptuous dinner" in the hotel dining room, before forming a line and marching to the train for the trip back to the city.[42] The Seidl Society's efforts on behalf of the Howard Orphan Asylum continued year-round. In November 1889, it gave a Thanksgiving dinner for the children, as well as for residents of the Zion Home for the Colored Aged, which was affiliated with the orphanage. This event enacted a reversal of racial and class hierarchies. "Beautiful women dressed in handsome silks, which were covered with aprons, waited on them. These women were members of the Seidl Society, and they would not allow any of the colored attachés of the asylum to do any of the work. For three days previous they had been busy preparing for the feast, and were assisted by two professional cooks from New York. All the cakes and delicacies were made by the women themselves."[43] The following year, after Seidl Society members had served Thanksgiving dinner, children from the orphanage put on an elaborate program of music and recitations. The *Daily Eagle* reported that "it might do credit to children of another race and far better condition in life. The singing was particularly good." The superintendent of the orphanage, the Reverend F. W. Johnson, thanked the benefactors, saying that "the color line had been blotted out in connection with the aid given to the asylum."[44]

In January 1890, the Seidl Society gave a musical entertainment at Plymouth Church to raise money for these institutions. "General O. O. Howard introduced the pianist and composer, Silas G. Pratt." Curiously, Pratt spoke about the transmigration of the tune of Stephen Foster's "My Old Kentucky Home," a song whose lyrics recalled slave life on a plantation.[45] Despite such ironies, the Seidl Society was crossing racial barriers at a period generally considered to be the nadir of race relations in the United States.

Not everyone, however, supported the beach excursions for African American children. In July 1891, an article in the *Brooklyn Daily Eagle* suggested that because "the polished ebony limbs of the inmates of the Howard Orphan Asylum do not this summer flash in the surf behind the music pavilion," attendance at Brighton Beach had increased. Some "well dressed guests who stroll about the piazza and order lunches in sight of the rolling waves" were glad that they were no longer "confronted suddenly with visions of nursery industries in spots not too remote from the promenade."[46] Holloway-Langford disputed the article's implication that the children had disturbed the other guests. Those from Howard Orphan Asylum were, she wrote, "among the best behaved and most grateful of children. It is an institution for which I make myself responsible and personally supply luncheons and tax my friends for money to help me pay the bills. So far we have been enabled to take these children down several times each season." She concluded. "We are trying daily to live and serve that we may hasten the day," and then she quoted from a poem popular among pulpit orators:

When man to man united,
And every wrong thing righted,
The whole world shall be lighted,
As Eden was of old.[47]

On August 27–29, 1895, the Seidl Society sponsored a children's festival. Five hundred children were recruited "without regard for sex" to sing in the choir. Hermann Rothschild donated the use of a large building for rehearsals. The festival was attended by "over a thousand youngsters, boys and girls, from institutions in this city, and added to their number were many who came with parents and guardians." They sang patriotic hymns, including "America," "Columbia, the Gem of the Ocean," and "The Star-Spangled Banner." The Howard Orphan Asylum was not among the participants.[48] It was, instead, the Hebrew Orphan Asylum that drew particular notice in the press.[49] The next summer, a free concert was given on four Mondays in August for children from orphanages, including Jewish, Catholic, and Protestant institutions. Once again, the Howard Orphan Asylum apparently was not invited.

During its first years, the Seidl Society, under Laura Holloway-Langford's leadership, tried to implement what were, for the times, radical notions of equality, attempting to bring holiday excursions and musical culture to all citizens of Brooklyn, irrespective of social class, religion, or race. The evidence suggests that more conservative forces in the Seidl Society eventually prevailed. For three years, Holloway-Langford brought African American children to the beach, but their visits were separate from those of other children. Just as her ambitious plan to bring poor women to Brighton Beach had been modified, likewise in later years her support for the Howard Orphan Asylum became less visible. In her leadership of the Seidl Society, Laura Holloway-Langford anticipated a New Age where racial as well as sexual and economic inequalities would be transcended, but America in the 1890s was not yet prepared to realize such a vision.

WORSHIP AT THE SHRINE OF WAGNER

Laura Holloway-Langford was often quoted as saying that the Seidl Society was established for "music and good works." Many people, however, believed that it was formed to promote the music of Richard Wagner. Undoubtedly, her interest in Anton Seidl was spurred by his close connection to Wagner. For several years, Seidl had lived with the Wagner family in Bayreuth, where he worked as Wagner's secretary and assisted at the music festivals.[50] By 1885, when he accepted the position of conductor of the Metropolitan Opera, Seidl was renowned as the premier interpreter of Wagner's music.

During 1882–1883, Anton Seidl had conducted Wagner's *Ring* cycle throughout Europe, performing it, as well as *Die Meistersinger* and *Tristan und Isolde,* in London. When Laura Holloway-Langford traveled to Europe, she discovered that Theosophists were among the most active Wagner enthusiasts. Gatherings at the home of A. P. Sinnett often featured performances of Wagner's music. After hearing *Lohengrin* there in early summer 1884, one Theosophist remarked that it was music she had "heard somewhere long, long ago," as if in a mystical past.[51] Arthur Gebhard, the son of Holloway-Langford's friend Mary, was "one of the first patrons of Wagner's musical dramas, at Bayreuth, Bavaria, recognizing their occult significance."[52] Many other Theosophists traveled to Bayreuth as if on a religious pilgrimage to participate in a sacred rite. Some even suggested a mystical connection between the founding of the Theosophical Society in fall 1875 and the first full performance of the Nibelungen operas in Bayreuth during the summer of 1876. Both, they thought, indicated the opening of a New Age when ancient wisdom and occult knowledge would be revealed.[53]

William Ashton Ellis, a member of the Royal College of Surgeons and sometime physician to Helena Blavatsky, had discovered Wagner in 1875, and in 1885 he joined the Universal Wagner Society. Ellis was also a member of the London Lodge of the Theosophical Society, which in 1886 published his "Theosophy in the Works of Richard Wagner."[54] Later, Ellis lectured on "Richard Wagner, as Poet, Musician and Mystic" to the London Society for the Encouragement of the Fine Arts at a meeting chaired by A. P. Sinnett. From 1888–1895, Ellis edited the *Meister,* a journal where he published translations of Wagner's writings, discussions of his dramas, and reviews of books and performances. The *Meister* printed a long article on *The Ring* by the Theosophist William C. Ward, who argued that the true subject of the opera was "the gradual progress of the human Soul, its contests, its victories and defeats, and its ultimate redemption by the power of Divine Love," an interpretation shared by William Ashton Ellis and most Theosophists.[55]

Wagner was a hot topic of discussion among spiritual seekers both in Europe and the United States. Clara Kathleen Rogers recalled: "It was in the Summer of 1886, following our intercourse with Arthur Gebhardt [*sic*], that we first went to worship at the shrine of Richard Wagner." She traveled to Bayreuth, where she saw *Tristan und Isolde* and was present for the funeral of Liszt. But it was *Parsifal* that left her with the greatest impression:

> I experienced an acute sense of reverence transcending anything I had
> ever known. . . . As I look back, I realize that such a representation of
> Parsifal offers a religious experience that can hardly be duplicated in
> any church. And yet, incredible as it may seem, there were actually both
> American and English people in the audience who inveighed against it
> as being shockingly *sacrilegious*! I know of many different instances of
> the deep and lasting impression made by Parsifal on individuals whom
> one would hardly have expected to be susceptible to such emotions. The
> ardent Theosophist, Arthur Gebhardt [*sic*], told me that up to the time
> when he first went to Bayreuth he was merely a physical and intellectual
> creature; that it was Parsifal which searched out and lighted in him the
> divine spark.[56]

That same year, Gebhard spoke on "Richard Wagner's Ideals and Theosophy" at a meeting of the New York branch of the Theosophical Society. He
recounted how "he had been lead [*sic*], through a study of the Wagnerian
treatment of the old legends, and through a personal acquaintance with
Wagner himself, to theosophical research. He described the field of work
in Oriental literature and occultisms, and he glorified Wagner."[57] Laura
Holloway-Langford missed by only a few weeks the first performance of
Parsifal in London, where, in November 1884, it was sung as an oratorio
by the Royal Albert Hall Choral Society.[58]

Theosophists viewed Wagner as a member of the Adept Brotherhood
who had been sent to teach the way to perfection, just as had the Buddha,
Jesus, Zoroaster, and Helena Blavatsky. A correspondent to the *Daily Eagle*
reporting on a musical lecture "under the auspices of the Brooklyn Theosophical Society" found this elevation of Wagner to be "repulsive, sacri-
legious and abhorrent."[59] Laura Holloway-Langford, in contrast, would
not have hesitated to include Wagner among the great spiritual adepts. At
Brighton Beach, on August 30, 1888, she recited a poem "To Herr Anton
Seidl," that she authored. It makes explicit her belief that Wagner was a
Master who revealed ancient wisdom in his operas and whose spirit in-
fused Anton Seidl, who had been chosen to pass on the mystical teachings.

> Rhineland gods, 'tis said no more
> Disport themselves on sylvan shore.
> The muses all their silence keep,
> The fairies and the elfins sleep.

Echoes only fill the air,
Mute that voice of power rare,
Which sang of Odin and his band,
Mystic King of Valhal land.

Singers many lisp his song,
For his mantle myriads long,
Yet but one has come to be
True teacher of his minstrelsy.

Only one with kindling heart
Can his secrets deep impart,
But for him in western world
Wagner's banner would be furled.

Master loved this pupil well,
Leads him now by magic spell;
For, last night, in 'Siegfried Idyl,'
He was incarnate in thee, Seidl.[60]

The programs that she designed for the Seidl Society reflected Holloway-Langford's spiritual interests. In September 1891, Henry S. Olcott spoke on "The Power of Music in Psychic Development."[61] A meeting of the Society in February 1892 began with violin-piano duets adapted from Wagner and performed by the German violinist Carl Venth, founder and director of the Brooklyn Symphony Orchestra, and his wife. A newspaper account, which compared the secretiveness of the Seidl Society to the "mysteries of Isis," chided the Society for its pretentiousness and Carl Venth for a lack of manliness: "These pieces are by 'Vogner.' Not Wagner, but 'Vogner.' Mr. Venth . . . came away from home yesterday and forgot his hairpins. He played very nicely, in spite of the fact that his wrist had a nervous chill whenever he had a long note to play." Kate Hillard, a Theosophist and an early president of the Brooklyn Woman's Club, then read a "long and highly uninteresting paper on 'The Twin Doctrines of the East,' meaning Reincarnation and Karma, two very important and useful things to know. No housekeeper should be without them." To belittle the work of the Society, the reporter resorted to gendered language, feminizing both its musical and intellectual endeavors and concluding: "The common, brutal man, who is accustomed to hear folks say something when they make speeches, was ineffably bored by it all. But the Seidlites were delighted—or said they were."[62] Derision in the press did not inhibit Holloway-Langford, who shared her religious ideas with none other than Anton Seidl, who wrote to her in his imperfect English, "I am now read The Karma, it interesting me very much."[63] One cannot help but wonder if Holloway-Langford had presented Herr Seidl with a copy of A. P. Sinnett's book by that name, the novel in which Holloway-Langford is incarnated as the character Mrs. Lakesby.

THE *PARSIFAL* ENTERTAINMENT

Less than a year after the formation of the Seidl Society, Laura Holloway-Langford suggested that it sponsor a "*Parsifal* Entertainment." It was a brilliant and audacious proposal. The opera had generated great excitement since the publication of the libretto in 1877, with an English translation available by 1879. *Parsifal* had premiered in Bayreuth in July 1882, but Wagner's family had forbidden any full-scale performance of the opera at other locations. In the United States, concert performances by the Oratorio Society of New York in 1886 had been disappointing. Thus, the prospect of bringing *Parsifal* to Brooklyn under the baton of the renowned Wagner interpreter Anton Seidl was greeted with enthusiasm.[64]

In *Parsifal*, Wagner tells the story of King Amfortas, guardian of the Holy Grail at the Castle of Monsalvat. He has been wounded by the lance that once pierced the Savior and so can be healed only by its touch. The lance, however, is possessed by Klingsor, an evil magician who also controls Kundry, a woman cursed to wander the world because she laughed at the Savior on the Cross. Through innocence and sexual renunciation, Parsifal, the "holy fool," obtains the lance from Klingsor, delivers Kundry from the curse, and heals the dying Amfortas. In the final scene, Parsifal ascends the altar and elevates the sacred chalice. A white dove descends and hovers over the new king, as voices sing: "Wondrous work of mercy! Salvation to the Savior!"

To prepare Brooklynites for the "*Parsifal* Entertainment," Holloway-Langford invited Henry E. Krehbiel, music critic for the *New York Tri-*

bune, to give four lectures in November 1889 devoted to "Richard Wagner and His Lyric Dramas." They were held at the Historical Hall, Brooklyn, and the admission fee of $1 per lecture was donated to the building fund for a future music hall.[65] Like many Victorians, Krehbiel invoked woman's spiritual superiority and the power of her redemptive love. Consequently, he judged *Parsifal* a "monstrous perversion of womanhood, and a wicked degradation of womankind." The notion that "all human virtues are summed up in celibate chastity" was to him completely opposed to a modern, civilized understanding of the relations between the sexes. He asserted that in *Parsifal* Wagner had fallen prey to "monkish theologians under the influence of fearful moral depravity and fanatical superstitions, as far removed from the teaching and example of his original hero [Christ] as are the heavens from the earth."[66] Later, Krehbiel wrote that in *Parsifal* Wagner had resorted to "the quietism or indifferentism of the old Brahmanic religion in which holiness is to be attained through an ascetic life of speculative contemplation. In Buddhism, which is reformed Brahmanism, there appears . . . a tender pity for the misfortunes of everything in nature." He found it "comforting to know that there are elements in the work which were in existence long before Christian symbolism was grafted upon the old tales of the quest of a magic talisman."[67] Krehbiel, therefore, did not accept *Parsifal* as a dramatization of the Passion, but rather as an amalgamation of ancient tales, superstitions, folklore, and Eastern philosophy forced into Christian garb. Perhaps to offer a more positive view of the religious significance of *Parsifal,* Holloway-Langford arranged for a free lecture on "*Parsifal,* the Finding of Christ through Art" by Albert R. Parsons. Taking place the week before the performance, the lecture consisted of long quotations from the works of Wagner, proving too rarefied for many in the audience who walked out.[68]

Nonetheless, by March 1890, *Parsifal* was all the rage in Brooklyn. The public library complained "that books on Wagner cannot be kept in the building longer than it takes to transfer them from one set of readers to another." *Parsifal* was the social highlight of the season, and newspapers speculated about the fashions that women would display at the performance. An "enterprising milliner . . . named a new spring style the 'Parsifal' toque." The *Daily Eagle* reported that "the affair will be quite unutterably swell from a social point of view, and the ladies are already mixing

a truly feminine anxiety about gowns with their raptures over 'Parsifal.'"
As the time for the opera approached, a ticket was selling for as much as
$25. Laura Holloway-Langford predicted the price might go higher, be-
cause seating capacity at the Brooklyn Academy of Music was limited. By
March 23, it was reported that "well-known Brooklynites . . . with money
and influence" had pledged $250,000 toward the construction of "a build-
ing to be devoted to music, with a conservatory made available for the
middle-class American children, and a hall suitable for concerts."[69]

Wagner had described *Parsifal* as a *Bühnenweihfestspiel*, a festival play
for the consecration of the stage, and critics had followed suit, deeming
it a sacred drama or a miracle play. William James Henderson, Holloway-
Langford's brother-in-law, wrote: "'Parsifal' is no opera. It is not even a
lyric drama. It is what the great tragedies of the Greeks were—a religious
ceremony."[70] The last scene of the opera was set on Good Friday, portraying the ceremony of the Holy Grail as the Eucharist, with Parsifal as
the Savior. Holloway-Langford was shrewd enough to know that *Parsifal*
would attract many people who ordinarily did not attend classical concerts. She chose the date for the performance as Monday, March 31, between Palm Sunday and Easter, situating it so that the event itself suggested a Holy Week ritual.

On the day of the performance, "pilgrims" crossed the Brooklyn Bridge
in a shower of snow, heading "up the hill to the Festal Nibelungen Theatre,
now, alas! commonly known as the Academy of Music."[71] There they entered a lobby whose floors had been covered with rich carpets and whose
walls were hung with silken draperies. Some areas had been transformed
into "veritable miniature magic flower gardens," suggesting a scene from
the opera where Parsifal is tempted by earthly delights. The Christian
connotations were reinforced by the stage set, painted in raspberry red
and pale green, which portrayed a "Romanesque cathedral, stretching
away, arch after arch, until the intersection of the transept and chancel
was reached," where an altar was screened with Easter lilies.[72]

Anton Seidl had assembled an outstanding cast. Lilli Lehmann sang
the part of Kundry. Her young husband, the tenor Paul Kalisch, was Parsifal. The performance began at 5:00 PM, but broke off at 6:30 for "a dainty little dinner of six courses." No alcoholic beverages were permitted. Patrons
were summoned back to the opera by a bugle, and even though Wagner's
score had been reduced by 25 percent, the performance continued until

10:00 PM. The evening concluded with a supper hosted by the Seidl Society. The audience "represented the best social and intellectual life of the city." It included former President Grover Cleveland; Alfred C. Chapin, mayor of Brooklyn; George Foster Peabody, banker and philanthropist; Stephen V. White, Congressman from Brooklyn; and Dr. Lyman Abbott, the minister who succeeded Henry Ward Beecher at Plymouth Church.[73] Abbott was so moved by the opera that the next year he preached about Kundry and Parsifal in his Holy Week sermon.[74]

The "*Parsifal* Entertainment" was a resounding success. In less than two years, Laura Holloway-Langford had transformed an idea about opening Brighton Beach concerts to single women into a major cultural force in Brooklyn. She was at the height of her influence on the intellectual and cultural life of the city, and she had reached a new level of social prominence. Only a few of her close friends realized, however, that for Holloway-Langford the success of the "*Parsifal* Entertainment" was not only a musical but also a religious triumph. To her mind, what had been witnessed at the Brooklyn Academy of Music was no less than a revelation of the essence of Divine Wisdom.

THEOSOPHICAL INTERPRETATIONS OF *PARSIFAL*

Despite its Christian trappings, *Parsifal* was considered by many Theosophists to be Wagner's most profound expression of esoteric knowledge. William Ashton Ellis conceded that much had been "borrowed from the rites of the Christian Church," but he excused Wagner on the grounds that this "was absolutely necessary in order to exercise a mystic and religious influence upon an audience accustomed to those rites. Had Wagner's compatriots been, as a whole, Mohammedans, Buddhists, or ancient Hellenes," then he would have cast his play into that form of worship. In *Parsifal,* Ellis discerned the merger of Christian symbolism into three greater truths of theosophy: sympathy, universal brotherhood, and renunciation of desire. These doctrines, Ellis believed, were taught by both Gautama Buddha and Jesus Christ.[75]

To Theosophists, the Grail represented occult knowledge that had been brought from the Himalayas to "Monsalvat, in the Pyrenees, in order to spread its light and wisdom in Western lands. When the mission was concluded, the Brotherhood returned once more to the East with the sacred vessel."[76] William Ashton Ellis found a correspondence to theosophical ideas in each character and scene of the opera. The old King, Titurel, was a Mahatma who had been visited by the Chohans—theosophical archangels—who brought him the Grail, the holy vessel that had received the blood of the crucified savior, and the spear that had pierced his side. The Grail, however, was not the chalice of the Eucharist, but rather a holy crystal that the Knights contemplated in order to gain spiritual knowledge. The lance represented occult power, which could defeat enemies, but could also be dangerous when it fell into evil hands. For Ellis, the knights of the Grail constituted a "body of occultists similar to the band of Mahatmas and Chelas of the East," only a few of whom were sufficiently pure to be accepted into the sacred brotherhood. The wounded king, Amfortas, was an occultist who had veered "from the right path, and whose desires, represented by the spear, or the will," put him under the power of the "Dweller on the Threshold." His wound could not heal until a Buddha appeared who taught "the renunciation of all desire, by the casting aside of the lower self, and entering upon the path where earthly objects are without attachment for them." Ellis believed that Wagner directly referred to Buddhism in the scene where Parsifal murdered a swan, because it was the sight of a bleeding swan shot by one of his companions that aroused compassion in the mind of the Buddha. When asked his name, Parsifal replied, "Many have I had, but all of them forgot," evidence to Ellis that Wagner depicted Parsifal as having passed through many previous incarnations. Only after many lives would he find "the paths which the initiate alone could tread.... He is spoken of as 'the fool,' in accordance with the old legends, and because Wagner wishes to emphasize the fact that not from the intellectual but from the astral or intuitive side can the greatest occult truths be approached."[77]

According to Ellis, Kundry represented the material world which Parsifal must renounce. She was his lower-self. When Parsifal received his baptism, or initiation, he entered "the service of the Buddhi, or spiritual soul." When he restored Amfortas to wholeness, Parsifal reunited the spear and the Grail, joining occult power with occult knowledge. Kundry, as an emblem of Parsifal's body, dissolved, leaving only the purified savior. But Ellis suggested that Kundry and Parsifal merged into a spiritual union.[78] He wrote: "Thus has Matter, brought to rest, passed from the illusory form, the *Maya* of the Vedas, of which Kundry in her protean external appearance was the type, into the divine essence of the Spirit."[79] The white dove which descended over Parsifal was "the Atmá, the Divine Spirit . . . which knits all others into a harmonious union with itself; and thereby Nirvána is gained."[80] In a similar manner, William C. Ward interpreted Kundry as "the irrational soul of man, the animal nature, helpful in its lawful state of service to the higher soul, but fraught with such deadly peril when allowed to rule when it should obey." To Ward, Kundry's death signified that in "the pure life of the spirit the animal faculties are no longer needed, and are reabsorbed into the source whence they came."[81]

Curiously, Helena Blavatsky's assessment of *Parsifal* was more in accord with its Christian critics than with the adulation given it by other Theosophists. She expressed doubts about the opera's wisdom, claiming that its popularity was due to depiction of the "fantastical" elements of "Christian legends," rather than its expression of universal truths. She judged *Parsifal* "childish in the extreme," describing Parsifal as an "innocent, irresponsible idiot" who because of "his blind, unreasoning faith" became a Savior who was still a "simpleton." She rejected the idea that salvation came through a "half-witted but *blindly believing* knight." To Blavatsky, blind faith without study or knowledge, and intuition without intellect was the path of fools, holy or not, rather than the way to salvation. Kundry, "a fallen woman, accursed by God and the embodiment of lust and vice," was in Blavatsky's opinion a more interesting character, but still preposterous. She wrote:

> Strangely enough Kundry loves *good*—by nature and in her sleep. But no sooner does she awake in the morning than she becomes awfully wicked. We have personally known other persons who were very good—when asleep. . . . She falls in love with Parsifal, who does not love her, but who allows her to wash his feet and wipe them Magdalene-like with the tresses of her long hair, and then proceeds to baptize her. Whether from the effects of this unexpected ceremony or otherwise, Kundry dies immediately, after throwing upon Parsifal a long look of love which he heeds not, but recovers suddenly his lost wits! *Faith* alone has performed all these miracles. The "Innocent" had by the sole strength of his piety, saved the world. Evil is conquered by Good.

Blavatsky was skeptical. She thought that the opera's handling of sacred truths was "a sheer debasement, a sacrilege, and a blasphemy." In her opinion, Wagner had turned the sublime ideals of Christianity into a degrading spectacle that pandered to the tastes of the music hall.[82]

Other Theosophists, however, tended to agree with Alice Cleather, who termed *Parsifal* "a blend of all that is best in the two great religions of the East and West—Buddhism and Christianity." In May 1897, over 200 people gathered in Brooklyn to hear Cleather speak on the theosophical understanding of the "Legend of the Holy Grail," with excerpts from "Lohengrin" sung by Basil Crump, the secretary of the English Theosophical Society. Cleather found the essence of theosophical teaching in Wagner and other geniuses, such as Emerson and Walt Whitman, who "preached brotherhood and the essential divinity of man. They were mystics, that is, they got their knowledge and their impulse to uplift humanity from within themselves."[83]

LAURA HOLLOWAY-LANGFORD AND *PARSIFAL*

In later years, *Parsifal* became a morality play through which some Theosophists interpreted what they termed the "great betrayal" of Helena Blavatsky by A. P. Sinnett, Annie Besant, Charles W. Leadbeater, and others. This view was expressed by Basil Crump, who pointed to *Parsifal* as an allegory about the dangers of misusing occult power. Crump compared A. P. Sinnett to Klingsor. Both were evil magicians who sought revenge for not having been accepted as a disciple of the Mahatmas. To Crump, Kundry represented "the plastic elemental female principle" who had no will of her own and succumbed to male power. "Awake she is the humble serving messenger of the royal brotherhood; but, unknown to them, the black magician, Klingsor, can throw her into a hypnotic trance and compel her to serve his various ends." Likewise, he suggested that when conscious, Holloway-Langford was a disciple of the Mahatmas, but when hypnotized she became an instrument for Sinnett's evil designs. The drama of *Parsifal* then helped Crump understand Laura Holloway-Langford's conflict with A. P. Sinnett: "The terrible danger to sensitive and hysterical women of being subjected to this process by an unscrupulous male hypnotizer cannot be exaggerated; and men like Sinnett, who have recourse to such evil practices in the pursuit of their selfish ends, are black magicians of the worst description, and are a menace to humanity."

Crump admitted that in subsequent years there had been other "self-styled 'initiates'" who claimed that their superior wisdom overrode the accepted moral code, and he mentioned in particular Charles Leadbeater's "operations with boys." Crump implied, however, that A. P. Sinnett used hypnotic power to dominate Laura Holloway-Langford sexually as well as psychically. He believed that theosophy had been led astray and that regeneration would come only with the appearance of a messianic figure. Crump wrote that the whole of *Parsifal* "may be taken as a drama of the Theosophical Society, which may now be said to be under the dominion of Klingsor, and still awaiting the coming of its Parsifal who can shatter the vast fabric of psychic illusion."[84]

It is, of course, impossible to know whether Laura Holloway-Langford read *Parsifal* as a fable about her own experience. Kundry was not a model either for the New Woman seeking self-determination or for a woman with spiritual aspirations. However, Laura Holloway-Langford and the women of the Seidl Society may have identified with the portrayal of a woman deeply conflicted over her sexuality, struggling to be free from the control of outside forces but finding herself caught in a cultural narrative that labeled her deepest desires as evil. Female Theosophists like Alice Cleather acknowledged that Parsifal alone was "a perfect being; there is no female figure on, or near, his level."[85]

Perhaps Holloway-Langford, like Cleather, rationalized that the eradication of all sexual desire would make gender irrelevant. Cleather had interpreted Kundry's baptism as a sign that she had been accepted into the holy community; nevertheless, there was no place for her at the Round Table. Locked into a female body, Kundry could not achieve perfection on earth, and only in death was she released from her role as sexual temptress and the object of male desire.[86] Like Kundry, Holloway-Langford could find no place among the Theosophical brotherhood; but she rejected the notion that women were the tools of men, and she fashioned her own life, demonstrating a will that was as strong as any man's. She realized that Wagner's portrayal of Kundry accentuated rather than resolved contradictions in gender ideology. Yet she had no words with which to conceptualize the problem and offer a feminist critique. Laura Holloway-Langford, like other late Victorian women, was circumscribed by the language of moral superiority and social purity, which precluded discussion of the price exacted by the idealization and concomitant demonization of woman.

DREAMS DASHED

After a two-year hiatus, the Brighton Beach concerts resumed during the summer of 1894. The following summer there was another dustup over finances. When the hotel refused to fund the concerts, the Seidl Society agreed to take on financial responsibility, ending the season with a substantial deficit. In January 1896, a dispute with Seidl erupted over scheduling conflicts. The Society voted to incorporate under a new name, the Brooklyn Symphony Society, and to engage Theodore Thomas to conduct concerts in March. According to the *New York Times,* in the seven years of its existence the Seidl Society had given "315 grand orchestral concerts, for which it spent $200,000."[87] But by late spring the spat with Seidl was resolved. On May 1, he resumed the concerts with a performance by Lillian Nordica. Holloway-Langford threatened to suspend the summer concerts entirely unless those who gained publicity from them—the railway and the hotel—contributed substantially to the project. Her efforts resulted in a $12,000 subsidy, enabling Anton Seidl to conduct at Brighton Beach for the last time during the 1896 summer season.

In May 1896, the Seidl Society incorporated, with a capital stock of $20,000. The incorporators were eight women, five of whom served as officers, with Laura Holloway-Langford as President of the Board of Directors.[88] The purpose of the corporation was to build and manage a "people's music hall" in Brooklyn. Holloway-Langford may have been influenced by her friend Imogene Fales, who was active in the cooperative movement. Whatever the inspiration, the requirement that the corporation stock could be purchased only by women was truly visionary. The corporation would be totally managed and controlled by women, who would reap the rewards of their own investments. The model proposed by the Seidl Society differed substantially from nineteenth-century women's benevolent organizations. Instead, it closely resembled a nonprofit business with a cultural and philanthropic mission. Significantly, the incorporation of the Seidl Society indicated that Brooklyn women had the resources to raise capital for an ambitious undertaking. There is no way to determine how much of her own money or, indirectly, that of Edward Langford, may have been invested in this venture, but as President of the Board of Directors, Holloway-Langford was surely one of the major contributors to the company's capital.

This dream was shattered. On October 12, 1896, a hurricane struck the coast of New York, and Brighton Beach was "desolated." The music stage was a mass of rubble, with huge beams up to fifty feet in length littering the ground. "The west wing of the music stand, made famous in late years by Seidl's orchestra, is entirely gone." The red leather chairs of the auditorium floated away and were found washed up along the beach.[89] Edward Langford may well have suffered significant financial loss because of the damage to the hotel and music pavilion. Certainly, the Seidl Society could no longer plan the next season at Brighton Beach, and Anton Seidl spent the summer of 1897 in Europe, where he conducted *Parsifal* at Bayreuth. The Seidl Society, however, continued to sponsor winter concerts at the Brooklyn Academy of Music.

Then, on March 28, 1898, after a lunch of shad roe which he had "eaten rather heartily," Seidl suddenly took ill, and died at 10:15 PM from food poisoning. He was only forty-seven. A member commented to the *Daily Eagle*, "It is an hour of desolation for the Seidl Society."[90] A memorial concert sponsored by the Society was held on May 2 at the Brooklyn Academy of Music. Most poignant for Holloway-Langford must have been the performance of a song, "Good Night," that Anton Seidl had composed for the children's chorus. The lyrics were taken from a poem written by her friend, Edna Dean Proctor.[91] After a decade of work building up and managing the Seidl Society, Holloway-Langford's plans for even greater accomplishments came to an abrupt end.

10

"Dear Friend and Sister"

The years following the demise of the Seidl Society were difficult for Laura Holloway-Langford. Not only had she lost her position at the center of Brooklyn social and cultural life, but in the late 1890s her husband suffered financial setbacks. In January 1901, her sister, Anne Catherine Terry, died, and in summer 1902, after a long period of declining health, Edward Langford passed away. During this time of loss and uncertainty, she renewed her friendship with the Shakers at Mount Lebanon, New York. The Shakers welcomed her attention, finding that "Friend Laura" could assist in their dealings with "the world." In particular, they enlisted her to write newspaper articles publicizing their mission and contradicting negative reports about the Society.[1]

Some Shakers in the North Family dared to hope that Holloway-Langford might join their ranks as a sister, but she remained an outsider. She agreed with them that a new spiritual age was commencing, but she disagreed on how to bring it about. For the Shakers, celibacy, not philanthropy, was the essential requirement of the spiritual life. It entailed separation from the world so that members could pursue lives of perfection. Holloway-Langford, in contrast, thought that rather than limiting their role to examples of personal purity, Shakers should welcome into their communities all those who needed physical as well as religious renewal. When she purchased a farm that had been the home of the Upper Canaan Shakers, Holloway-Langford expected that her physical proximity to Mount Lebanon would be mirrored in a spiritual kinship. Rather than bringing her closer to the Shakers, however, the purchase led to misunderstandings over the property and to estrangement from them. Despite these conflicts, Holloway-Langford popularized the Shakers among the seekers of alternative religion, promoting an image of them as feminists and social reformers. At the same time, she spread ideas from Theosophy and Eastern religious traditions to the Shakers. Never an original thinker, Holloway-Langford mediated among disparate religious traditions, recombining them in ways that became characteristic of an emerging American spirituality.

SHAKER FRIENDSHIPS

In the 1870s, Laura Holloway-Langford had corresponded with Frederick W. Evans and Antoinette Doolittle, the leaders of the North Family Shakers. She sent at least one impoverished child to them, and she proposed that city children who would benefit from rural living, fresh air, and healthy food come to Mount Lebanon for summer holidays. The Shakers, however, rejected this idea. Evans reminded her that the Shaker mission was not to provide for the city's poor, and that they only accepted children who were of "the better class."[2] While in Germany in 1884, Holloway-Langford wrote Evans, claiming that she had represented Shakerism to the "vegetarians & temperance philosophers" with whom she was living. On returning to the United States, she told the Shakers about a mind cure that was of great interest to Evans, who hoped to employ it in his community.[3] She also debated concepts such as reincarnation with the Shakers, arguing that human suffering was the result of an individual's karma, caused by his or her own actions. Alonzo Hollister of Mount Lebanon was not convinced. He wrote:

> I see no necessity for those whose one incarnation has been to them an unspeakable affliction, coming back to try it over, & perhaps again & again. To say everything we suffer here is a punishment for sins previously committed by us, seems to me neither based on positive nolej [sic] nor provable nor reasonable, nor probable. The appearance of things is that the best people suffer most for the sins of others—or from causes they never set in motion. . . .
>
> If a man gets angry at me & strikes me in a way to break my arm, it does not mend nor mitigate my suffering, for him to get served in the same

manner. If he kills me, it does not aid me an atom, to know that he must be killed to atone for his crime.[4]

Holloway-Langford, nevertheless, persisted, presenting Hollister with a copy of *The Gospel of Buddha* by Paul Carus.[5]

Despite these early interactions, in the years after Antoinette Doolittle's death in 1886 Laura Holloway-Langford had only intermittent contact with the Shakers. In 1901, however, she wrote the North Family inquiring once again about their policy on taking children. Eldress Anna White reiterated the Society's position: "We take children but not all kinds, they need sorting. We have taken Asylum children, but the Asylum trait was upon all of them. Most of them were from the slums, and the change was too much for them, and too much for us with their slang . . . jeer and scoffings."[6] In her next letter, Holloway-Langford was more candid about her situation, revealing that her younger sister, Anne Catherine Terry, a widow, had died, leaving a son, Charles Erastus Terry. White replied: "As you suggest, have your nephew come to us for a visit of a week and then upon acquaintance the brethren will decide what shall be done."[7]

On March 16, 1902, Charles Terry arrived at the North Family, accompanied by Edward Langford.[8] Less than six weeks later, Anna White wrote Holloway-Langford:

> The poor boy seems very unhappy. . . . One evening he was very determined to go down in the village of New Lebanon and when Elder Levi refused him he was very much put out about it and was quite insolent. . . . To our mind he needs stronger discipline, a firmer hand than we can give. . . . I know it will pain you to hear of our decision not to keep Charlie. We feel exceedingly sorry it has turned in this way, but we have done our best. We are fearful he will run away and make trouble.[9]

Charles Terry was not a child, but a young man of nineteen who, in his aunt's words, was "feeble minded." After leaving the Shakers, he returned to Brooklyn and apparently lived with Holloway-Langford for the rest of her life.[10]

In July 1902, Holloway-Langford wrote Anna White to inform her that her husband, Edward, was gravely ill. White replied that Edward's spirit had been with the Shakers at Mount Lebanon, conversing with Elder Levi. "We have always regretted that Colonel Langford's stay with us was not longer. He only had a glimpse of our home and yet he seemed to understand the inner workings that produced the outward order and beauty he so much admired." White praised Colonel Langford as "a conqueror who rose above base passion and thus fulfilled the higher law of his being," apparently convinced that Edward and Laura had shared a spiritual, rather than physical, union. She predicted that after Edward "passes over" he would meet "some of our people" in the spirit land, where he would learn more about Shakerism. She offered reassurance that Edward would continue to communicate with Laura: "You will miss his bodily presence; that can never be replaced, but the spirit may be so quickened as to know him better even than when in the body."[11] In the years between Edward's death on July 25, 1902, and the death of Anna White in December 1910, Holloway-Langford's relationship with the Shakers was at its most intense.

NEWSPAPER REPRESENTATIONS OF THE SHAKERS

Even though Holloway-Langford did not visit Mount Lebanon until summer 1904, she began to publish articles about the Shakers in various New York newspapers.[12] In one she presented in interview format Anna White's views on temperance, vegetarianism, and the fate of poor children in the city—all issues of particular interest to Holloway-Langford. White criticized those who gave up liquor while at the same time "they are indulging in the body and mind debasement of swine and other flesh eating. How can people, calling themselves Christians—who ask mercy of God for themselves, expect it when they treat animals without mercy?" White recalled that "Elder Frederick always commended the Buddhists for making the first article of their religious creed 'Thou shalt not kill' because they assumed that the killing of inferior animals leads to murder—to war—the killing of human beings."[13]

Holloway-Langford then asked if Frederick Evans was "opposed to women in general having the equal rights that Shaker women possess." White replied: "He wanted women to have the rights of citizenship, the right to vote & to hold office, and he said, at all times, that if she had these responsibilities, she would soon cease to befoul herself with the feathers & plumes of dead birds." Holloway-Langford also brought up her *idée fixe*, asking White: "Why do you not take children here to educate them? If the people generally knew what an ideal country home you Shakers have, how beautifully clear and wholesome life is here, how much opportunity for manual training, for both boys and girls there is here, I am sure you would have hundreds and thousands of applications." Anna White again replied that the Shakers took only the "right kind of children." Nevertheless, Holloway-Langford concluded the article with a refrain that remained constant throughout her relationship with the Shakers:

> Looking over the broad fields, the great orchards, the sleek & well fed horses and cows, the large poultry yards, and the commodious houses occupied by this Family of Shakers, we wished from the bottom of our hearts, that the hundreds of nervous, tired little girls and boys who are penned up in flats in greater New York sent to overcrowded schools, could be released from such a penitentiary as a city is to a child, & given a lease on a new life, in the quiet country and in the home of these pure, upright and loveable people—the Shaker family of Mt. Lebanon.[14]

White was so pleased with how Holloway-Langford had represented Shakerism that she distributed the article to visitors to "give publicity to our home and its life." She declared, "You have done this in the best way it has ever been done, some say and all who have read approve." Holloway-Langford had succeeded in gaining the trust of Anna White, who wrote: "I feel honored, my dear friend, in being held in your friendship and love."[15]

The Shaker leadership was grateful to have found a supporter who had connections to the New York press and who, as a journalist, was able to pronounce opinions that could exert far more public influence than the Shakers could by themselves. Consequently, on July 15, 1903, they made a formal request to Holloway-Langford for assistance in their plea for tax exemption from the New York legislature. In response, she wrote an article for the *New York Sun,* arguing that the Shakers "should share the privileges of the other religious denominations in the State." Curiously, the Shakers included among the reasons that they should receive this exemption "their long service to the State in the unaided care, protection and education provided to friendless children and youth,"[16] a statement that justified their classification as a charitable institution, but one which also reinforced Holloway-Langford's view of the Shaker mission.

Anna White deemed the article acceptable, but she took issue with Holloway-Langford's statement that there were no new recruits among the Shakers, pointing out two recent converts of remarkable capacity (one of these was Leila Taylor, a former schoolteacher). She continued: "Years of experience have taught us caution; people have taken advantage in ways detrimental to the prosperity of the society, so that now we watch with a jealous eye those who apply. It is not the lack of applicants, but rather the lack of quality in them that is wanting." White concluded the letter with an expression of gratitude for her "hearty sympathy and promise of help," and she urged Holloway-Langford to visit Mount Lebanon so that she could "know the Shaker life by personal contact." Then White added a postscript, in which she admitted that the Society as an organization "may dwindle and become extinct in the course of years," but she declared that one might "as well talk of the mountains becoming extinct, or the ocean becoming dry" as to speak of Shakerism declining. "There are more Shakers to day on the earth, I claim, than ever before and if we read the signs of the times right they will bear us out in it."[17] To Anna White's way of thinking, Laura Holloway-Langford might be among the true Shakers, even while living in the world.

By fall 1903, Laura Holloway-Langford had established a warm relationship not only with Anna White, but also with M. Catherine Allen and Daniel Offord, both of whom visited her in Brooklyn, where she introduced them to her friends.[18] When Shaker sisters faced an emergency in the city, they asked Elder Daniel Offord who might help them. He answered, "Laura is the one, she will attend to whatever is wanting."[19] Additionally, she aided individual Shakers who had problems with the world, and she tried to find markets for Shaker products.[20] Thus, a pattern in the relationship was established: Shakers turned to Holloway-Langford for help in their dealings with the world, and she depended on them to preserve an image of herself as woman of benevolence who was devoted to the spiritual life. Shaker sisters lavished praise on Holloway-Langford as one who possessed a "rich gift" of "bearing the burden with and for others."[21] In their letters from these years, the Shakers reflected back to Holloway-Langford an idealized image of herself.

A SHAKER SCHOOL FOR GIRLS

By late 1903, Laura Holloway-Langford had begun to think about how unoccupied Shaker buildings might be put to benevolent use. Her first idea was that the North Family should establish a residential school for girls. She recommended her friend Elizabeth P. Chapin as its headmistress.[22] For more than a decade, Chapin had been a teacher at the Wilson Industrial School, established in 1855 as the nation's first effort to train poor girls in domestic accomplishments. In June 1893, however, a scandal erupted when it was discovered that Theosophy had made inroads among the teachers. The school was non-sectarian, but all the same it sent Bible teachers to the children's homes and held regular services at a mission church.[23] When the school demanded that teachers renounce membership in the Theosophical Society, Elizabeth Chapin refused. Even though she testified that she was a Christian, women from the School Committee were disturbed by her defense of Helena Blavatsky, whom they considered a "woman of vile character" who threatened the moral and spiritual welfare of children. In addition to Chapin, the matron, Mrs. E. I. Armstrong, resigned, protesting that even her own Church did not "prescribe what books I should read, what lectures I should hear, or through what means I should seek truth." Chapin sued for breach of contract, and she was defended by the famous freethinker Robert G. Ingersoll. Although they were paid through the end of the school year, the teachers were not reinstated at the Wilson School. Theosophists deplored such an "outburst of religious hatred," and they designated Chapin and Armstrong martyrs to the cause of Theosophy and religious freedom.[24]

From Holloway-Langford's perspective, a girl's school on Shaker property could serve a dual purpose, bringing poor children from the tenements to live among the Shakers, while at the same time reinstating her friend Lizzie Chapin to the teaching profession. She expected the Shakers to embrace eagerly a philanthropic project that also could demonstrate the superiority of the Shaker way to both children and spiritually inclined adults. Anna White tactfully but firmly rejected the proposal: "While we very much appreciate your suggestions made toward the training of young minds, we find ourselves in the same dilemma as at a previous suggestion. . . . We must keep open doors and hearts to all sincere, honest-hearted applicants and further we cannot go."[25]

ANN LEE COTTAGE

In early 1904, Holloway-Langford reformulated her idea, suggesting that rather than a school, the Shakers should establish a summer boardinghouse. The Ministry at Mount Lebanon approved the project, with the understanding that Holloway-Langford would "get outside friends whom she believed to be in sympathy with the principles of our Order and who desire board in the country during summer, to patronize this place, where they will have opportunity to attend our meetings and become enlightened relative to aims and organic life of Believers. In short the experiment is to be as an *Outer Court*."[26] Anna White recommended that the former residence of the Center Family, which had been dissolved in 1896, might serve this purpose. The building contained eleven rooms plus a kitchen and attic. She wrote: "The plan meets the approval of nearly all, some objections were raised to small children on the ground of the danger of losing fruit. Shaker villages are quiet places and too rampageous youngsters would not be acceptable, but of course you will select a good class of children." She concluded the letter, "Hoping all our interests may prosper and that a summer with you and your friends awaits us."[27] Thus it was at Laura Holloway-Langford's instigation that Shakers, in summer 1904, first experimented with bringing the world's people to live at what she first called "St. Ann's Inn," after Ann Lee, the founder of Shakerism. Anna White preferred the name "Mountain Home," explaining, "The name Mountain indicates loftiness and Home all that is attractive and sweet, while St. strikes one with awe and Ann had no meaning until explained, while we have two or three 'Inns' around us."[28] Finally, they agreed upon the name "Ann Lee Cottage."

The Shakers were persuaded that Holloway-Langford would send to the Society the right sort of spiritually advanced people whom they were seeking as converts. In early June, shortly before the first guests were due to arrive, Holloway-Langford visited Mount Lebanon for the first time. After she left, Anna White wrote: "You have made your mark, you have left behind a favorable impression how could you do otherwise with the spirit you carry? We understand you, *we* who have known you for years as being true to high living, true to the Christ within you.... We look to you as a leader in the forth-coming cycle to open anew the spiritual avenues and help build up this cause which is to redeem the world."[29]

Soon the sisters at Mount Lebanon were overwhelmed by the hard work required to make Ann Lee Cottage a reality. Water closets had to be installed in two bathrooms; extension tables, table cloths, eleven single bedsteads, and one double bed were needed. Anna White praised

Holloway-Langford's intentions, but insisted that they must work out those "minor things—of so much importance in this earth life." The Society could not furnish sheets and pillowcases, hand-enameled oil cloth, canned goods, or soap for laundry. They would, however, supply crocheted mats, basic groceries, and the labor to wash and press the sheets.[30] Some members of the Society were alarmed by Holloway-Langford's boundless enthusiasms, which included plans for a "retreat to those who want rest and who will care to become acquainted with our people," a school for boys and girls, and a model kindergarten. Feeling rebuffed, Holloway-Langford accused the Shakers of being afraid to make changes that would ensure their own survival and bring the New Age to fruition. Anna White cautioned her to be patient and plan for the future:

> Your large heart would take in the whole world and mother it . . . but, the law of limitation is as true as is the law of love. . . . There are two distinct elements existing in this little village of ours diametrically opposite, the one rigid conservatism, the other extreme radicalism, both dangerous when unbalanced by the other. . . . In view of this, it is my judgment, dear Laura, . . . to move slowly—slowly but surely—not to project beyond what we can perform beyond what will be acceptable.

Nevertheless, Anna White reaffirmed her belief in Holloway-Langford's mission to the Shakers: "To organize and establish a family—a society—such as you shall represent, that shall be an outer court—an outer wheel in God's providence calls for sacrifice, it calls for brave hearts true and strong who see the end from the beginning and are willing and glad and rejoice to help and administer." But she stressed that an outer court would become a reality only if they proceeded with care and prudence. White did, however, endorse Holloway-Langford's desire to publish a magazine similar to *The Shaker* that would aid in recruiting supporters.[31] In a subsequent letter, White elaborated: "I look to you as one selected and prepared by the spirit intelligences to perform and establish at Mt. Lebanon a work that shall be the means of perpetuating the Shaker organization, by bringing to its aid men and women ripe for the resurrection order and who will be able to train the rising generation to respect, revere and sustain that order."[32]

Anna White believed Holloway-Langford to be an instrument for the continuation of the Society, but she nevertheless struggled to keep her zeal in check, warning that "large bodies move slowly. We must bear this in mind and hold on to the reins of our ambition, or we may meet with an upset." She begged "Friend Laura" not to send any more persons to Mount Lebanon, since the current guests were already proving a burden. Elder Daniel Offord had made "several fruitless journeys to the station to meet those who were to come but did not," and one guest even demanded a horse to ride through the Berkshire countryside, but as it was harvest time it was impossible for the Shakers to break up a team. Before White could post this letter, four more letters from Holloway-Langford arrived. One of them announced the arrival of another family which had four children. Exasperated, White wrote that Catherine Allen was "puzzled to know how to arrange for all the people you want to send," and she asked Holloway-Langford to decline the family, repeating the Society's objections to having noisy, meddlesome children on the premises. She wrote: "The best of them will bear watching lest they get into mischief, especially boys. We have machine shops and machinery, and to have children wandering around the premises, prying, as children will pry, into every place, would not be borne. The brethren object decidedly and the sisters . . . are not far behind."[33] Yet neither Anna White nor Catherine Allen was a match for Holloway-Langford's determination, and the family took up residence at the Ann Lee Cottage.

The Shakers had earlier rejected the proposal to use their buildings for a year-round school, but since, in addition to the adult boarders, nine children lived at the Cottage, they allowed Holloway-Langford to establish a summer school. Children from Shaker families and the children of hired help also attended the school, which served twenty-two children ages three to twelve. Lizzie Chapin and Katherine Edwards, who were boarding at Ann Lee Cottage, ran the school. The youngest children were cared for by Sister Sarah Burger. Anna White was so impressed when she visited that she thought "it would be an excellent plan to keep the school open all winter if it would not infringe upon the district school."[34] Other Shakers were less enthusiastic, and the school closed at the end of the summer.

Holloway-Langford wanted the Shakers to offer the boarders a Fourth of July celebration; she had requested an organ or piano and a company of Shakers to sing.[35] Anna White was relieved when Holloway-Langford relinquished this idea and agreed instead to commemorate Mother Ann's landing in America, which was much more in tune with Shaker ideas than

a holiday that glorified nationalism. Held on August 7, 1904, this celebration was the Society's first venture in hosting conferences for the public,
with speakers including J. P. MacLean, Shaker collector and historian,
and Paul Tyner, formerly editor of *The Arena,* and a member of the North
Family from 1890–1893.[36]

At the close of the season, Anna White wrote Holloway-Langford, "With
regrets do we part with the dear friends at the Cottage, they seem to be
one with us as if we had always known them."[37] Many of the women whom
Holloway-Langford had recruited as guests at the Ann Lee Cottage were
connected to both Theosophy and the Vedanta Society. The only one to
become a Shaker, Alice Crane, had been the housekeeper at the Vedanta
headquarters on East 58th Street in New York when Vivekananda stayed
there in 1900.[38] In spring 1905, Anna White wrote Holloway-Langford that
Crane had "disconnected herself from the Vedanta Society never more
to return, she says. When notified she would leave them their treatment
was very unkind."[39] Crane continued to live at the North Family even
after becoming a Christian Scientist, which, unlike Vedanta, met with
Anna White's approval, and in later years she was in charge of the family's honey operation.[40] White continued to hope that several of the other
summer guests might return to live permanently at Mount Lebanon, but
she confessed that she never expected that "all those cottagers" would
turn Shakers.[41]

Many Shakers felt that the peace and order of their lives had been dis-
rupted by an enterprise that neither garnered converts nor made a profit.
Trustee Emma Neale wrote: "The matters at Annlee [sic] Cottage are rather
muddled for real business and I shall have to lump the wreckage somewhat
as things have not come to me in the time of occurance [sic]." She concluded her statement with a list of articles that had been broken, including
a looking glass, a covered dish, and a chair. "I can hardly place an estimate.
The chair was an easy little rocker. I think I will call all $1.50 & let it go if
this is satisfactory."[42] When Holloway-Langford expressed her own criticisms of the Shaker part in the endeavor, Emma Neale retorted: "All our
experiments in this life must ever be open to improvements. Were they
perfect at the beginning we should have nothing to aim for. We will call
our summer a success in many ways."[43] It was Leila Taylor, however, who
put the summer's cooperative venture into perspective, urging Holloway-

Langford to be sensitive to internal tensions in the Society at Mount Lebanon. In this letter, for the first time, Holloway-Langford was addressed as "Sister Laura":

> It has been a perfect miracle-play to me to see you manipulate people, and bring such diverse elements into harmonious action. That so much peace and so little friction and so few mistakes should have marked the first season's work at Mt. Lebanon, is the surprise, not that all matters have not gone just "according to Hoyle." . . . It is by adding whole-souled, earnest, devoted women workers to our inner circle that true advance will be made. The outer ring of the nebulae will take care of itself if there is a live heart of fire at the centre. . . . Dear Laura, there are many among us who feel that you are in a special sense the one sent to lead us in the effort that alone can bring the opening of the new day to our Order.[44]

By fall of 1904, many of Holloway-Langford's projects involving the Shakers were going awry. She had tried to establish an outlet in the city for Shaker fancy-work, but the Shakers were not able to meet the demand. Her effort to take extra apples from Shaker orchards to the city for the poor was foiled by an early frost. She and Eldress Anna White had intended for Ann Lee Cottage to be occupied year-round to keep pipes from freezing, but the family Holloway-Langford recruited was judged unsuitable. Consequently, the former Center Family residence was closed for the winter.[45] By late December, White needed a decision about whether the Ann Lee Cottage would be rented during the coming summer.[46] Holloway-Langford requested that improvements be made on the house, but Sister Emma Neale balked at the cost. Anna White wrote that even though the North Family wished to reopen the cottage, they did not control the buildings. Additionally, some of the brethren "were very decided not to have the house occupied the coming season," because Robert Valentine, a former Trustee of the Church Family, wanted to use the property for a dairy. With regret White added: "Some fail to see the luminous rays of light that are transmitted by coming in contact with illumined souls, they fail to hear the sounds 'Gather my saints together.'"[47] Anna White blamed conservative Shakers for failing to realize that spiritual light was spreading into the world through saints like their "Friend Laura." This disagreement was, to some extent, theological. Nevertheless, the decision to close Ann Lee Cottage indicated opposition to Holloway-Langford's schemes, which required Shaker labor and financing but did not give Shakers control.

Holloway-Langford was outraged that the decision to close the Cottage had been made by the Shaker Brothers rather than the Sisters, and she apparently confronted Robert Valentine head-on. According to Leila Taylor, "Laura tipped over her dish, &, so to speak, drove the cat up the tree by her own harangue in the last meeting she attended. It is, so my observation goes, entirely possible to manage the masculine being, but it is not a good plan to put it too plainly beforehand that you're going to do it."[48] Holloway-Langford not only felt unappreciated, but she was also disillusioned to discover that even among the Shakers sexual equality was more an ideal than a reality. Consequently, her correspondence with the North Family slowed from a flood to a trickle.

Despite the mixed results of its first season of operation, Trustee Emma Neale decided to revive Ann Lee Cottage in summer 1906, but she limited Holloway-Langford's role to recruiting the right kind of "inmates." Non-Shakers would not be allowed to run the enterprise. Holloway-Langford agreed to publicize the Cottage, but her article printed in the *Daily Standard Union* did little to entice mature single women to the North Family. Once again, she portrayed Shaker communities as a sanctuary for destitute city children, writing: "To this good work of rescuing homeless children the Shakers owe much of their genuine popularity with the public. . . . That not more boys and girls are sent among them is due to the fact that this custom of theirs is not known."[49] Anna White could barely restrain her anger, and her reply was sharp: "The article . . . is admirably written and will attract attention and awaken interest, but the assertion at the heading of it,—'Shakers at Mt. Lebanon open doors to city children,' is misleading and is untrue, for the idea has never once entered our minds. . . . So please counteract the movement for the 'fresh-air children.' . . . It might prevent applications, explanations or the whys and wherefores, and correspondence that would lead to nothing."[50]

The Ann Lee Shaker Cottage reopened in the summer of 1906, with Sister Emma Neale charging $2 per day, about twice what had been asked in 1904. By summer's end, all were relieved to see the boarders depart. Anna White wrote Holloway-Langford: "They were a queer lot, uninteresting and fault finding. Sister Emma has had her hands full, she is asking if it is best to continue another year. I doubt it very much, doubt if it pays and doubt as to the propriety—the wisdom of so doing. Your scheme is far ahead of any yet made and we pray most fervently for your success."[51] The doors to Ann Lee Cottage were closed permanently.

SHAKERISM: ITS MEANING AND MESSAGE

During 1904, in the midst of operating the Ann Lee Cottage, Anna White and Leila Taylor had completed Shakerism: Its Meaning and Message, a book that scholars consider the "crowning intellectual achievement" of Shaker sisters and "the most comprehensive historical statement ever written by members of the Society."[52] Seeking a publisher for the book, Anna White turned to Holloway-Langford, who recommended Funk & Wagnalls. The company had put out several of her own works; in addition, the company's founder, Isaac Kaufman Funk, was a spiritualist who, in spring 1904, produced his own collection of extrasensory experiences, in which he argued that soon science would confirm the existence of spiritual vibrations.[53] White submitted the Shakerism manuscript to Funk & Wagnalls in early March. Six weeks later she sent a letter that she hoped would "hurry them up a little, as we have other wires to pull if the connection fails in their case."[54] After two months without a response, White demanded that Funk & Wagnalls express-ship the manuscript to Holloway-Langford, whom she asked to read the book "with the eye of a critic, knowing the way to the ear, eye and heart of the public, remembering also that we write not only for the public but for the Shaker world as well. This double focus has sometimes made matters difficult for our collator and she fears lest aiming at two marks she has hit neither." White added: "Any changes, omissions or additions that you might suggest, we should gratefully accept and consider."[55] In mid-May White finally received an offer from Funk & Wagnalls to publish the book on the condition that it be condensed and rearranged.[56] Apparently Holloway-Langford offered to undertake this task, but White determined that only a Shaker, not an outsider, even one as close to the community as Holloway-Langford, should revise the book.[57] While White and Taylor made final changes in the manuscript, another friend of the Shakers, John Patterson MacLean, arranged for it to be published by Fred J. Heer, of Columbus, Ohio.[58]

During this time, Holloway-Langford was composing pieces about the Shakers which she thought would appeal to the public. In 1904, she published *The Story of a Piano,* which had a Shaker motif but was written as a promotion for the well-known piano manufacturer Otto Wissner.[59] The North Family agreed to distribute the small monograph to local Sunday school classes. Holloway-Langford was also collecting anecdotes about Shaker encounters with spirits. In "Spirit Visitors to the Shakers at Mount Lebanon," she described how an apparition of Antoinette Doolittle had warned Believers that explosives had been left in one of their buildings. She described a "little squaw" who was a troublesome spirit, but one who ferreted out mischief among Believers. And she told of a recent Shaker convert who did not believe in spirit manifestations until his son, who had died of drowning, materialized in his room.[60]

These writings were amusing but insubstantial pieces in the popular mode of local color fiction. In contrast, in *Shakerism: Its Meaning and Message,* White and Taylor situated Shaker spiritism historically and theologically. For them, spiritism evoked profound meanings. To use the historian Molly McGarry's term, it was a "technology of memory" that returned the dead to the living.[61] The spirits not only reinforced memories about personages important in Shaker history, but they created common bonds among the members of the Society, erasing the boundaries between the material and the spiritual worlds. In effect, spiritism enlarged the community of Believers, reassuring Shakers like Anna White that although the number of Believers on earth might be few, they were nevertheless part of a vast and vibrant heavenly sphere. Spiritism melded Shakers, past and present, into a single community.

PEACE, PURITY, AND SWAMIS

The following summer, during which the Ann Lee Cottage was not in operation, the Mount Lebanon Shakers sponsored a Peace Convention, held on August 31, 1905. It was organized by Amanda Deyo, an ordained Universalist minister and "thorough, radical peace advocate" who lived off and on with the Shakers for several years.[62] Anna White invited Laura Holloway-Langford to address the convention, but she declined—not surprisingly, perhaps, since her brothers and son had pursued military careers.[63] She recommended, however, that White invite Ponnambalam Ramanâthan, Solicitor General of Ceylon. Ramanâthan was touring the United States hosted by Myron H. Phelps, a Theosophist and self-proclaimed American Hindu, who had spent a year under Ramanâthan's tutelage.[64] Phelps publicized Ramanâthan's arrival, praising "the breadth and liberality of his view. As he knows but one God, so he regards all religious systems as equally paths to Him, each adapted to the differing needs of various portions of mankind, each a facet of the One Religion which is the essence of all."[65] Moncure Conway, who also had met Ramanâthan on his "Pilgrimage to the Wise Men of the East," wrote that he reconciled "Brahmanism, Buddhism, and Christianity by giving them all a new birth" for the purpose of "individual self-renunciation, atrophy of the senses to enlarge the soul, and absorption of the soul in deity. The old religions are not entirely lost, but folded away as a sheath under a glowing spiritual flower in which their essence is expressed."[66]

Anna White extended Ramanâthan "a cordial invitation" to address the Convention and to be the guest of the North Family.[67] On August 22, she wrote Laura Holloway-Langford asking that she meet Ramanâthan and Myron Phelps at the Pittsfield railway station and escort them to Mount Lebanon.[68] Holloway-Langford immediately contacted White with troubling information about the men's personal lives. She refused to attend the Convention, and apparently she persuaded White to rescind her invitation to Ramanâthan, since there is no evidence of a "Hindu" visitor.[69]

Anna White thought that Holloway-Langford had made a mistake in missing the Convention. She wrote:

> After we heard from you of Mr. Phelps and Ramanathan we thought to let them severely alone, we had no use for such whether Christian or heathen. It is only character which tells, the private life must be above censure to exert any kind of an influence over the public mind. Surely you will not have any fears of meeting them now, they will not molest us with their presence. What a scar, what a blot is this upon civilized nations! when men of that stamp have no restraint over themselves.[70]

Most likely Laura Holloway-Langford had been alarmed to learn that Myron Phelps was accompanying Ramanâthan to Mount Lebanon. She knew that Phelps was the companion of Marie de Souza Canavarro, a former Theosophist who, in 1897, under the influence of Anagarika Dharmapala, became the first American woman to convert to Buddhism. Sister Sanghamitta, as she was subsequently known, left her husband and children to move to Ceylon, where she founded a convent school. After a falling out with Dharmapala, rumored to be over her lack of monastic chastity, she was expelled from Ceylon in 1900 and returned to the United States, where she founded branches of the Maha Bodhi Society. In about 1902, Canavarro and Phelps began living together on a New Jersey farm. In explaining her relationship with Phelps, Canavarro argued that spiritual affinity, not legality, determined a true marriage, and she defined adultery as sharing an intimate relationship without a spiritual bond.[71]

All of this, including the spiritualist justification for free love, was hardly news to Holloway-Langford. She had known Phelps for many years, from the time when she had been active in Theosophical activities in Brooklyn. A lawyer, Phelps had defended William Q. Judge against accusations of fraud by Annie Besant and Henry S. Olcott. It seems reasonable to assume that Phelps knew a great deal about Holloway-Langford's private life, including her relationship with Judge and her escapades in Europe.[72]

Holloway-Langford may not have known that on his tour of America, Ramanâthan was also accompanied by his secretary, the Australian-born R. L. Harrison. A wealthy heiress, Harrison had gone to Ceylon in the 1890s "in a state of religious uncertainty, although convinced that Christianity was empty of truth." Ramanâthan, with whom she was studying, told her "not to dismiss the Bible so lightly."[73] She transcribed his oral interpretation of the Gospels, and then edited and published them as commentaries on *Matthew* and *John,* identifying her teacher as Sri Paránanda, Supreme Bliss.[74] In 1906, after the death of his first wife, Ramanâthan married Harrison, who converted to Hinduism and became Lady Leelawathy Ramanâthan.[75]

For years Holloway-Langford had associated with people who followed alternative paths, many of whom did not equate spirituality with celibacy. In the world of Theosophy and Eastern gurus, spiritual affinities often found physical expression. When women like Canavarro talked about a "pure spiritual nature" and "surrendering worldly ties," these words meant something quite different than Shakers' use of similar vocabulary. Holloway-Langford enjoyed acting as a conduit among different religious worlds and relished her skill in adapting to their different languages and codes of behavior, but even so she needed to keep these spheres separate.

She had presented herself to the Shakers as a devotee of purity, which to Anna White's mind entailed renunciation of sexuality. But the language of spiritual purity was slippery, and Holloway-Langford used its ambiguity to mask aspects of her life. But whatever her private thoughts or behavior, in public Laura Holloway-Langford would not risk being associated with advocates of free love.

The strains in Holloway-Langford's Shaker friendships reflected grave concerns about the future of Shakerism that permeated the Society after the turn of the century. With an aging population and few new members, it faced difficult decisions. For more than a decade, a few members of the North Family had discussed whether, in order to assure the survival of the Society, some core beliefs might be modified. According to Stephen J. Paterwic, in the 1890s Elder Daniel Offord had proposed that progressive members from Mount Lebanon move to California, where they would practice "Social Shakerism," that is, live communally but without the requirement for celibacy. In late 1895, Offord briefly left the Society, accompanied by a Shaker sister, only to be readmitted three years later.[76] These discussions were ongoing around the time of the Peace Convention. In November 1905, Anna White wrote to Holloway-Langford: "Everybody wants their own way and their own say, which is all very well if in accordance with the celibate communistic life. To compromise is dangerous."[77] White's solution to this problem was for the Society to offer two levels of religious commitment, the inner court consisting of those who were celibate and lived communally according to the covenant of the Society, and an outer court made up of sympathetic friends like Laura Holloway-Langford who were not able to cut all ties with the world.

Yet the Ramanâthan incident raised the question of what sort of people the Shakers should cultivate. Certainly, many of Holloway-Langford's friends held ideas that were incompatible with Shakerism. Some believed in a Mother-Father God, but by way of spiritualism, Theosophy, or Vedanta rather than Mother Ann. Holloway-Langford believed not only in reincarnation, but also in esoteric knowledge communicated by living adepts. Other Shaker friends were Christian Scientists and New Thought practitioners, whose influence was more readily accepted by members of the North Family than were ideas from Eastern religions. Consequently, the appropriate role of supporters like Holloway-Langford, who admired

the Shakers but did not fully share their commitments, remained controversial within the Society.

ELDER ERNEST PICK AND THE CHALLENGE
TO SHAKER COMMUNALISM

Elder Ernest Pick was an anomaly among the Shakers. An Austrian Jew,
Pick was a university graduate with expertise in financial matters. He had
joined the Shakers as a young man and lived at Mount Lebanon, where he
was responsible for their sweet corn business. In spring 1909, the North
Family solicited Holloway-Langford's help in responding to a scandal that
had erupted when Pick, an elder of the Second Family, was expelled from
the Society by M. Catherine Allen, head of the Ministry, for improper
behavior with Eldress Lillian Barlow. The *New York Sun* had published two
articles that presented an unflattering portrait of what it termed "Shakerdom." The newspaper suggested that self-righteous members of the North
Family had wielded undue influence on Allen, a former member of that
family, pressuring her to "defrock" Pick. And it painted a pathetic picture
of Pick weeping "when his few simple belongings were placed in a sleigh
and he walked out of the White Buildings into the world, as the Shakers
call that sphere outside of their community."[78]

Another article in the *Sun* blamed new members from Switzerland
whom Pick had recruited to the Society. It reported that, with Pick's financial support, a carpenter named Otto Thuemmel, his wife, and a young
man named Carl Koeber had come to live at Mount Lebanon. According to the *Sun,* Koeber spoke only German, so Sister Lillian Barlow had
been assigned to teach him English. Koeber accused Barlow of becoming
"very ardent" and "laying hands upon him."[79] It was Koeber, however, who
was dismissed from the Society, disgruntling Thuemmel, who believed
his fellow countryman had been mistreated. In this version of events,
Thuemmel tried to get even with Barlow by spreading rumors about her
relationship with Pick.

Ernest Pick and Lillian Barlow admitted some small indiscretions (reportedly they had held hands in public), but denied the accusation of serious sin. Once again, however, it was the male Shaker who received the

harsher punishment. Pick was dismissed from the Shakers, while Barlow was allowed to remain, but stripped of her authority. Perhaps Shakers, especially in a time when the Society was overwhelmingly female, were predisposed to see male desire as the culprit in any infringement of the rules of sexual separation; or perhaps the popular press tended to view Shaker female leaders as vindictive prudes. However this may be, the Shakers were anxious that the full story be aired in the press, and they enlisted Laura Holloway-Langford's help.

On April 11, 1909, the *Sun* published a substantial article, with many photographs, by Holloway-Langford. She asserted that, after years of laxity, M. Catherine Allen had decided to enforce the requirements of the Shaker covenant more stringently. She wrote that in addition to sexual misconduct, Pick had failed to accept the commitment to communalism by refusing to give up personal control of an inheritance of $15,000. "As the Shakers are an order of communism and as everyone without exception is required to turn in all earthly possessions to the common fund this refusal was open rebellion." Thus, she implied that instead of Pick being sent away with no compensation for his work, he was, in fact, a wealthy man.

At the same time, Holloway-Langford sympathized with Pick's belief that he should be allowed to keep personal property. She claimed that communalism, not celibacy, was the major stumbling block to Shaker survival, because it attracted only the poor or elderly. She argued that unless the Shakers were willing to allow "personal financial independence" there would be no new generation of Shakers to inherit their extensive landholdings, buildings, and wealth. According to Holloway-Langford, "The older Shakers oppose any change from the ancient order of things, though as one of their elders, Daniel Offord, recently said, 'The best state for Shakers is that of poverty, for in poverty there is union.'" But given that a return to the poverty of the Society's early years was not an option, Holloway-Langford advised the Shakers to adopt the cooperative plan which "might result in such a growth as Ann Lee in her most hopeful mood never anticipated. It would overthrow the present form of government . . . and it would necessitate wise management; but by this plan the Shakers might renew their former successes."[80] What she had in mind was apparently something akin to the Rochdale Cooperative Principles that were advocated by her friend Imogene C. Fales. Members would contribute equitably to a cooperative which they controlled. Despite Anna White's suggestion at the conclusion of *Shakerism: Its Meaning and Message* that the Society's governance and financial management should be democratized, there is no evidence that the Shakers seriously considered abandoning their commitment to communalism.

Laura Holloway-Langford received a note of thanks for the article from Eldress Anna White: "You are our Aaron—our mouth-piece. You do more in defense of the Cause than can we, in one way. Some will read and believe what an outsider says where it would be useless for us to combat. In this case, which was peculiary [*sic*] trying, we thought it wisest to keep still. . . . Now that the public have aired their skirts they are in a better condition to listen don't you think so?"[81] White did not comment on Holloway-Langford's proposed changes in Shaker governance and economic organization. As was often the case, Holloway-Langford's defense of the Shakers proved a mixed blessing; while she told their side of the story regarding Ernest Pick, at the same time she blamed Shaker rigidity and the "inelasticity of the covenant which binds members" for Shaker decline. Once again, it was clear that despite her admiration for the Shakers and her friendships with individual members, she was far from accepting the principles of the Society. Much to Anna White's disappointment, and despite her designation as "Friend and Sister," Holloway-Langford would never "make a Shaker."

THE UPPER CANAAN FARM

Since 1903, Laura Holloway-Langford had proposed schemes to use the empty buildings and farmland that had formerly been the home of the Upper Canaan Family.[82] After attempting to sell the farm for several years, the Shakers reduced their asking price to $12,000. In 1906, Holloway-Langford suggested that the Shakers donate the property for use as a celibate sanitarium. When this scheme was rejected, she proposed to lease the farm for ten years, with an option to purchase at any time for $10,000. Finally, she accepted a counteroffer from the Shakers to buy Upper Canaan for $8,000, with $1,000 down and $500 paid each year without interest.[83] In July 1906, Holloway-Langford put down $100 earnest money on the property. It was not until August of that year, however, that she set foot on the land she was purchasing. At that visit, Anna White had hoped to discuss thoroughly "the responsible situation" that her friend was taking, but Holloway-Langford left hurriedly because some of the North Family sisters had made her feel that she was imposing on their hospitality.[84] Holloway-Langford later recounted the condition of the Upper Canaan farm:

> I found there was not a habitable house on the place and to put the big house in order for Sanitarium purposes would cost as much as to build a new one—since it was . . . in a sad state of decay & dilapidation. . . .

> It was a forlorn place, altogether. The grounds were littered with debris, old beer & whisky bottles by the hundreds, tin cans & broken crockery lying about in every direction.[85]

Nevertheless, in late December she remitted $900 to complete the initial payment on the property. At this point, she believed that Dr. Burrows, who had prescribed a milk diet for several Shakers, including Anna White, would collaborate with her to establish a sanitarium modeled on those in vogue among city folk who were troubled, as one advertisement said, by "dyspepsia, neurasthenia, morphinism, or a nervous, run-down state of health."[86] Shortly after she had completed purchase of the property, the partnership with Dr. Burrows dissolved, and Holloway-Langford found herself solely responsible for a large farm requiring costly repairs. All the sewers were clogged, water pipes were broken, and stone fences were crumbling. She confided her troubles to Anna White, who offered spiritual encouragement but no concrete help: "Dear child, you are compassed on every hand with difficulties, but from them you will arise stronger to surmount them. . . . You are fortunate in possessing a certain sort of grit—an ingrediant [sic] very necessary—in carrying out plans and meeting with cross-currents, and then you are helped from an invisible source, visible to *you,* from which I am sure you derive strength and courage."[87]

At that point, Holloway-Langford decided that she would turn the Canaan property into a larger version of the Ann Lee Cottage. She enlisted Catherine Allen's help in supplying Shaker furniture for the smaller of the two houses on the farm. Additionally, Allen agreed to stock a library with books, and she gave Holloway-Langford permission to use the Shaker name. Allen wrote her: "We appreciate your desire to work in unison with the spirit and principles of our order and when ever we can co-operate with you to assist in any way within our strength we shall feel that it is all for the same Cause and gladly prove to you the relationship of Sisterhood."[88] Perhaps Holloway-Langford really believed that she could inaugurate a Shaker "outer court," composed of single women who admired the Shakers but were not inclined to give up individual autonomy. Even this project, however, was beyond her capacity. In the summer of 1904, Shaker sisters had been at her beck and call to perform the many tasks required to get the Ann Lee Cottage up and running. Left to her own resources, however, Holloway-Langford was unable to establish either a summer boardinghouse or a health spa on the Canaan property.

DEATH AND DISAPPOINTMENTS

On January 30, 1910, Eldress Anna White, the "beloved little Mother," fell, fracturing her left arm. Laura Holloway-Langford was also ill that year, undergoing serious surgery and residing in a sanitarium until she returned to Canaan early that summer. It was during these last months of Anna White's life that Holloway-Langford's problems with the Canaan Farm came to a head. The Berkshire Industrial School had demanded access to a spring that appeared on both its deed to the Lower Canaan property and the deed to the Upper Farm. Holloway-Langford had responded by installing an iron gate and lock on the road that led to the spring.[89] Both parties engaged lawyers. M. Catherine Allen admitted that there had been some "little misunderstanding" among the Shaker Trustees as to the property lines, but since all of those who had a hand in the transactions had passed away, she urged Holloway-Langford to be patient. Holloway-Langford was not appeased, and she demanded that the Shakers buy back the farm for $11,000, the $8,000 price she had paid plus an additional $3,000 for improvements. Allen replied: "That simply would be beyond the possible in our present circumstances. You have had the means to put far more on that little farm than the North family have been able to do for theirs." Allen reminded her that it was the responsibility of the purchaser of property to have the title searched.[90] Holloway-Langford then threatened to sue the Shakers, whom she claimed had misrepresented the property. Eventually, the matter was settled out of court, and the Berkshire Industrial School was given the right to install a pipe to tap into water from the spring on Holloway-Langford's land.[91] However, with the threat of legal action against the Shakers in summer 1910, Laura Holloway-Langford's relationship with the North Family suffered irreparable harm.

Perhaps the Mount Lebanon Ministry protected frail Eldress Anna White from knowledge of the escalating acrimony with Holloway-Langford, or perhaps White's sympathy was wide enough to embrace her friend despite these troubles. In any case, White's affection for Holloway-Langford never faltered. In one of her last letters to "My Dear Laura," she wrote: "It is only this body of flesh, I should say bones, that keeps me from you. I am praying and helping in other ways as best I can. . . . Your work is our work, Believers on the other side are helping."[92] On December 16, 1910, Elder Daniel Offord sent a telegram to Brooklyn: "Eldress Anna passed away seven thirty five this afternoon."[93] On February 23, 1911, he wrote Holloway-Langford: "Dear Friend. . . . We miss Eldress Anna very much: and nothing would give us more pleasure than to hear from you and her. If you have any communications from her, will you not let us hear from you!"[94] Three days later, Holloway-Langford received a letter informing her of Offord's sudden death. It was signed, "Yours in a common & yet for each a separate sorrow—Leila."[95] The deaths of Anna White and Daniel Offord within less than three months were a devastating loss to the North Family. It was, wrote Leila Taylor, "an orphaned house." She confided that Elder Daniel and Eldress Anna had been heard singing in meeting, evidence that their spirits were near to help and sustain the remaining members of the family.[96]

Holloway-Langford wrote a lengthy obituary for Anna White, intended for publication on Sunday, December 18, the day of her funeral. Rather than praising White's lifelong commitment to Shakerism and her example as a spiritual leader, Holloway-Langford emphasized the externals of White's life. She noted that White "was of aristocratic birth" and "the daughter of a wealthy Quaker of English ancestry." She described White's "bright, vivacious" personality and her "extremely comely" personal appearance: "Dainty of dress, as are all Shaker women, she had a taste so individual that even the severe plainness of the Shaker costume could not conceal her ideas of beauty & fitness in ornament." Holloway-Langford wrote that White was "a social magnet" who drew to the North Family "visitors from all parts of the country, and, as well from abroad." While failing to acknowledge White's commitment to celibacy and communalism, she mentioned her dedication to the peace movement and to vegetarianism, issues more important to outsiders than to most Shakers. She stressed White's role in humanitarian and reform organizations and her large following among the "best type of people." She portrayed White as a talented writer, a woman of "mental force and executive ability." Remarkably, this tribute ignored both White's unwavering faith in Shakerism and her role in leading the United Society of Believers. Instead, the obituary closed with a paean to Shaker women, who were portrayed as examples for the New Woman of the twentieth century:

> They are all capable, industrious, self-supporting, money earning, intelligent and aspiring people. And in a day when so much is being said about the larger opportunities required for women, these Shaker Sisters are shining examples of what women can do in the way of creating opportunities for themselves. Certainly they are living proof of the natural ability of women to achieve results for themselves, in all ways commendable and honorable.[97]

Holloway-Langford's view of Anna White was refracted through the prism of her own belief in individualism, self-reliance, and female independence. The obituary thus captured little of the Shaker life that Anna White had lived for more than half a century.

In his last letter to "Friend Laura," Elder Daniel Offord had written: "We hope prosperity has attended you; for your prosperity is our prosperity."[98] But by 1911, Laura Holloway-Langford had exhausted her financial resources, and her life had begun a downward emotional and economic spiral from which she would never recover. That January she sent the Shakers only $250, rather than the expected $500 payment on the farm. She mailed an additional check in March.[99] In June, she requested a loan from the North Family. Leila Taylor replied:

> We would very much like to assist you, if only for love's sake, but, dear Laura, it is utterly impossible. Our own family must come first, and we have small sums or great, absolutely no money to lend. We are hard

pressed ourselves to meet the necessary expenses and are closing eyes & ears to repairs and demands on every hand, barns, farm and family, for needed things. We simply cannot do it. We can only struggle on ourselves hoping & trusting for better days.[100]

A MEMORIAL TO ELDRESS ANNA WHITE AND ELDER DANIEL OFFORD

Shortly after the deaths of Anna White and Daniel Offord, Leila Taylor set to work on a memorial volume to commemorate their lives. She asked Laura Holloway-Langford to loan the letters she had received from them: "I would very much like to have some of the gems in your collection to weave in." Additionally, Taylor asked Holloway-Langford to contribute a personal estimate of Anna White: "Your side of her would be what we would like."[101] Almost a year later, Sarah Burger wrote to Holloway-Langford: "Sister Leila is working on the memorial, is trying to get it into the publisher's hand by the first of March, but we have not seen or heard anything from our dear Laura for the book." Burger added wistfully, "I suppose you see the dear ones very often and get their messages of love and sympathy, how I wish I was blessed with the gift."[102] Whether or not Holloway-Langford was in touch with the spirits of Eldress Anna and Elder Daniel, she did not contribute to the book, which went to press with no memorial from White's closest friend outside the United Society of Believers.

It is striking that in the *Memorial* Leila Taylor mentions many of White's associates, but Laura Holloway-Langford's name does not appear. Nevertheless, Taylor surely referred to her when she described projects that "were advanced by outside friends." She wrote:

> One was to open a home for little children, aiming not only to relieve the stress among city workers for that class, but to prepare the way for such children to become useful men and women and recruits for Shakerism. Eldress Anna, open in her philanthropic heart to every good cause, never lost sight of the fact that the work in her hands was not institutional, for the relieve [sic] of suffering bodies or starved minds of the many, but spiritual, for the evolution of men and women. . . . Very few, even among the most enlightened of her friends and outside helpers, could see this

or realize her point of view. . . . It was not easy to refuse, apparently to be unwilling to assist in the so-called plain duty of humanity to its suffering brothers and sisters. But . . . [she] held to her conviction that she had no right nor authority to use the Shaker homes and the spiritual plant, established by generations of faithful toilers, for any other purpose than that for which, under divine direction, they had been given.[103]

REASSESSING SHAKERISM

In 1911, Laura Holloway-Langford wrote an article that made clear her growing ambivalence toward the Shakers.[104] She declared it painful to witness the decline of the Society, which was "burdened with the old and the weak of will," as well as those who were worn out by "the stress and strain of modern life." She concluded that their efforts to keep themselves apart from the world were in vain because their village was "over run by hired help." Her disillusionment with Shakerism ran deeper than the problems caused by a lack of members. She was also reassessing Shaker commitment to feminism and spiritualism. She wrote that although the Shakers claimed that in their Societies men and women were equal, this had never been true. The male Trustees had managed the property and resources of the order, making business deals without the knowledge of the women, who "were never consulted beforehand, and were never asked to participate in any enterprise outside of their departments. The women were kept in ignorance of the outside transactions of 'the Brethren,' unless they were invited to take their share of the consequences of some of the ill-starred ventures of the Trustees." Holloway-Langford blamed "male leadership" for financial mismanagement, most likely referring to Robert Valentine, the Shaker Brother who had blocked her plans for the Ann Lee Cottage. While a Trustee at Mount Lebanon, Valentine had been guilty of engaging in deceitful and illegal real estate speculation without the community's knowledge and for his personal benefit, resulting in damage to its financial stability and its reputation for honest dealings.[105]

Laura Holloway-Langford was also disappointed that Shakers did not hold fast to their spiritual traditions. Even though she herself had been a major purveyor of new religious ideas to the Shakers, she had harsh words for the North Family's openness to the influence of Mary Baker Eddy, the founder of Christian Science. She wrote: "Shakerism no longer satisfies the Shakers. They have gone out seeking new idols, and have taken to their hearts Eddyisms and all that it stands for today. They are Christian Scientists—believing more ardently in Mrs. Eddy than they do in 'Mother Ann.' They are zealous converts accepting all the tenets of the Christian Science creed, and having for their teachers people who, whatever else they are, are not Shakers."[106]

There is something ironic and sad in Laura Holloway-Langford's complaint that the Shakers had not lived up to *her* expectations. Yet her bond had been with individuals; it had never entailed a commitment to Shakerism as a religion or to the community of Believers as a whole. Holloway-Langford neither claimed Shakers as her spiritual ancestors, nor did she take to heart the theological import of Shaker spiritism. Even though she professed to be able to contact Shakers who had passed to the other side, she did not feel herself a part of Shaker history or a member of the larger spiritual community that encompassed both living and dead Shakers.

After Anna White's death, not only did Holloway-Langford's spiritual optimism diminish, but her financial situation continued to deteriorate. After her son George retired from the U.S. army on disability in 1911, he moved to Canaan, where he took over management of the farm.[107] The following year, Holloway-Langford gave up her residence in Brooklyn, possibly in an effort to economize, and moved permanently to Canaan. Three years later, unable to keep up the mortgage payments on the property, she was sued by Emma J. Neale, Trustee of the Shakers. In June 1914, the matter was settled avoiding foreclosure.[108] Only a few weeks later, George died suddenly from heart disease.[109] At this point, Holloway-Langford sank into a depression; she sequestered herself on the farm, having little contact with her neighbors or her old friends from Brooklyn. By the 1920s, she was living "like a hermit" with her brother Vaulx Carter and her disabled nephew Charles Terry.[110] She had no assets other than the Canaan farm, which had been mortgaged several times and which had an assessed value of only $7,500, less than what she had originally paid for the property.[111]

Laura Holloway-Langford had been attracted to a progressive version of Shakerism that had been promulgated by the leaders of the North Family at Mount Lebanon. Yet the Shaker dream that liberal feminists would flock to the Society was misplaced. By emphasizing the universal aspects of the Christ spirit while minimizing the demanding require-ments of the Shaker path, the leaders of the North Family encouraged a ro-manticized view of Shakerism that contributed to an emerging American spirituality, but that did little to strengthen Shaker communities. When Holloway-Langford saw vacant buildings and fallow farmland, she had visions of benevolent institutions—whether homes for orphans, schools for impoverished children, summer retreats for religious seekers, or health spas for weary city-dwellers. Repeatedly, she was frustrated by the Shaker refusal to put their resources to use in benefiting the world. She came to believe that the Shakers focused selfishly on their own welfare when they should be concerned about others. In all her writings about the Shakers, she never seriously engaged Shaker theological claims of a Mother in the Divinity. She did not address the power dynamics of patriarchy, either within or outside of Shakerism. And she failed to take seriously the Shaker critique of American capitalism. In the final analysis, Shakers could call on Holloway-Langford for publicity, but they could not control how she represented them.

Laura Holloway-Langford's relationship with the Shakers also reveals aspects of her character that are less than flattering. She was often stub-born, obsessive, and self-centered, demanding that the Shakers accept her ideas rather than adapting herself to their needs. To her mind, spirituality was an individual, not a communal, undertaking. She was entrepreneurial, enterprising, and self-promoting. Her aim as a writer was not depth, but finding an angle that would reach a wide audience. All this said, for many years Laura Holloway-Langford was a dependable friend to the North Family Shakers. She gave time and energy to promoting their writing, their products, and their welfare. Her devotion to Anna White was deep and sincere. Perhaps in the Shakers Laura Holloway-Langford recognized an integrity and discipline of spiritual practice that was lacking in her own life, despite her varied spiritual journeys.

It is impossible to completely untangle the threads of spiritual longing and personal desire in Laura Holloway-Langford's character; however, her attraction to the Shakers was based as much on a need for personal validation as on a spiritual quest. The Shakers, especially Anna White, reaffirmed that Holloway-Langford was endowed with extraordinary gifts and devoted to the higher life. Holloway-Langford's metaphysical pursuits during the 1880s had ended in disappointment not only with the Theosophical Society, but also with her own prospects as a clairvoyant. The person whom she had chosen as a mentor, Helena Blavatsky, had dismissed her as a failure. The Shakers, however, never questioned her psychic powers. Additionally, Holloway-Langford's connection to the Shakers obliterated any hint of disrepute that may have tainted her ventures in spiritualism and Theosophy. Christians in Brooklyn, like those in charge of the Wilson Industrial School, might consider Helena Blavatsky an immoral woman, and the Society for Psychical Research might label her a fraud, but no one could accuse Anna White or M. Catherine Allen of such failings. For almost a decade, the Shakers became Holloway-Langford's spiritual guides. They nourished and sustained her faith in a New Age and her place in it. With Anna White's death, however, these dreams also passed away.

11

Who Tells the Tale?

Struggles over the leadership and direction of a new religious movement are stored in competing narratives. Where does the story begin? Who are the essential actors? What texts are sacred? How such questions are answered determines the shape of the narrative and interprets the movement. Telling the story of the Theosophical movement is particularly challenging because there is little agreement on essential issues. The status of Helena Blavatsky is contested. There are only a few principles that all members accept, and there is no canon of authoritative texts. The role of the Tibetan Masters and the value of their communications remain highly controversial. Yet, even among those who doubt the existence of the Mahatmas, their letters, especially those written during Blavatsky's lifetime, retain special significance. In the first decades of the twentieth century there was no consensus about whether the Mahatma letters should be made public; but their recipients nevertheless wielded extraordinary influence on how the early days of the Theosophical Society would be remembered.

In the 1920s, Laura Holloway-Langford and another Theosophist, Hildegard Henderson, battled for control of correspondence from the Master Koot Hoomi that had been written more than thirty-five years earlier. When Henderson and her colleague Alice Cleather realized that Holloway-Langford possessed these seminal documents, her status increased in their eyes from a minor figure in the movement to one who had the power to shape the Theosophical narrative. The struggle that ensued culminated in a lawsuit over a manuscript in which Holloway-Langford quoted extensively from the letters of Koot Hoomi. As a result, her historical reconstruction of Theosophical history was destroyed, even though some portions of it were illegally copied and preserved. The conflict between Laura Holloway-Langford and Hildegard Henderson serves as a cautionary tale about the fragility and ambiguity of historical documents, and about the loves, hates, and jealousies—as well as the hopes and disappointments—which inform their creation. It also demonstrates that the surviving story of a religious movement is, at best, at the mercy of chance, and, at worst, may be the result of suppression, intimidation, and intrigue.

REHABILITATING BLAVATSKY

After the turn of the century, Laura Holloway-Langford stayed clear of the struggle for control of the leadership of the Theosophical Society. She did not identify publicly as a Theosophist, preferring to call herself a mystic, but privately she remained loyal to Helena Blavatsky and to William Q. Judge. She disliked Annie Besant, who had risen to prominence in the Society after Blavatsky's death in 1891. Besant, along with Henry S. Olcott, had accused Judge of forging Mahatma Letters. Holloway-Langford's contempt for Besant increased when, soon after becoming president of the Theosophical Society, Adyar, in 1907, she readmitted to membership Charles W. Leadbeater, who had been expelled from the Society for teaching young men to masturbate. Holloway-Langford claimed to have foreseen that Besant would damage the Theosophical movement. Her friends Elizabeth Chapin and Maude Ralston testified that one afternoon, while at a Brighton Beach concert, she had a vision of Blavatsky "standing upon the platform beside Anton Seidl," the conductor of the orchestra. In "furious tones" the astral form of Blavatsky said "'Damn her [Besant], she's gone into the Catholic Church.'" Laura Holloway-Langford then said quietly, "*Watch Mrs. Besant's career.*"[1] Always fiercely opposed to Roman Catholicism, Holloway-Langford was dismayed when, some years later, Leadbeater and Besant became associated with the Liberal Catholic Church.[2]

Since 1912, Laura Holloway-Langford had lived year-round on the former Shaker farm in Canaan, New York, where she planned to spend her
remaining years with her son, George. She recalled that his sudden death
in August 1914 swept over her life like a cyclone. In her grief, Holloway-
Langford retreated to the big Shaker house with no company except that
of her disabled nephew, Charles Terry. She had little contact with her
previous friends, including her Shaker neighbors. Her situation was com-
pounded by grave financial difficulties.[3] She earned a pittance doing freelance writing, placing a few articles in newspapers and publishing anonymously in the Theosophical journal *The Word* until it ceased publication
in 1917. She may have even tried to support herself through fortune-telling
by correspondence.[4] By 1920, her brother, Vaulx Carter, whose marriage
had failed and who had filed for bankruptcy, was living with her. Her sav-
ings had been depleted by maintenance on the dilapidated farm, which
never produced the income that she had anticipated. Owing years of back
wages to a Swedish couple who managed it, she had given them a mortgage
on the property. On October 7, 1920, she wrote to her friend Edna Dean
Proctor asking for financial assistance. Proctor replied:

> I am grieved to hear death has taken away so many of your friends, espe-
> cially your son to whom you were so devoted, but this is the way of life for
> all. I am the last of my family. I am very sorry for our anxieties and cares
> and should be very glad if I could aid you as you wish, but it is not possible.
> Let me enclose a small check, begging you to accept and use it for any little
> thing you may fancy in memory of old Brooklyn days.[5]

Increasingly desperate, Holloway-Langford on October 28, 1921, issued
another mortgage to Josephine W. Jackson to secure the sum of $3,000. By
this time, according to her own estimate, Holloway-Langford had a yearly
income of about $400, an amount not sufficient even to supply her basic
necessities, much less to pay the interest on the mortgages.

PERSONAL RECOLLECTIONS BY OLD FRIENDS

Falling deeper and deeper into debt, Holloway-Langford decided that
she could pull herself back from the brink of insolvency by writing a book
on Helena Blavatsky. This idea had been prompted by a correspondence
that began in fall 1919 with the Theosophist Alice Cleather. Cleather, who

had recently moved to India, had known Blavatsky in London in the late 1880s, and she was promoting a "Back to Blavatsky Movement" in opposition to what she called the "Neo-theosophy" of Annie Besant. Holloway-Langford told Cleather that her aim in writing a book was to rehabilitate "H. P. B.'s personality as known to those who never wavered in their faith that she was the inspiration of the movement, and remains such."[6] Cleather believed that in Laura Holloway-Langford she had found an important ally in her effort to undermine Annie Besant and to restore Blavatsky to the center of the Theosophical narrative.

At first, Holloway-Langford proposed to collect reminiscences from persons who had met Blavatsky while she lived in New York, many of whom had also been her own friends. This task proved difficult: nearly half a century had passed, along with many of the persons who had known Blavatsky. She then decided to write her own "history of the friendships formed by [Blavatsky] in this country," including sketches of William Quan Judge; General Oliver Otis Howard; Isabella Mitchell, Henry S. Olcott's sister; "Mrs. Waters, wife of the Boston publisher, who brought Mohini to this country"; and many others.[7] Her title for the book was *Helena Petrovna Blavatsky: Personal Recollections by Old Friends.* She asked Alice Cleather to contribute an essay to the volume.[8] In May 1922, Cleather wrote her personal recollections about the "great Soul" and mailed them to Laura Holloway-Langford for inclusion in her book, which, Cleather assumed, would be published later that year, at about the same time as two books of her own, *H. P. Blavatsky: Her Life and Work for Humanity* and *H. P. Blavatsky: A Great Betrayal.* After another year had passed and Holloway-Langford's book still had not appeared, Cleather decided to publish the piece she had written, "H. P. Blavatsky As I Knew Her," as a separate monograph. In her preface to this work, Cleather announced that Holloway-Langford's *Personal Recollections* had been completed and that it would be "in the printer's hands not later than July."[9]

In the meantime, Hildegard Henderson, a Theosophist who had been Alice Cleather's pupil in London, traveled to India, where she visited Cleather in Darjeeling. In their conversation, Cleather informed Henderson about the book that Holloway-Langford was writing and suggested that Henderson visit her. When Henderson returned to the United States, she wrote Holloway-Langford, suggesting that an unspecified person in India desired them to meet. Sensitive to Holloway-Langford's aversion to the Theosophical Society, Adyar, Henderson offered assurances that she, too, was a follower of Blavatsky's original teachings and that she was not affiliated with Annie Besant. Holloway-Langford replied, but did not invite Henderson to call upon her.[10]

Henderson next visited the office of *The Word*, where Harold W. Percival told her that Laura Holloway-Langford "was so sick of the fighting & back biting & the traitors" in the Theosophical Society that she wanted nothing to do with it and that even "the word 'Theosophist' . . . would call up vibrations that would be disturbing." Nevertheless, Percival gave Henderson Holloway-Langford's address. In September 1921, she drove to Canaan, New York, with her son Malcolm, whom she sent to the farm with a note requesting permission for an interview. Holloway-Langford's brother Vaulx Carter informed Malcolm that his sister was "in such straits, & so ill" that he himself could hardly get an "audience" with her, much less strangers. Holloway-Langford weighed less than one hundred pounds, and Henderson believed her condition was the result of "the dangers these psychics are exposed to —& is a lesson in the tragedy of broken vows, & the inevitable fate of 'looking back' after having put one's hand to the plow." She concluded that Holloway-Langford was "the same, sensitive tortured psychic as in her early days," but one who, she felt sure, still believed in the Masters.[11]

"PECUNIARY EMBARRASSMENT"

After her failed attempt to visit Laura Holloway-Langford, Hildegard Henderson moved to Victoria, British Columbia, where she lived until her death in 1948. However, for several years she and Holloway-Langford carried on a correspondence.[12] Letters from both Henderson and Holloway-Langford are extant, making it possible to reconstruct a relationship built around the sometimes converging, sometimes conflicting desires of the two writers. Early in the correspondence, in what would become a familiar refrain, Holloway-Langford appealed for financial assistance. She wrote that her book on Blavatsky had been delayed because she had not been able to find a financial sponsor, even though she had approached several people. In a long, rambling letter, she confided the details of her despair:

What I have been of late yrs I do not like to admit. . . . I am in debt, & with
pecuniary embarrassment came a morbid distaste for life itself. I have
been morbid, I am morbid, living now as I do under the shadow of a mortgage on this place of 6,000 due in October, & which can not be renewed.
. . . Only today I received notice . . . that it wd. have to be pd. together with
interest overdue. I have tried in every way to sell the property, a valuable
farm of 450 acres, with both mountain & water scenery . . . but I have not
succeeded.

Holloway-Langford even proposed to Henderson that the farm might
"be used as a home for the friends of H. P. B.," a desperate fantasy that a
wealthy benefactor would buy the former Shaker property and turn it into
a retirement home for aging Theosophists.[13]

In response to this plea, Hildegard Henderson sent $850 to Holloway-
Langford for the purpose of getting the book into print. On October
5, 1922, Henderson further demonstrated her faith in Laura Holloway-
Langford by remitting money to pay on the mortgage and avoid foreclosure on the Canaan Farm. In a letter that became crucial evidence in a
later lawsuit, Henderson wrote:

> If the offer of $1,000 would tide over the present crisis for you, I do not
> want to let it be one more weight around your neck, for I know from what
> you have told me of your feeble-minded nephew that you must feel the ne-
> glect of debt to hang very heavily—and if you will put this so-called loan
> right out of your head as an obligation, and should you be unable to repay
> it, reconcile yourself to accepting it in the name of our common faith and
> effort.[14]

A few months later, Holloway-Langford wrote Henderson that the interest on the mortgage had been paid, but that she still owed $195 in taxes on
the farm. In order to convince Henderson that she was trying to solve her
financial problems, Holloway-Langford reported that she had contacted
the Governor of New York, a Roman Catholic, who was said to be interested in establishing new institutions. She offered to sell the farm to him
to be used for an orphans' home.[15] Henderson again came to Holloway-
Langford's aid, this time with a check for $100.

By early 1923, Henderson had begun to pressure Holloway-Langford
about the book's publication. Holloway-Langford replied that "no contract can be signed until I have turned over the entire work, but my old

publishers—The Funk & Wagnalls Company of New York—are ready to undertake it as soon as all the illustrations & copy are estimated." In the same letter, however, she wrote that she was trying to get a firm in Albany to take the book.[16] In mid-March 1923, Eleanor Curtis, a Theosophist and friend of Hildegard Henderson, had visited Holloway-Langford, prompted by "anxiety to know about the book and when it would be published." Curtis had braved the snow to find Holloway-Langford living in a cold house, with only an oil heater in one room.[17] Perhaps as a result of this visit, and at the time unbeknownst to Henderson, Eleanor Curtis contributed $1,000 to the Canaan farm's mortgage.

A. P. SINNETT'S RECOLLECTIONS

In spring 1923, however, their attention, like that of Theosophists everywhere, was focused on posthumous publications by A. P. Sinnett: *The Early Days of Theosophy in Europe* came out in late 1922 under the auspices of the Theosophical Publishing House, with ties to Annie Besant. Causing even greater consternation among those in the "Back to Blavatsky" movement was *The Mahatma Letters to A. P. Sinnett,* edited by A. Trevor Barker and published in 1923. Cleather was outraged at Sinnett's portrayal of Blavatsky as "an ordinary medium, and a fraudulent one at that."[18] She was also opposed to claims to authority based on letters from the Mahatmas— whether by A. P. Sinnett, William Q. Judge, Katherine Tingley, Charles W. Leadbeater, or Annie Besant—believing that all communication with the Masters had ceased with Blavatsky's death.

After reading *The Early Days of Theosophy in Europe,* Holloway-Langford wrote Henderson that she was "amazed to read of myself as a medium and one who 'claimed to be the Master's mouthpiece.'" She continued, "I never realized how greatly I was favored by the Masters, & by H. P. B., but I did occasionally feel that others envied me—and sometimes I was made unhappy by manifestations of jealousy." She told Henderson that she was determined to publish "every one of [her] Mahatma letters," in order to contradict Sinnett's version of events. As an example, she enclosed an excerpt from a July 1884 letter from Koot Hoomi to Francesca Arundale which included Koot Hoomi's assessment: "Let her [Holloway-Langford] obtain self control over her self and her too great sensibility and she may become the most perfect—as the strongest pillar of the Theosophical Society."[19] Shortly thereafter, Holloway-Langford received a cablegram from Alice Cleather, saying that Sinnett's "false statements concerning you and Blavatsky must be refuted in your book."[20]

Certainly, the publication of *The Mahatma Letters to A. P. Sinnett* had shown Cleather and Henderson that the Master Koot Hoomi had taken much greater interest in Laura Holloway-Langford during the summer of 1884 than they had recognized. They knew that in 1912 she had published "The Mahatmas and Their Instruments," which had included excerpts from Koot Hoomi letters, but only in 1923 did they seem to grasp that Laura Holloway-Langford possessed original letters from Koot Hoomi and from Blavatsky. Thus, she was one of the few people who could authoritatively contradict A. P. Sinnett's posthumous claims. At the same time, Henderson and Cleather were nervous about whether these letters would vindicate charges against Blavatsky and, if they would, as Holloway-Langford claimed, expose "the awful deceit and selfishness of Mrs. Besant."[21] Holloway-Langford tried to reassure them, declaring "that H. P. B. had repeatedly reminded me of the promise I had given her to defend, when the time came, the cause she represented, and the Masters who gave the Teachings. I had almost despaired of ever having occasion to do this, and I had reached a point where I refused to be called a Theosophist so hateful was the reputation Theosophy had acquired through the degrading Leadbeater scandals." But now, Holloway-Langford asserted, she and Alice Cleather together "could make history. . . . H. P. B. is at work now; has never ceased to work, and please God, a few realize this fact."[22]

Ironically, although Hildegard Henderson interpreted Sinnett's revelations as casting doubt on Holloway-Langford's character, the publication of his books undoubtedly raised the value of the letters that she possessed. Realizing this, she began to tempt Hildegard Henderson with choice tidbits from Koot Hoomi letters. An April 1923 letter declared: "It is a bitter dose for me who am naturally unpretentious, to blazon to the whole world that I have had so much attention from the Great Lodge; but it will cost me real grief if I have to expose the real reason for Mr. S's [Sinnett's] hatred of H. P. B. . . . I am like one from the ranks of the dead, but I bring with me credentials that will be respected by everyone who believes in the Masters."[23] In addition to letters from the Masters, Holloway-Langford alluded to correspondence from Blavatsky, B. J. Padshah, Subba Row, Damodar Mavalankar, and Mohini Chatterji, as well as to papers from Blavatsky's sister Vera. As if to forestall any doubts that she owned these materials, Holloway-Langford mailed to Henderson some of her mementos, including a card from William Q. Judge.

STALL TACTICS

Not receiving any information about Holloway-Langford's book, Hildegard Henderson sent her a telegram on July 4, 1923, demanding to know its status. In reply, she received another rambling letter, in which Holloway-Langford confided that she had not, after all, submitted her manuscript to Funk & Wagnalls, because she had learned that the firm was publishing Roman Catholic propaganda. Holloway-Langford stressed that since she had made only a verbal agreement, she was not legally committed to Funk & Wagnalls, which, she claimed, was under investigation. "When I receive the affidavits expected, I shall put my book in the hands of another publisher (already selected) and he will announce it."[24] Holloway-Langford must have counted on the patronage of Adam Willis Wagnalls without taking into account the fact that Wagnalls was then over eighty years old and had given up control of the company. In another letter, she confessed to Henderson that her previous dealings had been through Isaac K. Funk, who had been a spiritualist, but who had been dead for more than a decade.[25] In the nineteenth century, Funk & Wagnalls had a strong list of books on religion and mysticism, but by the 1920s, it specialized in dictionaries and encyclopedias. It seems probable that Wagnall's successors had so informed Holloway-Langford, who was loath to admit to Henderson her difficulty in finding a publisher.

Holloway-Langford also realized that Henderson shared her prejudice against Roman Catholicism, and she used this knowledge to buy time for her book. Despite her frustration with Holloway-Langford's evasiveness, Henderson was ready to believe that Funk & Wagnalls was an agent of the Catholic Church. She replied that it was her responsibility to avoid "any firm with a taint of the real 'enemy.'" She believed the Jesuits were occultists of the left-hand path. "Such important work as your book with Masters' letters hitherto unpublished—would be a target they would spare no pains to hit. I really feel very anxious to know *who* publishes your book—& how far you were able to sift the warnings your friend gave you re your old publishers."[26] In other words, Henderson believed that the Jesuits were a powerful enemy who might employ black magic against Holloway-Langford's book.

During the summer and early fall of 1923, Holloway-Langford's letters to Hildegard Henderson exhibited both paranoia and delusions of grandeur. She warned of Catholic conspiracies, writing Henderson that "all evil will come to this country if the Protestants, Masons and other organizations do not wake up to the dangers" of the Roman Catholic Church. She described being harassed about the mortgage by an Irish Catholic lawyer, who she suspected wanted her property as the location for a religious institution. At the same time, she made grandiose claims for her own importance, asserting that she had kept vital secrets, waiting for the time designated by the Masters before revealing them: "I went into exile after the summer of 1884 . . . and have to all practical purposes remained in the wilderness of Silence for forty years. At the end of this self-inflicted exile I was promised the opportunity to serve the Masters in a way that no other could."[27]

Holloway-Langford's entreaties for financial help became increasingly frantic. She mailed snapshots of laurel blooming on the mountains surrounding the farm, suggesting that Henderson buy the mortgage and use the property to build bungalows on Lake Queechy for summer tourists. She claimed that the title to the property was "absolutely perfect" and that there was ample water for "any kind of manufacturing," perhaps fearing that Henderson had gotten wind of the fact that there had been problems with the title to the farm and the water supply.[28] Hildegard Henderson suspected that Laura Holloway-Langford was becoming senile and incapable of producing the book, but Holloway-Langford was more calculating than Henderson realized. On August 31, 1923, just at the time when Henderson was pressuring her to return the money she had advanced, Holloway-Langford made a will. It made no mention of the mortgages, nor did it acknowledge any debts to Henderson or Curtis. Additionally, it specified that any copyrights in her name were to be sold, with the proceeds going to her nephew Charles Terry. The will was witnessed by Maude Ralston Sharman and Elizabeth P. Chapin, who then lived in Detroit and were visiting Holloway-Langford in Canaan.[29] As Theosophists themselves, Chapin and Sharman were surely privy to their friend's troubled relationship with Hildegard Henderson, and they may well have advised her on the need for a will.

From the beginning of their correspondence, Holloway-Langford lured Hildegard Henderson with excerpts from Koot Hoomi letters. Additionally, she claimed to have many letters that would shed light on the mysterious relationship between William Q. Judge and Katherine Tingley, who succeeded Judge as head of the American Section of the Theosophical Society.[30] By 1924, in her desperation not to lose Henderson's support, Holloway-Langford claimed that prophecies made by Blavatsky in 1884 were now being fulfilled. She described seeing a vision on board the ship as she prepared to return to the United States:

> The room was filled with a blazing light that came like a flood upon me. Two Masters stood in the midst of this light and conversed with me. It was the most transcendent Vision I had ever seen, or shall hope to see again, and while these enlightened Beings were with me they instructed me regarding my future. They informed me I would outlive Mr. Sinnett and would answer his final conclusions regarding H. P. B.

> Many surprising prophecies were confided to me, one that will interest you was that when I was ready to emerge from the retirement of this long period, I should have word of a sister in India who would reveal her identity to me, and together we would serve.

Having asserted that she had been chosen for a special mission by these "glorified Beings" (one of whom she identified as Blavatsky, while implying that the other was the Master Koot Hoomi), Holloway-Langford then pressed Henderson for "one or two thousand in cash" to appease the mortgage holder, to whom $5,000 was due in October. Once again, she proposed the establishment of a Blavatsky Lodge, which she promised to help run.[31]

Henderson replied that, although she sympathized with the wish to avoid foreclosure, she had hoped that the $1,000 she had donated the previous year would buy time so that the place could be sold. She wrote that contributing any more money would be "like pouring water into a sieve." She even suggested that it might be a good thing for Holloway-Langford to give up the place, so that she would not have to spend another winter cut off from the world and in a house that was so cold that it made her ill. "If the place should be turned into a Blavatsky Lodge by your friends then I hope more warmth would be available, and that you would be enabled to stay on and work happily with them. I could not take part in such a scheme—I 'belong' to nothing—to no organization of any kind."[32]

The next month, October 1923, Henderson demanded assurance that the $850 provided to publish the book had been deposited in a bank and that the $1000 given toward the mortgage would be paid back when Holloway-Langford's property was settled, whether before or after her death.[33] Laura Holloway-Langford did not respond to either demand. By late March 1924, Henderson's tone turned icy, writing to Holloway-Langford that it had become plain that she was accepting money for purely personal reasons. She continued: "The hour has gone by for your book to do its work. The contract being, therefore, null & void you cannot evade the duty of returning to me the capital sum, with or without interest." She then warned Holloway-Langford that she was considering legal redress for "money obtained under false pretenses."[34]

In reply to these accusations, Holloway-Langford wrote a rambling missive about her experiences during 1884 and enclosed a copy of a letter written to her by Helena Blavatsky. She acknowledged neither Henderson's threat of legal action nor her assertion that the book was no longer needed. Only in her last sentence did Holloway-Langford allude at all to the project: "I must publish now, what is practically the third book I have prepared, and shall be very grateful to you, if, in the kindness of your heart, you will wait yet longer for me to meet your expectations in every respect."[35] In another letter, Holloway-Langford explained that she had written two books. The first presumably contained the recollections about Blavatsky and her friends. The second dealt with the Mahatma Letters, and it was designed to answer "Sinnett's book more effectually than personalities could or would. With these Letters will appear a prophecy foretold thirty-nine years ago, to the effect that I should be chosen to testify of the deeds I had witnessed when—as a child in occultism—I moved among the actors of a drama staged by the Masters themselves."[36] In her final letter to Henderson, on June 20, 1924, Holloway-Langford once again wandered from topic to topic, memories from forty years previous intermingled with current gossip. Finally, she offered another explanation for the delay in publishing the book: she had not been able to find the Koot Hoomi letters and other original documents and had thought them lost or stolen. Recently, however, her brother had discovered them packed in the bottom of a cedar chest, where they had been since the time she had moved from Brooklyn to Canaan, New York. Now, she said, the book could be completed.[37]

LEGAL ACTION

It was, however, too late for any more excuses. Hildegard Henderson and Eleanor Curtis engaged the services of Sidney P. Henshaw, a lawyer with the firm of Lazenby and Biglow in New York. Ostensibly demanding repayment of money, Henderson had other purposes in bringing legal action. In a statement of facts that she submitted to Henshaw, she wrote:

> I now come to the point of my reason for taking up this matter. It is of very real importance to me to see her manuscript, if it exists, or to have proof that it does not exist.
>
> The idea is that failing her being able to repay me even the money furnished for her book, she might be made to see that I have a right to her MS. It could be represented to her that I would undertake to destroy it—it could even be destroyed in the presence of Mrs. Curtis but I would *prefer* to read it first if that were possible.
>
> Another alternative would be to have it sent to me to read and return to her, failing a better arrangement.
>
> The actual reason for wishing to see the MS is that another book on the same subject is to be written and it is almost impossible for this to be done until, and unless we know just what Mrs. Langford's book says on certain points for we regretfully realise that she is not truthful or reliable and might publish something highly injurious to the matter which I and my friends hold dear.[38]

This statement makes clear that Henderson did not intend for the manuscript to be destroyed before she had a chance to read or, perhaps, copy it. She had come to fear that Holloway-Langford might produce documents that would injure Blavatsky's reputation or that would undermine teachings about the Masters. Her claim that someone else was preparing a book on the same subject was nothing more than a rationalization of her aims. Henderson's apprehensions about what Laura Holloway-Langford might write had increased when she read *The Mahatma Letters to A. P. Sinnett.* Not only did Henderson believe that Laura Holloway-Langford was a "tool of the Dugpas," but she also was convinced that Holloway-Langford had been a "Sex Maya" who had seduced A. P. Sinnett and probably tried to work her charms on Mohini Chatterji as well.[39]

Sidney Henshaw wrote Holloway-Langford, trying to determine whether the book had been written and if so whether it had been submitted for publication.[40] Vaulx Carter responded on behalf of his sister, asserting that the valuable documents and manuscripts were possibly worth more than the claims against them.[41] At this point, Henshaw suggested that Sheridan R. Cate, an attorney from Pittsfield, Massachusetts, be authorized to negotiate on behalf of Henderson and Curtis. After a four-hour interview with Vaulx Carter, Cate wrote Henshaw that he believed there was little reason to press monetary claims against Holloway-Langford. In the first place, she had no money and would leave no estate. Her property was assessed for $7,500, but there were two mortgages outstanding, plus a chattel mortgage on personal property. Additionally, there was evidence in a letter from Hildegard Henderson to Holloway-Langford that the money had been given as a gift, not a loan. Vaulx Carter told Cate that a finished manuscript for a 450-page book was ready for publication. His sister refused to give it up, but she was willing to have a copy made for Hildegard Henderson, with the proviso that it not be published.[42] As Vaulx Carter seemed to have realized, Henderson had hoped to obtain more than just a copy of the manuscript.

Henderson later recounted:

> I, eventually, put a lawyer onto the brother with threats of prosecution for obtaining money under false pretence—not that I expected, or had any intention of demanding money to be refunded, but as we knew that L. C. H. had Letters in Master K. H.'s handwriting, I had hoped to get possession of these in compensation, but the brother and his sister were too sharp for me, and as I was not on the spot all my lawyer could obtain were copies in Mrs. L.'s handwriting of the Master's Letters. I have a box full of these but I place no reliance on them, as I feel sure that all rebukes from the Master would have been omitted, and probably much material added to gloss over the bare truth of her complete failure.[43]

The Koot Hoomi letters were not mentioned in the legal agreement that on April 28, 1925, was entered into by "Laura C. Langford," Mrs. Hildegard Henderson, and Mrs. Eleanor Curtis. It stated that "'Helena Petrovna Blavatsky, Personal Recollections of Old Friends', which manuscript has never been published, and of which only one copy, which for the most part is in the handwriting of the said party of the first part, exists," was to be submitted to the plaintiffs, in lieu of Laura C. Langford being released from all debts, contracts, or liabilities. Holloway-Langford had given in to the demand that she surrender her manuscript, but she made her own stipulations: neither Hildegard Henderson and Eleanor Curtis nor their agents were permitted to publish the manuscript "in whole or in part, either in the words of the manuscript or in substance, nor any quotations there from, nor allow any others to do so."[44] Additionally, Holloway-Langford had resisted any attempt by Henderson to take possession of original documents in her possession. Such copies as Henderson had of the Koot Hoomi letters were either those that Holloway-Langford had sent her over the three years of their correspondence or ones that she had included in the book manuscript. Taking into account the more than $500 that they spent on legal fees, Hildegard Henderson and Eleanor Curtis had purchased Laura Holloway-Langford's book at a cost of close to $4,000.

AGREEMENT VIOLATED

After Hildegard Henderson read the manuscript, she wrote Alice Cleather that their fears about Holloway-Langford's portrayal of Blavatsky had been unfounded: "Nowhere is there anything antagonistic to H. P. B., not even a veiled sleight." In fact, Henderson believed that the book would have served to discredit A. P. Sinnett, revealing "how poisonous he really was." She was amazed that Holloway-Langford had included nine letters from Koot Hoomi, complete with "reproofs which she had carefully eliminated in the copies she used to send us," believing that they showed that Holloway-Langford had failed the test of obedience to the Masters. Henderson wrote that she did not regret the legal row, since it had been "the means of our getting the MS." She wanted Cleather to read the book and find a way to publish it, despite the legal agreement. Henderson requested that Cleather pressure Holloway-Langford to publish the Koot

Hoomi letters "complete and unaltered—with as much of her own stuff as you consider would be desirable (if *any*)." She suggested that Holloway-Langford's name could appear as author, but that she not be allowed any financial profit. Henderson continued: "She will naturally understand that after the large sums advanced and put by her to other purposes than publishing, she would not expect to have expectation of our entering on any further financial dealing *with her*—all business would have to be between us and the publishers *direct*."[45] Alice Cleather's response to this letter is unknown. Surely, however, Laura Holloway-Langford would not have reacted kindly to a request to publish, without compensation, material on which she had labored for several years and which included copies of letters that were her most precious possessions.

Laura Holloway-Langford lived the last decade of her life in dire poverty. She had relinquished the only copy of her manuscript, but she retained the original Koot Hoomi letters, including a few which had never been copied. At her death, these letters remained among her papers, and at least some, if not all, of them came into the hands of Edward Deming Andrews, who subsequently donated them to the Winterthur Library.[46] To be sure, neither Laura Holloway-Langford nor Hildegard Henderson emerge from this story untainted; each manipulated the other, and perhaps each underestimated the guile of the other. But by 1925 Laura Holloway-Langford's Theosophical journey was finished. Her last contacts with living Theosophists had ended in another row, the very reason that for years she had disassociated herself from the Society.

THE FATE OF THE MANUSCRIPT

What became of Laura Holloway-Langford's manuscript remains a mystery. In *The Complete Works of H. P. Blavatsky*, published in 1933, A. Trevor Barker quoted several times from this document, but each time he noted that the manuscript had been destroyed. Clearly, Hildegard Henderson had allowed others to read the manuscript, taking notes on it or even copying it in full. Twice, Barker reproduced a portrait of Madame Blavatsky with a fan.[47] He said this was taken by Laura Holloway-Langford; it was not, in fact, but she owned many portraits of Blavatsky, and she may have included this one in the book manuscript. There is no doubt that Hildegard Henderson did not abide by the legal agreement not to let others quote from the manuscript, either in words or in substance; however, she may have refrained from allowing publication from its contents until after Holloway-Langford's death in 1930. Even if the original manuscript was destroyed, it is still possible that one or more copies were made. In 2000, the Blavatsky Study Center online published Daniel Caldwell's "Mrs. Holloway and the Mahatmas," in which he quotes several times from "an unpublished autobiographical manuscript by Mrs. Holloway."[48] If this manuscript is indeed extant, it has not been made public so that it can be inspected by scholars.

CONTROLLING THE NARRATIVE

The struggle between Laura Holloway-Langford and Hildegard Henderson underscores the challenges in writing the history of the Theosophical movement. It may seem obvious that what history gets written depends on what documents are preserved. Any historical reconstruction is based on partial information. Nevertheless, historians have a responsibility to assess whose perspective the surviving documents represent. The case of Laura Holloway-Langford and Hildegard Henderson demonstrates how the historical narrative may be deliberately skewed by what gets saved, what gets destroyed, what remains private, and what reaches the eyes of the public. Holloway-Langford's story raises additional issues. Her articles have been mined by historians for evidence about the early days of Theosophy, even though her sketches of Blavatsky, Judge, and Olcott were crafted in order to take a stand on contemporary controversies about leadership in the Theosophical Society. In her letters and in other articles Holloway-Langford offered tantalizing excerpts from early documents, but excluded material that might have raised questions about her own character or actions. Rather than publishing in full correspondence from the Masters, she presented edited passages in "The Mahatmas and Their Instruments." "A Master and His Pupils," published in *The Word* in 1912, was a fictionalized spiritual autobiography about the teachings of her Master. Yet some historians of Theosophy have relied extensively on Laura Holloway-Langford's imaginative productions in the effort to write the early history of the movement.[49]

How should scholars evaluate material that has been excerpted from documents that are not available for scrutiny? On the one hand, important information that is unavailable elsewhere can hardly be ignored. On the other hand, it is dangerous to use excerpts irrespective of knowledge of the fuller context of their production. Holloway-Langford's manuscript may have contained primary material that has vanished from the historical record, but it nevertheless was part of a larger political project that aimed to restore Helena Blavatsky to the center of Theosophical history. Laura Holloway-Langford's perspective on the early days of the Theosophical Society has been lost. Had her interpretation of the events of 1884 changed over the years? Did she have any deeper insight into the personalities and conflicts of that time? Did she still accept the existence of the Masters of Wisdom and their letters as authoritative? Had her view of Blavatsky developed? Perhaps someday a copy of *Helena Petrovna Blavatsky: Personal Recollections by Old Friends* will turn up, so that we can assess whether she, at long last, had developed a full grasp of the issues which arose during the months that she lived among Theosophists.

The evidence from the last years of Holloway-Langford's life suggests that she continued to admire Helena Blavatsky and to believe that she was a channel for esoteric knowledge. Whether or not Holloway-Langford accepted the existence of the Masters on a literal level, she valued the letters that placed her among a select few who had received such communications during Blavatsky's lifetime. Throughout her life, Holloway-Langford sustained an interest in the occult, but she did not identify with any organized group or any particular metaphysical perspective. Her Theosophical experiences had become a commodity. Alice Cleather and Hildegard Henderson had demonstrated that both her memories and the documents in her possession had value, and she used them adroitly as bargaining chips. Then in her eighties, Laura Holloway-Langford was no longer striving to be accepted among the upper echelons of society. Living in poverty and isolation, her one concern was how to make the most of the resources she possessed. Still, if she had knowledge about how the Mahatma letters were produced and disseminated, she was not willing to barter this information for monetary gain. She had no loyalty to the Theosophical Society as an organization, but by preserving silence on these matters she remained faithful to Blavatsky and the Masters.

Epilogue: Seeking Laura

For over a decade I have lived in Nashville, Tennessee, where I teach at Vanderbilt University. In 2005, I began research on Eldress Anna White, whose sharp intellect and devotion to progressive causes I had long admired. I discovered that the Edward Deming Andrews Shaker Collection at the Winterthur Library contained many letters from White to someone named Laura Langford. When I realized that Laura (in this final chapter, we are on a first-name basis) had been born in Nashville, my interest was piqued. In the local history room of the Nashville Library, Carol Kaplan located a vertical file with clippings about the hometown daughter who had made good as the author of *Ladies of the White House*. From it, I first got wind of the persona Laura had fashioned for the public: she was born in 1848 on a plantation; her father, Samuel Carter, had been governor of Tennessee; she began publishing at age eleven; she married Junius B. Holloway while "yet a school girl," and she was widowed while very young.

NASHVILLE

I headed across the Legislative Plaza to the Tennessee State Archives. A librarian there looked at me in astonishment when I asked about Samuel Carter, governor of Tennessee. I was embarrassed to learn that no such governor existed. It soon turned out that almost none of my original information about Laura was true. Laura O. Carter was born on August 22, 1843. Her father owned a small farm not far outside of Nashville. During much of Laura's childhood, he managed a racetrack and a hotel. Her earliest publications were in local newspapers around 1860. She married in June 1862 when she was almost nineteen—certainly no child-marriage by nineteenth-century standards. Most shocking to discover was that Laura was not a widow. Junius B. Holloway lived until 1915. I was hooked. Who was this woman and why had I, in just a few days, turned up so many discrepancies in her life story? Thus began my search for the "real" Laura Carter Holloway-Langford.

Each discovery complicated the emerging portrait. I soon realized that in her lifetime Laura concealed the failure of her marriage by shearing five years from her age. Other pretenses soon began to crumble. I could find no record of a divorce from Junius Holloway, and there were no direct references to him in surviving letters. I concluded that Junius's imprisonment as a possible traitor to the Union revealed a flawed character. Still, Laura's secrecy remained puzzling, since her New York and Brooklyn friends included many women who were divorced or who led unconventional sexual and social lives. Because, in her early fiction, Laura wrote about the perils of marriage for young women, I could not help but wonder what she might have contributed to the debate over women's rights if she had been open about her own experience. Confession might have healed her soul, but widowhood aroused sympathy and provided a justification for her professional life. Delving into the story of Junius B. Holloway also might have raised troubling questions about her political loyalties during the Civil War. Her New York friends would more readily forgive a failed marriage than her support for the Confederacy.

Laura's unease about her Southern past is suggested by her claim to Quaker heritage and her assertion that her slaveholding father had been a lifelong abolitionist. Neither contention is supported by the facts. In "Between the Lines," a presentation that she gave to the YWCA in 1895, Laura portrayed herself during the war years as an innocent youngster who was concerned about a lack of fashionable clothing, not as a married woman whose husband had been taken prisoner. Sensitive to the mood of post-

Reconstructionist America, she knew that life on a plantation would seem glamorous to Northern eyes. The unresolved contradictions in Laura's story, I concluded, were emblematic of a nation that chose to ignore portions of its history in order to preserve the impression of reconciliation. Likewise, Laura refashioned her past in order to establish a new life, not only for herself, but also for her son and her siblings.

Still, I wondered whether Laura's belief in national unity included a commitment to racial equality. The evidence is sparse. During her youth in Nashville she could not have escaped the prevalent belief in white superiority. Yet Nashville in the 1850s was not segregated in the way that it became after Reconstruction. Laura interacted on a daily basis not only with slaves but also with free blacks who ran the city transport (hack) service and who owned and operated the most popular ice cream parlor and bakery. A quasi-free black man, Frank Parrish, was hired out as a barber in the St. Cloud hotel where Samuel Carter was proprietor. Laura's brother William recalled climbing to the roof of the hotel with Parrish to watch the Union troops enter Nashville. Perhaps it is not surprising, then, that, in contrast to A. P. Sinnett, Laura was never reproached for racism by the Mahatmas. She admired Oliver Otis Howard, the former head of the Freedmen's Bureau who was considered one of the nation's most radical proponents of racial equality. As President of the Seidl Society, Laura not only raised funds to support the Howard Colored Orphan Asylum, but she also included its children in outings to Brighton Beach. Laura's racial attitudes, I found, were more open than I had anticipated and more liberal than those of most of her Northern-born friends.

There were more surprises, each of which raised its own set of questions. Laura's first book turned out to be a melodramatic tearjerker, *Laure, the History of a Blighted Life,* published under her initials and later misattributed. In a letter from Anna White, I found a reference to a semiautobiographical account of spiritualism, *Beyond the Sunrise,* that Laura published anonymously. Another letter led me to an article by S. E. Archer, "Unequal Marriages," in the pages of the *Brooklyn Magazine.* Discovery of this pseudonym was an important piece of information that enabled identification of other writings. The full corpus of her work, I was beginning to realize, was beyond my grasp, since much of it had appeared in newspapers and magazines without a byline.

CANAAN, NEW YORK

In spring of 2006, I visited the Old Chatham, New York, Shaker Museum and Library. Jerry Grant, Director of Research, brought out materials that he had acquired some months earlier when property from the former Shaker farm in Upper Canaan, New York, had been auctioned. Remarkably, the house where Laura lived until her death in 1930 still contained her books and papers, many of them what Grant termed "spiritualist stuff." He had obtained a few items that belonged to Laura, including a small Bible presented to her "For correct recitation at one time of the whole of the 'Westminster Assembly's Shorter Catechism,' May 3rd, 1856." Additionally, he had acquired several pamphlet publications; a photograph of Vivekananda; a copy of the *Buddhist Diet-Book* with Laura's handwritten corrections; and an 1868 edition of the *New Illustrated Self-Instructor in Phrenology and Physiology,* with the "Chart and Character of Mrs. L. Holloway," signed "S. R. Wells Jan 13/69." A most surprising find among Laura's possessions was a copy of *Little Essays of Love and Virtue,* published in 1922 by Havelock Ellis. Denying that procreation was the purpose of marriage, Ellis discussed sex as "Divine play." He argued that every woman had a right to erotic pleasure, for she was "a real human being, with sexual needs and sexual responsibilities."[1] In such documents I detected the major themes of Laura's life: women's rights, sexuality, and spirituality.

Grant suggested that I stop by Welcome Home, an antique shop in Chatham, New York, because its owner, Kathy Stumph, had also purchased materials from the Canaan farmhouse. When I introduced myself, Stumph exclaimed, "I heard you were working on Laura and I wondered when you'd show up." To my amazement, she began bringing out boxes full of magazines and books. I made a modest bid for the whole lot, having no idea what I might be getting, and filled my Jeep Cherokee with Laura memorabilia. Laura, I felt sure, had guided me to take some leaves from her life back home with me to Nashville. Among these was a book of women's poetry titled *Atlanta Souvenir* that had been given to Laura's mother before her marriage. It was inscribed, "Presented to Anne Catherine Vaulx by her Father. 1831." Another item was an album of Confederate sheet music that Laura had collected when she was a student at the Nashville Female

Academy. Its cover depicted a Southern belle dancing the polka with a cadet from Nashville's Western Military Institute, which trained officers for the Confederacy. There were textbooks that had been in the family since the 1830s, and others that her son George had used at West Point. I brought these finds back to Nashville, where they have a new home in the Tennessee State Library and Archives.

Most important for understanding Laura's early life was a scrapbook that she had kept during the 1860s. It contained many sentimental, but not overtly religious, poems about love and death that she had clipped from magazines and newspapers. The scrapbook revealed that Laura had a number of suitors. A letter from "Your true friend Louis D. Hurly" ran: "I would very much I could be with you once more, all I ask of thee is that the memory of my name shall not be entirely forgotten." In pencil, Laura had corrected his punctuation (little chance that he would win her heart!). The scrapbook contained a calling card: "Thos. B. Manlove compliments to Miss Carter, and respectfully solicits the pleasure of calling upon her to day. Thursday morning. April 4th, 1861." Beside his initials, "T. M.," she had pasted a cut-out flower. In a newspaper clipping from April 1863, Laura marked a passage indicating that Manlove had moved his family from Vicksburg to Brandon, Mississippi. "Everything, save articles absolutely necessary is sacrificed, and Manlove from great wealth has sunk to poverty. His case is a type of all."

The War looms over the pages of the scrapbook. There are clippings about General Lee, obituaries of soldiers, and a poem set during the Battle of Nashville. By this time, I had learned that in 1865 Laura's father, Samuel Carter, ran for Congress on the Radical Republican ticket (he lost badly), but it took a newspaper clipping from the scrapbook to reveal his political opinions. Carter counseled reconciliation of Tennessee with the Union, but he did not believe that former slaves should be given suffrage or be allowed to testify in court. This information helped me understand how Laura could initially have been a "little rebel," supporting the Confederacy, but then have married a Union officer who was occupying Nashville.

I was also struck by what the scrapbook did not contain: no clippings about her wedding, and not a single mention of her husband, Junius B. Holloway, or her son, George, who had been born in 1864. Many of the scrapbook's pages are loose, and some sections obviously were cut out.

Laura apparently removed and destroyed any references to her brief marriage. However, she retained a page featuring a picture of the Madonna with the child Jesus at her knees. Below it, Laura had written: "Thus ends the old life. A new begins from this point. New York, 1866, 67, 68, 69." George would not yet have been three years old when she started her new life as a single mother. The image of Mary with the young boy must have given Laura comfort and strength.

After finding so much misleading information about Laura, I distrusted the claim that she had lived in the White House, especially, as some sources had it, for three years. But the scrapbook served to caution me that not everything about her biography was a pretense. It contained a bit of stationery engraved with her name and "Executive Mansion." Her handwritten note added: "Jany & Febr. 1869." I speculated that Martha Patterson, Andrew Johnson's daughter, had invited Laura to visit her while she completed work on *Ladies of the White House*. As I continued my research, I began to appreciate that the personae Laura created succeeded because they were based partially on fact. Instead of directly asserting falsehoods, she embellished the details, suggesting interpretations that bolstered her status. I also realized that Laura had managed to maintain a boundary between her public and her private life that today would be impossible. No one probed into the details of her marriage to Junius Holloway; no one pointed out inconsistencies in the various anecdotes she told about the writing of *Ladies of the White House;* and no one investigated the reason she traveled to Europe in the summer of 1884. Maintaining the posture of a "lady," Laura kept her personal life off-limits for discussion in the press. Thus, the scrapbook offered a glimpse of Laura in the years before she embarked on a life of self-invention. From it, I envisioned a young woman who was bright and inquisitive but also conventional; romantic and sentimental but not pious; literary in inclination but unoriginal in taste.

The trauma that Laura experienced during the 1860s explains much about her subsequent history. For example, it illuminates why her most heartfelt philanthropic work concerned homeless children and why her advocacy of the economic rights of women never wavered. I began to admire Laura for what Anna White rightly termed her "grit." She was tough and hard-working. When she latched on to a project, she pushed it through, no matter who or what got in the way. She was an immensely productive but facile writer. Her managerial and organizational skills were prodigious. Given the obstacles she faced as an independent woman in a culture that was still Victorian, Laura's accomplishments were impressive.

THE LIBRARY OF CONGRESS

Just as my admiration for Laura was increasing, I came across a "Finding Aid" to the Andrew Johnson Papers that the Library of Congress put online in 2009. There I discovered that around 1900, when she was ostensibly writing a biography of Andrew Johnson, Laura sought access to presidential papers owned by his daughter, Martha Patterson, of Greeneville, Tennessee. A trunk of material was shipped to her in Brooklyn. When time passed without progress on the book, Patterson requested that Laura return the documents. She complied, but according to the President's grandson, Andrew Johnson Patterson, "some of the most important papers were never returned."[2] I immediately contacted Claudia J. Keenan, who had also been pursuing Laura. Claudia knew about this episode. With her usual generosity, she mailed me copies of correspondence from the Library of Congress. It revealed that a few months after Martha Patterson died in July 1901 Laura wrote to John Hay, Secretary of State, asking his help in identifying two letters signed by Lincoln, but not in his hand. She hoped that they had been transcribed by Hay, since "their value will be greatly enhanced if they prove to be in your handwriting."[3] She also wanted to determine whether other letters in her possession had been included by Hay in his works on Lincoln. Clearly, Laura wanted to determine the monetary value of the documents, which would be greater if they were unpublished.

In 1907, just after her purchase of the Shaker farm at Upper Canaan, Laura sold some of the correspondence in her custody to George S. Hellman, who immediately resold five Lincoln letters to J. Pierpont Morgan.[4] However, these were only a few of the presidential documents that she held. In 1919, Hellman put on the market more correspondence that he had purchased earlier from Laura. It was described as "the most remarkable collection ever offered for public sale relating to a President of the United States." George D. Smith purchased the collection, which included thirteen "of the longest and most discursive letters written by Johnson on family and political matters," for $1,700.[5] It is uncertain how many documents Laura pilfered, but she was savvy enough to have selected those that would bring the best price. She made no secret of the fact that she possessed presidential correspondence, but she claimed that the materials had been given to her. Martha Patterson, of course, was not alive to contest Laura's account.

Certainly there was no justification for her actions. Still, I tried to understand them within the context of Laura's life. I knew that she harbored a long-standing fear of poverty, one that was realized in her later years. Just like people who experienced the Depression in the 1930s and forever after were penny-pinching, Laura's insecurity stemmed from the family's loss of wealth and property in Nashville after the War. When she married Edward Langford, Laura surely thought that her financial worries were over. In the late 1890s, however, he suffered an economic reversal when the Brighton Beach hotel went bankrupt and the railway was forced into foreclosure.[6] A few days after his death, the *Brooklyn Daily Eagle* observed:

> It is one of the injustices of fate that Colonel Edward L. Langford, who was buried on Monday, should not have made a fortune out of Brighton Beach. He was one of the few who believed in the future of that resort in its darkest days. He was much more than an officer of the Brighton Beach Company. He invested his money in the enterprise and he tried, vainly, to get capital to realize the possibilities which he saw so clearly. Yet, after the property passed to other hands, the prosperity which he had always known was there began to be realized.[7]

I concluded that Edward Langford's bankruptcy rekindled Laura's early fears. Nevertheless, whatever the underlying psychology, the episode of the Lincoln-Johnson papers raised questions about her character. In some ways, however, this incident was not inconsistent with other things that I knew about Laura. She was skillful at manipulating people to her own advantage; and she was prone to self-justification, seeming to take the moral high ground while blaming others for her own shortcomings. She was a woman who, for better or for worse, would go to great lengths to get what she wanted.

I remained puzzled about Laura's determination to purchase the Upper Canaan farm despite her fear of poverty and Shaker warnings that it was a risky venture. Perhaps owning a large country estate was to Laura a mark of social distinction, a way to restore symbolically her lost life in Tennessee. Or perhaps her ambition to achieve renown as a philanthropist clouded her judgment. Then again, Laura may have believed that the purchase of the farm would seal her relationship with the Shakers in an intimate bond of neighborliness and shared spirituality. Misplaced hopes, all. I suspect that even Laura did not understand fully what compelled her to acquire property that would drain her emotionally and financially for the rest of her life.

WINTERTHUR, DELAWARE

To backtrack a bit, when I began to pursue Laura seriously, her name turned up most frequently in connection with Theosophy, where she appeared as a minor character in the 1880s. Histories of the movement, however, often took a condescending tone, describing her either as a failure or as a troublemaker. It was far from clear, however, in what way she had failed or what kind of trouble she had caused. At first, I tried to ignore the Theosophical piece of her life. Not only was the material confusing and contradictory, but evaluating the credibility of sources was daunting. On a visit to the Winterthur Museum and Library, however, I saw the certificate that Laura received when she joined the Society in late 1883. I also transcribed strange letters written in blue pencil signed by a Mahatma called "Koot Hoomi."

When I found a preponderance of esoteric publications in the materials I acquired from Welcome Home in Chatham, New York, I knew that the Theosophical collection at the Winterthur Library was crucial evidence for understanding Laura. Theosophy was not just a blip in her story; rather, spiritual seeking was its central theme. Surely there had originally been much more "spiritualist stuff" among Laura's belongings that had been destroyed years ago or dispersed when the house's contents were auctioned. What I possessed were the leftovers. Nevertheless, they included Theosophical pamphlets, a copy of Henry Steel Olcott's Presidential Address, November 17, 1875, and an 1884 copy of the "Rules of the Theosophical Society," as well as copies of *The Theosophist; Lucifer; The Theosophical Forum; The Path;* and *The Word*. I had presumed that by the turn of the century, her interest in Theosophy had waned, but this proved not to be the case. Even in the late 1920s, she subscribed to *Theosophy: A Magazine Devoted to the Path,* a publication of The United Lodge of Theosophists in Los Angeles. In many of these publications, Laura had marked articles or passages that she found significant, sometimes adding her own notes.

Most important among the Theosophical materials was an early edition of *Light on the Path* by Mabel Collins, signed "William Q. Judge August 22, 1886," Laura's birthday. This confirmed not only a special bond between Laura and Judge, but a friendship that survived the events of 1884. Their relationship remains a puzzle. My best guess is that she and Judge shared the notion popular among spiritualists that sexual liaisons were justified by spiritual affinity. Claiming that they had been united in past lives, Laura led Judge to imagine that once away from Brooklyn they might develop a sexual as well as spiritual connection. She used this enticement to gain an introduction to Helena Blavatsky and an opportunity to become a disciple of the Masters. Evidently, at about the same time, Judge was making overtures to a much younger woman. Blavatsky wrote to him about "the shameful story . . . about you & your drama with Mrs. B's daughter," referring to the child of Laura's friend, the medium Mary Hollis-Billing.[8] Whatever the complications in his private life, however, I like to imagine that without Laura's inspiration William Q. Judge would not have had the courage to leave New York and stake out a place for himself as a major figure in the history of the Theosophical movement.

Among the materials donated by Edward Deming Andrews to the Winterthur Library was an autographed portrait of Judge, as well as one of Henry S. Olcott signed "To my dear and valued friend and colleague L. C. Holloway H. S. Olcott Elberfeld, Germany." Laura owned many photographs of Helena Blavatsky, one of which was inscribed: "To my faithful 'Barkis' who, I hope will now be *willing* from her devoted friend H. P. Blavatsky." It is dated July 1884, London. Also at the Winterthur was a postcard from Elizabeth Chapin, picturing thirteen members of the "India Society," a group of turbaned Indian men and American women in big flower-strewn hats.

In the 1890s, Laura's friend Lizzie Chapin and her cousin Maude Ralston had been Theosophists, but in the following decade they embraced Vedanta and supported Indian independence. In 1908, Chapin worked for the India House that Myron H. Phelps established in New York.[9]

There she met the Swami Premananda Das, one of the original disciples of Ramakrishna. The following year Chapin established the India Society of Detroit, where she lived with Ralston, who had married Thaker Dev Sharman, an immigrant from India.[10] While Ralston claimed that "high caste" Indians did not encounter racial prejudice, she nevertheless advised that in the United States it would be wise to wear turbans in order not to be mistaken for Negroes.[11] A poet, Ralston wrote "The Charkha," which begins: "Spin, spin, a nation is waking, A fresh dawn is breaking, a new day is born."[12] Gandhi used the spinning wheel to campaign for national self-sufficiency, and Ralston's poem holds a place in the literature of India's struggle against colonialism.

In the materials auctioned from her house at Canaan, New York, there was evidence that Laura, too, followed developments in the Ramakrishna movement and the struggle for Indian independence. She owned portraits of Swami Vivekananda, founder of the Ramakrishna Mission, and Swami Abhedananda, who headed the Vedanta Society in New York. Another photograph appears to be a portrait of the young Mahatma Gandhi in European dress. Yet the evidence is scanty, and Laura's attention at the turn of the century was fixed more on the Shakers than on Ramakrishna.

HPB LIBRARY, TORONTO

One of the most frustrating aspects of my research has been that few letters from Laura have survived, even though she was an almost compulsive correspondent, writing frequently to Judge, Olcott, Chatterji, Anna White, and many others. I have thus been forced to reconstruct her story primarily through the perspective of her correspondents. The one exception was the interchange in the 1920s with Hildegard Henderson, who saved Laura's letters, which eventually found a home in the HPB Library in Toronto. However, I am acutely aware that my portrayal of Laura is partial, a picture composed of widely connected dots. I like to hope that someday a cache of Laura's letters will be found tucked away in an attic trunk or unnoted in a private library. If this were to happen, it would be both a historian's dream come true and a bit of a nightmare—a test of the interpretations of her life that I have had the temerity to venture.

Despite all these discoveries, the real Laura remains elusive, hard to pin down even on those issues that were most important to her. She believed strongly that women's economic independence, not suffrage, was the key to their autonomy. She never relinquished a belief in a spiritual world beyond the material, although the characteristics of that realm shifted over time. On some level, she continued to have faith in the Adept Brotherhood, but how much of this belief was literal and how much metaphorical is unclear. Whatever she thought about how the Koot Hoomi letters were produced, she prized them and the recognition they had accorded her.

I feel less confident, however, about Laura's attitude toward sexuality. There are tantalizing hints that she sometimes shared her home with other women, even perhaps, if we are to believe *Beyond the Sunrise,* that she bought the Schermerhorn property with a female friend. Yet if this were true, it nevertheless says little about Laura's sexual orientation, since women who wanted to remain economically independent from men often pooled their resources. Her doubts about marriage and heterosexual relationships were strengthened by interaction with Helena Blavatsky, who, like many occultists, advocated sexual abstinence "as the distinguishing mark of the perfected life."[13] In subsequent years, Laura convinced the Shakers that she shared their commitment to celibacy, even though, as the incident with Myron Phelps and Ramanâthan showed, there could be widely differing interpretations of the meaning of purity. Laura was forty-six when she married Edward Langford; he was five years her senior (though he, no doubt, thought that the age difference was ten years). It seems unlikely, although not impossible, that theirs was a marriage in spirit only. Even in her later years, however, Laura sought information about female sexuality and the new science of psychology in the work of Havelock Ellis and his wife. For Laura, sexuality and its relationship to spirituality remained an irresolvable problem.

HANCOCK SHAKER LIBRARY

Laura's religious ideas also proved unexpectedly difficult to pin down. She supported a number of progressive causes—temperance, sex education, and housing for single working women, but she believed that the New

Age would be ushered in by spiritual means rather than through political or social reform. Her leadership of the Seidl Society was an important phase of her life, but it lasted for less than a decade, while the pursuit of spirituality remained a constant refrain. Nevertheless, Laura was reluctant to express her religious ideas openly. She avoided putting them into print where they could be examined and questioned. She may have feared that her unconventional beliefs would compromise her social status. Only in works published anonymously or under a pseudonym did she dare to express her own perspective.

Visiting the Hancock Shaker Library in spring 2006, I came across a letter to Laura from M. Catherine Allen, who in 1907 was manager of the North Family Shaker store. Referring to a little book, *As It is Written of Jesus the Christ,* Allen observed: "In writing that you were lifted up, heart and mind together receiving the divine influx. Many may teach, but to each heart separately must come the revelation—the clear vision as to Peter when he said 'Thou art the Christ'. We of North Family will take one hundred of the books to have in our store the coming season."[14] Thus, Allen judged the book consistent with the Shaker message, selling it alongside publications written by Believers. No reference to the volume appears in standard bibliographic sources, but I was able to purchase a copy from an antiquarian book dealer. When I received the book, authored by "The Helpers," I was excited to discover that the copyright was held by S. E. Archer, one of the pseudonyms used by Laura.

AS IT IS WRITTEN OF JESUS THE CHRIST

Because it provides the most direct evidence of her religious beliefs, I want to describe the contents of Laura's last book in some detail. An emblem on the cover portrays a circle containing a cross, but with the addition of a double loop on the horizontal bar that suggests the first letter of the "Aum," the Hindu symbol of the absolute.[15] This image encourages the association with Theosophy, but the book's first pages made me wonder if Laura had reverted to her Christian roots. The introductory chapter presents Jesus as "the Master." Subsequent chapters are organized around "The Way," "The Truth," and "The Life," with all quotations coming either from biblical or apocryphal texts. Laura, however, soon shifted from this familiar ground to challenge the tenets of mainstream Protestantism. She asserted that what a person believed was not important and that only actions were of consequence. She depicted an evolution of the self that was based on a belief in reincarnation, although she avoided the term. She eschewed any mention of crucial Christian concepts such as sin, redemption, and atonement. Perhaps most significantly, she did not represent Jesus as a personal savior.

She began with her own interpretation of the tree of life in Genesis. She portrayed the tree as an image of a human being, much as it had been depicted in Kabbalistic literature. But she went further, declaring that the four rivers flowing into the Garden of Eden represented the digestive, the respiratory, the circulatory, and the generative systems, while the nervous system was the scaffolding of the tree. Laura argued that the most important of these streams was the reproductive, which she declared "lies at the roots of the tree of life. It supplies the tree with the very virility itself."[16] She argued that this force, apparently masculine in nature, must be sublimated in order to create not only physical, but also spiritual and psychic strength. In much the same way that Blavatsky depicted the *Fohat,* the prototype of Eros that on earth becomes "Life-electricity," Laura described the generative force as divine electricity.[17] Thus, she concluded that Jesus' life revealed that the key to immortality was control of sexual energy.

Her rendering of the tree of life was also influenced by the rituals of the Hermetic Order of the Golden Dawn. In ritual ceremonies, aspirants of the Golden Dawn followed paths of the four elements that connected the *Sephirot,* or the emanations of the Divine, on the tree of life, depicted as the human body. In this narrative, human consciousness, which had been lowered by the fall in the Garden of Eden, could progress through occultism to reach the "Higher Self" and "the God within."[18] For Laura, however, secret knowledge did not reside in occult rituals so much as in the example set by Jesus. In her interpretation, his life revealed that in order to become divine it was necessary to be "sexless." She explained that "in heaven there is no marrying or giving in marriage. . . . Therefore, it is plain from His words, as well as His life, that one must eliminate sex to come to the kingdom."[19] In a version of the nineteenth-century theory of spermatic economy, she maintained that reproductive force must be conserved and directed from the physical plane to the spiritual. When fully controlled, this divine energy would convey humans "unscathed, conscious, full-armed through that dread change called death."[20] Laura, I began to suspect, had heard discussions of sexual magic, perhaps even ideas from Tantric Buddhism. She argued that if sexual energy were completely controlled by the will it would "transmute a lower into a higher power by the alchemy of divine love."[21] Humans could thus become gods and obtain eternal life.[22]

I was most surprised by how Laura's interpretation was gendered. Not only did she perceive the Divine in masculine terms, but she also described religious aspirants as men who must direct their generative power into spiritual channels. It was male, not female, sexuality that energized the universe. Her theology appeared to be influenced by a desire to apply the ideals of social purity equally to men as to women. In this view, women were spiritually superior beings who endeavored to transform male sexuality so that the New Age could be realized. Surprisingly, the Shaker belief in the feminine as well as the masculine in the deity did not resonate with Laura. Even Blavatsky had written about the Mother and Father as divine manifestations. Laura also knew writings by the Christian Theosophists Anna Kingsford and Edward Maitland, who declared that both humans and the Godhead were of dual sex, partaking of both masculine and feminine features.[23] As a subscriber to *Lucifer,* she would have read "The Future of Woman," in which Susan E. Gay argued that souls were reincarnated in both male and female bodies until they reached a "spiritual equilibrium of duality" perfected by Christ.[24] Laura herself in *Man: Fragments of Forgotten History* had suggested that Jesus embodied the feminine as well as the masculine. To some extent, Laura was influenced by the Kabbalistic notion that the female would be absorbed into, and subsumed by, the male to produce apparently androgynous but essentially masculine archetypal beings. Yet at the same time she was convinced that all sexual and gender differences must be eradicated in order to reach a state of bodiless spirituality that was not androgynous, but rather sexless.

Laura's esoteric interpretation of Christ was deeply theosophical.[25] She accepted the existence of adepts who lived in remote places. She wrote that they were "the repositories of the world's greatest knowledge. They prolong their earthly existences beyond the allotted span of life, and acquire powers little short of divinity." She argued that Jesus was "the great

Psychic," who had a superior power because he commanded: "He who loveth God, loveth his brother also."[26] The book reiterated Blavatsky's judgment that the "true esoteric SAVIOR—is no man, but the DIVINE PRINCIPLE in every human being" and that this "Christ Spirit" was available to all who were willing to "rise" from the material to the spiritual through their "own spiritual labour."[27] This message had been proclaimed by Mohini Chatterji on his tour of the United States in the 1880s. A version of it animated *Shakerism: Its Meaning and Message* by Anna White and Leila Taylor. It would also have been familiar to many ultra-liberal Protestants of the late Victorian period.[28]

Yet despite Laura's assertion that the "Christ Spirit" was available at all times and places, she mentioned no other example of its manifestation: neither the Buddha nor Mother Ann appear in the book's pages. I began to suspect that despite the influence of Helena Blavatsky, Laura's spiritual synthesis was quintessentially American. Her perspective remained Christ- and Bible-centered. She had combined the occult injunction to develop the will with the perfectionist strain in American Protestantism. Arguing that the physical must be perfected in order to bring the spiritual into being, she focused on the health and discipline of the human body. In addition to sexual renunciation, Laura recommended pure air and a vegetarian (preferably milk) diet. Self-development, then, was neither a psychological nor an intellectual process, but rather a physical one that was in essence also spiritual. I suspect that if she were writing today, Laura would add physical exercise to her list of requirements for bodily perfection. She was, in effect, the forerunner of popular books such as *What Would Jesus Eat?*[29] She stressed that each person must exercise power over the body: mental and spiritual progress, as well as future existence, depended on it. This message had great appeal, especially to women burdened by hierarchies that excluded them from full participation in religious, political, or social institutions.

As It is Written of Jesus the Christ concluded with a messianic plea, warning that it was only the followers of this redefined Christ who would enter the New Age:

> It is only for the humble seeker after Christ that the light shineth. It is to the simple and trusting child of Faith that is revealed the psychic power and the spiritual wisdom, which united, enable a man to travel the straight

and narrow path that leads to emancipation, and to make manifest the possession of such gifts of seeing and hearing and doing as shall compel humanity to know that His prophets are still among us, that His messengers are now in the world to herald His coming.

COME QUICKLY, LORD![30]

To be sure, theosophy had not been immune to its own version of millennialism. Blavatsky had predicted the end of the Kali Yuga, the Dark Age of spiritual decline, at the turn of the century. Some theosophists anticipated the arrival of a great World Teacher, or Messiah, who would usher in the New Age.[31] Still, despite the radical assertions of *As It is Written of Jesus the Christ,* in the end Laura appeared to proclaim that salvation would come only through the return of Christ. Christian readers would have recognized that her conclusion echoed the book of Revelation 22:20: "He which testifieth these things saith, Surely I come quickly. Amen. Even so, come, Lord Jesus." They might be reassured that Laura, after all, was one of them. At the same time, occultists would look for the esoteric meaning of the Second Coming, and Shakers would be comfortable with the notion that it would take place within each person. Laura, once again, demonstrated her knack for absorbing popular ideas and presenting them in such a way that disparate readers could feel that she confirmed, rather than challenged, their own presuppositions.

Laura envisioned a millennial age when social and political systems would be perfected, but she believed that it would be realized only through individual, not collective, effort. Perfection would be achieved through an evolutionary process entailing many incarnations before the material was completely transformed into the spiritual. Like the now infamous Sheila in Robert Bellah's *Habits of the Heart,* written more than half a century later, Laura created her own religion.[32] She drew on multiple sources— spiritualism, Shakerism, and theosophy—and recombined them into a distinct metaphysics. Her knowledge of sacred texts and religious history was superficial, but she did not hesitate to select elements that she found evocative while ignoring those that she did not find congenial. Her spirituality was rooted neither in particular traditions nor in a community of practice. She replaced the Calvinist compulsion to search for evidence of salvation with just as demanding an impulse to discipline the body through the exercise of will, confirming the presence of psychic power. In *As It is Written of Jesus the Christ,* she did not interpret the tree of life as a metaphor for community as the Shakers had done. Rather, she imagined it as an image of a single person, who looked within for spiritual knowledge. She even argued that Christ was the son of God because he was true to the demands "of His Own Being."[33] In this perspective, traditions and institutions, particularly religious ones, were the enemy of "truth." Hence, the Master that she followed founded no movement or community; he had little to say about how society should be organized or how the world could be repaired. Jesus—whether as the Christ Spirit or the Chief Adept—showed the way to self-perfection and immortality.

As It is Written of Jesus the Christ shares many elements with American spirituality as it developed in the twentieth century. It emphasizes the persistence of the individual soul. It asserts that physical energy can be transformed into spiritual. It suggests that Ascended Masters light the path of religious seekers. It understands bodily perfection as a mark of spirituality, while proclaiming the reality of esoteric healing. These ideas were common currency among many theosophists, and a few years later they would be popularized through the writings of Alice Bailey and others. Most tellingly, Laura claimed that each person had the potential for divinity and could become her own Christ. These ideas evoked Emerson and the Transcendentalists, and they resonated with those seeking alternatives to organized religion, both in the nineteenth century and beyond.

THE SEARCH CONTINUES

The "real" Laura Carter Holloway-Langford still seems hidden behind the masks that she so carefully crafted. We are all many different selves, in different times and places, within different contexts and in relation to different people; yet this does not imply deliberate concealment. As a young woman Laura was displaced socially, economically, and geographically. Early on in New York she was brash and ambitious, but she learned the penalties women paid for asserting themselves in public. It was not her spiritual beliefs that led her to avoid radical social and political activity, but rather her social experience as a woman. She longed for the power to command. Had she been a man, Laura might have made a general, like her brother William Harding Carter, and won accolades for these qualities. Instead, she stood apart, often criticizing others for not meeting her ideals—frustrated, I suspect, because she lacked the means to realize her dreams. It was through groups controlled by women that Laura was most successful in promoting new religious ideas. Certainly, her success in running the Seidl Society suggests what she could accomplish when given free rein. Most often her spirituality was expressed privately, but it was never divorced from her yearning for a New Age when women would play an equal role in both the material and spiritual realms.

Laura was a late Victorian religious seeker whose spirituality focused on the internal processes of self-development. By temperament, however, she preferred a life of action to one of contemplation. She attributed political and social progress to divine forces, and she saw no conflict between her spiritual search and her efforts for social reform. Spiritualism, theosophy, and Shakerism all suggested to her that change depended on the perfection of the individual. Thus, her pursuit of the occult did not result in disengagement from the world; rather, it coexisted with a longing to reconstruct society.

Laura Holloway-Langford's spiritual journey was a solitary undertaking. Spiritualism and theosophy provided neither a lasting community nor opportunity for leadership. Among the Shakers, however, Laura found a depth of friendship that sustained her spirit. Even so, she resisted living their communal life. In the end, her desire to transform the world had to be satisfied by a personal quest for a New Age of individual perfection.

ABBREVIATIONS

DeWint Henry Francis du Pont Winterthur Museum, Winterthur, Delaware. All material comes from the Edward Deming Andrews Memorial Shaker collection. Folder 1202 contains LHL material, including Shaker correspondence and scrapbooks. Folder 1198 contains materials relating to the Theosophical Society, including letters from the Mahatmas.

DLC Manuscript Division, Library of Congress.

HPB HPB Library, Toronto, Canada, LIIL file.

MPH Hancock Shaker Village Library, Pittsfield, Massachusetts.

NBPu Brooklyn Public Library. Brooklyn Room, LHL Papers.

NHi New York Historical Society.

NN New York Public Library. Shaker Manuscript Collection.

NNC-RB Columbia University Rare Books & Manuscripts Library. Seidl Society Papers.

NOC Emma B. King Library, Shaker Museum, Old Chatham, New York.

NyBLHS Brooklyn Historical Society Library. Anton Seidl Records.

OClWHi Western Reserve Historical Society, Cleveland, Ohio.

T Tennessee State Library and Archives.

TN Public Library of Nashville and Davidson County.

NOTES

INTRODUCTION

1. For example, see Marion Meade, *Madame Blavatsky: The Woman Behind the Myth* (New York: G. P. Putnam's Sons, 1980); Edward Deming Andrews and Faith Andrews, "The Shakers and Laura Langford," in *Fruits of the Shaker Tree of Life: Memoirs of Fifty Years of Collecting and Research* (Stockbridge, Mass.: Berkshire Traveller Press, 1975), 175–181; Thomas A. Tweed, *The American Encounter with Buddhism, 1844–1912: Victorian Culture and the Limits of Dissent* (Bloomington: Indiana University Press, 1992); and Joseph Horowitz, *Wagner Nights: An American History* (Berkeley: University of California Press, 1994). Horowitz added significant new material in his study of LHL's leadership of the Seidl Society.

2. Claudia J. Keenan, "Laura Carter Holloway Langford, 1843–1930," *Tennessee Encyclopedia of History and Culture,* http://tennesseeencyclopedia.net/entry.php?rec=1623; Diane Sasson, "'Dear Friend and Sister': Laura Holloway-Langford and the Shakers," *American Communal Societies Quarterly* 1, no. 4 (Oct. 2007): 170–190; Diane Sasson, "The Self Inventions of Laura Carter Holloway," *Tennessee Historical Quarterly* 67, no. 3 (Fall 2008): 178–207.

3. The term "New Age" was used in this sense at least from the 1840s. See, for example, "Declarations Concerning the New Associative Era," *New Age, Concordium Gazette and Temperance Advocate* 1 (Oct. 1844): 294–297. By the 1870s, the term "New Age" appeared frequently in publications promoting spiritualism, mental healing, and social reform.

4. For most of the nineteenth century, the term "feminist" meant the characteristics of womanhood. By the 1890s it was used to designate those who supported equal political, economic, and social rights for women. In this study, however, I apply the label to women like LHL who supported women's autonomy. The work which most directly addresses the link between feminism and new forms of spirituality in the late Victorian period is Catherine Tumber, *American Feminism and the Birth of New Age Spirituality: Searching for the Higher Self, 1875–1915* (Lanhan, Md.: Rowman & Littlefield Publishers Inc., 2002). Tumber uses the term "gnostic feminism" to describe women's cultivation of "special powers" in a search for a higher self, with their attendant rejection of the material world. Her analysis, however, is marred by her "robust disapproval" of their spiritual quest (2, 13).

5. Leigh Schmidt, *Restless Souls: The Making of American Spirituality* (San Francisco: HarperSanFrancisco, 2005).

6. Hal D. Sears, *The Sex Radicals: Free Love in High Victorian America* (Lawrence: University Press of Kansas, 1977).

7. See Joanne E. Passett, *Sex Radicals and the Quest for Women's Equality* (Urbana: University of Illinois Press, 2003), 158–162, for a discussion of these issues.

8. Allison P. Coudert, "Angel in the House or Idol of Perversity? Women in Nineteenth-century Esotericism," *Esoterica* 9 (2007): 14.

9. William Giles Harding Carter, *Giles Carter of Virginia: Genealogical Memoir* (Baltimore, Md.: The Lord Baltimore Press, 1909). LHL's mother was Samuel Carter's second wife, and a member of a prominent Middle Tennessee family. Her maternal grandfather was William Vaulx, who was from a prominent Nashville family; her maternal grandmother, Mary Hays, was the daughter of Charles Hays, a prosperous farmer and founder of the Baptist Church at Antioch.

10. On May 3, 1856, she received a Bible from A. G. Adams, Superintendent of the 2nd Presbyterian Church Sunday School in Nashville, inscribed: "Presented to Laura Carter For correct recitation at one time of the whole of the Westminster Assembly's Shorter Catechism." Emma B. King Library, Shaker Museum, Old Chatham, N.Y., hereafter NOC.

11. Alfred Leland Crabb, *Nashville: Personality of a City* (Indianapolis: The Bobbs-Merrill Co., Inc., 1960), 174, 195; Francis Garvin Davenport, "Cultural Life in Nashville on the Eve of the Civil War" (Ph.D. dissertation, Vanderbilt University, 1936), 75.

12. "Education" in Tennessee: A Guide to the State, http://newdeal.feri.org/guides/tnguide/ch12.htm, quotes Rev. Elliott. "The Nashville Female Academy," typescript, vertical file, Tennessee State Library and Archives, hereafter T.

13. Davenport, *Cultural Life*, 49, 139–187.

14. "Saint Cloud Hotel," *The Daily American* [Nashville], 27 Aug. 1889, 2.

15. Ben C. Truman, "Memories of Many Years," *New York Times*, 29 June 1890, 17; Benjamin C. Truman, "Anecdotes of Andrew Johnson," *Century Magazine* 85 (1913): 437.

16. Truman, "Memories."

17. Andrew Johnson, *The Papers of Andrew Johnson*, ed. Leroy P. Graf, Ralph W. Haskins, and Paul H. Bergeron, vol. 6, 1862–1864 (Knoxville: University of Tennessee Press, 1983), 249–250.

18. LHL to Andrew Johnson, 15 June 1863, *The Papers of Andrew Johnson*, vol. 6, 248–249.

19. Truman, "Memories," mentions a divorce, but there is no record of one in Davidson County, Tenn. Grounds for divorce varied from state to state. See Norma Basch, *Framing American Divorce: From the Revolutionary Generation to the Victorians* (Berkeley: University of California Press, 1999).

20. 64th Congress, House of Representatives, Report no. 118, "Widow of Junius B. Holloway," 4 Feb. 1916.

21. Newspaper clipping, n. d., scrapbook in the author's possession.

21. Thomas Benjamin Alexander, *Political Reconstruction in Tennessee* (New York: Russell & Russell, 1950), 81.

23. Ronald G. Machoian, *William Harding Carter: A Soldier's Story* (Norman: University of Oklahoma Press, 2006), 12.

24. Anson Nelson, "Brief Annals of Nashville from Its Foundation to 1875," in *Old Times in Tennessee: With Historical, Personal, and Political Scraps and Sketches*, ed. Jo. C. Guild (Nashville: Tavel, Eastman, & Howell, 1878), 496.

25. LHL to Andrew Johnson, 7 Sept. 1868, *The Papers of Andrew Johnson, Sept.1868–April 1869*, vol. 15 (Knoxville: University of Tennessee Press, 1999), 31–32.

26. Samuel Carter died in March 1873; Anne Vaulx Carter died in August 1874.

27. Federal Census, 1880. The handwriting is not legible; consequently LHL's name has been transcribed into Ancestry.com as "Lause C. Holaway," who was boarding with the family of Aaron Brinkerhoff at 179 Schermerhorn. George Holloway was living with Sam Lee and his wife Ahlo, who were born in China.

28. In 1866 and 1867, she lived at 147 East 17th St.; in 1868 and 1869, her address was 34 East 19th St.; and in the later part of 1869 and early 1870, the family resided at 106 E. 25th St.

29. Stephen Pearl Andrews, Horace Greeley, and Henry James, *Love, Marriage and Divorce, and the Sovereignty of the Individual: A Discussion* (New York: Stringer & Townsend, 1853).

30. "The Cooper Union for the Advancement of Art and Science," *Harper's Weekly*, 30 March 1861, 200.

31. "Southern Destitution," *New York Times*, 26 Jan. 1867, 1–2.

32. "Working Women's Protective Union," *New York Times*, 28 Feb. 1867, 8.

33. "Nothing Unreasonable," *New York Times*, 29 May 1869, 4.

34. "The Mighty Dead at Cooper Institute—a Séance and a Scene," *New York Times*, 20 Sept. 1869, 8; "Advent of Modern Spiritualism," *New York Times*, 1 April 1869, 1.

1. SEX, SUFFRAGE, AND RELIGIOUS SEEKERS

1. See "The New Woman as Androgyne: Social Disorder and Gender Crisis, 1870–1936," in Carroll Smith-Rosenberg, *Disorderly Conduct: Visions of Gender in Victorian America* (New York: Alfred A. Knopf, 1985), 245–296. Mary Farrell Bednarowski, in "Outside the Mainstream: Women's Religion and Women Religious Leaders in Nineteenth-Century America," *Journal of the American Academy of Religion* 48, no. 2 (June 1980): 207–231, discusses why women turned to alternative religious traditions.

2. Anne Ruggles Gere, *Intimate Practices: Literacy and Cultural Work in U. S. Women's Clubs, 1880–1920* (Urbana: University of Illinois Press, 1997); Karen J. Blair, *The Club Woman as Feminist: True Womanhood Redefined, 1868–1914* (New York: Homes and Meier Publishers, 1980); and Anne Firor Scott, *Natural Allies: Women's Associations in American History* (Urbana: University of Illinois Press, 1991).

3. Smith-Rosenberg, *Disorderly Conduct*, 245.

4. William Leach, *True Love and Perfect Union: The Feminist Reform of Sex and Society* (New York: Basic Books, Inc., 1980), 23.

5. The title of this journal varies. In the text I refer to it as *The Phrenological Journal*.

6. "Free Religion in America," *The Phrenological Journal and Life Illustrated* 58 (March 1874): 201–203. In the 1850s, *The Phrenological Journal* had as many as 50,000 subscribers. See Lisle Woodruff Dalton, "Between the Enlightenment and Public Protestantism: Religion and the American Phrenological Movement" (Ph.D. dissertation, University of California, Santa Barbara, 1998), 171.

7. Ruth Putnam, ed., *Life and Letters of Mary Putnam Jacobi* (New York: G. P. Putnam's Sons, 1925), 58, 310–311.

8. Ann Braude, *Radical Spirits: Spiritualism and Women's Rights in Nineteenth-Century America*, 2nd ed. (Bloomington: Indiana University Press, 2001), 30.

9. Barbara Goldsmith, *Other Powers: The Age of Suffrage, Spiritualism, and the Scandalous Victoria Woodhull* (New York: Alfred A. Knopf, 1998).

10. Joy Dixon, *Divine Feminine: Theosophy and Feminism in England* (Baltimore, Md.: Johns Hopkins University Press, 2001).

11. LHL [L. C. H.], *Laure: the History of a Blighted Life* (Philadelphia: Claxton, Remseyn & Haffelfinger, 1869, repr.1872). The *National Union Catalog* originally attributed the book to "Laura C. Holloway." After Lyle Wright listed the author as "L. C. Hill" in his book *American Fiction 1851–1875* (San Marino, Calif.: Huntington Library, 1957), the *National Union Catalog* changed the attribution in its revised edition.

12. Sara Payson Willis Parton published *Ruth Hall: A Domestic Tale of the Present Time*, under the pen name "Fannie Fern" (New York: Mason Brothers, 1855).

13. LHL, *Laure*, 219.

14. Ibid., 370–371.

15. Andrew Johnson to LHL, n. d., folder 5, Brooklyn Public Library, Brooklyn Collection, hereafter NBPu.

16. LHL [Laura C. Holloway], *The Ladies of the White House* (New York: United States Publishing Company, 1869, repr. 1870), 4; *The Ladies of the White House; or, in the Home of the Presidents. Being a Complete History of the Social and Domestic Lives of the Presidents from Washington to the Present Time—1789–1881* (Philadelphia: Bradley & Co., 1881).

17. Claudia J. Keenan, "Laura Carter Holloway and the First Lady's Story," *White House Studies* 8, no. 4 (2009): 468–469, 473.

18. LHL to Andrew Johnson, 10 May 1871, Andrew Johnson Papers, Manuscript Division, Library of Congress, hereafter DLC. There is no evidence that President Johnson complied with her request, and *Homes of Famous Americans* was never published.

19. [Eliza Putnam Heaton],"For Girls Who Scribble: Chats with Mrs. Laura Holloway and Mrs. Frank Leslie," *Washington Post*, 25 Dec. 1887, 9.

20. Carolyn Kitch, "Women in Journalism," in *American Journalism: History, Principles, Practices*, ed. W. David Sloan and Lisa Mullikin Parcell (Jefferson, N.C.: McFarland & Co., 2002), 87–89.

21. Newspaper clipping, "Frou-Frou," n. d., Scrapbook 1870, Henry Francis du Pont Winterthur Museum, Winterthur, Delaware, Edward Deming Andrews Memorial Shaker Collection, hereafter DeWint.

22. Lisa Tetrault, "The Incorporation of American Feminism: Suffragists and the Postbellum Lyceum," *The Journal of American History* 96, no. 4 (March 2010): 1027–1056.

23. Clippings, *New York Sun*, 8 Feb. 1870; *Brooklyn Daily Eagle*, 7 and 16 Feb. 1870; both in Scrapbook 1870, DeWint. Tickets cost fifty cents. In these years, Cooper Union was commonly referred to as "Cooper Institute." For consistency, I have used "Cooper Union" throughout.

24. Newspaper clipping, [Jan. 1870], Scrapbook 1870, DeWint.

25. The lecture's contents are known only from newspaper reports. In 1882, LHL published *An Hour with Charlotte Brontë: or, Flowers from a Yorkshire Moor* (Philadelphia: J. W. Bradley, 1882). Reviews were poor, noting that LHL offered nothing new about Brontë's life.

26. "Afternoon Mail Morsels," *Brooklyn Daily Eagle,* 28 Feb. 1870, 4.

27. P. P. [Parker Pillsbury], clipping, [Feb. 1870]; *The Revolution* 5 (3 March 1870), Scrapbook 1870; both in DeWint.

28. LHL to Susan B. Anthony, 19 Feb. 1870, reprinted in *The Revolution* 5 (3 March 1870). Excerpts from the *Boston Advertiser's* accounts of these events along with comments by Parker Pillsbury (see n27) were also published there. Patricia G. Holland and Ann D. Gor-

don, eds., *The Papers of Elizabeth Cady Stanton and Susan B. Anthony* (Wilmington, Del., Scholarly Resources, 1991, microfilm), vol. 2, 179.

29. P. P. [Parker Pillsbury], "The Lecturer on Charlotte Bronte," *The Revolution* 5 (3 March 1870).

30. LHL [Laura C. Holloway], *The Revolution* 6 (12 Oct. 1871) quoted in *The Revolution in Words: Righting Women, 1868–1871,* Women's Source Library 4, ed. Cheris Kramarae and Lana F. Rakow (London: Routledge, 1990), 98–99.

31. Edward W. Bok, ed., *Beecher Memorial: Contemporaneous Tributes to the Memory of Henry Ward Beecher* (Brooklyn, N.Y.: Privately Printed, 1887), 54.

32. Madeleine B. Stern, *Heads & Headlines: The Phrenological Fowlers* (Norman: University of Oklahoma Press, 1971), 34–35.

33. Ibid., 42.

34. Ibid., 170.

35. Ibid., 57–61.

36. Ibid., 167.

37. David S. Reynolds, *Walt Whitman's America: A Cultural Biography* (New York: Alfred A. Knopf, 1995), 209.

38. Samuel R. Wells, *Wedlock; or, the Right Relations of the Sexes: Disclosing the Laws of Conjugal Selection, and Showing Who May, and Who May Not Marry* (New York: S. R. Wells, 1869), 8–9, 114–124.

39. Christopher G. White, "Minds Intensely Unsettled: Phrenology, Experience, and the American Pursuit of Spiritual Assurance, 1830–1880," *Religion and American Culture: A Journal of Interpretation* 16, no. 2 (Summer 2006): 233.

40. Orson S. Fowler and Lorenzo N. Fowler, *New Illustrated Self-Instructor in Phrenology and Physiology; with Over One Hundred Engravings; Together with the Chart and Character of Mrs. C. Holloway, As Marked by S. R. Wells Jan. 13/69* (New York: Fowler and Wells, 1868), NOC.

41. "To Our Readers," *Brooklyn Daily Eagle,* 9 Dec. 1870, 3.

42. "Southern Women's Bureau," *The Phrenological Journal and Life Illustrated* 51 (Oct. 1870): 293–294.

43. "Southern Women's Bureau," *New York Times,* 8 June 1870, 5.

44. Newspaper clipping, 24 June 1870, Scrapbook 1870, DeWint.

45. "Southern Women's Bureau—'Women's Rights' Discussed," *New York Times,* 24 June 1870, 8.

46. *Brooklyn Daily Eagle,* 24 June 1870, 2.

47. LHL [Laura C. Holloway], "The Women of the South," *The Phrenological Journal and Life Illustrated* 51 (Sept. 1870): 208–209.

48. "To Our Readers," *Brooklyn Daily Eagle,* 9 Dec. 1870, 3.

49. "Perils of the Hour—Lecture by Laura C. Holloway," *New York Times,* 17 Dec. 1870, 4. This is the last record I have found of the Southern Women's Bureau.

50. "Perils of the Hour," *Brooklyn Daily Eagle,* 17 Dec. 1870, 3.

51. Edward Deming Andrews to Edward T. Jones, 18 Sept. 1963, Folder 1202, DeWint.

52. Jane Cunningham Croly, *The History of the Woman's Club Movement in America* (New York: H. G. Allen and Co., 1898), 18.

53. Ibid., 15–16.

54. Ibid., 25.

55. Newspaper clipping, n. d., Scrapbook 1887, DeWint, erroneously lists her as a member of

Sorosis. The New England Women's Club of Boston was the second-oldest women's club.

56. "Woman's Club, History of the Brooklyn Organization," *Brooklyn Daily Eagle*, 10 Feb. 1890, 2.

57. Ibid.

58. "The Brooklyn Woman's Club," *Brooklyn Daily Eagle*, 25 Oct. 1870, 2.

59. "The Ladies of Election Day. Interesting Meeting of the Woman's Club," *Brooklyn Daily Eagle*, 9 Nov. 1870, 4.

60. "The Woman's Club," *Brooklyn Daily Eagle*, 29 Oct. 1870, 6.

61. "The Brooklyn Woman's Club Again," *Brooklyn Daily Eagle*, 14 Dec. 1870, 2.

62. "Women. Work Being Done by Them in Brooklyn," *Brooklyn Daily Eagle*, 3 Oct. 1874, 2.

63. E. A. Thackray, "Mrs. Laura Holloway Langford," *The Writer: A Monthly Magazine for Literary Workers* 5 (June 1891): 119–120.

64. For example, she reviewed the *History of Woman Suffrage*, vol. 1, *Brooklyn Daily Eagle*, 20 June 1881, 1.

65. "A Slow, Steady Growth. Shown by the Report of the Brooklyn Kindergarten Association," *Brooklyn Daily Eagle*, 25 Oct. 1893, 7.

66. "Seeking to Displace Men," *New York Times*, 2 June 1887, 4; *The Standard Union*, 2 June 1887, Scrapbook 1887, DeWint.

67. Mary Putnam Jacobi, *The Question of Rest for Women During Menstruation* (New York: G. P. Putnam's Sons, 1877); Sears, *The Sex Radicals*, 238.

68. "Brooklyn Woman's Club. New Quarters in the Young Women's C. A. Building," *Brooklyn Daily Eagle*, 24 Jan. 1893, 8.

69. *Brooklyn Daily Eagle*, 25 Oct. 1870, 2.

70. Debbie Applegate, *The Most Famous Man in America: The Biography of Henry Ward Beecher* (New York: Doubleday, 2007), 302–305. There were reports that Beecher had raped Proctor in the 1850s. In 1874, when Francis Moulton published a letter from Proctor as evidence of Beecher's bad character, Proctor sued him for defamation of character. The suit was settled without going to trial. *Brooklyn Daily Eagle*, 17, 18, 21 Sept. 1874; 10, 16, 17 Dec. 1874.

71. LHL [Laura C. Holloway], "Would Women Vote? Over Thirty of Our Most Famous Women Answer the Question," *New Orleans Picayune*, 28 Oct. 1888, 13.

72. "Brooklyn's Only Lady Journalist," *Paper People*, 5 July 1874, Scrapbook 1870, DeWint.

73. "The Women's Peace Party," *Brooklyn Daily Eagle*, 3 June 1873, 4; "Universal Peace," *Brooklyn Daily Union*, 3 June 1873.

74. David W. Blight, *Race and Reunion: The Civil War in American Memory* (Cambridge, Mass.: Belknap Press of Harvard University Press, 2001).

75. Edwin Arnold, *The Light of Asia; or, The Great Renunciation (Mahâbhinishkramana): Being the Life and Teachings of Gautama, Prince of India and Founder of Buddhism* (New York: A. L. Burt, 1879); clipping, *New York Star*, n. d., Scrapbook 1887, DeWint. LHL, of course, had never traveled to "Oriental lands."

76. "The Brooklyn Ethical Association," *Popular Science*, March 1893, 672.

77. "Buddha's Birthday," *Brooklyn Daily Eagle*, 17 May 1897, 7.

78. Portrait in the author's possession.

79. John L. Thomas, *Alternative America: Henry George, Edward Bellamy, Henry Demarest Lloyd, and the Adversary Tradition* (Cambridge, Mass.: Harvard University Press, 1983).

2. "A CLAIRVOYANT OF THE FIRST WATER"

1. Henry James, "Spiritualism, New and Old," *Atlantic Monthly* 29 (March 1872): 358–362; Henry James, "Spiritualism, Modern Diabolism," *Atlantic Monthly* 32 (Aug. 1873): 219–224; Frederick W. Evans, "Autobiography of a Shaker," *Atlantic Monthly* 23 (1869): 415–426, 593–605.

2. Mrs. H. B. Stowe, "Spiritualism," *The Phrenological Journal and Life Illustrated* 51 (Nov. 1870): 351–357.

3. Braude, *Radical Spirits,* 36–37.

4. For a discussion of the relationship between spiritualism and social reform, see R. Laurence Moore, "The Rise and Fall of Spiritualist Reform," in *In Search of White Crows: Spiritualism, Parapsychology, and American Culture* (New York: Oxford University Press, 1977), 70–101.

5. Imogene C. Fales, "The New Age," *Religio-Philosophical Journal,* 31 May 1884, 6. See also, Fales, *The Religion of the Future* (Boston: Esoteric Publishing Company), 1889.

6. Braude, *Radical Spirits,* 26, notes the importance of communities of readers and writers among spiritualists.

7. For a full account, see Goldsmith, *Other Powers.*

8. LHL [Mrs. L. C. Holloway], "The Angel Guide," *American Phrenological Journal* 48 (Dec. 1868): 214.

9. Clipping, "Lines Inscribed to the Grand-daughter of President Johnson," n. d., Scrapbook 1870, DeWint.

10. Andrew Jackson Davis, *A Stellar Key to the Summer Land,* pt. 1 (Boston: William White and Company, 1868), 8.

11. LHL [Laura C. Holloway], "A Prayer of Thanks," *The Phrenological Journal and Life Illustrated* 51 (Aug. 1870): 137; LHL [Laura C. Holloway], "Morning Land," *Inter Ocean,* 7 Aug. 1875, 7. The title of this poem suggests Thomas Lake Harris, *A Lyric of the Morning Land* (New York: Partridge and Brittan, 1856).

12. Andrew Jackson Davis, *The Great Harmonia: Being a Philosophical Revelation of the Natural, Spiritual, and Celestial Universe,* vol. 5 (New York: J. S. Redfield, 1850), 171. For an exploration of his vision of conjugal union and its social implications, see Catherine L. Albanese, "On the Matter of Spirit: Andrew Jackson Davis and the Marriage of God and Nature," *American Academy of Religion* 60, no. 1 (Spring 1992): 1–17.

13. Clipping, n. d., Scrapbook 1870, DeWint. Mary Love Davis was a member of Sorosis, and the club women of New York rallied in her defense when in 1885 Andrew Jackson Davis had their marriage annulled.

14. Suzanne Thurman has pointed out that this theory was not only popular among spiritualists, but was also advocated by a heterodox group of Shaker sisters. Suzanne Thurman, "Shaker Women and Sexual Power: Heresy and Orthodoxy in the Shaker Village of Harvard, Massachusetts," *Journal of Women's History* 10 (Spring 1998): 70–87.

15. LHL [S. E. Archer], "Some Famous Unequal Marriages," *Brooklyn Magazine* 4 (Jan. 1887): 156–159; Mary Farrell Bednarowski, "Women in Occult America," in *The Occult in America: New Historical Perspectives,* ed. Howard Kerr and Charles L. Crow (Urbana: University of Illinois Press, 1983), 179–183, discusses the preoccupation of spiritualists with the reformation of sexual arrangements.

16. LHL [Laura C. Holloway], "Jane Hadley," *Phrenological Journal and Life Illustrated* 60 (Feb. 1875): 100–104; "Hettie Malvern," *Phrenological Journal and Life Illustrated* 61

(July 1875): 24–26; "Agnes Worth," *Phrenological Journal and Life Illustrated* 59 (July 1874): 31–36.

17. Leach, *True Love and Perfect Union*, 293–294.

18. LHL [Laura C. Holloway], *The Hearthstone: Or, Life at Home: A Household Manual* (Philadelphia: Bradley & Co., 1883), 368.

19. Catherine Esther Beecher and Harriet Beecher Stowe, *The American Woman's Home: Or, Principles of Domestic Science: Being a Guide to the Formation and Maintenance of Economical, Healthful, Beautiful, and Christian Homes* (New York: J. B. Ford and Company, 1869), 18, 203.

20. LHL, *Hearthstone*, 368, 367.

21. Her ideas were similar to those espoused by the Free Religious Association, as well as by many Unitarians. See David B. Parke, ed., *The Epic of Unitarianism: Original Writings from the History of Liberal Religion* (Boston: Skinner House Books, 1957).

22. Antoinette Doolittle, "Address of Antoinette Doolittle," 14 March 1872, *Shaker* 2 (June 1872): 42–43.

23. Emma Hardinge [Britten], *The Place and Mission of Women* (Boston: Hubbard W. Swett, 1859), 3. Although she originally published under the name "Hardinge," WorldCat catalogs all of her books under the married name "Britten," which she assumed in the 1870s. I have followed this practice in the bibliography to this book, but enclosed the later surname in brackets.

24. Patients at the "Home" engaged in "gymnastics, movement cure, lifting cure, Turkish, electric, vapor, or Russian baths, with all other forms of bathing and exercises known; each patient following out the course as directed by the attending physician." "Correspondence," *The Ohio Medical and Surgical Reporter* 5 (May 1871): 142.

25. Eli P. Miller, *Vital Force: How Wasted and How Preserved* (New York: Miller, Haynes & Co., 1872). The book is a catalogue of such "abuses," including Chapter IV, "Abuse of the Sexual Function: A Prime Cause of Derangements."

26. James M. Peebles had published a popular book, *Seers of the Ages: Embracing Spiritualism, Past and Present. Doctrines Stated and Moral Tendencies Defined* (Boston: William White and Company, 1869). He had a lifelong friendship with the Shakers, particularly with Frederick Evans, whom he had accompanied on a missionary tour to England in 1871.

27. Antoinette Doolittle to LHL, 10 Oct. 1874, DeWint, refers to having met her in New York. The *Brooklyn Daily Eagle* did not report on the Shaker meeting.

28. Letter addressed to "Elder F. W. Evans, Messenger of the Lord—the Female in the Deity" from "The Travailing Daughters of Zion, in New York City," 24 Nov. 1873, *Shaker and Shakeress* 4 (Jan. 1874): 4.

29. The letter from the Daughters of Zion provoked a lively discussion in the *Shaker and Shakeress* 4 (July 1874). One Shaker sister condemned the writers' "malice and envy" toward men; another supported their claim to an equal role in "humanity's cause"; while a third claimed that only the "inalienable rights of Virgins" could guarantee the position of a "truly enfranchised woman."

30. Antoinette Doolittle to LHL, 17 May 1874, DeWint. With the letter, Doolittle sent a picture of herself, calling it her "shadow," and one of Frederick Evans.

31. Anna White to LHL, 21 July 1902, DeWint; Daniel Offord to LHL, 15 Nov. 1908, NOC; Anna White to LHL, 23 Nov.1905, DeWint; Anna White to LHL, 27 Sept. 1905, DeWint.

32. Alvin Boyd Kuhn, *Theosophy: A Modern Revival of Ancient Wisdom* (New York: H. Holt and Company, 1930), 60, says that Lovell was the first person to pay the $5 initiation fee to the Theosophical Society. LHL, *Beyond the Sunrise: Observations by Two Travellers* (New York: John W. Lovell Company, 1883).

33. "The Bookshelf," *The Continent: A Weekly Illustrated Magazine*, 10 Oct. 1883, 474; Anna White to LHL, 13 May 1901, photocopy, Library Collection, Hancock Shaker Village, Pittsfield, Mass., hereafter MPH. I suspect that the "Two Travellers" are the characters Mona and Cleo, and that LHL is the book's sole author.

34. Antoinette Doolittle to LHL, 10 Oct. 1874, DeWint.

35. F. W. E., "Beyond the Sunrise," *Shaker Manifesto* 13 (Oct. 1883): 233.

36. LHL, *Beyond the Sunrise*, 8–9.

37. Ibid., 109.

38. Ibid., 108.

39. Ibid., 179.

40. Ibid., 9–10.

41. Ibid., 16–19.

42. Most of Cleo's story about her mother is taken from LHL's life. Only a few details are changed. In *Beyond the Sunrise*, the mother travels to Georgia rather than Tennessee. Cleo's younger brother is eight years old, while Vaulx Carter was thirteen when his mother died.

43. LHL, *Beyond the Sunrise*, 28.

44. Anne Vaulx was born June 18, 1818, and Samuel Carter was born Jan. 3, 1803.

45. One of the children was no longer living at the time of their marriage: Watson M. Carter was born on Dec. 16, 1826 and died May 3, 1828; Jordon B. Carter was born on Nov. 14, 1828 and died May 12, 1843; and Eliza S. Carter was born on May 3, 1831 and died Jan. 10, 1888.

46. LHL, *Beyond the Sunrise*, 29–35, 40, 49–64. The text explained that Cleo's sister could reproduce a detailed record of her mother's last days because she took down her impressions in shorthand. The census confirms that LHL's sister, Irene, was a stenographer.

47. Ibid., 179–182.

48. Ibid., 180–186.

49. The character of Honor may have been loosely based on that of LHL's colleague, Hester M. Poole, who was both an outspoken feminist and an admirer of the Shakers.

50. LHL, *Beyond the Sunrise*, 152–160.

51. Ibid., 165–166.

52. Ibid., 165–166, 173–174.

53. Ibid., 170.

54. Ibid., 212–215.

55. Ibid., 229.

56. Ibid., 196.

57. "Mrs. Laura Holloway Langford," *The Writer* 5 (1891): 120, indicates that Proctor lived at 181 Schermerhorn. A glowing description of Proctor's character by LHL in the *Graphic* was reprinted in *Current Literature* 1 (July 1888): 15–16. According to this article, in earlier years Proctor had lived with her relative, the "late" Charles Storrs, while more recently she spent "the greater part of her time" with a sister in South Framingham, Mass. After Charles Storrs died in 1884, Proctor probably lived with LHL when in Brooklyn. "A Coachman's

Excursion," *New York Times*, 7 Aug. 1889, 8, indicates that Dr. Lucy M. Hall then lived at 181 Schermerhorn. By the early 1890s, when she was a vice-president of the Seidl Society, Lucy Hall-Brown had married, and she was living on 158 Montague Street, Brooklyn.

58. Henry James, *The Bostonians* (New York: The Century Co., 1884).

59. Lillian Faderman, *To Believe in Women: What Lesbians Have Done for America—a History* (New York: Houghton Mifflin, 1999), 15, 22–23, 25–26.

60. Holloway-Langford reportedly edited *George Eliot's Poetry and Other Studies* (New York: Funk & Wagnalls, 1885) which appeared under Rose Elizabeth Cleveland's name. In 1886 they briefly co-edited a magazine, *Literary Life*. On Cleveland's lesbian relationship, see Lillian Faderman, *Odd Girls and Twilight Lovers: A History of Lesbian Life in Twentieth-Century America* (New York: Columbia University Press, 1991), 32.

61. *Beyond the Sunrise* also includes an account of a mining venture, which apparently depicts William Q. Judge, who was a member of this Sunday evening gathering.

3. "BETTER COME"

1. In this way she was similar to Helena Blavatsky, Annie Besant, and Katherine Tingley. See Robert S. Ellwood and Catherine Wessinger, "The Feminism of 'Universal Brotherhood': Women in the Theosophical Movement," in *Women's Leadership in Marginal Religions: Explorations Outside the Mainstream*, ed. Catherine Wessinger (Urbana: University of Illinois Press, 1993), 68.

2. These included Mary Hollis-Billing, a spiritualist medium; William E. S. Fales, son of her friend, Imogene, and translator of Blavatsky's testimony in a court case; William M. Ivins, a lawyer who had represented Blavatsky; and Charles Sotheran, one of the original members of the Theosophical Society. LHL was also a friend of Isabella [Belle] Olcott Mitchell, Henry Olcott's sister, but it is unclear whether they were acquainted prior to LHL's trip to Europe.

3. Henry Steel Olcott, *People from the Other World* (Hartford, Conn.: American Publishing Company, 1875), 293–313.

4. Emma Hardinge [Britten], *Modern American Spiritualism: A Twenty Years' Record of the Communion Between Earth and the World of the Spirits* (New York: Published by the Author, 1870).

5. Henry S. Olcott, *Old Diary Leaves*, vol. 1 (New York and London: G. P. Putnam's Sons, 1895), 120–121, 135.

6. James Santucci, "Women in the Theosophical Movement," *Explorations: Journal for Adventurous Thought* 9, no. 1 (Fall 1990): 71–94. Available at the Theosophical History Website: www.theohistory.org.

7. Josephine Ransom, *A Short History of the Theosophical Society* (Adyar, India: The Theosophical Publishing House, 1938; repr. 2007), 103–104.

8. Olcott, *Old Diary Leaves*, vol. 1, 120.

9. For Peebles's description of the "Calcutta Spiritualists," see J[ames] M[artin] Peebles, *Around the World: Or, Travels in Polynesia, China, India, Arabia, Egypt, Syria, and Other "Heathen" Countries*, 2nd ed. (Boston: Colby and Rich, 1875), 251–253.

10. Ransom, *A Short History of the Theosophical Society*, 98.

11. The first American branch of the Society was not formed until 1882, in Rochester, New York, followed by one in St. Louis. The New York Branch was inaugurated in December 1883. The major expansion of Theosophy in the United States, however, came after William Q. Judge became the General Secretary of the American Section of the Society

in December 1886. By 1891, when Helena Blavatsky died, fifty-four branches of the Society had been established in the United States. Michael Gomes, *The Dawning of the Theosophical Movement* (Wheaton, Ill.: Theosophical Publishing House, 1987), 14–15.

12. For information about Hollis-Billing, see Napoleon Bonaparte Wolfe, *Startling Facts in Modern Spiritualism* (Cincinnati: N. B. Wolfe, 1874).

13. Olcott, *Old Diary Leaves*, vol. 1, 483.

14. Olcott, *Old Diary Leaves*, vol. 1, 142; Ransom, *A Short History of the Theosophical Society*, 124–125.

15. Gomes, *The Dawning of the Theosophical Movement*, 14.

16. Helena Petrovna Blavatsky, *Isis Unveiled: A Master-Key to the Mysteries of Ancient and Modern Science and Theology* (New York: J. W. Bouton, 1877).

17. H. P. Blavatsky, "Elementaries," *Religio-Philosophical Journal* 23 (Nov. 1877), reprinted in *Blavatsky: Collected Writings*, vol. 1, ed. Boris de Zirkoff (Wheaton, Ill.: Theosophical Publishing House, 1950), 265–271. She contrasted these "elementaries"—"disembodied, vicious, earth-bound yet human spirits"—with "elementals, nature spirits." For an account of the relationship between spiritualism and the early days of Theosophy, see Gomes, *The Dawning of the Theosophical Movement*, 19–61.

18. Mark Bevir, "The West Turns East: Madame Blavatsky and the Transformation of the Occult Tradition," Journal of the American Academy of Religion 62, no. 3 (Autumn 1994): 751.

19. Cathy Gutierrez, "The Elusive Isis: Theosophy and the Mirror of Millennialism," in *The End That Does: Art, Science, and Millennial Accomplishment*, ed. by Cathy Gutierrez and Hillel Schwartz, Millennialism and Society 3 (London: Equinox, 2006), 120.

20. Moore, *In Search of White Crows*, 229. Moore discusses the similarities between spiritualism and Theosophy, 227–236.

21. Stephen Prothero, "From Spiritualism to Theosophy: 'Uplifting' a Democratic Tradition," *Religion and American Culture* 3 (Summer 1993): 198. Like the recruits to Theosophy studied by Prothero, LHL's social status was situated on what he terms the "border zone between populism and elitism," (202). Thomas Bender, *New York Intellect: A History of Intellectual Life in New York City, from 1750 to the Beginnings of Our Own Time* (New York: Alfred A. Knopf, 1987), terms this class a "metropolitan gentry," but in his study, women's cultural and intellectual activities are ignored.

22. Kirby Van Mater, "William Quan Judge: A Biographical Sketch," *Sunrise Magazine*, April/May, 1996, quotes a letter, "WQJ to Sarah W. Cape, Oct. 1891[3?]; photocopy, Archives, Theosophical Society, Pasadena." Available at the Theosophy Northwest website: www.theosophy-nw.org.

23. For more information on Hermeticism, see Nicholas Goodrick-Clarke, *The Western Esoteric Traditions: A Historical Introduction* (New York: Oxford University Press, 2008).

24. John Patrick Deveney, "An 1876 Lecture by W. Q. Judge on His Magical Progress in the Theosophical Society," *Theosophical History: A Quarterly Journal of Research* 9 (July 2003): 12–20.

25. H. P. Blavatsky to A. N. Aksakov, 15 June 1877, quoted in Vsevolod S. Solovyov, *A Modern Priestess of Isis*, abridged and translated by Walter Leaf (London: Longmans, Green, and Co., 1895; repr. New York: Arno Press, 1976), 276.

26. William Q. Judge to A. P. Sinnett, 1 Aug. 1881, letter 158 in A. Trevor Barker, ed., *The Letters of H. P. Blavatsky to A. P. Sinnett*, (Pasadena, Calif.: Theosophical University Press, 1973), 312.

27. William Q. Judge to Damodar K. Mavalankar, 1 March 1880, *The Theosophist* 52 (Feb. 1931): 325– 326.

28. H. P. Blavatsky to A. Wilder, [ca. 6 Dec. 1876], letter 75 in John Algeo, ed., *The Letters of H. P. Blavatsky, 1861–1879* (Wheaton, Ill.: Quest Books, 2004), 281.

29. William Q. Judge to Henry S. Olcott, 3 Dec. 1870 [*sic*, actually 1879], "Letters of W. Q. Judge," *The Theosophist* 52 (Jan. 1931): 212.

30. William Q. Judge to Henry S. Olcott, 9 April 1879, "Letters of W. Q. Judge," *The Theosophist* 52 (Jan. 1931): 211.

31. William Q. Judge to Damodar K. Mavalankar, 26 July 1881, in *Damodar and the Pioneers of the Theosophical Movement,* Sven Eek (Adyar, India: The Theosophical Publishing House, 1965), 63.

32. William Q. Judge to Henry S. Olcott, 16 Jan. 1882, *The Theosophist* 52 (May 1931): 194–195.

33. Ibid., 197.

34. William Q. Judge to Henry S. Olcott, 26 Sept. 1881, *The Theosophist* 52 (March 1931): 464.

35. William Q. Judge to Henry S. Olcott, 21 Jan. 1882, *The Theosophist* 52 (June 1931): 356.

36. William Q. Judge to Henry S. Olcott, 7 Jan. 1882, *The Theosophist* 52 (May 1931): 192. There are a number of other references to thoughts of suicide in Judge's letters to Olcott and LHL.

37. William Q. Judge to New York Theosophists, 18 March 1882, *The Theosophical Forum,* 15 Sept. 1932, 8; online edition at: http://blavatskyarchives.com/judgeletter1882.htm. Judge went to Venezuela in fall 1881 and again in March 1882; he returned to New York on July 24, 1882, but left soon afterwards for Mexico.

38. William Q. Judge to Henry S. Olcott, 1 Aug. 1882, *The Theosophist* 52 (Sept. 1931): 752–753.

39. William Q. Judge to Henry S. Olcott, 15 May 1863 [*sic*, actually 1883], *The Theosophist* 52 (Sept. 1931): 755–756.

40. William Q. Judge to Henry S. Olcott, 16 Jan. 1882, *The Theosophist* 52 (May 1931): 197.

41. "Chronological Survey," in *Blavatsky: Collected Writings,* ed. Zirkoff, vol. 4, xxviii. The editor notes that this information is from "Holloway MSS destroyed some years ago."

42. William Q. Judge to Henry S. Olcott, 14 Sept. 1880, *The Theosophist* 52 (March 1931): 461. Blavatsky also asked Hollis-Billing to communicate with Judge through a Native American spirit, "Ski." See H. P. Blavatsky to Mrs. Hollis-Billing, 2 Oct. 1881, *The Theosophical Forum* (May 1936): 343–346. Available at: http://blavatskyletters.net/.

43. [LHL], "Buddhism in India: Mr. Sinnett's *Esoteric Buddhism,*" *Brooklyn Daily Eagle,* 23 Sept. 1883, 5.

44. LHL, "William Quan Judge, A Reminiscence," *The Word* 22 (Nov. 1915): 82–83.

45. Van Mater writes: "Judge had continued corresponding with Damodar K. Mavalankar, and on the back of Mavalankar's letter of 11 June 1883 was a message: 'Better come M.' (The original of WQJ's letter in reply to Damodar's letter, on the back of which M sends his message, is in the Archives of the Theosophical Society, Adyar; Damodar's letter is missing)."

46. William Q. Judge to Damodar K. Mavalankar, 11 June 1883, in Eek, ed. *Damodar and the Pioneers of the Theosophical Movement,* 76.

47. Michael Gomes, "Abner Doubleday and Theosophy in America, 1879–1884," *Sunrise Magazine,* April/May 1991, http://www.theosociety.org/pasadena/sunrise/40-90-1/th-tsgom.htm. Gomes notes that the word "Aryan" did not, at that time, have the racist overtones that it has since acquired.

48. LHL, "William Quan Judge, A Reminiscence," 81–82, 84.

49. William Q. Judge to Henry S. Olcott, 24 April 1884, *The Theosophist* 53 (Nov. 1931): 197.

50. Marlene Tromp, "Spirited Sexuality: Sex, Marriage, and Victorian Spiritualism," *Victorian Literature and Culture* (2003): 68, 78.

51. The certificate is dated "the Second Month of its Eighth Year," probably Dec. 1883 (DeWint).

52. Grace F. Knoche, "Our Directives, Study of the Evolution of the 'Objects of the T.S.' —from 1875 to 1891," *The Theosophical Forum* (Oct. 1947): 582–587; online edition (Theosophical University Press online), http://www.theosociety.org/pasadena/gfkforum/ourdir.htm.

53. Like all new members, however, LHL was placed on trial until she could demonstrate her commitment to the Society and its principles. In the papers left after her death was the pamphlet [Theosophical Society], *Rules of the Theosophical Society, Together with an Explanation of Its Objects and Principles* (Madras, India: Printed at the Scottish Press, 1884). LHL's copy is in the author's possession. For a summary of early Theosophical ideas in the American context, see Robert S. Ellwood, "The American Theosophical Synthesis," in *The Occult in America,* ed. Howard Kerr and Charles L. Crow, 111–134.

54. The word "chela" is derived from the Hindu meaning "servant"; in English, it refers to a religious disciple. The nature of "chelaship" was debated among Theosophists. See Helena P. Blavatsky, "Chelas," *The Theosophist* 6 (Oct. 1884), http://www.blavatsky.net/blavatsky/arts/Chelas.htm.

55. Handwritten note in LHL's hand, inserted in *The Theosophist* 8, no. 87 (Dec. 1886), in the author's possession.

56. Santucci, "Women in the Theosophical Movement."

57. Ransom, *A Short History of the Theosophical Society,* 152–153.

58. Dixon, *Divine Feminine,* 62, estimates that in England throughout the 1890s two-thirds of the Theosophical Society's members were male.

59. LHL, "Extracts From Letters Written by William Q. Judge from London in the Spring of 1884. To A Long-Time Friend," *The Word* 14 (March 1912): 325.

60. Ibid., 331.

61. Ibid., 329–330. Judge and LHL still looked to Egypt, rather than India, as the source of ancient knowledge, as had Blavatsky during the first years of Theosophy.

62. Joy Dixon, "Sexology and the Occult: Sexuality and Subjectivity in Theosophy's New Age," *Journal of the History of Sexuality* 7, no. 3 (Jan. 1997): 427, shows how Theosophists located "inappropriate desires" in distant times and places to create "an imaginary space in which the boundaries imposed by bourgeois norms could be transgressed with apparent impunity."

63. LHL, "Extracts from Letters," (March 1912), 326–327.

64. Ibid., 324–325. Judge had sent LHL and the two other "disciples" portions of letters that Sinnett had received from the Masters. LHL's letter to Mavalankar is not extant, but some of its contents can be surmised from his reply.

65. Damodar K. Mavalankar to LHL, 11 May 1884, DeWint, SA1318.1b1.

66. LHL, "Teachings of the Master. Recorded by One of the Authors of 'Man: Fragments of Forgotten History,'" *The Path* 1 (Dec. 1886): 278–279.

67. Olcott, *Old Diary Leaves,* vol. 3, 90.

68. LHL, "Extracts From Letters Written by William Q. Judge," *The Word* 14 (April 1912): 22, 17, 18.

69. Ibid., 24.

70. William Q. Judge to Henry S. Olcott, 24 April 1884, *The Theosophist* 53 (Nov. 1931): 197.

71. H. P. Blavatsky to LHL, 24 April 1884, DeWint, SA1318.1e1. A typescript of this letter is in the HPB Library, Toronto, hereafter HPB.

72. William Q. Judge to Henry S. Olcott, 30 April 1894, *The Theosophist* 53 (Nov. 1931): 201–202. Adam Willis Wagnalls was a partner in Funk & Wagnalls, which from 1883–1886 published a number of LHL's works.

73. Louise Chandler Moulton to LHL, Nov. 30 [1883], NBPu. This letter suggests that LHL had begun making plans to leave the United States by late fall 1883.

74. Oliver Otis Howard, *Autobiography of General Oliver Otis Howard, Major General United States Army*, vol. 2 (New York: The Baker & Taylor Co., 1907), 524.

75. Daniel H. Caldwell, "Mrs. Holloway and the Mahatmas: Published and Unpublished Mahatma Letters," available at the Blavatsky Archives Online: www.blavatskyarchives .com. Caldwell quotes LHL from an unpublished manuscript:

> The impelling motive that occasioned my trip to Europe in the spring of 1884 was the receipt of a letter from [Madame Blavatsky]. . . . But for Mr. Judge's many and insistent assurances of a welcome I would never have met her, for there was no allurement for me in an ocean voyage, and I had pen work to do that would occupy so much time I did not anticipate much if any of a summer vacation away from it. But I longed to know her, and to learn from her the meaning of some of the psychic experiences I had before Mr. Judge left America. Finally with a friend and her young son we went to Europe.

76. Olcott, *Old Diary Leaves*, vol. 3, 162.

77. Ransom, *A Short History of the Theosophical Society*, 203, indicates that Judge left England in late June, arriving in Bombay on July 15.

4. "THE FIRST BOMB-SHELL FROM THE DUGPA WORLD"

1. Helena Blavatsky to A. P. Sinnett, 17 March 1886, letter 141 in Trevor A. Barker, ed., *The Mahatma Letters to A. P. Sinnett from the Mahatmas M. and K. H.* (Theosophical University Press Edition: http://www.theosociety.org/pasadena/mahatma/ml-hp.htm). In citing *The Mahatma Letters*, I have used the online edition, which is a facsimile of the 2nd ed., 1926, with additional material from Margaret Conger, *Combined Chronology for Use with the Mahatma Letters and the Letters of H. P. Blavatsky to A. P. Sinnett* (Pasadena, Calif.: Theosophical University Press, 1973). Most of the Mahatma letters are undated. Inferred dates are supplied in brackets. Information about dates comes both from Barker and from *The Mahatma Letters to A. P. Sinnett, Chronological Edition, Theosophical Classics*, CD-ROM (Manila, Philippines: Theosophical Publishing House, 2002).

2. Society for Psychical Research "Report of the Committee Appointed to Investigate Phenomena Connected with the Theosophical Society," *Proceedings of the Society for Psychical Research* 3 (1885): 207.

3. The Dugpas were sorcerers who lived in Tibet and practiced malicious magic. They could be identified by their red hats.

4. H. P. Blavatsky to A. P. Sinnett, 17 March 1886, letter 141 in Barker, *The Mahatma Letters to A. P. Sinnett*.

5. Koot Hoomi in a letter to A. P. Sinnett, [rec. 10 Oct. 1884], letter 66 in Barker, *The Mahatma Letters to A. P. Sinnett*, remarked that the "unpleasantness" of the summer of 1884

could have been avoided if Laura Holloway-Langford had stayed in Paris until the end of June, when Madame Blavatsky went to London.

6. The fullest exploration of attitudes toward gender and sexuality among early Theosophists is Siv Ellen Kraft, "The Sex Problem: Political Aspects of Gender Discourse in the Theosophical Society 1875–1930" (Thesis, University of Bergen IKRR, Dept. of the History of Religions, 1999).

7. LHL, "Helen Petrovna Blavatsky. A Reminiscence," *The Word* 22 (Dec. 1915): 147. LHL's recollection of Blavatsky's words after a quarter of a century may have been colored by her subsequent opposition to the leadership of Annie Besant.

8. "Conversations on Occultism with H.P. B," in *Blavatsky: Collected Writings*, vol. 5, 269.

9. In most cases, letters from Koot Hoomi were not dated; but sometimes there is a record of when a specific letter arrived. In other instances, the date of a letter can be inferred only by internal evidence. I have enclosed the date in brackets when the date of a letter has been inferred.

10. For example, see Bruce F. Campbell, *Ancient Wisdom Revived: A History of the Theosophical Movement* (Berkeley: University of California Press, 1980), 56–57.

11. Catherine Wessinger, "Democracy vs. Hierarchy: The Evolution of Authority in the Theosophical Society," in *When Prophets Die,* ed. Timothy Miller (Albany: State University of New York Press, 1991), 93–106. Wessinger focuses on the struggle for power that emerged after Blavatsky's death, especially the conflicting claims to occult authority by William Q. Judge and Annie Besant.

12. Sylvia Cranston, *HPB: The Extraordinary Life and Influence of Helena Blavatsky, Founder of the Modern Theosophical Movement* (New York: G. P. Putnam's Sons, 1993), 208.

13. Olcott, *Old Diary Leaves*, vol. 2, 28–29, 136.

14. Biography of Sinnett from the Theosophy Forward website: http://www.theosophyforward.com/index.php/theosophical-encyclopedia/351-sinnett-alfred-percy-1840-1921.pdf.

15. Anna Kingsford and Edward Maitland, *The Perfect Way: or, The Finding of Christ* (London: Field & Tuer, 1882).

16. Alfred Percy Sinnett, *The Early Days of Theosophy in Europe* (London: G. Redway, 1922), 47, 44–45.

17. Ibid., 48–50.

18. A. P. Sinnett to Helena P. Blavatsky, [Fall 1883], letter 28 in Barker, *The Letters of H. P. Blavatsky to A. P. Sinnett,* 65.

19. Koot Hoomi to Mohini Chatterji, [Sept. 1882], in C. Jinarajadasa, comp., *Letters from the Masters of the Wisdom,* 2nd series (Adyar, India: Theosophical Publishing House, 1925) / *Theosophical Classics,* letter 58. Chatterji was also forbidden to pronounce the name of the other chelas.

20. J. Barton Scott, "Miracle Publics: Theosophy, Christianity, and the Coulomb Affair," *History of Religions* 49, no. 2 (2009): 181. This claim is based on a letter by Chatterji, "The Theosophical Mahatmas," published in the *Pall Mall Gazette,* 2 Oct. 1884, and reflects a later need to defend Blavatsky in light of the Coulomb accusations.

21. Koot Hoomi to Mohini M. Chatterji, n. d., in Jinarajadasa, *Letters from the Masters of the Wisdom,* 1st series / *Theosophical Classics,* letter 15.

22. K. Paul Johnson, *The Masters Revealed: Madame Blavatsky and the Myth of the Great White Lodge* (Albany: State University of New York Press, 1994), 6.

23. Mohini Mohun Chatterji, "The Himalayan Brothers—Do They Exist?" *The Theosophist* 5 (Dec. 1883), repr. in [LHL and Mohini Mohun Chatterji, ed.], *Five Years of Theosophy: Mystical, Philosophical, Theosophical, Historical, and Scientific Essays Selected from The Theosophist* (London: Reeves & Turner, 1885), 459–469.

24. For his account of first discerning the presence of the Masters at Theosophical Headquarters, see "Mohini Chatterji's Deposition to the Society for Psychical Research, 1884," http://www.blavatskyarchives.com/chatterjideposition.htm, reprinted from the Society for Psychical Research, "First Report," 1884, Appendix 2, 62–74. Chatterji translated from the Sanskrit a dialogue, Atmanatma Viveka, attributed to Sankara Acharya, the eighth-century Hindu philosopher, entitled "Discrimination of Spirit and Not-Spirit," *The Theosophist* 4 (Nov. 1882) and 5 (Dec. 1883); repr. in [LHL and Chatterji] *Five Years of Theosophy,* 394–407. In "Matter and Force, from the Hindu Standpoint," *The Theosophist* 4 (Dec. 1882): 66–67, he argued against Western analytical reasoning, while at the same time alluding to European philosophical and literary sources.

25. Koot Hoomi to Mohini Chatterji, [rec. March 1884], in Jinarajadasa, *Letters from the Masters of the Wisdom,* 2nd series / *Theosophical Classics,* letter 62.

26. Charles W. Leadbeater, *How Theosophy Came to Me* (Madras: Theosophical Publishing House, 1930), 41.

27. Alan Trevithick, "The Theosophical Society and Its Subaltern Acolytes," *Marburg Journal of Religion* 13, no. 1 (May 2008): 1–32, argues that orientalism was fundamental to the Theosophical Society, which sought out "little dark helpers" who were thought to be idealistic, susceptible, loyal, and submissive.

28. Ransom, *A Short History of the Theosophical Society,* 198.

29. Koot Hoomi to Mohini M. Chatterji, [spring 1884], in Jinarajadasa, *Letters from the Masters of the Wisdom,* 1st series / *Theosophical Classics,* letter 13.

30. William Q. Judge to Henry S. Olcott, 30 April 1884, *The Theosophist* 53 (Nov. 1931): 200.

31. Isabelle de Steiger, *Memorabilia: Reminiscences of a Woman Artist and Writer* (London: Rider & Co., 1927), 249, 261, 260. Chatterji's wife was a member of the wealthy Tagore family of Bengal. She was the granddaughter of Debendranath Tagore, founder of the Brahmo Samaj, one of the most important Indian reform movements, and her uncle was the writer Rabindranath Tagore. Steiger's book contains many errors of fact, but it is useful for descriptions of people and the times. For example, she misidentifies LHL as "Mrs. Warrington," but describes her as a beautiful and interesting American woman who was clairvoyant and clairaudient . . . and a medium "well received by the Theosophists in general. Somehow she incurred the displeasure of H. P. B. . . . Shortly afterwards Mrs. Warrington's hitherto friendly circle collapsed and she returned to New York without carrying with her the affectionate feelings with which she was received" (268).

32. Leadbeater, *How Theosophy Came to Me,* 27.

33. Solovyov, *A Modern Priestess of Isis,* 17–18. Steiger also remarked on "the entire absence of the familiar handshake on all occasions," 260.

34. Supplement to *The Theosophist* 5 (Sept. 1884): 131.

35. Koot Hoomi to A. P. Sinnett, [rec. after 1 Dec. 1880], letter 5 in Barker, *The Mahatma Letters to A. P. Sinnett.*

36. Master Morya to A. P. Sinnett, [rec. Jan 1884], letter 96 in Barker, *The Mahatma Letters to A. P. Sinnett.*

37. H. P. Blavatsky to A. P. Sinnett, 17 March 1886, letter 141 in Barker, *The Mahatma Letters to A. P. Sinnett.*

38. LHL, "Extracts From letters Written by William Q. Judge," *The Word* 14 (March 1912): 324–330.

39. Master Morya to A. P. Sinnett, [rec.15 April 1884], letter 61 in Barker, *The Mahatma Letters to A. P. Sinnett*. "Pays" probably refers to the French for "country."

40. Ibid.

41. LHL, "The Theosophists. Something About Madame Blavatsky, the High Priestess of the Society. Her Approaching Visit to This Country With Colonel Henry S. Olcott. A Most Gifted Woman—Her Circle of Distinguished Friends in London," *The Leader*, 14 Oct. 1888, 14. (Blavatsky Study Center online edition, copyright 2004.)

42. Koot Hoomi to H. P. Blavatsky, in Caldwell, "Mrs. Holloway and the Mahatmas," letter 2. He dates this letter to early July 1884. I have not found it in other collections.

43. Sinnett, *Early Days of Theosophy*, 58.

44. A. P. Sinnett, *The Rationale of Mesmerism* (Boston: Houghton Mifflin and Company, 1892), 232, discusses "astral" clairvoyance, in which the medium sees and converses with entities not visible to ordinary persons. See Alex Owen, *The Darkened Room: Women, Power, and Spiritualism in Late Victorian England* (Philadelphia: University of Pennsylvania Press, 1990), for a discussion of the relationship between the sexual vulnerability and the sexual power of the medium.

45. According to Joscelyn Godwin, *The Theosophical Enlightenment* (Albany: New York State University Press, 1990), 196, Blavatsky suggested to Olcott the existence of living beings that had been sent to change the world. In *People from the Other World*, Olcott attributed the outbreak of spiritualism to these agents.

46. Sinnett, *Early Days of Theosophy*, 59.

47. Ibid., 60.

48. Koot Hoomi to H. P. Blavatsky, [early July 1884], letter 2 in Caldwell, "Mrs. Holloway and the Mahatmas."

49. Koot Hoomi to H. P. Blavatsky, [mid-July 1884], DeWint, SA1318.20h. This letter appears to be the original. It was copied by LHL in a letter to Hildegard Henderson, 28 April 1923, HPB. Caldwell, "Mrs. Holloway and the Mahatmas," publishes portions of it as five separate letters, nos. 4, 5, 6, 7, and 8. The likely explanation is that LHL copied excerpts in a number of documents. For information on the Kama-loka, see William Q. Judge, *The Ocean of Theosophy*, 11th ed. (Los Angeles, Calif.: The United Lodge of Theosophists, 1922), 99–108.

50. Koot Hoomi[?] to H. P. Blavatsky, n. d., DeWint, SA1318.20g. The letter quotes from DeWint, SA1318.20h, so can be dated to mid-July 1884. This letter has, to my knowledge, never been published.

51. Koot Hoomi to LHL, [late Aug. 1884], DeWint, SA1318.21b-c; letter 17 in Caldwell, "Mrs. Holloway and the Mahatmas." LHL to Hildegard Henderson, 28 April 1923, HPB, contains portions of this letter, but LHL omitted the incriminating section.

52. Ibid.

53. Koot Hoomi to H. P. Blavatsky, [mid-July 1884], DeWint, SA1318.20g.

54. Meade, *Madame Blavatsky*, 305.

55. LHL [L. C. L.], "The Mahatmas and Their Instruments. Madame Blavatsky and the Masters—Precipitated Letters and Their Recipients," *The Word* (May 1912), 70.

56. Koot Hoomi to Francesca Arundale, [late July 1884], letter 9 in Caldwell, "Mrs. Holloway and the Mahatmas."

57. Koot Hoomi to H. P. Blavatsky, [late July or early Aug., 1884], DeWint, SA1318.20e; letter 11 in Caldwell, "Mrs. Holloway and the Mahatmas."

58. Master Morya to H. P. Blavatsky, [mid-July 1884], DeWint, SA1318.20j. This MS begins on the second page. The first paragraph is also provided in Caldwell, "Mrs. Holloway and the Mahatmas," letter 5; and Jinarajadasa, *Letters from the Masters of the Wisdom*, 1st series / *Theosophical Classics*, letter 40. "Zinzin" is a French expression meaning "crazy."

59. Letter 38 in Barker, *The Letters of H. P. Blavatsky to A. P. Sinnett*, 91.

60. Sinnett, *Early Days of Theosophy*, 62.

61. Koot Hoomi to LHL, [July 1884], in Jinarajadasa, *Letters from the Masters of the Wisdom*, 1st series / *Theosophical Classics*, letter 35.

62. Koot Hoomi to A. P. Sinnett, [rec. 18 July 1884], letter 62 in Barker, *The Mahatma Letters to A. P. Sinnett*.

63. Koot Hoomi to A. P. Sinnett, [rec. 5 Nov. 1880], letter 4 in Barker, *The Mahatma Letters to A. P. Sinnett*.

64. H. P. Blavatsky to A. P. Sinnett, [written soon after 18 July 1884], letter 133 in Barker, *The Mahatma Letters to A. P. Sinnett*.

65. Gauri Viswanathan, "The Ordinary Business of Occultism," *Critical Inquiry* 27 (Autumn 2000): 2–3.

5. FANTASIZING THE OCCULT

1. Sinnett, *Early Days of Theosophy in Europe*, 48.

2. Dixon, *Divine Feminine*, 23–24.

3. Blavatsky, *Isis Unveiled*, 285–286.

4. Ibid., 358.

5. A. P. Sinnett, *The Occult World* (London: Trübner and Co., 1881), 23.

6. Ibid., 24.

7. *Current Literature* 2 (June 1889): 455.

8. Sinnett, *The Occult World*, 151–152. The first use of "pansy" to refer to a homosexual male was recorded in the 1920s; however, this quotation suggests that "pansy" may have been associated with effeminate behavior much earlier.

9. Francis Marion Crawford, *Mr. Isaacs: A Tale of Modern India* (New York: Grosset & Dunlap, 1882), 6.

10. "Interview with Madame Blavatsky—Paris, 1884, with an Introduction and Notes by Michael Gomes," *The Canadian Theosophist* 67 (Nov./Dec. 1986): 103; online edition, http://theosophy.katinkahesselink.net/canadian/Vol-67-5-Theosophist.htm. According to Gomes, Ward joined the London Lodge of the Theosophical Society in April 1883.

11. Koot Hoomi to A. P. Sinnett, [rec. Jan. 1883], letter 56 in Barker, *The Mahatma Letters to A. P. Sinnett*.

12. "Interview with Madame Blavatsky—Paris, 1884": 101.

13. H. P. Blavatsky, "Mr. Isaacs," *The Theosophist* 4, no. 5 (Feb. 1883), in *Blavatsky: Collected Writings*, vol. 4, 339.

14. Ibid., 340.

15. Crawford, *Mr. Isaacs*, 120.

16. Blavatsky, "Mr. Isaacs," 341.

17. Ibid., 342.

18. Crawford, *Mr. Isaacs*, 298.

19. Ibid., 119.

20. Ibid., 120.

21. Blavatsky, "Mr. Isaacs," 342.

22. Koot Hoomi to A. P. Sinnett, [Jan. 1883], letter 56 in Barker, *Mahatma Letters to A. P. Sinnett.*

23. Dixon, *Divine Feminine,* 27. Dixon quotes from Koot Hoomi to A. P. Sinnett [mid-Sept. 1882], letter 24b in Barker, *The Mahatma Letters to A. P. Sinnett.*

24. Rosa Campbell Praed, *Affinities: A Romance of To-day,* revised ed. (London: George Routledge & Sons, 1886 [first ed. 1885]); Praed, *The Brother of the Shadow: A Mystery of To-day* (London: George Routledge & Sons, 1886).

25. Angela Kingston, *Oscar Wilde as a Character in Victorian Fiction* (New York: Palgrave Miller, 2007), 48–56. Kingston explains that Rosa Campbell Praed refashioned gossip that was circulating about Oscar Wilde's marriage to Constance Lloyd in May 1884; Wilde was rumored to have continued his friendship with the artist Louise Jopling after the wedding.

26. Olcott, *Old Diary Leaves,* vol. 3, 165–166.

27. Praed, *Affinities,* 195.

28. Ibid., 213–214.

29. Ibid., 243–244.

30. Ibid., 243.

31. Ibid., 310–311.

32. Ibid., 249.

33. Ibid., 204.

34. Ibid., 231.

35. Ibid., 238.

36. Ibid., 311–312.

37. Ibid., 312.

38. "Notes on Novels," *The Dublin Review* 14 (July 1885): 196–197.

39. A. P. Sinnett, *Karma, A Novel,* 2 vols. (London: Chapman and Hall, 1885).

40. Sinnett, *Karma,* vol. 1, 199–200.

41. Ibid., 49–50.

42. Ibid., 211.

43. Ibid., 220.

44. Ibid., vol. 2, 94, 99–103.

45. "Esoteric Buddhism," *Lucifer* 1, no. 3 (Nov. 1887): 229–230.

46. *The Dublin Review* 15 (March 1886): 182–183.

47. *The Critic: a Weekly Review of Literature and the Arts* 8 (2 July 1887): 183.

48. H. P. Blavatsky to A. P. Sinnett, 19 Aug. 1885, letter 46 in Barker, *Letters of H. P. Blavatsky,* 107.

49. Ibid.

50. The most enduring literary portrayal of Mohini Chatterji appears in the poetry of William Butler Yeats. Yeats's encounter with Chatterji inspired several poems, including "Anashuya and Vijaya," "The Indian Upon God," and "The Indian to His Love." In 1928, Yeats published "Mohini Chatterjee," which drew directly on the words that Chatterji had spoken to Yeats in Dublin in April 1886. See Alexander Norman Jeffares, *W. B. Yeats: Man and Poet* (New Haven, Conn.: Yale University Press, 1949), 27.

51. Theories about electricity as an occult force and as a treatment for mental and spiritual problems appear in popular novels such as Marie Corelli, *A Romance of Two Worlds* (London: Bentley, 1886).

52. Praed, *Brother of the Shadow,* 16.

53. Ibid., 20.

54. The term "Inner Asia" denoted the far reaches of the Himalayas and Tibet. The kingdom of Shambhala, the Buddhist "Pure Land," where ancient wisdom was preserved and all inhabitants were enlightened, was said to be located there.

55. Praed, *Brother of the Shadow*, 17.

56. Ibid., 16.

57. Ibid., 22.

58. Ibid., 44.

59. Ibid., 16–17.

60. Ibid., 48–50.

61. For a description of the "electric bath," see Jean Baptiste Alexandre Baille and John W. Armstrong, *The Wonders of Electricity* (New York: Scribner, Armstrong, and Co., 1872), 206–209.

62. Rachel P. Maines, *The Technology of Orgasm: "Hysteria," the Vibrator, and Women's Sexual Satisfaction* (Baltimore & London: The Johns Hopkins University Press, 1999). Today it seems preposterous that so little was known about women's sexual response that many doctors as well as their patients seemed unaware or unwilling to admit that the treatments produced sexual orgasm.

63. Praed, *Brother of the Shadow*, 104.

64. Ibid., 44.

65. Ibid., 63.

66. Ibid., 68–69.

67. Ibid., 144.

68. Marie Corelli. *A Romance of Two Worlds.*

69. See Dixon, "Sexology and the Occult," for a full discussion of these issues.

6. "OUR GOLDEN WORD: *TRY*"

1. According to Gauri Viswanathan, as occultism was professionalized, it eschewed phenomena, whether the tinkling of bells or the supernatural transmittal of letters, in favor of the publication of metaphysical texts ("The Ordinary Business of Occultism," 14). For a discussion of the "literary bias within modern Western conceptions of religion," see Richard King, *Orientalism and Religion: Postcolonial Theory, India, and 'The Mystic East'* (London: Routledge, 1999), 62.

2. Helen Sword, "Necrobibliography: Books in the Spirit World," *Modern Language Quarterly* 60 (March 1999): 85–113, discusses the "modernist obsession" with reading, writing, authorship, and publication in occult literature.

3. H. P. Blavatsky to LHL, n. d., DeWint, SA1318.24.

4. [Koot Hoomi] to Upasika [H. P. Blavatsky], n. d., DeWint, SA1318.20i. In this letter, Koot Hoomi quotes LHL's questions. Her original letter is not extant. Letter 23 in Caldwell, "Mrs. Holloway and the Mahatmas," contains extracts of this document, but does not contain LHL's queries.

5. Koot Hoomi to H. P. Blavatsky, n. d., DeWint, SA1318.20c. This document, written in blue script, begins in mid-sentence. The conclusion is apparently DeWint, SA1318.20d, which is signed "K. H."

6. Koot Hoomi to Henry S. Olcott, [late Aug. 1884], Jinarajadasa, *Letters from the Masters of the Wisdom*, 1st series / *Theosophical Classics*, letter 37.

7. Francesca Arundale, *My Guest— H. P. Blavatsky* (Adyar, India: Theosophical Publishing House, 1932), 42–44.

8. Godwin, *The Theosophical Enlightenment*, 261.

9. Koot Hoomi to LHL, 22 Aug. 1884, DeWint, SA1318.21b-c.

10. LHL and Koot Hoomi, [late July or early Aug., 1884], DeWint, SA1318.19. The blue pencil crossed through LHL's suggested title, "Bygones or Cameos," leaving the phrase "of Forgotten History (Fragments)." LHL also asked: "Shall names be used." Koot Hoomi answered "no" and indicated that the book should be attributed to "Two Chelas."

11. [LHL and Mohini Mohun Chatterji], Two Chelas in the Theosophical Society, *Man: Fragments of Forgotten History* (London: Reeves and Turner, 1885), ix–xiii.

12. Ibid., xv–xxvi.

13. Koot Hoomi to Mohini M. Chatterji, [late July or early Aug., 1884], Jinarajadasa, *Letters from the Masters of the Wisdom*, 1st series / *Theosophical Classics*, letter 52.

14. LHL and Chatterji, *Man*, 57.

15. Ibid., 67.

16. Blavatsky, *Isis Unveiled*, pt. 2, 2.

17. Diana Burfield, "Theosophy and Feminism: Some Explorations in Nineteenth Century Biography," in *Women's Religious Experience*, ed. Pat Holden, 27–56 (London: Croom Helm Ltd, 1983), 36.

18. LHL and Chatterji, *Man*, 70–71.

19. Ibid., 72–73.

20. Kraft, *Sex Problem*, 81–86, discusses Blavatsky's attitudes.

21. Helena Petrovna Blavatsky, "The Future Occultist," *The Theosophist* 5, no. 11 (Aug. 1884): 263–264. She states that the "inner man is neither male, nor female.... [A] WOMAN-ADEPT can produce high occultists— a race of 'Buddhas and Christs,' born 'without sin.' The more and the sooner the animal sexual affinities are given up, the stronger and the sooner will be the manifestation of the higher occult powers which alone can produce the 'immaculate conception.' And this art is practically taught to the occultists at a very high stage of initiation."

22. Helena Petrovna Blavatsky, *The Secret Doctrine: The Synthesis of Science, Religion, and Philosophy*, 2 vols. (London· The Theosophical Publishing Company, 1888).

23. Koot Hoomi to LHL, [Aug. 1884], DeWint, SA1318.21b-c.

24. Hildegard Henderson to Alice Cleather, 13 July 1925, HPB. Henderson said that LHL's copies of the Koot Hoomi letters had omitted "stern reproofs." She wrote Cleather: "Is'nt that the limit! She must correct the Master's version of her motive!"

25. Santucci, "Women in the Theosophical Movement."

26. Ransom, *A Short History of the Theosophical Society*, 150, 170.

27. Koot Hoomi to A. P. Sinnett, [rec. mid-Sept. 1882], letter 111 in Barker, *The Mahatma Letters to A. P. Sinnett*.

28. Koot Hoomi to H. P. Blavatsky, [Aug. 1884], DeWint, SA1318.20i.

29. Koot Hoomi to [Francesca Arundale], [Aug. 1884], Jinarajadasa, *Letters from the Masters of the Wisdom*, 1st series / *Theosophical Classics*, letter 20.

30. According to Lynn Teskey Denton, *Female Ascetics in Hinduism* (Albany: State University of New York Press, 2004), menstruating women were barred from temples, dharma, and prayer or worship. When menstruating, a woman was considered to belong to the lowest class.

31. LHL and Chatterji, *Man*, 66.

32. Ibid., 63.

33. Helena Blavatsky, "Chelas and Lay Chelas," *The Theosophist* 4 (supplement to no. 10, July 1883): 10–11, gives the most detailed explanation of what "chelaship" entailed. Although the issue of the sex of a chela is not explicitly addressed, the assumption throughout the article is that the chela is male.

34. Sword, "Necrobibliography," 87.

35. LHL had been a supporter of sex education from the time of her association with phrenology. Many of her friends, including Charlotte Fowler Wells, Dr. Anna D. French, and Dr. Mary Jacobi, lobbied for sex education and rejected the notion that women's activities must be limited when menstruating.

36. Koot Hoomi to LHL, [late Aug. 1884], Jinarajadasa, *Letters from the Masters of the Wisdom*, 1st series / *Theosophical Classics*, letter 38. LHL quoted it in "The Mahatmas and Their Instruments," *The Word* (July 1912): 201.

37. Koot Hoomi to Henry S. Olcott, [late Aug. 1884], Jinarajadasa, *Letters from the Masters of the Wisdom*, 1st series / *Theosophical Classics*, letter 37.

38. Koot Hoomi to A. P. Sinnett, [rec. 8 Nov. 1884], letter 64 in Barker, *The Mahatma Letters to A. P. Sinnett*. Blavatsky was often referred to as "Upasika," or the "one who sits close by" the Masters.

39. Helena Blavatsky, "To the Theosophists," 7 Nov. 1885, in *Blavatsky: Collected Writings*, vol. 6, 412.

40. Letter 40 in Barker, *The Letters of H. P. Blavatsky to A. P. Sinnett*, 93.

41. Helena Blavatsky, "Re-Classification of Principles," *The Theosophist* 8, no. 95 (Aug. 1887): 651–655.

7. THE LADY MRS. X

1. M. [Master Morya] to [Francesca Arundale, summer 1884], Jinarajadasa, *Letters from the Masters of the Wisdom*, 1st series / *Theosophical Classics*, letter 3.

2. Society for Psychical Research, "First Report of the Committee of the Society for Psychical Research, Appointed to Investigate the Evidence for Marvellous [sic] Phenomena Offered by Certain Members of the Theosophical Society" (London: n. p., 1884). Available at: http://www.blavatskyarchives.com/sprrpcontents.htm.

3. Richard Hodgson had been sent to India by the S. P. R. in fall 1884. His report, presented at its May and June 1885 meetings, was published as "Report of the General Meeting," *Journal of the Society for Psychical Research* 3 (London), June 1885, 418–424; and July 1885, 451–460. Available at http://www.blavatskyarchives.com/spr52985.htm, and http://www.blavatskyarchives.com/spr62685.htm, respectively. The "Statements of Conclusion of the Committee" appeared in the " *Proceedings of the Society for Psychical Research* 3 (1885): 201–207, followed by Richard Hodgson, "Account of Personal Investigations in India, and Discussion of the Authorship of the 'Koot Hoomi' Letters," *Proceedings of the Society for Psychical Research* 3 (1885): 207–317, 318–380. LHL owned a copy of this report, in which she marked passages that pertained to her experience. In the author's possession.

4. S. P. R., "First Report," 1884.

5. Mohini M. Chatterji, "On the Higher Aspect of Theosophical Studies," *The Theosophist* 6 (March 1885): 140–144; and Chatterji, "Transcendental Senses," *The Theosophist* 6 (June 1885): 217–219.

6. S. P. R., "First Report," 1884.

7. LHL, "The Mahatmas and Their Instruments," (May 1912), 70.

8. Meade, *Madame Blavatsky*, 308. They stayed for several days in a small hotel near the Union Society. Blavatsky had testified before Eleanor and Henry Sidgwick, Richard Hodgson, and others.

9. LHL, "The Theosophists. Something About Madame Blavatsky" (1888), 14.

10. Caldwell, "Mrs. Holloway and the Mahatmas," letter 14, n10. Caldwell says this is "quoted from an unpublished draft of the 1884 'First Report of the Committee of the Society for Psychical Research.'"

11. Arundale, *My Guest*, 34–35.

12. LHL, "Blavatsky's Mesmerism," *Current Literature* (March 1889): 243–244. A longer version of this article was published in *The Daily Inter Ocean*, 28 Oct. 1888, as "Psychic Phenomena."

13. LHL, "The Mahatmas and Their Instruments" (May 1912), 71, 69.

14. Olcott, *Old Diary Leaves*, vol. 3, 162–163.

15. M[orya] to H. P. Blavatsky, [July 1884], DeWint, SA1318.20j.

16. John Patrick Deveney, *Paschal Beverly Randolph: A Nineteenth-Century Black American Spiritualist, Rosicrucian, and Sex Magician* (Albany, N.Y.: State University New York Press, 1997), 298, says that Blavatsky was introduced to hashish in Egypt in the 1850s when traveling with A. L. Rawson and that she probably used the drug in Paris and in New York in the 1870s. Hashish was reported to be particularly effective in creating an "elevated mental condition in which the soul, freed from the confines of the body and spirit, could traverse the limitless universe of the soul world at will" (96).

17. LHL, "The Mahatmas and Their Instruments," printed the word as "beginner," which makes no sense. LHL, however, knew German and surely she commanded Schmiechen "to begin" in his native tongue.

18. LHL, "The Mahatmas and Their Instruments" (July 1912), 204–205.

19. A.P. Sinnett wrote to Charles Leadbeater that Blavatsky admitted that during the 1884 crisis "the Masters had stood aside and left everything to various chelas, including freedom to use the blue handwriting," C. Jinarajadasa, *The "K. H." Letters to C. W. Leadbeater* (Kessinger's Publishing Photocopy Edition: 2010; originally published Madras, India, Theosophical Publishing House, 1941), 75. LHL may have believed that Chatterji had written some of the Koot Hoomi letters, but she accepted Blavatsky's explanation that few occult letters were written "by the hand of the Master in whose name" they were sent. Rather, Blavatsky explained, "when a Master says, 'I wrote that letter,' it means only that every word in it was dictated by him and impressed under his direct supervision." Helena Blavatsky, "Lodges of Magic," in *Blavatsky: Collected Writings*, vol. 10, 129–130.

20. David Anrias [Brian Ross], *Through the Eyes of the Masters: Meditations and Portraits* (London: George Routledge & Sons, Ltd., 1932), 34. The sketch of "Master Jesus," in contrast, portrays a figure with a darker beard, with his hair covered by a keffiyeh. Jack R. Lundbom, *Master Painter Warner E. Sallman* (Macon, Ga.: Mercer University Press, 1999), 1. In 1924, Sallman had made a charcoal sketch, "The Son of Man," which could have been known to Brian Ross.

21. See *Master Kuthumi, Ray 2 of Love and Wisdom*, no. 214, painted by Peter Fich Christiansen, http://www.zakairan.com/ProductsDivineLightImages/DivineLightImages.htm#JumptoImages.

22. Olcott, *Old Diary Leaves*, vol. 3, 171–172. On 27 July 1884, the Germania Theosophical Society had been founded in Elberfeld, with Mary Gebhard elected its vice-president. Corinna Treitel, *A Science for the Soul: Occultism and the Genesis of the German Modern* (Baltimore, Md.: Johns Hopkins University Press, 2004), 64, notes that "although the

professional element in the German occult movement was largely male," women like Gebhard "played a key role in introducing and spreading occultism."

23. Koot Hoomi to H. P. Blavatsky, [early Aug. 1884], DeWint, SA1318.20e.

24. Koot Hoomi to LHL, [2 Aug. 1884], DeWint, SA1318.1d. This message was written in blue ink diagonally across an invitation that LHL had received in a sealed envelope.

25. Koot Hoomi to LHL, [early Aug. 1884], DeWint, SA1318.21a. At this point, the Masters did not expect LHL to return to the United States.

26. Koot Hoomi to H. P. Blavatsky, [late Aug. 1884], DeWint, SA1318.20f.

27. While in Germany, LHL associated with several prominent Theosophists who later became critics of Blavatsky and the Theosophical Society. Among these were Vsevolod S. Solovyov; Frederic Myers, a member of the Society for Psychical Research; and Elliott Coues, who became William Q. Judge's rival for control of the U. S. branch of the Theosophical Society. Her most lasting relationship, however, was with Mary Gebhard. British by birth, Gebhard had lived in New York, where she met and married Gustav Gebhard, a silk manufacturer and banker. See Eek, *Damodar,* 593. LHL found a kindred spirit in Mary Gebhard and their friendship endured until Mary's death in 1892.

28. Sinnett, *Incidents in the Life,* 281–283.

29. Koot Hoomi to LHL, [Aug. 1884], DeWint SA1318.21b-c; typed copy, SA1318.1c.

30. H. P. Blavatsky to *Light,* 28 Sept. 1884, in *Blavatsky: Collected Writings,* vol. 6, 281.

31. Sinnett, *Early Days of Theosophy,* 72–73.

32. Koot Hoomi to LHL, [late Sept. 1884], letter 19 in Caldwell, "Mrs. Holloway and the Mahatmas." Caldwell says that "all published and never before published letters found in this web edition are taken from copies preserved in my personal library." I have not discovered an original of this document.

33. Koot Hoomi to A. P. Sinnett, [rec. summer 1884], letters 60, 62, and 63 in Barker, *Mahatma Letters to A. P. Sinnett.* Koot Hoomi asserted that his letters were private and that he would never consent to their publication. Furthermore, he informed Sinnett that from this time forward only the "chelas at the Headquarters" would be trusted to compose "a consistent and systematic philosophy" for Theosophical publications. Whether or not LHL was hostile to Sinnett, as this comment suggested, clearly Koot Hoomi was still anxious to undermine Sinnett's relationship with her.

34. Koot Hoomi to A. P. Sinnett, [rec. early Oct. 1884], letter 55 in Barker, *Mahatma Letters to A. P. Sinnett.*

35. Sinnett, *Early Days of Theosophy,* 73.

36. Koot Hoomi to A. P. Sinnett, [rec. early Oct. 1884], letter 55 in Barker, *Mahatma Letters to A. P. Sinnett.*

37. Koot Hoomi to LHL, [Sept. 1884, Elberfeld, Germany], typed copy, HPB.

38. LHL to Hildegard Henderson, 30 March 1924, HPB.

39. It was postmarked 9 Oct. 1884, Bromley, Kent, England. Although the envelope was addressed in an unfamiliar hand, the letter itself was in the Koot Hoomi script.

40. Koot Hoomi to A. P. Sinnett, [rec. 10 Oct. 1884], letter 66 in Barker, *Mahatma Letters to A. P. Sinnett.*

41. LHL to Koot Hoomi, with replies from Koot Hoomi to LHL, [Oct. 1884], DeWint, SA1318.22. The suggestion for a secret society was a reaction to the "Petition to the Masters for the Formation of an 'Inner Group,'" which had been approved in the summer by Koot Hoomi, but was restricted to members of the London Lodge. See *Blavatsky: Collected Writings,* vol. 6, 250–256.

42. LHL to Koot Hoomi, [Oct. 1884], DeWint, SA1318.22.

43. Ibid. LHL used this excerpt in "The Mahatmas and Their Instruments" (July 1912), with slight variations from the original.

8. DISSEMINATING NEW IDEAS

1. Accounts of these events are contested, but it is generally agreed that when Judge, Franz Hartmann, and Ananda Charloo removed the "Shrine," they discovered a sliding back panel, along with an aperture in the wall, recently plastered over, that would have permitted passage to Blavatsky's adjoining room. Judge later admitted that he removed the Shrine, which a few days later was broken into pieces and burned, but he denied that there had been any aperture in the wall.

2. In order to pay for his return passage, Judge solicited several hundred rupees from Damodar K. Mavalankar, the Recording Secretary of the Theosophical Society. At first reluctant, Mavalankar finally agreed, feeling Judge was entitled to the money because he had loyally defended Blavatsky and the Society. Helena Blavatsky to William Q. Judge, 1 May 1885, *Some Letters of H. P. Blavatsky to W. Q. Judge,* transcribed from the "Helena Petrovna Blavatsky Letters," Andover-Harvard Theological Library, bMS34, by Dara Ecklund and Nicholas Weeks, 1999; online edition, http://www.blavatskyarchives.com/hpbwqjtab.html.

3. Ibid.

4. William Q. Judge to H. P. Blavatsky, 16 May 1885, *Theosophical History* 6 (Jan. 1997): 164–166. Quoted in Ernest E. Pelletier, *The Judge Case: A Conspiracy Which Ruined The Theosophical Cause* (Edmonton, Canada: Edmonton Theosophical Society, 2004), 11.

5. Along with Judge, Mavalankar was traumatized by these events. He was interviewed by Richard Hodgson, who arrived in Adyar in mid-December 1884. In February, Mavalankar set out on a pilgrimage; he was last seen near the Tibetan border, where he reportedly froze to death.

6. H. P. Blavatsky to William Q. Judge, 1 May 1885, in Blavatsky, *Some Letters,* quoting a letter from Judge to Franz Hartmann.

7. William Q. Judge to Henry S. Olcott, 27 April 1886, in William Q. Judge, *Practical Occultism: From the Private Letters of William Q. Judge,* ed. Arthur L. Conger (Pasadena, Calif.: Theosophical University Press, 1951); online edition, http://www.theosociety.org/pasadena/prac-oc/po2.htm.

8. H. P. Blavatsky to A. P. Sinnett, [18 Oct. 1884], letter 39 in Barker, *Letters of H. P. Blavatsky,* 91–92. LHL's note paper previously had been used for messages from Koot Hoomi. See editor's notes, Koot Hoomi to A. P. Sinnett, [rec. early Oct. 1884], letter 55 in Barker, *Mahatma Letters to A. P. Sinnett.*

9. H. P. Blavatsky to A. P. Sinnett, 9 Nov. 1884, letter 137 in Barker, *Mahatma Letters to A. P. Sinnett.*

10. Blavatsky later described this tree as "the Queen of Beauty in the African forests," but one whose "atmosphere kills every living thing that approaches it." H. P. Blavatsky, "Our Cycle and the Next," *Blavatsky: Collected Writings,* vol. 2, 198.

11. Koot Hoomi to A. P. Sinnett, [8 Nov. 1884], letter 64 in Barker, *Mahatma Letters to A. P. Sinnett.* Although Virginia Hanson's annotations to the Chronological Edition of the *Mahatma Letters, Theosophical Classics* on CD-ROM suggest that Koot Hoomi was responding to a letter from LHL, it seems clear that he is in fact replying to a letter from Sinnett, who had repeated what Blavatsky termed the "crafty insinuations of [his] would-be

sibyl." Sinnett was instructed to keep the letter from Koot Hoomi "entirely private except for Mohini and F. A. [Francesca Arundale]."

12. H. P. Blavatsky to A. P. Sinnett, [late March 1886], letter 139 in Barker, *Mahatma Letters to A. P. Sinnett.*

13. H. P. Blavatsky to William Q. Judge, 1 May 1885, Blavatsky, *Some Letters.* While visiting Elberfeld, Germany, Howard had lectured Blavatsky on the falsity of her beliefs and the superiority of Christianity.

14. H. P. Blavatsky to A. P. Sinnett, 17 March 1885, letter 138 in Barker, *Mahatma Letters to A. P. Sinnett.*

15. William Q. Judge to H. P. Blavatsky, 22 March 1886, letter 160 in Barker, *The Letters of H. P. Blavatsky to A. P. Sinnett,* 314.

16. William Q. Judge to Henry S. Olcott, 27 April 1886, in William Q. Judge, *Practical Occultism.*

17. Pelletier, *The Judge Case,* 335. The question mark appears in the quotation.

18. H. P. Blavatsky to William Q. Judge, 1 May 1885, *Some Letters.*

19. "Teachings of the Master. Recorded by One of the Authors of 'Man: Fragments of Forgotten History,'" *The Path* 1 (Nov. 1886): 253–256; *The Path* 1 (Dec. 1886): 278–281. LHL likely published other articles anonymously in *The Path.*

20. [Mabel Collins], *Light on the Path: A Treatise Written for the Personal Use of Those Who are Ignorant of the Eastern Wisdom, and Who Desire to Enter within Its Influence. Written down by M. C.* (New York: Reprinted with Special Permission Aryan Theosophical Society, n. d.). This is an early version of *Light on the Path* which does not include added "Comments" (see Michael Gomes, *Theosophy in the Nineteenth-Century: An Annotated Bibliography* [New York and London: Garland Publishing Co., 1994], 447–448). This copy is signed "William Q. Judge August 22, 1886." In possession of the author.

21. "Brighton Beach Music Hall Programmes 1890–91," NBPu; "Literary Notes," *The Path* 2 (July 1887): 125; newspaper clipping, n. d., Scrapbook 1887, DeWint. Another advertisement appeared in LHL's *The Buddhist Diet-Book.*

22. Issues from more than a dozen occult and Theosophical journals dating from the mid-1880s until December 1929 were among LHL's papers and are in possession of the author.

23. Emil August Neresheimer, *Some Reminiscences of William Q. Judge,* Blavatsky Online Study Center, copyright 2003, http://www.blavatskyarchives.com/stokesneres.htm.

24. In addition to LHL, members of the Theosophical Society of New York included Dr. J. H. Salisbury, Donald Nicholson (managing editor of the *New York Tribune*), Harold W. Percival, and Dr. Alexander Wilder. When *The Word* ceased publication, the Theosophical Society of New York became dormant. John Garrigues, ed., *The Theosophical Movement 1875–1925: A History and a Survey* (New York: E. P. Dutton & Company, 1925), 682–683 (available at http://www.blavatskyarchives.com/garrtc.htm).

25. A. P. Sinnett, *Incidents in the Life of Madame Blavatsky* (London: G. Redway, 1886), 321.

26. LHL, "Colonel Olcott: A Reminiscence" and "Supplementary Letter," *The Word* 22 (Oct. 1915): 10–11.

27. LHL, "William Quan Judge, A Reminiscence," *The Word* 22 (Nov. 1915): 76, 79, 89.

28. Pelletier argues that before he left India in late Oct. 1884, Judge had been initiated into occult mysteries and thenceforth exercised paranormal power.

29. LHL, "Madame Blavatsky: A Pen Picture by An American Newspaper Writer," *The*

Word 14 (Feb. 1912): 264. See also "Helen Petrovna Blavatsky, A Reminiscence," *The Word* 22 (Dec. 1915): 136–153. "H. P. Blavatsky," *The Word* 25 (April 1917): 70–81 focuses on Blavatsky's early life.

30. LHL, "William Quan Judge, A Reminiscence," 78.

31. LHL [Laura C. Holloway], *Adelaide Neilson: a Souvenir* (New York: Funk & Wagnalls, 1885); [Laura C. Holloway], *Chinese Gordon: the Uncrowned King, His Character as It Is Portrayed in His Private Letters* (New York: Funk & Wagnalls, 1885); [Rose Elizabeth Cleveland], *George Eliot's Poetry and Other Studies* (New York: Funk & Wagnalls, 1885); [Laura C. Holloway], *Howard: the Christian Hero* (New York: Funk & Wagnalls, 1885); [Laura C. Holloway], ed., *Songs of the Master* (Philadelphia: J. W. Bradley, 1885).

32. LHL, *Songs of the Master* (1885), 3.

33. Thomas Wentworth Higginson, "The Sympathy of Religions," *The Radical* 8 (Feb. 1871): 1–23; "The Character of Buddha," *Index* 3 (16 March 1872): 81–83; "The Buddhist Path of Virtue," *The Radical* 8 (June 1871): 62.

34. Tweed, *The American Encounter with Buddhism*, 29.

35. After a lecture on "Buddhism and Theosophy" by Anagarika Dharmapala, C. T. Strauss, an immigrant of Jewish ancestry from Switzerland, took Buddhist vows. Tweed, *American Encounter with Buddhism*, 39.

36. "He Has a Formidable Name: The Distinguished Buddhist Who is Now in Brooklyn," *Brooklyn Daily Eagle*, 3 Sept. 1893, 20. This article gives a detailed description of Dharmapala, emphasizing his "mahogany color" and his "delicate, feminine-looking hands." The Ralston home at 464 Classon Avenue was for many years associated with alternative religion. In 1906, the church of the New Jerusalem Swedenborgian was located there, and in the 1930s it was the home of Father Divine.

37. LCH, Elizabeth P. Chapin, and Maude Ralston, *Atma Fairy Stories* (New York: Home Publishing Co., 1903).

38. "Group of prominent Theosophists just prior to attending the World's Parliament of Religions at the Chicago World's Fair in 1893," photo 37 in Pelletier, *The Judge Case*.

39. "Brooklyn Buddhists. Does the Light of Asia Shine in This City?" *Brooklyn Daily Eagle*, 10 Oct. 1886, 6.

40. "A Strange Theosophical Society," *Brooklyn Daily Eagle*, 23 June 1887, 5. I have found no evidence that such an organization was formed until much later.

41. "The Brooklyn Theosophists," *Brooklyn Daily Eagle*, 30 Sept. 1890, 2. This meeting took place in Robertson Hall, 166 Gates Avenue, Brooklyn.

42. "Brooklyn Theosophists. They Will Now Take Up the Consideration of the Second Course," *Brooklyn Daily Eagle*, 7 Oct. 1890, 1.

43. LHL [Laura C. Holloway], *The Buddhist Diet-Book* (New York: Funk & Wagnalls, 1886), 6–7.

44. For a history of vegetarianism among the Shakers, see Margaret Puskar-Pasewicz, "Kitchen Sisters and Disagreeable Boys: Debates over Meatless Diets in Nineteenth-Century Shaker Communities," in *Eating in Eden: Food and American Utopias*, ed. Etta M. Madden and Martha L. Finch (Lincoln: University of Nebraska Press, 2006), 109–124.

45. Russell T. Trall, *The New Hydropathic Cookbook: With Recipes for Cooking on Hygienic Principles* (New York: Fowler and Wells, 1854).

46. Karen Iacobbo and Michael Iacobbo, *Vegetarian America: A History* (Westport, Conn.: Praeger Publishers, 2004), 112–114.

47. LHL, *The Buddhist Diet-Book*, 16.

48. LHL [L. C. Holloway], "Buddhism vs. Christianity," *Current Literature* 2 (May 1889): 379–381.

49. John Wothold, "Where Books Are Made," *The Current* 7 (April 1887): 510–511.

50. Her name appears as editor in *The Lady's World* 1 (March 1887), Folder 1202, DeWint.

51. LHL's work on the magazine explains why her literary output during 1887 appears relatively meager. In fact it was enormous, since she authored much of the material in *The Lady's World*. The Winterthur Library contains a number of issues of the magazine; the June–December issues have been microfilmed by the Library of Congress.

52. The magazine was 12.5 inches by 9.5 inches, with each issue running approximately 60 pages.

53. "Special Propositions," *The Home Library Magazine* 1 (Oct. 1887).

54. "Publisher's Announcement," *The Home Library Magazine* 1 (Dec. 1887) reads: "After the December issue THE HOME LIBRARY MAGAZINE and THE WOMAN'S ARGOSY will be merged with THE WOMAN'S WORLD, published by the well-known house of Cassell & Co. (Limited), of New York and London. THE WOMAN'S WORLD will be conducted with the aid of the same staff of contributors."

55. *The Home Library Magazine* 1 (Aug. 1887): 441. LHL solicited contributions from many of her friends: Isabella Olcott Mitchell, Edna Dean Proctor, Ella Wheeler Wilcox, Hester Poole, and Rose Elizabeth Cleveland·

56. "How Women May Earn a Living," *The Home Library Magazine* 1 (June 1887): 315. This is the conclusion of an article that probably appeared in the May 1887 issue. Edward Willet[?] to LHL, n. d., DeWint, SA1305, confirms that this unsigned article was by LHL.

57. *The Home Library Magazine* 1 (July 1887): 369.

58. Inspired by Besant's description, in 1887 a "People's Palace" was established in London's East End. It contained a great hall with an organ, a library, and even a swimming pool. The "People's Palace" is now the Queen's Building, University of London. See http://www.victorianweb.org/art/architecture/london/125.html.

59. *The Lady's World* edited by LHL was published by R. S. Peale in Chicago, January–May 1887. There was another *The Lady's World* published by Cassell & Co. in London during the same year, which was renamed *The Woman's World* when Oscar Wilde became editor.

60. Stephanie Green, "Oscar Wilde's *The Woman's World*," *Victorian Periodicals Review* 30, no. 2 (Summer 1997): 102–105; John Sloan, *Oscar Wilde* (Oxford: Oxford University Press, 2003), 105. Holloway-Langford and Wilde probably met in London during summer 1884.

61. *The Home Library Magazine,* 1 (Sept. 1887): 530.

62. *The Home Library Magazine* 1 (Nov. 1887): 626–627. This incident has not appeared elsewhere in Theosophical literature. Blavatsky and LHL left Elberfeld with Rudolf Gebhard, who accompanied them to Flushing (the English name for Vlissingen, Netherlands), where he probably left them and returned home. They apparently spent the night there, arriving in London the following day. See Alice Leighton Cleather, *H. P. Blavatsky as I Knew Her: Her Life and Work for Humanity. A Great Betrayal* (Calcutta: Thacker, Spink & Co., 1923), 62.

63. Mohini Chatterji, "Duty and Sacrifice," *The Lady's World* 1 (March 1887): 138.

64. Jamal J. Elias, *Death Before Dying: The Sufi Poems of Sultan Bahu* (Berkeley: University of California Press, 1998). Ram Mohun Roy, Chatterji's great-grandfather, studied Persian and Arabic and was influenced by Sufism.

65. Eek, *Damodar,* 638.

66. Harbans Rai Bachchan, *W. B. Yeats and Occultism: A Study of His Works in Relation to Indian Lore, the Cabbala, Swedenborg, Boehme, and Theosophy* (Delhi: Motilal Banarsidass, 1965), 18.

67. Vivekananda was scornful of Theosophy, although he avoided condemning it publicly. See Steven F. Walker, "Vivekananda and American Occultism," in *The Occult in America,* ed. Howard Kerr and Charles L. Crow, 165.

68. William Q. Judge to H. P. Blavatsky, 5 Feb. 1886, letter 159 in Barker, *The Letters of H. P. Blavatsky to A. P. Sinnett,* 313. Evidently the Waters had, at some earlier time, joined the Theosophical Society, but had let their membership lapse.

69. Gebhard had become an American citizen in 1878, and for many years he represented his father's factory in New York.

70. Clara Kathleen Rogers, *The Story of Two Lives: Home, Friends, and Travels* (Norwood, Mass.: Plimpton Press, 1932), 154–155. Throughout this book, Rogers spells "Gebhard" as "Gebhardt." Mrs. Waters was said to be a frequent guest at the home of Louise Chandler Moulton. For a biographical sketch, see Jennifer Scanlon and Sharon Cosner, *American Women Historians, 1700s–1990s: A Biographical Dictionary* (Greenwood Publishing Group, 1996), 236–237. According to Angela V. John, *Elizabeth Robins: Staging a Life, 1862–1952* (London: Routledge, 1995), Mrs. Waters and Elizabeth Robins visited Helena Blavatsky in London in 1890 (112).

71. Chatterji declined Clara Waters's first invitation because he did not want to get involved in a "row" between Waters and Elliott Coues. H. P. Blavatsky to A. P. Sinnett, 23 Aug. 1886, letter 97 in Barker, *The Letters of H. P. Blavatsky to A. P. Sinnett.* Olcott had appointed Coues President of the American Board of Control of the Theosophical Society. In spring 1886, Coues had tried to shut down the Aryan Theosophical Society, the branch in New York headed by William Q. Judge. Waters supported Judge. William Q. Judge to Mrs. Waters, 28 May 1886, in Judge, *Practical Occultism.*

72. "A Teacher of Buddhism Mohini Mohun Chatterjee Coming to the United States," *St. Louis Globe-Democrat,* 7 Oct. 1886, 4.

73. "A Hindu Philosopher," *New York Times,* 23 Nov. 1886, 4; "A Scholar from India. Babu Mohini Mohun Chattergee [*sic*] Now in New York City," *Chicago Daily Tribune,* 28 Nov. 1886, 13, may have been written by LHL.

74. Clara Kathleen Rogers, *The Story of Two Lives: Home, Friends, and Travels* (Norwood, Mass.: Plimpton Press, 1932), 156–157.

75. "A Remarkable Career: A Woman Invents Theosophy to Further Political Schemes" *Chicago Daily Tribune,* 9 Jan. 1888, 9.

76. "The New Craze. Religious Longing for Oriental Types and Usages," *Brooklyn Daily Eagle,* 18 July 1886, 10.

77. Frances Weston Carruth Prindle, *Fictional Rambles In & About Boston* (New York: McClure, Phillips, and Company, 1902), 16.

78. "Society Topics of the Week," *New York Times,* 3 April 1887, 14.

79. She refers to a letter from Chatterji "to my dear Sister from her loving Brother, Mohini." LHL to Hildegard Henderson, 5 June 1923, HPB. I have not been able to locate any of Chatterji's letters to LHL.

80. Clipping, [30 March 1887], Scrapbook 1887, DeWint.

81. "He was Weary When He Left. A Brahmin Discussing Theosophy at Mrs. Holloway's House," *Brooklyn Daily Eagle,* 31 March 1887, 4.

82. *West Church Boston: Commemorative Services . . . on Tuesday, March 1, 1887* (Boston: Damrell & Upham, 1887), 68–70; Cyrus Bartol, n. t., *Christian Union* 35 (10 March 1887): 10. Chatterji's closing statement alluded to Ram Mohun Roy's death while in England among Unitarian friends.

83. After returning to India, he wrote an essay about his great-grandfather, "Raja Ram Mohun Roy As a Man of Lettres," praising his "love of truth" and his "reverence for freedom of thought." Sophia Dobson Collet, ed., *The Life and Letters of Raja Rammohun Roy*, 2nd ed. (London: Harold Collet: 1914), 259–262. For more on Roy and the influence of Indian reformers in America, see Carl T. Jackson, *The Oriental Religions and American Thought: Nineteenth-Century Explorations* (Westport, Conn.: Greenwood Press, 1981).

84. Ednah Dow Cheney, "Correspondence: A Letter from Boston," 10 Feb. 1887, *Open Court* 1 (3 March 1887): 52.

85. E. M. Chesley, "Universal Brotherhood. A Voice from the East," *Christian Union* 35 (14 April 1887): 6. This is Chesley's paraphrase of Chatterji's talk.

86. Mohini M. Chatterji, "Theories in Comparative Mythology," *The Theosophist* 8 (Jan. 1887): 193–204.

87. "Ticknor and Co. announce 'The Bhagavad Gita, or the Lord's Lay,' translated by the Hindoo scholar, Chatterji," *Brooklyn Daily Eagle*, 2 Oct. 1887, 4.

88. Mohini M. Chatterji, *The Bhagavad Gîtâ or The Lord's Lay: With Commentary and Notes, as well as References to the Christian Scriptures* (Boston: Ticknor and Company, 1887), v, vi, 275.

89. "Commentary on a Brahman Poem," *New York Times*, 11 Dec. 1887, 14.

90. Titus Munson Coan, "The Indian Classics in English," *New York Times*, 4 March 1888, 10. *The Literary World* judged the translation inferior to earlier renderings by Edwin Arnold and John Davies and the "Commentary and Notes" simplistic, making the poem more difficult rather than easier to understand. "The Bhagavad Gita," *The Literary World; A Monthly Review of Current Literature*, 12 Nov. 1887, 18, 23.

91. "Books and Authors. The Bhagavad Gita," *Christian Union*, 26 Jan. 1888, 118.

92. Eek, *Damodar*, 639; *The Path* 2 (Oct. 1887): 223.

93. Isabelle de Steiger, *Memorabilia: Reminiscences of a Woman Artist and Writer* (London: Rider & Co., 1927), 264–265.

94. *The Path* 2 (March 1888): 383. See also "Babu Mohini M. Chatterji" in *The Theosophist* 4 (supplement to no. 10, July 1888): xlvii.

95. "Chronological Survey," in *Blavatsky: Collected Writings*, vol. 10, xxiv.

96. He published at least one poem, "The Homesick," in the journal where LHL's later articles appeared: *The Word* 15 (April 1912): 39. Years later Chatterji became Vice President of the Calcutta Center of the Poetry Society, a London-based organization that published *The Poetry Review*. Stephen Phillips and Galloway Kyle, *The Poetry Review* (London: Poetry Society, 1934), vi.

97. *Crest-Jewel of Wisdom of Shree Shankaracharya* was first published sometime in the 1890s in Bombay by Rajaram Tukaram for the Theosophical Publication Fund, with many later editions using Chatterji's translation published under different titles. Chatterji also published *The Language of Symbols* (London: Theosophical Publication Society, 1894); *Manual of Deductive Logic* (Calcutta: Thacker, Spink & Co., 1906); *Indian Spirituality: or, the Travels and Teachings of Sivanarayan* (London: Luzac & Co., 1907); *History as a Science* (London: Butterworth, 1927); and a number of articles on aspects of Brahmanism. He translated texts into German and French as well as into Bengali and Hindi.

98. Jinarajadasa, *Letters of the Masters of the Wisdom*, 1st series / *Theosophical Classics*, compiler's note, letter 15.

99. Swami Vivekananda, "Address at the World's Parliament of Religions . . . 11 September 1893," in *The Complete Works of Swami Vivekananda*, pt. 1, 2nd ed. (Almora, Himalayas: Advaita Ashram, 1915), 2.

100. Catherine L. Albanese, *A Republic of Mind and Spirit: A Cultural History of American Metaphysical Religion* (New Haven & London: Yale University Press, 2007), 334.

101. Carl T. Jackson, *Vedanta for the West: The Ramakrishna Movement in the United States* (Bloomington: Indiana University Press, 1994), 92.

102. "Ole Bull Will Contest," *New York Times*, 13 Feb. 1911, 1. In addition to Chatterji, the Hindu recipients were Margaret E. Noble, known in India as "Sister Nivedita," Dr. Jagadis Chunder Bose, and the Swami Saradananda.

103. Myron H. Phelps, "Green Acre," *The Word* 1 (Nov. 1904): 52, lists, among others involved with the first conference: Edward Everett Hale, Ralph Waldo Trine, Henry Wood, Swami Vivekananda, Professor Ernest F. Fenollosa, Mrs. Ole Bull, Mrs. Margaret B. Peeke, William Dean Howells, Booker T. Washington, Professor C. H. A. Bjerregaard, Rabbi Charles Fleischer, Paul Carus, Annie Besant, Professor Nathaniel Schmidt, and Charles Johnston.

104. *The Metaphysical Magazine, A Monthly Review of the Occult Sciences* 4 (July 1886): 144.

105. Janet Young, ed. *Psychological Yearbook* (New York: Paul Elder and Company, 1905). This work also contains many quotations from the *Bhagavad Gita*.

9. MUSIC OF THE SPHERES

1. "Constitution and By-Laws of the Seidl Society, Brooklyn, 1889," Scrapbook, box 3, Brooklyn Historical Society Library, Anton Seidl Records, hereafter NyBLHS.

2. Anne Catherine married Charles Terry, and she was the mother of Charlie (see chapter 10). Ella Watson Carter was divorced from Henderson, who remarried in 1902. One of the country's leading proponents of Wagner and the "New Music," Henderson published *Richard Wagner, His Life and Dramas: A Biographical Study of the Man and an Explanation of His Work* (New York: G. P. Putnam's Sons, 1901).

3. LHL, *Beyond the Sunrise* (1883), 85.

4. W. Michael Ashcraft, *The Dawn of the New Cycle: Point Loma Theosophists and American Culture* (Knoxville: The University of Tennessee Press, 2002), 4, discusses the belief in a universal substance that holds levels of reality together.

5. Maude Ralston, "The Secret of Power," *Theosophical Forum* 4 (April 1899): 12.

6. Among LHL's papers were librettos for *Götterdämmerung, Die Meistersinger von Nürnberg, Das Rheingold, Die Walküre, Tristan und Isolde, Tannhäuser, Lohengrin,* and *Der Fliegende Hollände*. Most list Edmund C. Stanton as Director of the Opera, so they were performed between 1884 and 1891. In the author's possession.

7. Henry Theophilus Finck, *Anton Seidl: A Memorial by His Friends* (New York: Charles Scribner's Sons, 1899), 134.

8. Clipping, "Our Portrait Gallery, Portraits and Biographies of Distinguished Men and Women. Mrs. Laura Carter Holloway," newspaper from Atlanta, Georgia, 2 June 1888, Scrapbook 1887, DeWint. As a burgeoning Wagner enthusiast, LHL would have been especially thrilled to see a performance by Amalie Materna, who had been the first Kundry in the Bayreuth *Parsifal*.

9. *Annual Report of the Board of Railroad Commissioners*, vol. 2 (New York: Board of Railroad Commissioners, 1884), 753–754.

10. "A Brooklyn Authoress. Mrs. Laura Holloway-Langford and Her Writings," *Brooklyn Daily Eagle*, 21 Sept. 1890, 18.

11. The hotel was also a popular meeting place for Brooklyn Aldermen and democratic politicians. See the "Jury for Alderman M'Kee," *New York Times*, 30 May 1893, 5.

12. "Obituary. Colonel Edward L. Langford," *Brooklyn Daily Eagle*, 26 July 1902, 2. During 1888, Langford had negotiated the contractual arrangements with Seidl and his orchestra, and he continued to do so well after the Seidl Society was founded.

13. Clipping, n. d., Scrapbook, box 3, Seidl Society Records, NyBLHS.

14. "Constitution and By-Laws of the Seidl Society," NyBLHS.

15. "The Seidl Society of Brooklyn," *Harper's Bazaar* 24 (28 Dec. 1891): 995.

16. "A Musical Society," *Christian Union* 40 (15 Aug. 1889): 189.

17. Clipping, 28 June 1889, Scrapbook, box 3, Seidl Society Records, NyBLHS. Miss Louise M. Heuermann, a teacher at the Girls High School in Brooklyn, gave the opening address in German. She praised Anton Seidl for "revealing to us the poetic beauties and the genius of Wagner." Her talk was followed by remarks by Amelia Wing, the president of the Brooklyn Woman's Club; Mrs. John Thallon, a member of the music advisory board of the Brooklyn Institute of Arts and Sciences; and the actress and writer Abby Sage Richardson. A performance by The Sappho Club, a women's drama and music society, concluded the program. "A Boom for Anton Seidl. Enthusiastic Brooklyn Ladies Name a Society After Him," *Brooklyn Daily Eagle*, 16 June 1889, 2.

18. Clipping, n. d., Scrapbook, box 3, Seidl Society Records, NyBLHS. Although undated, the article was written prior to Holloway-Langford's marriage in spring 1890.

19. Books stamped "Seidl Society Library," in the author's possession. To my knowledge only the first book in the series was published: John P. Jackson, *The Bayreuth of Wagner* (New York: J. W. Lovell Co., 1891).

20. "We Need a Music Hall," *Brooklyn Daily Eagle*, 3 Feb. 1896, 6.

21. Newspaper clipping, n. d., Scrapbook, box 3, Seidl Society Records, NyBLHS. Although a member of the Brooklyn Presbytery, Sherwood was not active in pastoral work and was best known as a religious journalist.

22. "In the City of Spires," *New York Times*, 11 May 1890, 16.

23. "Close of the Seidl Season. Remarkable Enthusiasm at Brighton Beach Yesterday," *Brooklyn Daily Eagle*, 4 Sept. 1894, 7.

24. Isaac K. Funk, editor-in-chief, *A Standard Dictionary of the English Language*, 2 vols. (New York: Funk & Wagnalls, 1893–1895).

25. "The Literary World," *Washington Post*, 12 March 1893, 15.

26. William Tomlins, ed., *Children's Souvenir Songbook* (New York: Novello, Ewer, and Co, 1893); "Editorial Bric-a-Brac: June Music at the Fair," *Music: A Monthly Magazine Devoted to the Art, Science, Technic and Literature of Music* 4 (July 1893): 295–297; "The Literary World," *Washington Post*, 12 March 1893, 15. LHL was said to have authored a poem in German, "Wasser Rosen," for which Victor Herbert, the celebrated composer of operettas, wrote the music, but it does not appear in the *Children's Souvenir Songbook*.

27. A telegram to Susan B. Anthony is printed in Ida Husted Harper, *Life and Work of Susan B. Anthony*, vol. 2 (New York: Arno Press, 1969), 653.

28. *Brooklyn Daily Eagle*, 1 Sept. 1889, 8.

29. "Anna Dickinson's Case. It is Proposed to Raise $20,000 for her Benefit," *Brooklyn*

Daily Eagle, 8 March 1891, 20; "Labor of Love. The Brooklyn Movement to Help Anna Dickinson," *Brooklyn Daily Eagle,* 9 April 1891, 3; "A Little Fund Raised in Brooklyn for Anna E. Dickinson," *Brooklyn Daily Eagle,* 27 April 1891, 6.

30. "The Talk of New York," *Brooklyn Daily Eagle,* 28 July 1889, 15.

31. Clipping, n. t., n. d., Scrapbook, NyBLHS. The *Brooklyn Daily Eagle,* 26 May 1889, 7, reprinted this article but omitted the phrase "and irrepressible Laura C. Holloway is the chief priestess," perhaps out of deference to a former employee.

32. "Encouraging Mr. Seidl," *Brooklyn Daily Eagle,* 22 June 1889, 4.

33. Clipping, "A Seaside Music Hall. In the Brighton Beach Pavilions Strict Decorum Prevails," 27 Aug. 1894, Scrapbook, box 4, Seidl Society Records, NyBLHS.

34. "Wagner's 'Parsifal'. Forthcoming Performance of the Work in Brooklyn," *Brooklyn Daily Eagle,* 16 March 1890, 12–13.

35. "Rather Weary. Why the Seidl Society Runs no More Charitable Excursions," *Brooklyn Daily Eagle,* 14 July 1891, 6.

36. Gere, *Intimate Practices,* 88.

37. Clipping, n. d., Scrapbook, box 3, Seidl Society Records, NyBLHS.

38. "Rather Weary," 6.

39. "Seidl Society Charity," *Brooklyn Daily Eagle,* 16 July 1891, 4.

40. "Ridiculous, Says Bernstein," *Brooklyn Daily Eagle,* 17 July 1896, 2; "Little Mr. Bernstein Did It, Stirred up a Big Row in the Seidl Society's Orchestra," *Brooklyn Daily Eagle,* 14 July 1896, 14.

41. "Fresh Air Fund. The Colored Picnic." *Brooklyn Daily Union,* 24 Aug. 1872.

42. "The Colored Orphans Enjoy a Day at Brighton Beach as Guests of the Seidl Society," *Brooklyn Daily Eagle,* 15 Aug. 1889, 1.

43. Clipping, *New York World,* 29 Nov. 1889, Scrapbook, box 3, Seidl Society Records, NyBLHS.

44. "Colored Orphans. Thanksgiving Festival for the Inmates of the Brooklyn Howard Asylum," *Brooklyn Daily Eagle,* 29 Nov. 1890, 2.

45. "Musical Metempsychosis. Silas G. Pratt Illustrates the Migration of a Tune," *Brooklyn Daily Eagle,* 10 Jan. 1890, 2. The Seidl Society continued to hold an annual benefit concert, raising funds for a different Brooklyn orphanage each year.

46. "Rather Weary," *Brooklyn Daily Eagle,* 14 July 1891, 6.

47. "Seidl Society Charity," *Brooklyn Daily Eagle,* 16 July 1891, 4. The excerpt comes from the poem "What We Live For" by G. Linneaus Banks.

48. "Seidl Children's Festival," *Brooklyn Daily Eagle,* 25 Aug. 1895, 2.

49. "The Children's Festival," *Brooklyn Daily Eagle,* 28 Aug. 1895, 6.

50. There were rumors that Seidl was the illegitimate son of Franz Liszt, which would make him the half-brother of Cosima Wagner.

51. Steiger, *Memorabilia,* 266–267.

52. Eek, *Damodar,* 595.

53. Basil Crump, "Richard Wagner's Music Dramas," *Theosophy* (April 1896), http://www.theosociety.org/pasadena/theos/v11n01p23_richard-wagners-music-dramas.htm.

54. William Ashton Ellis, "Theosophy in the Works of Richard Wagner," *Transactions of the London Lodge* 11, 1886. This article was republished in two parts in *The Theosophist,* in vols. 7 (Dec. 1886): 162–169, and 8 (Jan. 1887): 222–228. LHL annotated these articles in her copies of the magazine. In possession of the author.

55. Quoted in Anne Dzamba Sessa, *Richard Wagner and the English* (Cranberry, N.J.:

Associated University Presses, 1979), 41. William Ashton Ellis translated into English all of Wagner's prose works and many of his letters. He also wrote several books on Wagner, including his biography.

56. Rogers, *The Story of Two Lives*, 162–169. She does not put *Parsifal* in quotation marks.

57. "Richard Wagner's Theosophy," *New York Times*, 12 March 1886, 2.

58. John Denison Champlin, Jr. and William Foster Apthorp, eds., *Cyclopedia of Music and Musicians*, vol. 3 (New York: Charles Scribner's Sons, 1893), 88.

59. *Brooklyn Daily Eagle*, 21 May 1897, 7.

60. LHL, "To Herr Seidl," 30 Aug. 1888, Scrapbook, DeWint, SA1305. Printed, probably in a program celebrating the end of the musical season at Brighton Beach.

61. Clipping, 28 Sept. 1891, box 4, Seidl Society Records, NyBLHS.

62. Newspaper clipping, "Seidlites All Serene," 24 Feb. 1892, Scrapbook, box 3, Seidl Society Records, NyBLHS.

63. Anton Seidl to LHL, 15 Sept. 1894, box 1, Seidl Society Records, NyBLHS.

64. Henry Edward Krehbiel, *Review of the New York Musical Season 1885–1886* (New York and London: Novello, Ewer & Co., 1886): 159–164. It was not until Dec. 1903, after the courts ruled that Bayreuth could not prevent its performance, that the Metropolitan Opera in New York presented a fully staged *Parsifal*. For the history of *Parsifal* in the United States, including the Seidl Society "Entertainment," see Joseph Horowitz, *Wagner Nights: An American History*, 181–239, 259–275.

65. "'Parsifal' in Brooklyn," *New York Sun*, 23 March 1890. Krehbiel repeated similar talks in February and March 1891 at the Metropolitan Opera House. *The Critic* 15 (28 Feb. 1891): 117.

66. Henry E. Krehbiel, *Studies in the Wagnerian Drama* (New York: Harper & Brothers, 1891), 164, 198.

67. Maurice Kufferath, *The Parsifal of Richard Wagner*, with an introduction by H. E. Krehbiel (New York: Henry Holt and Co., 1904): xi–xii.

68. "Wagner Found in His Music a Knowledge of the Son of God," *Brooklyn Daily Eagle*, 26 March 1890, 1.

69. Newspaper clippings, "Brooklyn's Big Festival," *The World*, 16 March 1890; "*Parsifal* in Brooklyn," *The Sun*, 23 March 1890; both in the Anton Seidl Collection, Columbia University Rare Books and Manuscripts Library, Seidl Society Papers, hereafter NNC-RB.

70. W. J. Henderson, *Preludes and Studies: Musical Themes of the Day* (London: Longmans, Green, & Co., 1891), 89.

71. Clipping, *The World*, 1 April 1890, Anton Seidl Collection, NNC-RB.

72. "'Parsifal.' A Notable Performance of Wagner's Last Work," *Brooklyn Daily Eagle*, 1 April 1890, 4.

73. Ibid.

74. Lyman Abbott, "Sunday Afternoon. The Suffering Servant of the Lord," *Christian Union* 43 (23 April 1891): 541.

75. William Ashton Ellis, "Wagner's 'Parsifal," *Theosophy* 7 (Jan. 1887): 227. See also Eduard Herrmann, "Parsifal," *The Word* 3 (Sept. 1906): 346–367. According to Hermann, "Parsifal" presents the Theosophical teachings of reincarnation, Karma, and the Masters.

76. Alice Leighton Cleather and Basil Woodward Crump, *Parsifal, Lohengrin, and the Legend of the Holy Grail* (New York: G. Schirmer, 1904), 35.

77. William Ashton Ellis, "Wagner's 'Parsifal,'" *Theosophy* 7 (Dec. 1886): 162–169. Ellis frequently compared the opera to *Zanoni* and *A Strange Story*, popular occult novels writ-

ten by Sir Edward Bulwer-Lytton. Wagner admired Bulwer-Lytton's novels, dramatizing an early opera based on his *Rienzi*.

78. William Ashton Ellis, "Wagner's 'Parsifal,'" *The Theosophist* 8 (Jan. 1887): 226.

79. William Aston Ellis, "Richard Wagner, as Poet, Musician, and Mystic," *Meister* 1 (1888): 123, quoted in Sessa, *Richard Wagner and the English*, 134.

80. William Aston Ellis, "Wagner's 'Parsifal,'" *The Theosophist* 8 (Jan. 1887): 228.

81. William C. Ward, *The Art of Richard Wagner* (London: The Theosophical Publishing Society, 1906), 24.

82. Helena Blavatsky, "From Keshub Babu to Maestro Wagner *via* the Salvation Camp," *The Theosophist* 4 (Feb. 1883), in *Blavatsky: Collected Writings*, vol. 4, 328, 330–333.

83. "Wagner as Mystic," *Brooklyn Daily Eagle*, 17 May 1897, 7.

84. Basil Crump, "A Posthumous Attack on H. P. B.," Addendum to Cleather, *H. P. Blavatsky as I Knew Her*, 64–65.

85. Quoted in Sessa, *Richard Wagner and the English*, 132.

86. Cleather and Crump, *Parsifal, Lohengrin, and the Legend of the Holy Grail*, 159.

87. "The Seidl Society No More," *New York Times*, 12 Jan. 1896, 3.

88. "Seidl Society Incorporated," *Brooklyn Daily Eagle*, 31 May 1896, 7.

89. "Ocean Front Wreck Strewn. Reports of Great Damage Done All Along the Atlantic Coast. Ravages Wrought at Coney Island," *Brooklyn Daily Eagle*, 13 Oct. 1896, 1.

90. "Plans for the Seidl Funeral. Service May be Held at the Metropolitan Opera House," *Brooklyn Daily Eagle*, 29 March 1898, 2.

91. "To the Memory of Seidl. A Concert in His Honor Tomorrow Night," *Brooklyn Daily Eagle*, 1 May 1898, 19.

10. "DEAR FRIEND AND SISTER"

1. For an overview of how outsiders viewed the Shakers, see Stephen J. Stein, *The Shaker Experience in America: A History of the United Society of Believers* (New Haven, Conn.: Yale University Press, 1992), 215–222.

2. Frederick W. Evans to LHL, 15 April 1874, DeWint, folder 1202. (All Shaker correspondence to LHL in the DeWint, Edward Deming Andrews Memorial Shaker collection, including all cited in this chapter, is contained in folder 1202.) Shakers had learned that taking in children was not an effective way to increase membership. Priscilla Brewer reported that out of 110 youngsters admitted to the Church Family at Mount Lebanon between 1871 and 1900 not a single one had converted. Brewer, *Shaker Communities, Shaker Lives* (Hanover, N.H.: University Press of New England, 1986), 179.

3. Frederick Evans to LHL, 12 Nov. 1884, DeWint. In Frederick Evans to LHL, 9 Feb. 1885, he asks LHL for the name of a medium who could offer this service.

4. Alonzo G. Hollister to LHL, 16 Dec. 1904, DeWint. Hollister had earlier written an article on Buddhism and Christianity, "Writing on the Sky," *Shaker Manifesto* 13 (May 1883): 97–100.

5. Paul Carus, *The Gospel of Buddha* (Chicago: Open Court Publishing Co., 1898). Copy inscribed "A. G. H.," NOC.

6. Anna White to LHL, 13 Nov. 1901, DeWint.

7. Anna White to LHL, 5 Jan. 1902, DeWint.

8. "North Family Visitor's Room, Mt. Lebanon, Columbia County, N. Y.," 1893–1903, MPH.

9. Anna White to LHL, 26 April 1902, DeWint.

10. LHL later asked the Shakers to hire Charlie, but they declined. Anna White to LHL, 22 Dec. 1904, DeWint. The 1930 Federal Census lists Charles E. Terry, nephew, living in LHL's household in Canaan, New York.

11. Anna White to LHL, 21 July 1902, NOC. A poem, probably written by LHL, and read at Edward's funeral, draws on the language of spiritualism and Theosophy, describing him "an adept in love's higher things." "In Memoriam," *Brooklyn Daily Eagle*, 29 July 1902, 5.

12. Since these articles do not have bylines, attribution is often possible only from references in other sources or from extant manuscripts.

13. LHL, "Eldress Anna White on Temperance and Vegetarianism; Women's Hats and Children," handwritten MS, DeWint. This "interview" was conducted by correspondence, with LHL posing questions and Anna White responding in letters.

14. Ibid.

15. Anna White to LHL, 9 June 1903, DeWint. White had read the article (she corrects an error that LHL made about her age), but I have not been able to locate where the article was published.

16. Anna White to LHL, 15 July 1903, DeWint; "Shakers to Seek Relief. Will Ask the Legislature for Exemption from Taxes," *New York Sun*, 16 Aug. 1903. A similar article, "Shakers Seek Tax Exemption," appeared in the *Chatham Semi-Weekly Courier*, 15 July 1903.

17. Anna White to LHL, 29 Aug. 1903, DeWint.

18. Anna White to LHL, 4 Nov. 1903, DeWint; M. Catherine Allen to LHL, 1 Oct. 1903, DeWint.

19. Anna White to LHL, 11 Dec. 1903, DeWint.

20. Ibid. LHL helped Sister Margaret Chubb, who was concerned about the fate of her children.

21. M. Catherine Allen to LHL, 1 Oct. 1903, DeWint.

22. Anna White to LHL, 4 Nov. 1903, DeWint.

23. "Charitable Work for Girls in New York City," *The Outlook*, 27 June 1903, 529–530.

24. *Lucifer* 12 (15 July 1893): 447–448; "No Place for Mrs. Chapin. As a Theosophist Not Fit to Teach Young Girls," *New York Times*, 5 June 1893, 1; "A Hotbed of Theosophy," *New York Times*, 6 June 1893, 9; "With Miss Chapin's Class: Exercises in a Theosophist Sunday School," *New York Times*, 12 June 1893, 5; "Split on Theosophy's Rock," *New York Times*, 26 June 1893, 1; "One Lady Manager Objected," *New York Times*, 27 June 1893, 8; "Mirror of the Movement," *Theosophy* 11 (May 1896): 63.

25. Anna White to LHL, 27 Aug. 1908, DeWint.

26. *Lebanon Records Kept by Order of the Church*, 18 June 1904, NOC.

27. Anna White to LHL, 23 April 1904, DeWint.

28. Anna White to LHL, 21 July 1904, DeWint. Shakers had opened a hotel at Pleasant Hill, Ky., in 1897, and even earlier an old farm at Tyringham, Mass., had become a resort. See G. W. Gustin, "An Old Shaker Farm. Turned into a Resort for Summer Visitors—The Ninety Year Old Traces of Industry and Taste—Fernside and Its Comforts," *Brooklyn Daily Eagle*, 7 Sept. 1880.

29. Anna White to LHL, 15 June 1904, DeWint.

30. Ibid.; Anna White to LHL, 20 June 1904, DeWint; Anna White to LHL, 21 July 1904, DeWint.

31. Anna White to LHL, 17 June 1904, DeWint. Like many of LHL's ideas, however, this project never materialized.

32. Anna White to LHL, 21 July 1904, DeWint.

33. Ibid.

34. Anna White to LHL, 19 Aug. 1904, DeWint, confirms that the Hyatte family was living at Ann Lee Cottage.

35. According to Jerry Grant, Director of Research and Library Services, at the Old Chatham Museum and Library, a story circulated that Holloway-Langford demanded that the Shakers perform songs and dances for her friends.

36. Anna White to LHL, 17 June 1904, DeWint; Anna White to LHL, 31 July 1904, DeWint.

37. Anna White to LHL, 5 Sept. 1904, MPH.

38. Jayanta K. Sircar, "The Vedanta Society of New York. A Review of the First Century," *Bulletin of the Ramakrishna Mission Institute of Culture* 48 (1997): 240–249; 294–305.

39. Anna White to LHL, 22 Dec. 1904, DeWint.

40. Anna White to LHL, 27 Nov. 1907, DeWint.

41. Anna White to LHL, 24 Oct. 1904, DeWint.

42. Emma Neal to LHL, 14 Sept. 1904, MPH.

43. Emma Neal to LHL, 23 Sept. 1904, DeWint.

44. Leila Taylor to LHL, 25 Sept. 1904, DeWint.

45. Anna White to LHL, 3 Oct. 1904, DeWint.

46. Anna White to LHL, 22 Dec. 1904, DeWint.

47. Anna White to LHL, 3 Feb. 1904, DeWint.

48. Leila S. Taylor to John P. MacLean, 30 April 1905, Western Reserve Historical Society, Cleveland, OH (hereafter OClWHi), A46.

49. "Shakers of Mt. Lebanon Open Doors to City Children: Former Brooklyn Woman Senior Eldress of Interesting Colony," *The Daily Standard Union*, 10 June 1906.

50. Anna White to LHL, 7 June 1906, DeWint. Anna White's reply is dated before the Sunday issue of *The Daily Standard Union*, because LHL had sent her an advance proof of the article.

51. Anna White to LHL, 12 Sept. 1906, DeWint.

52. Anna White and Leila S. Taylor, *Shakerism: Its Meaning and Message Embracing An Historical Account, Statement of Belief and Spiritual Experience of the Church from Its Rise to the Present Day* (Columbus, Ohio: Fred J. Herr, 1904); Stein, *The Shaker Experience*, 266–267.

53. Isaac Kaufman Funk, *The Widow's Mite and Other Psychic Phenomena* (New York and London: Funk & Wagnalls Company, 1904), ix–x. He quoted the inventor and Theosophist Thomas Edison, who claimed that "rays of vibration" were set in motion by an unseen force. Funk speculated that at high speed these vibrations would cause the human body to become invisible and capable of passing through solid matter "as Christ's resurrected body passed through the walls of the chamber at Jerusalem."

54. Anna White to LHL, 18 April 1904, DeWint.

55. Anna White to LHL, 23 April 1904, DeWint.

56. Anna White to LHL, 20 May 1904, DeWint. Funk & Wagnalls offered to sell the book for $1.50, with the Shakers receiving a 10 percent royalty. Additionally, the Shakers would be expected to purchase 1,000 copies at half the retail price.

57. If LHL made any suggestions for changes in the book, no record of them has been preserved.

58. Fred. J. Heer was the publisher of the *Ohio Archeological and Historical Quarterly*, where MacLean published a number of essays, and later Heer published MacLean's bibliography of Shaker literature.

59. LHL [Laura Holloway Langford], *The Story of a Piano* (Brooklyn, N.Y.: O. Wissner, 1904).

60. "Spirit Visitors to the Shakers at Mount Lebanon," *New York Sun,* 18 Dec. 1904. Anna White identified William Chubb as the Brother portrayed in the sketch. He had given LHL permission to recount his experience.

61. Molly McGarry, *Ghosts of Futures Past: Spiritualism and the Cultural Politics of Nineteenth-Century America* (Berkeley: University of California Press, 2008), 149.

62. Anna White to LHL, 24 Oct. 1904, DeWint.

63. Anna White to LHL, 25 July 1905, DeWint.

64. "T. S. Activities," *Theosophical Quarterly* 3 (July 1905): 260–261. Aleister Crowley, a member of the Golden Dawn and a practitioner of sexual magic, also studied with Ramanâthan. See Lawrence Sutin, *Do What Thou Wilt: A Life of Aleister Crowley* (New York: St. Martin's Press, 2000).

65. Myron H. Phelps, "Miscellaneous. A Representative Hindu," *The Open Court, a Quarterly Magazine* 19 (July 1905): 590.

66. Moncure Daniel Conway, *My Pilgrimage to the Wise Men of the East* (Boston: Houghton, Mifflin and Co., 1906), 159–160.

67. Anna White to LHL, 7 Aug. 1905, DeWint.

68. Anna White to LHL, 22 Aug. 1905, DeWint.

69. Deborah Escobar, "Shakers and Their Participation in the Peace Movement, 1870–1905" (Honors Thesis, Russell Sage College, Troy, N.Y., 1990).

70. Anna White to LHL, 11 Sept. 1905, DeWint.

71. Tessa J. Bartholomeusz, "Real Life and Romance: The Life of Miranda de Souza Canavarro," *Journal of Feminist Studies in Religion* 10 (Fall 1994): 27–47. In the Sri Lankan sources, her first name is Miranda, while in America she was known as Marie. In late 1902, the couple traveled to Acre in Palestine, where Phelps took down, through an interpreter, the words of the son of Baháu'u'lláh, the founder of the Bahá'i faith. In collaboration with Canavarro he wrote *Life and Teachings of Abbas Effendi,* published in 1903.

72. For many years, Phelps had been a co-worker in the Theosophical Society with LHL's friends Lizzie Chapin and Maude Ralston.

73. Richard Fox Young, *The Bible Trembled; The Hindu-Christian Controversies of Nineteenth-century Ceylon* (Vienna: Sammlung De Nobili, 1995), 161.

74. Sri Paránanda [Ponnambalam Ramanâthan], *An Eastern Exposition of the Gospel of Jesus According to St. Matthew,* ed. R. L. Harrison (London: Kegan Paul, 1898); Paránanda, *An Eastern Exposition of the Gospel of Jesus According to St. John,* ed. R. L. Harrison (London: William Hutchinson & Co 1902). Harrison performed a similar role during Ramanâthan's U.S. tour, where his lectures were published as *The Culture of the Soul Among Western Nations* (New York: G. P. Putnam's Sons, 1906).

75. "The Royal Family of Jaffna," http://www.jaffnaroyalfamily.org/ponnambalam.php.

76. Stephen J. Paterwic, *Historical Dictionary of the Shakers* (Lanham, Md.: The Scarecrow Press, Inc., 2008), 163.

77. Anna White to LHL, 23 Nov. 1905, DeWint.

78. "Shakers Shake as Shaker Bishop Catherine Presides at Unfrocking of Elder," *New York Sun,* 20 March 1909.

79. "The Shakeup in Shakerdom. Came Through Pick's Pick of Foreign Recruits," *New York Sun,* 21 March 1909.

80. LHL, "Future of the Shakers. Their Members Dwindling, Their Wealth Large," *New York Sun,* 11 April 1909.

81. Anna White to LHL, 14 April 1909, DeWint.

82. This Shaker family had been closed in 1897 and its members dispersed to other communities.

83. Daniel Offord to LHL, 28 June 1906, DeWint. Under this arrangement, LHL would not pay off the farm until 1921. The Shakers added the proviso that they would retain thirty-eight acres of timberland.

84. Anna White to LHL, 24 Aug. 1906, DeWint.

85. LHL, MS, n. t., n. d., DeWint.

86. Ibid. "The Sanitarium was to be on lines similar to the one at Summit New Jersey (formerly at Harrison New York) and was to run after the plan of Dr. Reinle—who had made a popular success of his institution. My knowledge of the said Sanitarium was nil, for I had never seen it, & never knew the Physician at the head of it. But I had met, & knew very well, several persons who had been greatly benefitted by the treatment given there." An advertisement for "Milk and Rest Cure. Dr. Reinle's System" appears in Health 9 (Sept. 1908): 511.

87. Anna White to LHL, 27 Nov. 1907, DeWint. Despite these problems, she purchased two additional pieces of land, buying 450 acres all told from the Mount Lebanon Shakers.

88. M. Catherine Allen to LHL, 10 March 1907, MPH.

89. LHL, MS, n. t., n. d. DeWint. The Lower Canaan Family had closed in 1884, and the property had been sold to Mr. and Mrs. Frederick G. Burnham of Morristown, N.J., who established a school for boys. Daniel Offord had problems obtaining a proper survey and map, but apparently had them completed by the time the deed was prepared.

90. M. Catherine Allen to LHL, 27 Aug. 1911, DeWint.

91. Philip Kaminstein, Berkshire Farms' archivist, telephone conversation, 2 July 2007.

92. Anna White to LHL, n. d., DeWint.

93. Daniel Offord to LHL, 16 Dec. 1910, Western Union telegram, DeWint.

94. Daniel Offord to LHL, 23 Feb. 1911, DeWint.

95. Leila Taylor to LHL, 26 Feb. 1911, DeWint.

96. Leila Taylor to LHL, 12 March 1911, DeWint.

97. LHL, "Eldress Anna White Dead," MS, n. d., DeWint. I have not been able to determine where this was published.

98. Daniel Offord to LHL, 23 Feb. 1911, DeWint.

99. Daniel Offord to LHL, 15 Jan. 1911, MPH; Leila Taylor to LHL, 12 March 1911, DeWint.

100. Leila Taylor to LHL, 30 June 1911, DeWint.

101. Leila Taylor to LHL, 12 March 1911, DeWint.

102. Sarah Burger to LHL, 26 Feb. 1912, DeWint.

103. Leila S. Taylor, A Memorial to Eldress Anna White and Elder Daniel Offord (Mount Lebanon, N.Y.: North Family of Shakers, 1912), 74–75.

104. LHL, MS, n. d., DeWint, SA1302.5. This eight-page document is incomplete, but after a gap it appears to continue in SA1302.3, 14–27. I have not been able to determine whether or not it was published.

105. Stein, Shaker Experience, 284.

106. LHL's vehemence against Christian Science was a reaction to Mary Baker Eddy, who portrayed spiritualism as a threat to order and good morals, writing: "Credulity, misguided faith, jugglery, fraud, are the foundations of mediumship." She went on to label belief in spirit communications "too ludicrous for serious argument." Eddy, Science and Health With Key to the Scriptures (Bedford, Mass.: Applewood Books, 1875), 240, 242.

107. "Army Orders," *The Washington Post*, 12 March 1911; *Brooklyn Blue Book and Long Island Society Register*, 1912, 135.

108. *Hudson New York Evening Register*, 8 June 1914, 1.

109. LHL lived at 181 Schermerhorn, Brooklyn, until May 1906, when she moved to 147 Willow St., Brooklyn, evidently in reaction to a robbery at her home the previous December. Anna White to LHL, 9 May 1906, DeWint; [Obituary for George Holloway], *Brooklyn Daily Eagle*, 8 Aug. 1914, and *New York Times*, 2 Aug. 1914, 5.

110. LHL to Hildegard Henderson, 18 Aug. 1922, HPB.

111. Sheridan R. Cate, Attorney at Law, to Sidney P. Henshaw, 26 Feb. 1925, HPB.

11. WHO TELLS THE TALE?

1. Typed MS, n. d., DeWint, SA1318.1a.

2. The Liberal Catholic Church reorganized in 1915–1916 from the British branch of the Old Catholic Church, which claimed apostolic succession not through Rome but through Utrecht, Holland. It was neither Protestant nor Roman Catholic, but its emphasis on ritual and mysticism appealed to many Theosophists.

3. LHL to Hildegard Henderson, 17 Aug. 1922, HPB.

4. [Hildegard Henderson] to Mr. Whiteman, "Extract from a letter to Mr. Whiteman," Sept. 1935, HPB.

5. Edna Dean Proctor to LHL, 18 Oct. 1920, NBPu.

6. LHL to Alice Cleather, 22 March 1922, HPB.

7. LHL to Hildegard Henderson, 9 Feb. 1923, HPB. LHL also promised to write about William M. Ivins, a lawyer who had represented Blavatsky; Charles Sotheran, one of the initial members of the Theosophical Society; Professor Hiram Corson, whom Blavatsky had visited in Ithaca, New York in 1874, and his son, Dr. Eugene Corson; Alexander Wilder, who had edited *Isis Unveiled*; Dr. Franz Hartmann, the German occultist; Donald Nicholson, formerly managing editor of the *New York Tribune*; C. H. A. Bjerregaard, chief of the reading room at the New York Public Library; Dr. Atwood; Harriet Brainard Moody (Mrs. William Vaughn Moody), who had hosted Rabindranath Tagore on his visit to the United States in 1913; and Harold W. Percival, editor of *The Word*.

8. LHL to Alice Cleather, 22 March 1922, HPB.

9. Alice Leighton Cleather, *H. P. Blavatsky as I Knew Her, with an Addendum by Basil Crump* (Calcutta: Thacker, Spink & Co., 1923), vii, ix. All three of Cleather's short books were then reprinted together as *H. P. Blavatsky as I Knew Her: Her Life and Work for Humanity: A Great Betrayal* (Calcutta: Thacker, Spink & Co., 1923).

10. Hildegard Henderson to Alice Cleather, 15 Sept. [1921], HPB.

11. Ibid. In her letter to Cleather, Henderson summarizes a series of events.

12. Although LHL's letters were given to the HBP Library in Victoria (now located in Toronto), most of Hildegard Henderson's letters to LHL did not survive. Henderson's letters to Alice Cleather became part of the HBP collection.

13. LHL to Hildegard Henderson, 17 Aug. 1922, HPB. LHL had executed a mortgage to Josephine W. Jackson on 28 Oct. 1921 for the sum of $3,000. After LHL's death in 1930, this mortgage was assigned to Florence G. Roberts. There was a second outstanding lien on the property for $3,000 plus interest. "Surrogates' Court County of Columbia. In the Matter of the Application of Florence G. Roberts of 557 Argyle Road, Brooklyn, New York, to obtain surplus moneys under a foreclosure upon property in the town of Canaan, N. Y., formerly of Laura C. Langford, deceased," Courthouse, Columbia County, NY.

14. Hildegard Henderson to LHL, 5 Oct. [1922], HPB. The date of the typed copy in the HPB Library is 5 Oct. 1925. This is incorrect. Mr. Cate, the lawyer, had noted that the original letter did not specify a year.

15. LHL to Hildegard Henderson, 9 Feb. 1923, HPB. LHL may have thought that a threat to sell the farm to a Roman Catholic would spur Henderson to send money.

16. Ibid.

17. LHL to Hildegard Henderson, 14 March 1923, HPB. LHL recounts details of Eleanor Curtis's visit.

18. Cleather, *H. P. Blavatsky As I Knew Her,* vii.

19. LHL to Hildegard Henderson, 7 March 1923, HPB.

20. LHL to Hildegard Henderson, 29 March 1923, HPB.

21. Ibid.

22. LHL to Hildegard Henderson, 2 April 1923, HPB.

23. LHL to Hildegard Henderson, 28 April 1923, HPB.

24. LHL to Hildegard Henderson, 5 July 1923, HPB.

25. HL to Hildegard Henderson, 21 July 1923, HPB.

26. Hildegard Henderson to LHL, 14 Sept. 1923, HPB.

27. LHL to Hildegard Henderson, 21 July 1923, HPB.

28. Ibid.

29. LHL [Laura C. Langford], 31 Aug. 1923, "Last Will and Testament, State of New York, County of Columbia, Surrogate's Office." In a letter to Sidney Henshaw, 4 Feb. 1925, Hildegard Henderson acknowledged that she had "never been able to make [LHL] state that her estate would be charged with any debt to me."

30. LHL to Hildegard Henderson, 21 July 1923, HPB.

31. LHL to Hildegard Henderson, 11 Sept. 1923, HPB.

32. Hildegard Henderson to LHL, 20 Sept. 1923, HPB.

33. Hildegard Henderson to LHL, 25 March 1924, HPB. Henderson's letter to LHL October 1923 is not extant, apparently having been submitted to the lawyer, but information about its contents is summarized in this letter. LHL had made her will on August 23, 1923, at a time when Henderson was pressuring her to acknowledge the debt in her estate. It is impossible to be sure whether Henderson's suspicion about the $850 publication subsidy was correct. However, in fall 1922, LHL owed $6,000 on her mortgage; the next year, the mortgage had been paid down to $5,000, but this reduction may have been due to Eleanor Curtis's $1,000.

34. Ibid.

35. LHL to Hildegard Henderson, 30 March 1924, HPB.

36. LHL to [Hildegard Henderson?], sometime in 1923, stray page of a letter, HPB.

37. LHL to Hildegard Henderson, 20 May 1924, HPB.

38. Hildegard Henderson, "Statement in regard to money supplied to Mrs. Laura C. Langford by Mrs. H. Henderson," enclosed in a letter to Sidney P. Henshaw, 2 Nov. 1924, HPB.

39. [Hildegard Henderson] to Mr. Whiteman, "Extract from a letter to Mr. Whiteman," Sept. 1935, HPB; Hildegard Henderson to Alice Cleather, 13 July 1925, HPB.

40. S. P. Henshaw to LHL, [Nov. 1924], copy of a letter, HPB.

41. Vaulx Carter to Sidney Henshaw, 13 Nov. 1924, HPB.

42. Sheridan R. Cate to Sidney P. Henshaw, 16 Feb. 1925, HPB.

43. [Hildegard Henderson], "Extract from a letter to Mr. Whiteman," Sept. 1935, HPB.

44. "Agreement and Release Laura C. Langford of the First Part And Hildegard Henderson and Eleanor Curtis of the Second Part. Sheridan R. Cate Attorney at Law Pittsfield, Mass.," HPB.

45. Hildegard Henderson to Alice L. Cleather, 13 July 1925, HPB.

46. It is possible that LHL's manuscript contained copies of letters that are no longer extant. The Winterthur Library holds five letters from Koot Hoomi to her. It is unclear whether four additional letters were lost, or whether Henderson included in this count letters from Koot Hoomi to Blavatsky and Francesca Arundale, and notes from Koot Hoomi written on other documents.

47. Blavatsky, *The Complete Works of H. P. Blavatsky*, vol. 1, ed. Trevor A. Barker (London: Rider & Co., 1933), 256. The editor refers to LHL's manuscript several times.

48. Available at the Blavatsky Study Center online: www.blavatskyarchives.com.

49. For example, Sylvia Cranston, *HPB: The Extraordinary Life & Influence of Helena Blavatsky, Founder of the Modern Theosophical Movement* (New York: G. P. Putnam's Sons, 1993) relies heavily on LHL's articles for evidence regarding the summer of 1884.

EPILOGUE

1. Havelock Ellis, *Little Essays of Love and Virtue* (New York: George H. Doran Company, 1922). In 1925, LHL wrote to Ellis inquiring about a pamphlet written by his wife, Edith Mary Oldham Ellis, "A Novitiate for Marriage" (1894). In her essays, Mrs. Ellis advocated a trial period for a couple to determine if they had a vocation for marriage, and she defended full personal and sexual development for homosexuals. Havelock Ellis to LHL, 9 Oct. 1925, NBPu.

2. Rev. J. S. Jones to Worthington C. Ford, 16 Dec. 1904, DLC, MS Division.

3. LHL to John Hay, 29 May 1903, John Hay Papers, General Correspondence May 20–31, 1902; LHL to John Hay, 2 June 1903, John Hay Papers, General Correspondence, June 1–10, 1903; DLC.

4. "Introduction," in Andrew Johnson, *Index to the Andrew Johnson Papers* (Washington, D.C.: Library of Congress Manuscript Division, 1963), vii. See also George S. Hellman, *Lanes of Memory* (New York: Alfred A. Knopf, 1927), 50–52.

5. "Hellman Book Sale Ends," *New York Times*, 27 Nov. 1919, 32. "Introduction," *Index to the Andrew Johnson Papers*, viii.

6. "Brighton Road Receivers," *Brooklyn Daily Eagle*, 14 Jan. 1898, 1; "Receiver for Brighton Beach," *Brooklyn Daily Eagle*, 24 July 1899, 14; "Case Involving the Furniture in the Brighton Beach Hotel," *Brooklyn Daily Eagle*, 31 Jan. 1899, 2; "Foreclosing on a Railroad," *Brooklyn Daily Eagle*, 12 June 1899, 18.

7. "On the Lookout," *Brooklyn Daily Eagle*, 29 July 1902, 5. I have been unsuccessful in locating a will for Edward Langford or determining the owner of the Schermerhorn property.

8. H. P. Blavatsky to William Q. Judge, 1 May 1885, Blavatsky, *Some Letters*.

9. Phelps founded the Indo-American National Association. The India House provided accommodations for Indian students in the United States. Phelps met Gandhi in India in 1909. Aravind Ganachari, "An Early American Contributor to India's Struggle for Freedom: Myron H. Phelps (1856–1916)," in *Nationalism and Social Reform in a Colonial Situation* (Delhi, India: Kalpaz Publications, 2005), 149–160.

10. The India Society hosted Indian students in American homes and raised money to support their education. Maude Ralston, "The India Society of Detroit," *Modern Review* 10 (1911): 234–237. Members of the Society are pictured on p. 235.

11. Ibid, 236.

12. Blanche Watson, *Gandhi and Non-violent Resistance: The Non-co-operation Movement of India: Gleanings from the American Press* (Madras: Ganesh & Co., 1923), 348–351.

13. Alex Owen, *The Place of Enchantment: British Occultism and the Culture of the Modern* (Chicago: University of Chicago Press, 2004), 91.

14. M. Catherine Allen to LHL, 10 March 1907, MPH. Allen served in the Shaker Central Ministry 1908–1922.

15. The sun-wheel symbol dates to prehistoric Europe. The insignia also hints at the connection between this book and Helena Blavatsky's *The Secret Doctrine,* which contains a chapter on the meanings of the "Circle and the Cross."

16. LHL, *As It is Written of Jesus the Christ. By The Helpers* (New York: Burr Printing House, 1907), 32.

17. H. P. Blavatsky, *The Secret Doctrine,* vol. 2, 69.

18. Owen, chapter 2, "Magicians of the New Dawn," in *The Place of Enchantment,* 43–76, discusses the Order of the Golden Dawn.

19. LHL, *As It is Written,* 60.

20. Ibid., 64.

21. Ibid., 85.

22. She owned a book by C. A. Stephens, *Natural Salvation: The Message of Science, Outlining the First Principles of Immortal Life on the Earth* (Norway Lake, Maine: The Laboratory, 1903), in which she underlined passages that suggested that mankind could evolve toward immortality and omnipotence. In possession of the author.

23. LHL was also inspired by later Christian Theosophical groups such as The Order of the Cross (originally called the Order of the Golden Age), whose publications she read with great interest.

24. S[usan] E. G[ay], "The Future of Women," *Lucifer,* Oct. 1890, 118.

25. In *The Secret Doctrine,* vol. 2, 561–562, Blavatsky declared that Adepts like Enoch and Elijah had reached such a high degree of purity and power that they died "only in the physical body," while still leading a conscious life in the "astral body." Blavatsky went on to say that even today there were yogis in India and some Christian monks who were transfigured in a like manner.

26. LHL, *As It Is Written,* 84, 81, 85.

27. H. P. Blavatsky, *The Esoteric Character of the Gospels,* vol. 5, *Studies in Occultism: Series of Reprints from the Writings of H. P. Blavatsky* (Boston: New England Theosophical Corporation, 1895); originally published in *Lucifer* (1887), 231.

28. In the following decades, however, many occultists asserted that Jesus was more than an example of the "Christ Spirit": he was, they claimed, the greatest Adept of the Brotherhood.

29. Don Colbert, *What Would Jesus Eat? The Ultimate Program for Eating Well, Feeling Great, and Living Longer* (Nashville: Thomas Nelson, 2003).

30. LHL, *As It Is Written,* 85.

31. Only a short time after LHL published *As It is Written of Jesus the Christ,* Charles Leadbeater proclaimed that Jiddu Krishnamurti was this Teacher.

32. Robert N. Bellah et al., *Habits of the Heart: Individualism and Commitment in American Life* (Berkeley: University of California Press, 1985).

33. LHL, *As It Is Written,* 80.

BIBLIOGRAPHY

Publications of Laura Holloway-Langford (Arranged Chronologically)

Books and Monographs

1869. L. C. H. *Laure: The History of a Blighted Life*. Philadelphia: Claxton, Remsen & Haffelfinger.

———. Laura Carter Holloway. *The Ladies of the White House*. New York: United States Publishing Co. Reprinted 1870 and 1872; 1875 under title *In the Home of the Presidents*.

1880. *The Ladies of the White House; or, In the Home of the Presidents. Being a Complete History of the Social and Domestic Lives of the Presidents from Washington to Hayes—1789–1880*. Philadelphia: Bradley & Co.

1881. *The Ladies of the White House; or, In the Home of the Presidents. Being a Complete History of the Social and Domestic Lives of the Presidents from Washington to the Present Time 1789–1881*. Philadelphia: Bradley & Co. Repr. AMS Press, 1976.

1882. Laura C. Holloway. *An Hour with Charlotte Brontë: or, Flowers from a Yorkshire Moor*. Philadelphia: J. W. Bradley, 1882. Repr. New York: Funk & Wagnalls.

1883. *Beyond the Sunrise. Observations by Two Travellers*. New York: John W. Lovell Company.

———. Laura C. Holloway. *The Hearthstone: Or, Life at Home: A Household Manual*. Philadelphia: Bradley & Co.

———. Laura C. Holloway. *The Mothers of Great Men and Women, and Some Wives of Great Men*. Baltimore, Md.: Wharton.

1884. Laura C. Holloway. *Famous American Fortunes and the Men Who Have Made Them: A Series of Sketches of Many of the Notable Merchants, Manufacturers, Capitalists, Railroad Presidents, Bonanza and Cattle Kings of the Country*. Philadelphia: Bradley & Co.

———. Laura C. Holloway. *Biographical Sketch of Charles Storrs, of Brooklyn, N. Y.* Philadelphia: Bradley & Co. Repr. from *Famous American Fortunes and the Men Who Have Made Them*.

———. L. C. Holloway. *The Home in Poetry*. Compiled by L. C. Holloway. New York: Funk & Wagnalls.

1885. Laura C. Holloway. *Adelaide Neilson: a Souvenir*. New York: Funk & Wagnalls.

———. Laura C. Holloway. *Chinese Gordon: The Uncrowned King, His Character as it is Portrayed in His Private Letters*. New York: Funk & Wagnalls.

———. [Ed. with Mohini Mohun Chatterji]. *Five Years of Theosophy: Mystical, Philosophical, Theosophical, Historical, and Scientific Essays Selected from The Theosophist*. London: Reeves and Turner.

———. Rose Elizabeth Cleveland. *George Eliot's Poetry and Other Studies*. New York: Funk & Wagnalls. [Mildred Lewis Rutherford, *The South in History and Literature: A Hand Book of Southern Authors* (1907), 413, claims that "Mrs. Holloway edited Miss Cleveland's 'Poems of George Eliot,'" and it seems likely that this is accurate.]

———. Laura C. Holloway. *Howard: The Christian Hero*. New York: Funk & Wagnalls.

———. Two Chelas in the Theosophical Society [LHL and Mohini Mohun Chatterji]. *Man: Fragments of Forgotten History*. London: Reeves and Turner.

———. Laura C. Holloway, ed. *Songs of the Master*. Philadelphia: J. W. Bradley.

1886. *The Ladies of the White House; or, In the Home of the Presidents. Being a Complete History of the Social and Domestic Lives of the Presidents from Washington to Cleveland—1789–1886*. New York: Funk & Wagnalls.

———. Laura C. Holloway. *The Buddhist Diet-Book*. New York: Funk & Wagnalls.

1888. Laura C. Holloway, ed. *The Woman's Story, as Told by Twenty American Women*. New York: J. B. Alden.

1891. *The Yoga Way*. New York: Eastern Publishing Company. [I have not been able to verify this publication or locate a copy, but it was advertised in several venues].

1893. Ed., with William Tomlins. *Children's Souvenir Songbook*. New York: Novello, Ewer, and Co.

1893–1894. Laura C. Holloway-Langford, co-editor, Department of Music. *A Standard Dictionary of the English Language*. New York: Funk & Wagnalls.

1903. Laura C. Holloway-Langford, Elizabeth P. Chapin, and Maude Ralston. *Atma Fairy Stories*. New York: Home Publishing Co.

———. Laura Holloway Langford. *The Magic Fan*. New York: O. Wissner. Repr. from *Atma Fairy Stories*.

[1904?]. Laura Holloway Langford. *How the Fairies Spent Christmas Eve*. New York: O. Wissner.

1904. Langford, Laura Holloway. *The Story of a Piano*. Brooklyn: O. Wissner.

1907. *As It is Written of Jesus the Christ. By The Helpers*. New York: Burr Printing House. Copyright S. E. Archer.

Periodical Publications and Contributions to Books

Laura Holloway-Langford wrote for many popular periodicals, often without attribution, and sometimes under the pseudonym, "S. E. Archer." I suspect that she used other pseudonyms. I know, for example, that she contributed to *Good Housekeeping* and *Drake's Magazine,* but it is difficult to identify specific articles that she authored.

1868. Mrs. L. C. Holloway. "The Angel Guide." *American Phrenological Journal and Life Illustrated* 48 (Dec.), 214.

1870. Laura C. Holloway. "The Duty of Mothers to Their Daughters." *The Phrenological Journal and Life Illustrated* 51 (Aug.): 101–102.

———. Laura C. Holloway. "A Prayer of Thanks." *The Phrenological Journal and Life Illustrated* 51 (Aug.): 137.

——. Laura C. Holloway. "The Women of the South." *The Phrenological Journal and Life Illustrated* 51 (Sept.): 208–209.

——. Laura C. Holloway, trans. "The Artist and His Master." Translated from the German. *The Phrenological Journal and Life Illustrated* 51 (Oct.): 257–258.

1871. L. C. H. "A Sketch of City Life." *The Phrenological Journal and Life Illustrated* 52 (March): 188–190.

1872. Laura C. Holloway. "The Homes of Famous Americans: Mount Vernon." *Phrenological Journal and Life Illustrated* 54 (April): 258–264.

——. Laura C. Holloway. "The Homes of Famous Americans: The Hermitage." *Phrenological Journal and Life Illustrated* 54 (May): 323–328.

——. Laura C. Holloway. "The Homes of Famous Americans: Monticello." *Phrenological Journal and Life Illustrated* 54 (June): 372–376.

1874. Laura C. Holloway. "Domestic Help." *Phrenological Journal and Life Illustrated* 58 (March): 172–174.

——. Laura C. Holloway. "Agnes Worth." *Phrenological Journal and Life Illustrated* 59 (July): 31–36.

——. Laura C. Holloway. "Personal Independence in Women." *Phrenological Journal and Life Illustrated* 59 (Nov.): 305–307.

1875. Laura C. Holloway. "Jane Hadley." *Phrenological Journal and Life Illustrated* 60 (Feb.): 100–104.

——. Laura C. Holloway. "Hettie Malvern." *Phrenological Journal and Life Illustrated* 61 (July): 24–26.

1884. Laura C. Holloway. "Our Forests and Tree Lore." *The Manhattan* 3 (March): 214–221.

1886. *Literary Life.* [For a few months in 1886, this journal was ed. Elizabeth Rose Cleveland and Laura Holloway-Langford.]

——. Laura C. Holloway. "Charles Storrs and the Storrs Genealogy." *Brooklyn Magazine* 4 (June): 119–122.

——. Laura C. Holloway. "Lady Burdett Coutts: Her Recent Birthday—In Good Health at Seventy-Two—Herself and Her Young Husband." *Frank Leslie's Popular Monthly* 22 (Aug.): 183–186.

——. "Teachings of the Master. Recorded by One of the Authors of 'Man: Fragments of Forgotten History,'" two installments. *The Path* 1 (Nov.): 253–256; 1 (Dec.): 278–281.

1887. Laura C. Holloway. "Miss Cleveland at Home." *Brooklyn Magazine* 4 (Jan.): 165–168.

——. S. E. Archer. "Some Famous Unequal Marriages." *Brooklyn Magazine* 4 (Jan.): 156–159. Repr. *The Daily Inter Ocean*, 23 Sept. 1888, 18.

——. Laura C. Holloway, ed. *The Lady's World. A Monthly Magazine of Home Literature* [Chicago] 1 (Jan.–May 1887); becomes *The Home Library Magazine: A Monthly Journal of Home Literature* 1 (June–Dec. 1887).

——. "Heredity and Practical Training." *The Lady's World. A Monthly Magazine of Home Literature* 1 (March): 140–141.

——. "The Children of the White House. President Washington's Family: The Custis Children." *The Lady's World: A Monthly Magazine of Home Literature* 1 (June): 307–309.

——. "How Women May Earn a Living." *The Lady's World: A Monthly Magazine of Home Literature* 1 (June): 315. [Continues a previous article, but I have not found extant copies of earlier issues.]

——. "Children of the White House. II." *The Home Library Magazine: A Monthly Journal of Home Literature* 1 (July): 383–384.

————. "Children of the White House. III." *The Home Library Magazine: A Monthly Journal of Home Literature* 1 (Aug.): 434.

————. "Ladies of Note. The Baroness Burdett-Coutts." *The Home Library Magazine: A Monthly Journal of Home Literature* 1 (Aug.): 438.

————. S. E. Archer. "A Day in an Old Holland Town." *The Home Library Magazine: A Monthly Journal of Home Literature* 1 (Nov.): 625–627.

————. "Mrs. Laura C. Holloway." In *Beecher Memorial: Contemporaneous Tributes to the Memory of Henry Ward Beecher,* ed. Edward W. Bok. Brooklyn, New York: Privately Printed, 1887, p. 54.

1888 [?]. "Daughters of America." *Drake's Magazine.* Clipping, Scrapbook 1888, DeWint.

1889. Laura C. Holloway. "Blavatsky's Mesmerism." *Current Literature* 2 (March): 243–244.

————. L. C. Holloway. "Buddhism vs. Christianity." *Current Literature* 2 (May): 379–381.

1890. L. C. H. "Mary Mathews Barnes." *The Magazine of Poetry* 2 (Jan.): 21.

————. Laura C. Holloway. "Memorial Day Story." "Annual Outing Number," *The Christian Union,* May 29.

1912. "Extracts from Man: Fragments of Forgotten History." *The Word* 14 (Feb.): 312–320.

————. "Madame Blavatsky: A Pen Picture by An American Newspaper Writer." *The Word* 14 (Feb.): 262–269.

————. "A Master and His Pupils—By One of Them," 4 installments. *The Word* 14 (Feb.): 286–295; 14 (March): 333–346; 15 (April): 33–39; 15 (May): 95–100.

————. "Extracts from Letters Written by William Q. Judge from Paris To A Long-Time Friend." *The Word* 14 (March): 324–332.

————. "Extracts from Letters Written By William Q. Judge from London in the Spring of 1884 To A Long-Time Friend." *The Word* 15 (April): 17–24.

————. S. E. Archer. "A Reincarnation Story. Strange Case of a Double Personality. Mite of a Girl Who Claims to be Two People." *The Word* 15 (April): 25–32.

————. L. C. L. "The Mahatmas and Their Instruments by L. C. L. Madame Blavatsky and the Masters—Precipitated Letters and Their Recipients," 2 installments. *The Word* 15 (May): 69–76; 15 (July) 200–206. Reprinted as: "Portraits of the Mahatmas," *The Path: A Theosophical Monthly* 3 (Oct.): 148–150. Reprinted as "The Portraits of the Two Masters," *The Theosophist* 69 (Sept. 1948): 365–370. These also appear in *Letters from the Masters of the Wisdom,* ed. C. Jinarajadasa, First Series, 4th ed., 201–215.

1915. "Colonel Olcott: A Reminiscence." (Oct.): 7–14. "Supplementary Letter." *The Word* 22 (Oct.): 14–19.

————. "William Quan Judge, A Reminiscence." *The Word* 22 (Nov.): 75–89.

————. "Helen Petrovna Blavatsky. A Reminiscence." *The Word* 22 (Dec.): 136–153.

1916–17. S. E. Archer and Laura C. Holloway-Langford. "Note Book of a Psychic." Published serially in *The Word,* Chapters 1–3 under the name S. E. Archer, and the remaining chapters under the name Laura C. Holloway Langford. Chapter 1, vol. 22 (March 1916): 342–352. Chapter 2, vol. 23 (April): 20–33. Chapter 3, vol. 23 (June): 135–149. Chapter 4, vol. 23 (July): 219–233. Chapter 5, vol. 23 (Aug.): 277–292. Chapter 6, vol. 23 (Sept.): 338–351. Chapter 7, vol. 24 (Oct.): 7–20. Chapter 8, vol. 24 (Nov.): 85–98. Chapter 9, vol. 24 (Dec.): 162–179. Chapter 10, vol. 24 (Jan. 1917): 199–213. Chapter 11, vol. 25 (March): 327–335. Chapter 12, vol. 25 (April): 37–52. Chapter 13, vol. 25 (May): 237–248. Chapter 14, vol. 25 (June): 237–248. Chapter 15, vol. 25 (Aug.): 297–306.

1917. "H. P. Blavatsky." *The Word* 25 (April): 70–81.

Newspaper Articles

Few of the many articles that Holloway Langford wrote for newspapers contained by-lines. Some can be attributed to her, however, because of references in other documents.

1873. L. C. H. "Mid-Autumn Fashions." *Brooklyn Daily Union*, Oct. 15.

1874. "Women. Work Being Done by Them in Brooklyn." *Brooklyn Daily Eagle*, Oct. 3, 2.

1875. "Andrew Johnson's Family." *Brooklyn Daily Eagle*, Feb. 24, 2,

———. "Dead. Ex-President Andrew Johnson." *Brooklyn Daily Eagle*, July 31, 4.

———. Laura C. Holloway. "Morning Land." *The Daily Inter Ocean*, Aug. 7, 7.

———. "Andrew Johnson's Family. The Marriage Yesterday of His Only Son—Recent Marriage of His Granddaughter." *Brooklyn Daily Eagle*, Nov. 26, 4.

1876. "The Death of Mrs. Andrew Johnson." *Brooklyn Daily Eagle*, Jan. 17, 2.

1878. "A Misjudged People." *Brooklyn Daily Eagle*, Jan. 20, 2.

———. "A Monument to Andrew Johnson." *Brooklyn Daily Eagle*, April 18, 2.

1881. "Suffragists. History of the Movement." *Brooklyn Daily Eagle*, June 20, 1.

1883. "Buddhism in India: Mr. Sinnett's *Esoteric Buddhism*." *Brooklyn Daily Eagle*, Sept. 23, 5.

1885. L. C. H. "The Ladies National Press Association." *Galveston Daily News*, May 19, 6.

1888. Laura C. Holloway. "Women upon the Stage. Why They Adopt the Dramatic Profession." *Morning Oregonian*, Feb. 19, 1.

———. Laura C. Holloway. "Margaret J. Preston. A Famous American Poet." *Washington Post*, Aug. 5, 11.

———. Laura C. Holloway. "Mrs. Gladstone. Incidents in the Life of a Worthy Helpmeet to a Great Man." *The Daily Inter Ocean*, Sept. 2.

———. Laura C. Holloway. "The Literary Women Who Religiously Stand by the Apostles' Creed." *The Galveston Daily News*, Sept. 18, 6.

———. Laura C. Holloway. "Unequal Marriages. The Romance of Strange Matches Made by People Well-Known in Society." *The Daily Inter Ocean*, Sept. 23, 18.

———. Laura C. Holloway. "Brother and Sister. A Pathetic Letter from Mrs. Stowe to Mrs. Beecher." *The Galveston Daily News*, Oct. 1, 2.

———. Laura C. Holloway. "The Theosophists. Something About Madame Blavatsky, the High Priestess of the Society. Her Approaching Visit to This Country with Colonel Henry S. Olcott. A Most Gifted Woman. Her Circle of Distinguished Friends in London." *The Leader*, Oct. 14, 14. Reprinted as "Hodgson's Karmic Destiny," *The Canadian Theosophist* 21 (Aug. 15, 1940): 179–180.

———. Laura C. Holloway. "The Theosophists. Laura S. [*sic*] Holloway Writes of Madame Blavatsky and Colonel Olcott." *The Daily Inter Ocean*, Oct. 14, 19.

———. Laura C. Holloway. "Psychic Phenomena. Laura C. Holloway Describes a Day with an Oriental Mystic." *The Daily Inter Ocean*, Oct. 28, 23.

———. Laura C. Holloway. "Would Women Vote? Over Thirty of Our Most Famous Women Answer the Question." *New Orleans Picayune*, Oct. 28, 13.

———. Laura C. Holloway. "Something about Cleopatra. Some Criticisms—A New Version of the Story of Lady Ellenborough." *The Galveston Daily News*, Nov. 21, 2.

———. Laura C. Holloway. "Ideas of Hereafter: Some Religious Views of Literary Women." *The Galveston Daily News*, Nov. 25, 10.

———. Laura C. Holloway. "A Woman on Cremation. She Believes a Higher Civilization Will Abolish Grave Yards." *Atchison Daily Champion,* Dec. 13, 7.

1891. Laura C. Holloway. "The Other Side: Some of the Many Industries Men Have Taken Away from Women." *Bismark Daily Tribune,* Feb. 3, 4 (reprinted from *Drake's Magazine*).

———. Laura C. Holloway Langford. "Anna Dickinson's Case." *New York Times,* March 8, 4.

1893. Laura Holloway Langford. "Christmas in the White House. How It Has Been Celebrated There During More Than Ninety Years." *L. A. Times,* Dec. 24.

1902. "How to Breathe." *Chat.* [A weekly newspaper published in Brooklyn. I have not been able to locate a copy of this article.]

1903. "Eldress Anna White on Temperance and Vegetarianism; Women's Hats and Children." MS, DeWint. [I have not been able to determine where this article was published.]

———. "Shakers Seek Tax Exemption." *Chatham Weekly Courier,* July 15.

———. "Shakers to Seek Relief. Will Ask the Legislature for Exemption from Taxes." *New York Sun,* Aug. 16.

1904. "Spirit Visitors to the Shakers at Mount Lebanon." *New York Sun,* Dec. 18.

1906. "Shakers of Mt. Lebanon Open Doors to City Children. Former Brooklyn Woman Senior Eldress of Interesting Colony." *The Daily Standard Union,* June 10.

1909. "Future of the Shakers. Their Members Dwindling, Their Wealth Large." *New York Sun,* April 11.

1910. "Obituary for Anna White." MS, DeWint. [I have not been able to confirm if this was published.]

Bibliography (Arranged Alphabetically)

Abbott, Lyman. "Sunday Afternoon. The Suffering Servant of the Lord.'" *Christian Union* 43 (23 April 1891): 541–543.

Albanese, Catherine L. "On the Matter of Spirit: Andrew Jackson Davis and the Marriage of God and Nature." *American Academy of Religion* 60, no. 1 (Spring 1992): 1–17.

———. *A Republic of Mind and Spirit: A Cultural History of American Metaphysical Religion.* New Haven, Conn.: Yale University Press, 2007.

Alexander, Thomas Benjamin. *Political Reconstruction in Tennessee.* New York: Russell & Russell, 1950.

Andrews, Edward Deming, and Faith Andrews. "The Shakers and Laura Langford." In *Fruits of the Shaker Tree of Life: Memoirs of Fifty Years of Collecting and Research,* 175–181. Stockbridge, Mass.: Berkshire Traveller Press.

Andrews, Stephen Pearl, Horace Greeley, and Henry James. *Love, Marriage and Divorce, and the Sovereignty of the Individual: A Discussion.* New York: Stringer & Townsend, 1853.

Annual Report of the Board of Railroad Commissioners, vol. 2. New York: Board of Railroad Commissioners, 1884.

Anrias, David [Brian Ross]. *Through the Eyes of the Masters: Meditations and Portraits.* London: George Routledge & Sons, Ltd., 1932.

Applegate, Debby. *The Most Famous Man in America: The Biography of Henry Ward Beecher.* New York: Doubleday, 2007.

Arnold, Edwin. *The Light of Asia; or, The Great Renunciation (Mahâbhinishkramana): Being the Life and Teachings of Gautama, Prince of India and Founder of Buddhism.* New York: A. L. Burt, 1879.

Arundale, Francesca. *My Guest—H. P. Blavatsky*. Adyar, India: Theosophical Publishing House, 1932.

Ashcraft, W. Michael. *The Dawn of the New Cycle: Point Loma Theosophists and American Culture*. Knoxville: The University of Tennessee Press, 2002.

Bachchan, Harbans Rai. *W. B. Yeats and Occultism: A Study of His Works in Relation to Indian Lore, the Cabbala, Swedenborg, Boehme, and Theosophy*. Delhi: Motilal Banarsidass, 1965.

Baille, Jean Baptiste Alexandre, and John W. Armstrong. *The Wonders of Electricity*. New York: Scribner, Armstrong, and Co., 1872.

Barker, A. Trevor, ed. *The Letters of H. P. Blavatsky to A. P. Sinnett*. London: T. Fisher Unwin Ltd., 1925. Repr. Pasadena, Calif.: Theosophical University Press, 1973.

———, ed. *The Mahatma Letters to A. P. Sinnett from the Mahatmas M. and K. H.* London: T. F. Unwin Ltd., 1923. Repr. Pasadena, Calif.: Theosophical University Press, 1975. Online edition at the Theosophical University Press Online: http://www.theosociety.org/pasadena/mahatma/ml-hp.htm. [The online edition is a facsimile of the 2nd ed. 1926 of *The Mahatma Letters*. It also incorporates material from Margaret Conger, *Combined Chronology for Use with the Mahatma Letters and the Letters of H. P. Blavatsky to A. P. Sinnett*. Pasadena, Calif.: Theosophical University Press, 1973.]

Bartholomeusz, Tessa J. "Real Life and Romance: The Life of Miranda de Souza Canavarro." *Journal of Feminist Studies in Religion* 10 (Fall 1994): 27–47.

Basch, Norma. *Framing American Divorce: From the Revolutionary Generation to the Victorians*. Berkeley: University of California Press, 1999.

Bednarowski, Mary Farrell. "Outside the Mainstream: Women's Religion and Women Religious Leaders in Nineteenth-Century America." *Journal of the American Academy of Religion* 48, no. 2 (June 1980): 207–231.

———. "Women in Occult America." In *The Occult in America: New Historical Perspectives*, ed. Howard Kerr and Charles L. Crow, 177–195. Urbana: University of Illinois Press, 1983.

Beecher, Catherine Esther, and Harriet Beecher Stowe. *The American Woman's Home: Or, Principles of Domestic Science: Being a Guide to the Formation and Maintenance of Economical, Healthful, Beautiful, and Christian Homes*. New York: J. B. Ford and Company, 1869.

Bellah, Robert N., Richard Madsen, William M. Sullivan, Ann Swidler, and Steven M. Tipton. *Habits of the Heart: Individualism and Commitment in American Life*. Berkeley: University of California Press, 1985.

Bender, Thomas. *New York Intellect: A History of Intellectual Life in New York City, from 1750 to the Beginnings of Our Own Time*. New York: Alfred A. Knopf, 1987.

Bevir, Mark. "The West Turns East: Madame Blavatsky and the Transformation of the Occult Tradition." *Journal of the American Academy of Religion* 62, no. 3 (Autumn 1994): 747–767.

Blair, Karen J. *The Club Woman as Feminist: True Womanhood Redefined, 1868–1914*. New York: Homes and Meier Publishers, 1980.

Blavatsky, Helena Petrovna. *Blavatsky: Collected Writings*. 15 vols. Ed. Boris de Zirkoff. Vol. 15, *Cumulative Index*, ed. Dara Eklund. Wheaton, Ill.: Theosophical Publishing House, 1950–1991. Also available on *Theosophical Classics* CD-ROM. Manila, Philippines: Theosophical Publishing House, 2003. The first four volumes previously appeared as *The Complete Works of H. P. Blavatsky*, ed. A. Trevor Barker, London: Rider, 1933–1936.

———. "Chelas." Blavatsky Online Study Center: http://www.blavatsky.net/blavatsky/ arts/Chelas.htm, repr. from *The Theosophist* (Oct. 1884).

———. "Chelas and Lay Chelas." *The Theosophist* 4 (supplement to no. 10, July 1883): 10–11.

———. *The Complete Works of H. P. Blavatsky,* 4 vols. Ed. A. Trevor Barker. London: Rider and Co., 1933–1936.

———. "Conversations on Occultism with H. P. B." *Blavatsky: Collected Writings,* vol. 5, comp. Boris de Zirkoff (Wheaton, Ill.: Theosophical Publishing House, 1940), 269.

———. "Elementaries." *Religio-Philosophical Journal* 23 (Nov. 1877), repr. in *Blavatsky: Collected Writings,* vol. 1, 265–271.

———. *The Esoteric Character of the Gospels.* Vol. 5 of *Studies in Occultism: Series of Reprints from the Writings of H. P. Blavatsky.* Boston: New England Theosophical Corporation, 1895.

———. "From Keshub Babu to Maestro Wagner via the Salvation Camp." *The Theosophist* 4 (Feb. 1883): 109–112.

———. "The Future Occultist." *The Theosophist* 5, no. 11 (Aug. 1884): 263–264.

———. *Isis Unveiled: A Master-Key to the Mysteries of Ancient and Modern Science and Theology.* New York: J. W. Bouton, 1877.

———. "Interview with Madame Blavatsky—Paris, 1884, with an Introduction and Notes by Michael Gomes." *The Canadian Theosophist* 67 (Nov./Dec. 1986): 98–103.

———. *The Letters of H. P. Blavatsky, 1861–1879,* vol. 1. Ed. John Algeo. Wheaton, Ill.: Quest Books, 2004.

———. "Lodges of Magic." In *Blavatsky: Collected Writings,* vol. 10, 129–130.

———. "Mr. Isaacs." *The Theosophist* 4, no. 5 (Feb. 1883), repr. in *Blavatsky: Collected Writings,* vol. 4, 339–344.

———. "Re-Classification of Principles." *The Theosophist* 8, no. 95 (Aug. 1887): 651–655.

———. *The Secret Doctrine: The Synthesis of Science, Religion, and Philosophy.* 2 vols. London: The Theosophical Publishing Company, Ltd., 1888.

———. *Some Letters of H. P. Blavatsky to W. Q. Judge.* Online edition at the Blavatsky Study Center: http://www.blavatskyarchives.com/hpbwqjtab.html. Transcribed from the "Helena Petrovna Blavatsky Letters," Andover-Harvard Theological Library, bMS34, by Dara Eklund and Nicholas Weeks, 1999.

Blight, David W. *Race and Reunion: The Civil War in American Memory.* Cambridge, Mass.: Belknap Press of Harvard University Press, 2001.

Bok, Edward W., ed. *Beecher Memorial: Contemporaneous Tributes to the Memory of Henry Ward Beecher.* Brooklyn, New York: Privately Printed, 1887.

Braude, Ann. *Radical Spirits: Spiritualism and Women's Rights in Nineteenth-Century America,* 2nd ed. Bloomington: Indiana University Press, 2001.

Brewer, Priscilla J. *Shaker Communities, Shaker Lives.* Hanover, N.H.: University Press of New England, 1986.

[Britten], Emma Hardinge. *Modern American Spiritualism: A Twenty Years' Record of the Communion Between Earth and the World of the Spirits.* New York: Published by the Author, 1870.

———. *The Place and Mission of Women.* Boston: Hubbard W. Swett, 1859.

Burfield, Diana. "Theosophy and Feminism: Some Explorations in Nineteenth Century Biography." In *Women's Religious Experience,* ed. Pat Holden, 27–56. London: Croom Helm Ltd, 1983.

Caldwell, Daniel H., ed. *The Esoteric World of Madame Blavatsky: Insights into the Life of a Modern Sphinx.* Wheaton, Ill.: Theosophical Publishing House, 2000.

———, ed. "Mrs. Holloway and the Mahatmas: Published and Unpublished Mahatma Letters." Online edition, copyright 2000, at the Blavatsky Study Center:. http://www
.blavatskyarchives.com/ml.htm.

Campbell, Bruce F. *Ancient Wisdom Revived: A History of the Theosophical Movement.*
Berkeley: University of California Press, 1980.

Carter, William Giles Harding. *Giles Carter of Virginia: Genealogical Memoir.* Baltimore,
Md.: The Lord Baltimore Press, 1909.

Carus, Paul. *The Gospel of Buddha According to Old Records.* Chicago: Open Court Publishing Co., 1898.

Champlin, John Denison, Jr., and William Foster Apthorp, eds. *Cyclopedia of Music and
Musicians.* Vol. 3. New York: Charles Scribner's Sons, 1893.

Chatterji, Mohini Mohun. *The Bhagavad Gîtâ: or The Lord's Lay: With Commentary and
Notes, as well as References to the Christian Scriptures.* Boston: Ticknor and Company,
1887.

———. *Crest Jewel of Wisdom of Shree Shankaracharya.* Bombay: Rajaram Tukaram for the
Theosophical Publication Fund, 189?

———. "Discrimination of Spirit and Not-Spirit." *The Theosophist* 4 (Nov. 1882) and 5
(Dec. 1883); repr. in [LHL and Chatterji] *Five Years of Theosophy,* 394–407.

———. "Duty and Sacrifice." *The Lady's World* [Chicago] 1 (March 1887): 138.

———. "The Himalayan Brothers—Do They Exist?" *The Theosophist* 5 (Dec. 1883). Repr. in
[LHL and Mohini Mohun Chatterji, ed.], *Five Years of Theosophy: Mystical, Philosophical, Theosophical, Historical, and Scientific Essays Selected from The Theosophist* (London:
Reeves & Turner, 1885), 459–469.

———. *History as a Science.* London: Butterworth, 1927.

———. "The Homesick." *The Word* 15 (April 1912): 39

———. *Indian Spirituality: or, the Travels and Teachings of Sivanarayan.* London: Luzac &
Co., 1907.

———, *The Language of Symbols.* London: Theosophical Publication Society, 1894.

———, and LHL. "Two Chelas in the Theosophical Society." *Man: Fragments of Forgotten
History.* London: Reeves and Turner, 1885.

———. *Manual of Deductive Logic.* Calcutta: Thacker, Spink & Co., 1906.

———. "Matter and Force, from the Hindu Standpoint." *The Theosophist* 4 (Dec. 1882): 66–67.

———. "On the Higher Aspect of Theosophical Studies." *The Theosophist* 6 (March 1885):
140–144.

———. "Theories in Comparative Mythology." *The Theosophist* 8 (Jan. 1887): 193–204.

———. "Transcendental Senses." *The Theosophist* 6 (June 1885): 217–219.

Chesley, E. M. "Universal Brotherhood. A Voice from the East." *Christian Union* 35 (April
14, 1887): 6.

Cleather, Alice Leighton. *H. P. Blavatsky as I Knew Her: Her Life and Work for Humanity. A
Great Betrayal.* Calcutta: Thacker, Spink & Co., 1923.

Cleather, Alice Leighton and Basil Woodward Crump. *Parsifal, Lohengrin, and The Legend
of the Holy Grail.* New York: G. Schirmer, 1904.

Colbert, Don. *What Would Jesus Eat: The Ultimate Program for Eating Well, Feeling Great,
and Living Longer.* Nashville: Thomas Nelson, 2003.

Collet, Sophia Dobson, ed. *The Life and Letters of Raja Rammohun Roy,* 2nd ed. London:
Harold Collet, 1914.

Collins, Mabel. *Light on the Path: A Treatise Written for the Personal Use of Those Who are
Ignorant of the Eastern Wisdom, and Who Desire to Enter within its Influence. Written*

down by M. C. Boston: Cupples, Upham and Co., 1886. Repr. with Special Permission, New York: Aryan Theosophical Society, 3rd ed.

Conger, Margaret. *Combined Chronology for Use with the Mahatma Letters and the Letters of H. P. Blavatsky to A. P. Sinnett.* Pasadena, Calif.: Theosophical University Press, 1973.

Conway, Moncure Daniel. *My Pilgrimage to the Wise Men of the East.* Boston: Houghton, Mifflin and Co., 1906.

Corelli, Marie. *A Romance of Two Worlds.* London: Bentley, 1886.

Coudert, Allison P. "Angel in the House or Idol of Perversity? Women in Nineteenth-century Esotericism." *Esoterica* 9 (2007): 8–48.

Crabb, Alfred Leland. *Nashville: Personality of a City.* Indianapolis: The Bobbs-Merrill Co., Inc., 1960.

Cranston, Sylvia. *HPB: The Extraordinary Life & Influence of Helena Blavatsky, Founder of the Modern Theosophical Movement.* New York: G. P. Putnam's Sons, 1993.

Crawford, Francis Marion. *Mr. Isaacs: A Tale of Modern India.* New York: Grosset & Dunlap, 1882.

Croly, Jane Cunningham. *The History of the Woman's Club Movement in America.* New York: H. G. Allen and Co., 1898.

Dalton, Lisle Woodruff. "Between the Enlightenment and Public Protestantism: Religion and the American Phrenological Movement." Ph.D. diss., University of California, Santa Barbara, 1998.

Davenport, Francis Garvin. *Cultural Life in Nashville on the Eve of the Civil War.* Ph.D. diss., Vanderbilt University, 1936.

Davis, Andrew Jackson. *The Great Harmonia: Being a Philosophical Revelation of the Natural, Spiritual, and Celestial Universe.* New York: J. S. Redfield, 1850.

———. *A Stellar Key to the Summer Land.* Boston: William White and Company, 1868.

Denton, Lynn Teskey. *Female Ascetics in Hinduism.* Albany: State University of New York Press, 2004.

Deveney, John Patrick. "An 1876 Lecture by W. Q. Judge on His Magical Progress in the Theosophical Society." *Theosophical History: A Quarterly Journal of Research* 9 (July 2003): 12–20.

———. *Paschal Beverly Randolph: A Nineteenth-Century Black American Spiritualist, Rosicrucian, and Sex Magician.* Albany: State University of New York Press, 1997.

Dixon, Joy. *Divine Feminine: Theosophy and Feminism in England.* Baltimore, Md.: Johns Hopkins University Press, 2001.

———. "Sexology and the Occult: Sexuality and Subjectivity in Theosophy's New Age." *Journal of the History of Sexuality* 7, no. 3 (Jan. 1997): 409–433.

Eddy, Mary Baker. *Science and Health With Key to the Scriptures.* Bedford, Mass.: Applewood Books, 1875.

Eek, Sven, ed. *Damodar and the Pioneers of the Theosophical Movement.* Adyar, India: The Theosophical Publishing House, 1965.

Elias, Jamal J. *Death Before Dying: The Sufi Poems of Sultan Bahu.* Berkeley: University of California Press, 1998.

Ellis, Havelock. *Little Essays of Love and Virtue.* New York: George H. Doran Company, 1922.

Ellis, William Ashton. "Wagner's 'Parsifal.'" *The Theosophist* 8 (Dec. 1886): 162–169; 8 (Jan. 1887): 222–228.

Ellwood, Robert S. "The American Theosophical Synthesis." In *Occult in America: New Historical Perspectives,* ed. Howard Kerr and Charles L. Crow, 111–134. Urbana, Ill.: University of Illinois Press, 1983.

Ellwood, Robert S., and Catherine Wessinger. "The Feminism of 'Universal Brotherhood': Women in the Theosophical Movement." In *Women's Leadership in Marginal Religions: Explorations Outside the Mainstream,* ed. Catherine Wessinger, 68–87. Urbana, Ill.: University of Illinois Press, 1993.

Escobar, Deborah. "Shakers and Their Participation in the Peace Movement, 1870–1905." Honors Thesis. Russell Sage College, Troy, New York, 1990.

Evans, Frederick W. "Autobiography of a Shaker." *Atlantic Monthly* 23 (1869): 415–426, 593–605.

Faderman, Lillian. *Odd Girls and Twilight Lovers: A History of Lesbian Life in Twentieth-Century America.* New York: Columbia University Press, 1991.

———. *To Believe in Women: What Lesbians Have Done for America—A History.* New York: Houghton Mifflin, 1999.

Fales, Imogene C. "The New Age." *Religio-Philosophical Journal,* 31 May 1884, 6.

———. *The Religion of the Future.* Boston: Esoteric Publishing Company, 1889.

Finck, Henry Theophilus. *Anton Seidl: A Memorial by His Friends.* New York: Charles Scribner's Sons, 1899.

Fowler, Orson S., and Lorenzo N. Fowler. *New Illustrated Self-Instructor in Phrenology and Physiology; with Over One Hundred Engravings.* New York: Fowler and Wells, 1868.

Funk, Isaac Kaufman. *The Widow's Mite and Other Psychic Phenomena.* New York and London: Funk & Wagnalls Company, 1904.

Ganachari, Aravind. *Nationalism and Social Reform in a Colonial Situation.* Delhi: Kalpaz Publications, 2005.

Garrigues, John, ed. *The Theosophical Movement 1875–1925: A History and a Survey.* New York: E. P. Dutton & Company, 1925. Online edition at the Blavatsky Study Center: http://www.blavatskyarchives.com/garrtc.htm

Gere, Anne Ruggles. *Intimate Practices: Literacy and Cultural Work in U. S. Women's Clubs, 1880–1920.* Urbana: University of Illinois Press, 1997.

Godwin, Joscelyn. *The Theosophical Enlightenment.* Albany: New York State University Press, 1990.

Goldsmith, Barbara. *Other Powers. The Age of Suffrage, Spiritualism, and the Scandalous Victoria Woodhull.* New York: Alfred A. Knopf, 1998.

Gomes, Michael. "Abner Doubleday and Theosophy in America, 1879–1884." *Sunrise Magazine,* April–May 1991. Online editions available from the Theological University Press Online: http://www.theosociety.org/pasadena/sunrise.

———. *The Dawning of the Theosophical Movement.* Wheaton, Ill.: Theosophical Publishing House, 1987.

———. *Theosophy in the Nineteenth-Century: An Annotated Bibliography.* New York and London: Garland Publishing Co., 1994.

Goodrick-Clarke, Nicholas. *The Western Esoteric Traditions: A Historical Introduction.* New York: Oxford University Press, 2008.

Green, Stephanie. "Oscar Wilde's *The Woman's World.*" *Victorian Periodicals Review* 30, no. 2 (Summer 1997): 102–120.

Gutierrez, Cathy. "The Elusive Isis: Theosophy and the Mirror of Millennialism." In *The End That Does: Art, Science, and Millennial Accomplishment,* Millennialism and Society 3, ed. Cathy Gutierrez and Hillel Schwartz, 119–137. London: Equinox, 2006.

Harper, Ida Husted. *Life and Work of Susan B. Anthony.* 3 vols. New York: Arno Press, 1969.

Harris, Thomas Lake. *A Lyric of the Morning Land.* New York: Partridge and Brittan, 1856.

Hellman, George S. *Lanes of Memory.* New York: Alfred A. Knopf, 1927.

Henderson, William James. *Preludes and Studies: Musical Themes of the Day.* London: Longmans, Green, and Co., 1891.

——. *Richard Wagner, His Life and Dramas: A Biographical Study of the Man and an Explanation of His Work.* New York: G. P. Putnam's Sons, 1901.

Higginson, Thomas Wentworth. "The Buddhist Path of Virtue." *The Radical* 8 (June 1871): 358–362.

——. "The Character of Buddha." *Index* 3 (March 16, 1872): 81–83.

——. "The Sympathy of Religions." *The Radical* 8 (Feb. 1871): 1–23.

Hodgson, Richard. "Account of Personal Investigations in India, and Discussion of the Authorship of the 'Koot Hoomi' Letters." *Proceedings of the Society for Psychical Research* 3 (1885): 207–317 + 15 Appendices, 318–380.

Holland, Patricia G., and Ann D. Gordon, eds. *The Papers of Elizabeth Cady Stanton and Susan B. Anthony.* Microfilm. Wilmington, Del., Scholarly Resources, 1991.

Horowitz, Joseph. *Wagner Nights: An American History.* Berkeley: University of California Press, 1994.

Howard, Oliver Otis. *Autobiography of General Oliver Otis Howard, Major General United States Army.* New York: The Baker & Taylor Co., 1907.

Iacobbo, Karen and Michael Iacobbo. *Vegetarian America: A History.* Westport, Conn.: Praeger Publishers, 2004.

Jackson, Carl T. *The Oriental Religions and American Thought: Nineteenth-Century Explorations.* Westport, Conn.: Greenwood Press, 1981.

——. *Vedanta for the West: The Ramakrishna Movement in the United States.* Bloomington: Indiana University Press, 1994.

Jackson, John P. *The Bayreuth of Wagner.* New York: J. W. Lovell Co., 1891.

Jacobi, Mary Putnam. *The Question of Rest for Women During Menstruation.* New York: G. P. Putnam's Sons, 1877.

James, Henry. *The Bostonians.* New York: The Century Co., 1884.

——. "Spiritualism, Modern Diabolism." *Atlantic Monthly* 32 (August 1873): 219–224.

——. "Spiritualism, New and Old." *Atlantic Monthly* 29 (March 1872): 358–362.

Jeffares, Alexander Norman. *W. B. Yeats: Man and Poet.* New Haven, Conn.: Yale University Press, 1949.

Jinarajadasa, C., ed. *The "K. H." Letters to C. W. Leadbeater.* Kessinger's Publishing Photocopy Edition: 2010. Originally published Madras, India: Theosophical Publishing House, 1941.

——, comp. *Letters from the Masters of the Wisdom,* 2 series. Series 1: 6th ed. Adyar, India: Theosophical Publishing House, 1988. Series 2: 1st ed. Adyar, India: Theosophical Publishing House, 1925. Both series also available as part of *Theosophical Classics,* CD-ROM. Manila, Philippines: Theosophical Publishing House, 2003.

John, Angela V. *Elizabeth Robins: Staging a Life, 1862–1952.* London: Routledge, 1995.

Johnson, Andrew. *Index to the Andrew Johnson Papers.* Washington, D.C.: Library of Congress Manuscript Division, 1963.

——. *The Papers of Andrew Johnson.* 16 vols. Ed. Leroy P. Graf, Ralph W. Haskins, and Paul H. Bergeron. Knoxville: University of Tennessee Press, 1967–2000.

Johnson, K. Paul. *The Masters Revealed: Madame Blavatsky and the Myth of the Great White Lodge.* Albany: State University of New York Press, 1994.

Judge, William Q. "Letters of W. Q. Judge," published serially in *The Theosophist.* Vol. 52 (Jan. 1931): 208–214; vol. 52 (Feb. 1931): 321–326; vol. 52 (March 1931): 458–464; vol. 52

(May 1931): 191–197; vol. 52 (June 1931): 355–358; vol. 52 (Sept. 1931): 752–756; vol. 53 (Oct. 1931): 67–69; vol. 53 (Nov. 1931): 196–202; vol. 53 (Dec. 1931): 304–308.

———. *The Ocean of Theosophy*, 11th ed. Los Angeles, Calif.: The United Lodge of Theosophists, 1922.

———. *Practical Occultism: From the Private Letters of William Q. Judge*. Ed. Arthur L. Conger. Pasadena, Calif.: Theosophical University Press, 1951. Online Edition at Theosophical University Press Online: http://www.theosociety.org/pasadena/prac-oc/po-hp.htm

Keenan, Claudia J. "Laura Carter Holloway Langford, 1843–1930." *Tennessee Encyclopedia of History and Culture*. http://tennesseeencyclopedia.net.

———. "Laura Carter Holloway and the First Lady's Story." *White House Studies* 8, no. 4 (2009): 467–488.

King, Richard. *Orientalism and Religion: Postcolonial Theory, India, and 'The Mystic East.'* London: Routledge, 1999.

Kingsford, Anna, and Edward Maitland. *The Perfect Way: or, the Finding of Christ*. London: Field & Tuer, 1882.

Kingston, Angela. *Oscar Wilde as a Character in Victorian Fiction*. New York: Palgrave Miller, 2007.

Kitch, Carolyn. "Women in Journalism." In *American Journalism: History, Principles, Practices*, ed. W. David Sloan and Lisa Mullikin Parcell, 87–89. Jefferson, N.C.: McFarland & Co., 2002.

Knoche, Grace F. "Our Directives, Study of the Evolution of the 'Objects of the T.S.' — from 1875 to 1891." *The Theosophical Forum* 25 (Oct. 1947): 582–587. Available at the Theosophical University Press Online: http://www.theosociety.org/pasadena/gfkforum/ourdir.htm.

Kraft, Siv Ellen. "The Sex Problem: Political Aspects of Gender Discourse in the Theosophical Society 1875–1930." Thesis. University of Bergen IKRR, Dept. of the History of Religions, 1999.

Kramarae, Cheris, and Lana F. Rakow, eds. *The Revolution in Words: Righting Women, 1868–1871*. Vol. 4 of *Women's Source Library*. London: Routledge, 1990.

Krehbiel, Henry E. *Review of the New York Musical Season 1885–1886*. New York: Novello, Ewer & Co., 1886.

———. *Studies in the Wagnerian Drama*. New York: Harper & Brothers, 1891.

Kufferath, Maurice. *The Parsifal of Richard Wagner*. With an introduction by Henry E. Krehbiel. New York: Henry Holt and Co., 1904.

Kuhn, Alvin Boyd. *Theosophy: A Modern Revival of Ancient Wisdom*. New York: H. Holt and Company, 1930.

Leach, William. *True Love and Perfect Union: The Feminist Reform of Sex and Society*. New York: Basic Books, Inc., 1980.

Leadbeater, Charles W. *How Theosophy Came to Me*. Madras: Theosophical Publishing House, 1930.

Lundbom, Jack R. *Master Painter Warner E. Sallman*. Macon, Ga.: Mercer University Press, 1999.

Machoian, Ronald G. *William Harding Carter: A Soldier's Story*. Norman: University of Oklahoma Press, 2006.

The Mahatma Letters to A. P. Sinnett, Chronological Edition. Theosophical Classics. CD-ROM. Annotated by Virgina Hanson. Manila, Philippines: Theosophical Publishing

House, 2003. [This text follows the revised edition by Humphreys and Elsie Benjamin from originals in the British Museum. Adyar: Theosophical Publishing House, 3rd. rev. ed., 1962, 1972, 1979.]

Maines, Rachel P. *The Technology of Orgasm: "Hysteria," the Vibrator, and Women's Sexual Satisfaction*. Baltimore, Md.: The Johns Hopkins University Press, 1999.

Mater, Kirby Van. "William Quan Judge: A Biographical Sketch." *Sunrise Magazine,* April–May, 1996. Available at: http://www.theosophy-nw.org/theosnw/theos/th-kvmj. htm.

McGarry, Molly. *Ghosts of Futures Past: Spiritualism and the Cultural Politics of Nineteenth-Century America*. Berkeley: University of California Press, 2008.

Meade, Marion. *Madame Blavatsky: The Woman behind the Myth*. New York: G. P. Putnam's Sons, 1980.

Miller, Eli P. *Vital Force: How Wasted and How Preserved*. New York: Miller, Haynes, & Co., 1872.

Moore, R. Laurence. *In Search of White Crows: Spiritualism, Parapsychology, and American Culture*. New York: Oxford University Press, 1977.

Nelson, Anson. "Brief Annals of Nashville from Its Foundation to 1875." In *Old Times in Tennessee: With Historical, Personal, and Political Scraps and Sketches,* ed. Jo. C. Guild. Nashville: Tavel, Eastman, & Howell, 1878.

Neresheimer, Emil August. *Some Reminiscences of William Q. Judge*. Online edition, 2003, at the Blavatsky Online Study Center: http://www.blavatskyarchives.com/stokesneres. htm.

Olcott, Henry Steel. *Old Diary Leaves*. 6 vols. Adyar: The Theosophical Publishing House, 1974–1975. [First published 1895–1935.]

———. *People from the Other World*. Hartford, Conn.: American Publishing Company, 1875.

Owen, Alex. *The Darkened Room: Women, Power, and Spiritualism in Late Victorian England*. Philadelphia: University of Pennsylvania Press, 1990.

———. *The Place of Enchantment: British Occultism and the Culture of the Modern*. Chicago: University of Chicago Press, 2004.

Paránanda, Sri [Ponnambalam Ramanâthan]. *The Culture of the Soul Among Western Nations*. New York: G. W. Putnam's Sons, 1906.

———. *An Eastern Exposition of the Gospel of Jesus According to St. John*. Ed. R. L. Harrison. London: William Hutchinson & Co., 1902.

———. *An Eastern Exposition of the Gospel of Jesus According to St. Matthew*. Ed. R. L. Harrison. London: Kegan Paul, 1898.

Parke, David B., ed. *The Epic of Unitarianism: Original Writings from the History of Liberal Religion*. Boston: Skinner House Books, 1957.

Parton, Sara Payson Willis [Fannie Fern]. *Ruth Hall: A Domestic Tale of the Present Time*. New York: Mason Brothers, 1855.

Passett, Joanne E. *Sex Radicals and the Quest for Women's Equality*. Urbana: University of Illinois Press, 2003.

Paterwic, Stephen J. *Historical Dictionary of the Shakers*. Lanham, Md.: The Scarecrow Press, Inc., 2008.

Peebles, J[ames]. M[artin]. *Around the World: or, Travels in Polynesia, China, India, Arabia, Egypt, Syria, and Other "Heathen" Countries,* 2nd ed. Boston: Colby and Rich, 1875.

———. *Seers of the Ages: Embracing Spiritualism, Past and Present. Doctrines Stated and Moral Tendencies Defined*. Boston: William White and Company, 1869.

Pelletier, Ernest E. *The Judge Case: A Conspiracy Which Ruined the Theosophical Cause*. Edmonton, Canada: Edmonton Theosophical Society, 2004.

Phillips, Stephen, and Galloway Kyle. *The Poetry Review*. London: Poetry Society, 1934.

Praed, Rosa Campbell. *Affinities: A Romance of To-day*. Revised ed. London: George Routledge & Sons, 1886.

———. *The Brother of the Shadow: A Mystery of To-day*. London: George Routledge & Sons, 1886.

Prindle, Frances Weston Carruth. *Fictional Rambles In & About Boston*. New York: McClure, Phillips, and Company, 1902.

Prothero, Stephen. "From Spiritualism to Theosophy: 'Uplifting' a Democratic Tradition." *Religion and American Culture* 3 (Summer 1993): 197–216.

Puskar-Pasewicz, Margaret. "Kitchen Sisters and Disagreeable Boys: Debates over Meatless Diets in Nineteenth-Century Shaker Communities." In *Eating in Eden: Food and American Utopias*, ed. Etta M. Madden and Martha L. Finch, 109–124. Lincoln: University of Nebraska Press, 2006.

Putnam, Ruth, ed. *Life and Letters of Mary Putnam Jacobi*. New York: G. P. Putnam's Sons, 1925.

Ralston, Maude. "The Secret of Power." *Theosophical Forum* 4 (April 1899): 12.

Ransom, Josephine. *A Short History of the Theosophical Society*. Adyar, India: Theosophical Publishing House: 1938. Repr. Adyar, India: The Theosophical Publishing House, 2007.

Reynolds, David S. *Walt Whitman's America: A Cultural Biography*. New York: Alfred A. Knopf, 1995.

Rogers, Clara Kathleen. *The Story of Two Lives: Home, Friends, and Travels*. Norwood, Mass.: Plimpton Press, 1932.

Santucci, James A. "The Notion of Race in Theosophy." *Nova Religio: The Journal of Alternative and Emergent Religions* 2, no. 3 (2008): 37–63.

———. "Women in the Theosophical Movement." *Explorations: Journal for Adventurous Thought* 9, no. 1 (Fall 1990): 71–94. Online edition at: http://www.theohistory.org/womenints.html.

Sasson, Diane. "'Dear Friend and Sister': Laura Holloway-Langford and the Shakers." *American Communal Societies Quarterly* 1, no. 4 (Oct. 2007): 170–190.

———. "The Self Inventions of Laura Carter Holloway." *Tennessee Historical Quarterly* 67, no. 3 (Fall 2008): 178–207.

Scanlon, Jennifer, and Sharon Cosner. *American Women Historians, 1700s–1990s: A Biographical Dictionary*. Westport, Conn.: Greenwood Publishing Group, 1996.

Schmidt, Leigh. *Restless Souls: The Making of American Spirituality*. San Francisco: HarperSanFrancisco, 2005.

Scott, Anne Firor. *Natural Allies: Women's Associations in American History*. Urbana: University of Illinois Press, 1991.

Scott, J. Barton. "Miracle Publics: Theosophy, Christianity, and the Coulomb Affair." *History of Religions* 49, no. 2 (2009): 172–196.

Sears, Hal D. *The Sex Radicals: Free Love in High Victorian America*. Lawrence: University Press of Kansas, 1977.

Sessa, Anne Dzamba. *Richard Wagner and the English*. Cranberry, N.J.: Associated University Presses, 1979.

Sinnett, Alfred Percy. *The Early Days of Theosophy in Europe*. London: Theosophical Publishing House, 1922.

————. *Esoteric Buddhism*. London: Trübner and Co., 1883.

————. *Incidents in the Life of Madame Blavatsky*. London: G. Redway, 1886.

————. *Karma, A Novel*. 2 vols. London: Chapman and Hall, 1885.

————. *The Occult World*. London: Trübner and Co., 1881.

————. *The Rationale of Mesmerism*. Boston: Houghton Mifflin and Company, 1892.

Sircar, Jayanta K. "The Vedanta Society of New York. A Review of the First Century." *Bulletin of the Ramakrishna Mission Institute of Culture* 48 (1997): 240–249; 294–305.

Sloan, John. *Oscar Wilde*. Oxford: Oxford University Press, 2003.

Smith-Rosenberg, Carroll. "The New Woman as Androgyne: Social Disorder and Gender Crisis, 1870–1936." In *Disorderly Conduct: Visions of Gender in Victorian America*, 245–296. New York: Alfred A. Knopf, 1985.

Society for Psychical Research. "First Report of the Committee of the Society for Psychical Research, Appointed to Investigate the Evidence for Marvellous [*sic*] Phenomena Offered by Certain Members of the Theosophical Society." London: n. p., 1884. Reproduced by permission of the Society for Psychical Research, London, at Blavatskty Study Center Online: http://www.blavatskyarchives.com/sprrpcontents.htm.

————. "Report of The Committee Appointed to Investigate Phenomena Connected with the Theosophical Society." *Proceedings of the Society for Psychical Research* 3 (1885): 201–207.

————. "Report of the General Meeting," *Journal of the Society for Psychical Research* (June, July 1885): 420–424, 451–460.

Solovyov, Vsevolod S. *A Modern Priestess of Isis*. Abridged and translated by Walter Leaf. London: Longmans, Green, and Co., 1895. Repr. New York: Arno Press, 1976.

Steiger, Isabelle de. *Memorabilia: Reminiscences of a Woman Artist and Writer*. London: Rider & Co.: 1927.

Stein, Stephen J. *The Shaker Experience in America: A History of the United Society of Believers*. New Haven, Conn.: Yale University Press, 1992.

Stephens, C. A. *Natural Salvation: The Message of Science, Outlining the First Principles of Immortal Life on the Earth*. Norway Lake, Maine: The Laboratory, 1903.

Stern, Madeleine B. *Heads & Headlines: The Phrenological Fowlers*. Norman: University of Oklahoma Press, 1971.

Stowe, Mrs. H. B. "Spiritualism." *The Phrenological Journal and Life Illustrated* 51 (Nov. 1870): 351–357.

Sutin, Lawrence. *Do What Thou Wilt: A Life of Aleister Crowley*. New York: St. Martin's Press, 2000.

Sword, Helen. "Necrobibliography: Books in the Spirit World." *Modern Language Quarterly* 60 (March 1999): 85–113.

Taylor, Leila S. *A Memorial to Eldress Anna White and Elder Daniel Offord*. Mount Lebanon, N. Y.: North Family of Shakers, 1912.

Tetrault, Lisa. "The Incorporation of American Feminism: Suffragists and the Postbellum Lyceum." *The Journal of American History* 96, no. 4 (March 2010): 1027–1056.

Thackray, E. A. "Mrs. Laura Holloway Langford." *The Writer: A Monthly Magazine for Literary Workers* 5 (June 1891): 119–120.

Theosophical Classics. CD-ROM. Manila, Philippines: Theosophical Publishing House, 2003.

[Theosophical Society]. *Rules of the Theosophical Society, Together with an Explanation of Its Objects and Principles*. Madras, India: Printed at the Scottish Press, 1884.

Thomas, John L. *Alternative America: Henry George, Edward Bellamy, Henry Demarest Lloyd, and the Adversary Tradition*. Cambridge, Mass.: Harvard University Press, 1983.

Thurman, Suzanne. "Shaker Women and Sexual Power: Heresy and Orthodoxy in the Shaker Village of Harvard, Massachusetts." *Journal of Women's History* 10 (Spring 1998): 70–87.

Tomlins, William, ed. *Children's Souvenir Songbook*. New York: Novello, Ewer, and Co., 1893.

Trall, Russell T. *The New Hydropathic Cookbook: With Recipes for Cooking on Hygienic Principles*. New York: Fowler and Wells, 1854.

Treitel, Corinna. *A Science for the Soul: Occultism and the Genesis of the German Modern*. Baltimore, Md.: Johns Hopkins University Press, 2004.

Trevithick, Alan. "The Theosophical Society and Its Subaltern Acolytes." *Marburg Journal of Religion* 13, no. 1 (May 2008): 1–32.

Tromp, Marlene. "Spirited Sexuality: Sex, Marriage, and Victorian Spiritualism." *Victorian Literature and Culture* (2003): 67–81.

Truman, Benjamin C. "Anecdotes of Andrew Johnson." *Century Magazine* 85 (1913): 437–438.

Tweed, Thomas A. *The American Encounter with Buddhism, 1844–1912: Victorian Culture and the Limits of Dissent*. Bloomington: Indiana University Press, 1992.

Tumber, Catherine. *American Feminism and the Birth of New Age Spirituality: Searching for the Higher Self, 1875–1915*. Lanhan, Md.: Rowman & Littlefield Publishers Inc., 2002.

Viswanathan, Gauri. "The Ordinary Business of Occultism." *Critical Inquiry* 27 (Autumn 2000): 1–20.

Vivekananda, Swami. "Address at the World Parliament of Religions . . . 11 September 1893." In *The Complete Works of Swami Vivekananda*, pt. 1, 2nd ed. Almora, Himalayas: Advaita Ashram, 1915.

Walker, Steven F. "Vivekananda and American Occultism." In *The Occult in America: New Historical Perspectives*, ed. Howard Kerr and Charles L. Crow, 162–176. Urbana: University of Illinois Press, 1983.

Ward, William C. *The Art of Richard Wagner*. London: The Theosophical Publishing Society, 1906.

Watson, Blanche. *Gandhi and Non-violent Resistance: The Non-co-operation Movement of India. Gleanings from the American Press*. Madras: Ganesh & Co., 1923.

Wells, Samuel R. *Wedlock; or, the Right Relations of the Sexes: Disclosing the Laws of Conjugal Selection, and Showing Who May, and Who May Not Marry*. New York: S. R. Wells, 1869.

Wessinger, Catherine. "Democracy vs. Hierarchy: The Evolution of Authority in the Theosophical Society." In *When Prophets Die*, ed. Timothy Miller, 93–106. Albany: State University of New York Press, 1991.

West Church Boston: Commemorative Services on the Fiftieth Anniversary of its Present Ministry. . . on Tuesday, March 1, 1887. Boston: Damrell & Upham, 1887.

White, Anna, and Leila S. Taylor. *Shakerism: Its Meaning and Message Embracing An Historical Account, Statement of Belief, and Spiritual Experience of the Church from Its Rise to the Present Day*. Columbus, Ohio: Fred J. Herr, 1904.

White, Christopher G. "Minds Intensely Unsettled: Phrenology, Experience, and the American Pursuit of Spiritual Assurance, 1830–1880." *Religion and American Culture: A Journal of Interpretation* 16, no. 2 (Summer 2006): 227–261.

Wolfe, Napoleon Bonaparte. *Startling Facts in Modern Spiritualism.* Cincinnati: N. B. Wolfe, 1874.

Wright, Lyle. *American Fiction 1851–1875.* San Marino, Calif.: Huntington Library, 1957.

Young, Janet, ed. *Psychological Yearbook.* New York: Paul Elder and Company, 1905.

Young, Richard Fox. *The Bible Trembled: The Hindu-Christian Controversies of Nineteenth-century Ceylon.* Vienna: Sammlung De Nobili, 1995.

INDEX

Abbreviations:
LHL: Laura Holloway-Langford
Man: Man: Fragments of Forgotten History

Page numbers in italics indicate illustrations.

DIANE SASSON

received her doctorate from the University of North Carolina
at Chapel Hill. She is the author of *The Shaker Spiritual Narrative*
(1983) and articles on American folklore and communal societies.
She was Director of the Master of Arts in Liberal Studies Program at Duke University, and served as President of the National
Association of Graduate Liberal Studies. For the last decade, she
has been on the faculty at Vanderbilt University.